Routes

ROUTES

*Travel and Translation
in the Late
Twentieth Century*

JAMES CLIFFORD

HARVARD UNIVERSITY PRESS

CAMBRIDGE, MASSACHUSETTS
LONDON, ENGLAND
1997

Copyright © 1997 by the President and Fellows of Harvard College

Printed in the United States of America

Library of Congress Cataloging-in-Publication Data

Clifford, James, 1945–
    Routes: travel and translation in the late twentieth century / James Clifford.
        p. cm.
    Includes bibliographical references (p. –) and index.
    ISBN 0–674–77960–6 (alk. paper)
    ISBN 0–674–77961–4 (pbk.)
    1. Ethnology—Philosophy. 2. Ethnology—Field work. 3. Travel—Philosophy.
4. Human geography. 5. Intercultural communication.
    I. Title.
    GN345.C54   1997
    305.8′001—dc20   96–38454

Patricia Zanelle

For Judith

Contents

Prologue: In Medias Res

"The Imam and the Indian," an autobiographical tale by Amitav Ghosh, is a parable for many problems I grapple with in this book. It tells of the encounter between an ethnographic fieldworker and some disconcerting inhabitants of an Egyptian village.

> When I first came to that quiet corner of the Nile Delta I had expected to find on that most ancient and most settled of soils a settled and restful people. I couldn't have been more wrong. The men of the village had all the busy restlessness of airline passengers in a transit lounge. Many of them had worked and travelled in the shiekdoms of the Persian Gulf, others had been in Libya and Jordan and Syria, some had been to the Yemen as soldiers, others to Saudi Arabia as pilgrims, a few had visited Europe: some of them had passports so thick they opened out like ink-blackened concertinas.

The traditional, rural village as airline transit lounge. It's hard to imagine a better figure for postmodernity, the new world order of mobility, of rootless histories. But not so fast . . .

> And none of this was new: their grandparents and ancestors and relatives had travelled and migrated too, in much the same way as mine had, in the Indian subcontinent—because of wars, or for money and jobs, or perhaps simply because they got tired of living always in one place. You could read the history of this restlessness in the villagers' surnames: they

1

had names which derived from cities in the Levant, from Turkey, from faraway towns in Nubia; it was as though people had drifted here from every corner of the Middle East. The wanderlust of its founders had been ploughed into the soil of the village: it seemed to me sometimes that every man in it was a traveller. (Ghosh, 1986: 135)

Amitav Ghosh—a native of India educated at an "ancient English university" who has done anthropological fieldwork in Egypt—evokes an increasingly familiar situation. This ethnographer is no longer a (worldly) traveler visiting (local) natives, departing from a metropolitan center to study in a rural periphery. Instead, his "ancient and settled" fieldsite opens onto complex histories of dwelling and traveling, cosmopolitan experiences. Since the generations of Malinowski and Mead, professional ethnography has been based on intensive dwelling, albeit temporary, in delimited "fields." But in Ghosh's account, fieldwork is less a matter of localized dwelling and more a series of travel encounters. Everyone's on the move, and has been for centuries: dwelling-in-travel.

Routes begins with this assumption of movement, arguing that travels and contacts are crucial sites for an unfinished modernity. The general topic, if it can be called one, is vast: a view of human location as constituted by displacement as much as by stasis. The essays gathered here aim to make some sense, or senses, of people going places. What worldly skills of survival and interaction can be recognized in all the coming and going? What resources for a diverse future? These essays are a few beginnings, attempts to trace old and new maps and histories of people in transit, variously empowered and compelled. They are concerned with human difference articulated in displacement, tangled cultural experiences, structures and possibilities of an increasingly connected but not homogeneous world.

Routes continues an argument with the concept of culture. In earlier books, especially *The Predicament of Culture* (1988), I worried about the concept's propensity to assert holism and aesthetic form, its tendency to privilege value, hierarchy, and historical continuity in notions of common "life." I argued that these inclinations neglected, and at times actively repressed, many impure, unruly processes of collective invention and survival. At the same time, concepts of culture seemed necessary if human systems of meaning and difference were to be recognized and supported. Claims to coherent identity were, in any event, inescapable in a contemporary world riven by ethnic absolutisms. Culture seemed a profoundly mixed blessing. I worked to loosen its constellation of common senses, focusing on processes of ethnographic representation. My levers for prying open the culture idea were expanded concepts of *writing* and *collage,* the former seen as interactive, open-ended, and processual, the latter as a way of making space for heterogeneity, for historical and political, not simply aesthetic, juxtapositions. Ethnographic practices of making and unmaking cultural meanings were discussed in a historical context of Euro-American colonial expansion and the unfinished contestations which, since 1945, have gone under the name of "decolonization."

During the course of this work, *travel* emerged as an increasingly complex range of experiences: practices of crossing and interaction that troubled the localism of many common assumptions about culture. In these assumptions authentic social existence is, or should be, centered in circumscribed places—like the gardens where the word "culture" derived its European meanings. Dwelling was understood to be the local ground of collective life, travel a supplement; roots always precede routes. But what would happen, I began to ask, if travel were untethered, seen as a complex and pervasive spectrum of human experiences? Practices of displacement might emerge as *constitutive* of cultural meanings rather than as their simple transfer or extension. The cultural effects of European expansionism, for example, could no longer be celebrated, or deplored, as a simple diffusion outward—of civilization, industry, science, or capital. For the region called "Europe" has been constantly remade, and traversed, by influences beyond its borders (Blaut, 1993; Menocal, 1987). And is not this interactive process relevant, in varying degrees, to any local, national, or regional domain? Virtually everywhere one looks, the processes of human movement and encounter are long-established and complex. Cultural centers, discrete regions and territories, do not exist prior to contacts, but are sustained through them, appropriating and disciplining the restless movements of people and things.

As I began to consider diverse forms of "travel," the term became a figure for routes through a heterogeneous modernity. In *The Predicament of Culture* I wrote about the Mashpee Indians of Cape Cod, Massachusetts, and their attempt to prove "tribal" identity in a court of law. I argued that their case was hampered by assumptions of rootedness and local continuity, notions of authenticity that denied them complex agency in an interactive, ongoing colonial history. The Mashpee medicine man had spent several years in Hawaii; many tribal members lived outside the traditional town; there was much coming and going; William Apess, the leader of a Mashpee rebellion for Indian rights in 1833, was an itinerant Methodist preacher of Pequot parentage. I began to see that such movements were not marginal to "tribal" life. I thought of *Moby-Dick's* harpooners, Tashtego the Gay Head Indian, Queequeg the South Sea Islander, and Daggoo the African—literary figures standing for real historical experiences. Such travels were evidently more than reactions to European expansion. For is not Queequeg, who shares his bed with Ishmael, clearly the more cosmopolitan of the two?

"Every man in [the village] was a traveller," Ghosh writes. And the passage continues: "Everyone, that is, except Khamees the Rat, and even his surname, as I discovered later, meant 'of Sudan.'" Khamees is unusual for his lack of wanderlust (he claims to have never even visited the nearest big city, Alexandria) and for having a mocking view of just about everything: religion, his family, the elders, and especially visiting anthropologists. But by the end of the story, after a series of painful and hilarious exchanges about the "barbaric" Hindu customs of cremation and cow worship, Khamees and the narrator have become friends. Despite his dogged homebody status, Khamees even imagines, in his joking-serious way, a possible visit to India. He probably won't go. But we realize that this homebody's view of the world is far from circumscribed. Literal travel is not a prerequisite of irony, critique, or distance from one's home culture. Khamees is a complicated "native."

Ghosh calls every man in the village a traveler, drawing attention to specific, largely male, experiences of worldliness, intertwined roots and routes. But in his late twentieth-century story, the long-established displacements and localizations occur within an increasingly powerful force field: "the West." The tale's climax is an ugly shouting match between the researcher and a traditional Imam—a healer he hopes to interview. All the barbs about Hindu cremation and cow worship have begun to rankle, and before he knows it the visiting scholar is embroiled in an argument with the Imam. Amid a growing crowd, the two men confront each other, loudly disputing whose country is better, more "advanced." They each end up claiming to be second only to "the West" in possessing the finest guns and tanks and bombs. Suddenly the narrator realizes that "despite the vast gap that lay between us, we understood each other perfectly. We were both travelling, he and I: we were travelling in the West."

The story delivers a sharp critique of a classic quest—exoticist, anthropological, orientalist—for pure traditions and discrete cultural differences. Intercultural connection is, and has long been, the norm. Moreover, these connections are channeled by powerful global forces. Ethnographer and native, Imam and Indian, are both "travelling in the West," a depressing revelation for the anticolonial anthropologist. For, as we learn in the book (1992) from which the story is excerpted, Ghosh seeks to map his own ethnographic voyage on older connections between India and Egypt, trade and travel relations which precede and partly bypass the world's violent polarization into West and East, empire and colony, developed and backward. This hope is shattered when he realizes that the only common ground he can find with the Imam is "in the West." But Khamees the Rat tugs against this bleak teleology, with his critical localism, his humor, and his friendly tolerance for a visitor from a land where, he says, "everything is upside down." Even his half-serious offer to visit the narrator in India suggests the possibility of "travelling East." This trajectory of a different cosmopolitanism is prefigured in a passing reference to the African Ibn Battouta, who visited the subcontinent in the fourteenth century. As old patterns of connection across the Indian Ocean, Africa, and West Asia are realigned along binary poles of Western modernization, are there still possibilities of discrepant movement? Ghosh poses, but does not foreclose, this critical question.

Moreover, when travel, as in his account, becomes a kind of norm, dwelling demands explication. Why, with what degrees of freedom, do people stay home? Common conceptions of local roots cannot account for a figure like Khamees the Rat. Indeed, his conscious choice *not* to travel—in a context of restlessness driven by Western institutions and seductive symbols of power—may be a form of resistance, not limitation, a particular worldliness rather than a narrow localism. And what of those who are not implicated at all in the statement "every man in [the village] was a traveller"? We hear little from women in the tale except a few, usually giddy, exclamations. Ghosh's story is quite clearly about relations between *men,* not cultural types, villagers, or natives. And the very partiality of his account raises important general questions about men and women, their specific, culturally mediated experiences of dwelling and traveling.

Women have their own histories of labor migration, pilgrimage, emigration, exploration, tourism, and even military travel—histories linked with and distinct from those of men. For example, the everyday practice of driving a car (a relatively new travel technology for masses of women in America and Europe) is forbidden to women in Saudi Arabia. This was a significant fact in the travel experiences of female U.S. soldiers in the 1991 Persian Gulf War. A woman driving a jeep in public was a potent symbol, a contested experience. Another example from the region: consider the very different "travel" histories (the term begins to break down here) of the thousands of female domestic workers who have come to the Middle East from South Asia, the Philippines, and Malaysia to clean, cook, and look after children. Their displacement and indenture have routinely included forced sex. These brief examples begin to suggest how specific histories of freedom and danger in movement need to be articulated along gender lines.

Do the women in Ghosh's village-cum-transit-lounge travel? If not, why not? What is the mix of choice and compulsion in the different mobilities of men and women? Are there significant class, racial, ethnic, or religious factors cross-cutting gender? Does a focus on travel inevitably privilege male experiences? What counts as "travel," for men and women, in different settings? Pilgrimage? Family visiting? Running a stall in a market town? And in those cases—common but not universal—where women stay home and men go abroad, how is "home" conceived and lived in *relation* to practices of coming and going? How, in such instances, does (women's) "dwelling" articulate, politically and culturally, with (men's) "traveling"? In relations of complementarity? Of antagonism? Both? Ghosh's story does not explore these issues. But it makes them inescapable by portraying complex experiences of dwelling and traveling, the roots and routes that constitute one small village. Many questions—empirical and theoretical, historical and political—arise from the statement, "every man. . . was a traveller."

The present book explores some of these questions. It tracks the worldly, historical routes which both constrain and empower movements across borders and between cultures. It is concerned with diverse practices of crossing, tactics of translation, experiences of double or multiple attachment. These instances of crossing reflect complex regional and transregional histories which, since 1900, have been powerfully inflected by three connected global forces: the continuing legacies of empire, the effects of unprecedented world wars, and the global consequences of industrial capitalism's disruptive, restructuring activity. In the twentieth century, cultures and identities reckon with both local and transnational powers to an unprecedented degree. Indeed, the currency of culture and identity as performative acts can be traced to their articulation of homelands, safe spaces where the traffic across borders can be controlled. Such acts of control, maintaining coherent insides and outsides, are always tactical. Cultural action, the making and remaking of identities, takes place in the contact zones, along the policed and transgressive intercultural frontiers of nations, peoples, locales. Stasis and purity are asserted—creatively and violently—*against* historical forces of movement and contamination.

When borders gain a paradoxical centrality, margins, edges, and lines of communication emerge as complex maps and histories. To account for these formations, I draw on emerging conceptions of translocal (not global or universal) culture. In anthropology, for example, new theoretical paradigms explicitly articulate local and global processes in relational, non-teleological ways. Older terms are complicated—terms such as "acculturation" (with its overly linear trajectory: from culture A to culture B) or "syncretism" (with its image of two clear systems overlaid). The new paradigms begin with historical contact, with entanglement at intersecting regional, national, and transnational levels. Contact approaches presuppose not sociocultural wholes subsequently brought into relationship, but rather systems already constituted relationally, entering new relations through historical processes of displacement. A few recent developments: Lee Drummond (1981) sees Caribbean societies as creolizing "intersystems"; Jean-Loup Amselle (1989), in his account of traditionally cosmopolitan West Africa, argues for an "originary syncretism"; Arjun Appadurai (1990) tracks cultural flows across five nonhomologous "scapes"—ethnoscapes, mediascapes, technoscapes, finanscapes, and ideoscapes; Nestor Garcia Canclini (1990) portrays the "hybrid cultures" of Tijuana as "strategies for entering and getting out of modernity"; Anna Lowenhaupt Tsing's account (1993) of "an out-of-the-way place" and Kathleen Stewart's ethnography (1996) of a "space on the side of the road" trouble established views of margin and center, maps of development. These are only a few signs of the times, limited to academic anthropology. Many more appear in the chapters that follow.

The book begins with a lecture, "Traveling Cultures," accompanied by the discussions it provoked at a cultural studies conference in 1990. The lecture introduces and locates my academic practice on the border between an anthropology in crisis and an emerging transnational cultural studies. It presents less a bounded topic than a transition from prior work—a process of translating, starting again, continuing. Subsequent chapters prolong, and displace, *The Predicament of Culture,* a continuity particularly evident in two major areas: a concern with ethnographic practice and with the display of art and culture in museums. These concerns are clustered in the first two parts of the book.

As a historical critic of anthropology, I have focused primarily on ethnographic fieldwork, a cluster of disciplinary practices through which cultural worlds are represented. In the book's first part, research in "the field" is portrayed as part of a long and now-contested history of Western travel. Where professional anthropology has erected a border, I portray a borderland, a zone of contacts—blocked and permitted, policed and transgressive. To see fieldwork as a travel practice highlights embodied activities pursued in historically and politically defined places. This worldly emphasis contributes to an opening of current possibilities, an extension and complication of ethnographic paths. For as the travelers and research sites of anthropology change in response to geopolitical shifts, so must the discipline.

The book's second part develops an earlier interest in strategies for the display of non-Western, minority, and tribal creations. Here I focus particularly on the museum as a place where different cultural visions and community interests are negotiated. Several essays explore developments in the current global proliferation of museums—from the highlands of New Guinea, to Native Canada, to diasporic urban neighborhoods. Something more is going on than the simple extension of a Western institution. In line with the book's general approach, museums and other sites of cultural performance appear not as centers or destinations but rather as contact zones traversed by things and people. This is both a description and a hope, an argument for more diverse participation in a proliferating "world of museums."

My approach to museums—and to all sites of cultural performance and display—questions those visions of global, transnational, or postmodern culture which assume a singular and homogenizing process. "Question" here suggests a genuine uncertainty, an ambiguity sustained. One cannot avoid the global reach of Western institutions allied with capitalist markets and the projects of national elites. And what could be a better symbol of this global hegemony than the proliferation of museums? What more bourgeois, conservative, and European institution? What more relentless collector and commodifier of "culture"? While recognizing the ongoing power of these legacies, my account of the current world of museums posits a global determination which works through, as much as against, local differences. The performance of culture involves processes of identification and antagonism that cannot be fully contained, that overflow national and transnational structures.

This concern with possibilities for resistance and innovation within and against global determinations is deepened in the book's third part, "Futures." Here I survey contemporary articulations of "diaspora," seen as potential subversions of nationality—ways of sustaining connections with more than one place while practicing nonabsolutist forms of citizenship. The history of diverse diasporas is reconfigured as a "prehistory of postcolonialism," a future far from guaranteed. Reflecting further on intersecting routes, I invoke Susan Hiller's reopening of a gathered life and its possessions in her recent installation at Sigmund Freud's London home, the Freud Museum. And I end—begin again—with a meditation written from my current location in northern California: an essay on transpacific contacts and a juxtaposition of different historical visions at Fort Ross, the furthest outpost of the Russian Empire in America. In these chapters, transnational travels and contacts—of people, things, and media—do not point in a single historical direction.

The world (dis)order does not, for example, clearly prefigure a postnational world. Contemporary capitalism works flexibly, unevenly, both to reinforce and to erase national hegemonies. As Stuart Hall (1991) reminds us, the global political economy advances on contradictory terrains, sometimes reinforcing, sometimes obliterating cultural, regional, and religious differences, gendered and ethnic divisions. Flows of immigrants, media, technology, and commodities have similarly uneven effects. Thus, recurring announcements of the obsolescence of nation-states in a brave new world of free trade or transnational culture are clearly premature. But at the same time—from India to Nigeria, to Mexico, to Canada, to the emerging European Union—the stability of national units is far from assured. The imagined communities called "nations" require constant, often violent, maintenance. Moreover, in a world of migrations and TV satellites, the policing of frontiers and collective essences can never be absolute, or not for long. Nationalisms articulate their purportedly homogeneous times and spaces selectively, in relation to new transnational flows and cultural forms, both dominant and subaltern. The diasporic and hybrid identities produced by these movements can be both restrictive and liberating. They stitch together languages, traditions, and places in coercive and creative ways, articulating embattled homelands, powers of memory, styles of transgression, in ambiguous relation to national and transnational structures. It is difficult to evaluate, even to perceive, the range of emerging practices.

In 1996 we are all too familiar with the virulent currency of nationalisms. If, in these essays, I emphasize cultural processes that complicate, cross, and cross-up national boundaries and communities, I do not mean to suggest that such processes exist outside the dominant orders of nationality and (largely capitalist) transnationality. And if one may find guarded optimism in subaltern and non-Western transcultural experiences (if only as possible alternatives to the one-way street of traveling "West"), there is no reason to assume that crossover practices are always liberatory or that articulating an autonomous identity or a national culture is always reactionary. The politics of hybridity is conjunctural and cannot be deduced from theoretical principles. In most situations, what matters politically is who deploys nationality or transnationality, authenticity or hybridity, against whom, with what relative power and ability to sustain a hegemony.

These essays are written under the sign of ambivalence, a permanently fraught hope. They discover, over and over, that the good news and bad news presuppose each other. It is impossible to think of transnational possibilities without recognizing the violent disruptions that attend "modernization," with its expanding markets, armies, technologies, and media. Whatever improvements or alternatives may emerge do so against this grim backdrop. Moreover, unlike Marx, who saw that the possible good of socialism depended historically on the necessary evil of capitalism, I see no future resolution to the tension—no revolution or dialectical negation of the negation. Gramsci's incremental and shifting "war of position," a politics of partial connections and alliances, makes more sense. In the tradition of Walter Benjamin's cultural criticism, these essays track emergence, new orders of difference. How are people fashioning networks, complex worlds, that both presuppose and exceed cultures and nations? Which forms of actually existing transnationalism favor democracy and social justice? What skills of survival, communication, and tolerance are being improvised in today's cosmopolitan experiences? How do people navigate the repressive alternatives of universalism and separatism? Posing such questions at the end of what will surely be the last "Western" millennium, we are beset with problems less of belatedness than of earliness. Hegel's Owl of Minerva flew at dusk. Where on the turning earth? What can be known at dawn? By whom?

Thinking historically is a process of locating oneself in space and time. And a location, in the perspective of this book, is an itinerary rather than a bounded site—a series of encounters and translations. The essays that follow attempt to be accountable for their own routes, their sites and times of production. Full accountability, of course, like the dream of self-knowledge, is elusive. The kind of situated analysis I have in mind is more contingent, inherently partial. It assumes that all broadly meaningful concepts, terms such as "travel," are translations, built from imperfect equivalences. To use comparative concepts in a situated way means to become aware, always belatedly, of limits, sedimented meanings, tendencies to gloss over differences. Comparative concepts—translation terms—are approximations, privileging certain "originals" and made for specific audiences. Thus, the broad meanings that enable projects such as mine necessarily fail as a consequence of whatever range they achieve. This mix of success and failure is a common predicament for those attempting to think globally—globally enough—without aspiring to overview and the final word. My expansive use of "travel" goes a certain distance and falls apart into nonequivalents, overlapping experiences marked by different translation terms: "diaspora," "borderland," "immigration," "migrancy," "tourism," "pilgrimage," "exile." I do not cover this range of experiences. And indeed, given the historical contingency of translations, there is no single location from which a full comparative account could be produced.

The essays gathered here are paths, not a map. As such, they follow the contours of a specific intellectual and institutional landscape, a terrain I have tried to evoke by juxtaposing texts addressed to different occasions and by not unifying the form and style of my writing. The book contains extended scholarly articles, supported and argued in conventional ways. It also includes a lecture, a book review, and several essays that respond to specific contexts of cultural display—museums and heritage sites—in immediate, sometimes frankly subjective ways. Experiments in travel writing and poetic collage are interspersed with formal essays. By combining genres I register, and begin to historicize, the book's composition—its different audiences and occasions. The point is not to bypass academic rigor. The sections of the book written in an analytic style will be judged by current critical standards. But scholarly discourse, an evolving set of conventions whose constraints I respect, condenses processes of thinking and feeling that may experiment in diverse forms. The book's mix of styles evokes these multiple and uneven practices of research, making visible the borders of academic work.

The purpose of my collage is not to blur, but rather to juxtapose, distinct forms of evocation and analysis. The method of collage asserts a relationship among heterogeneous elements in a meaningful ensemble. It brings its parts together while sustaining a tension among them. The present ensemble challenges readers to engage with its parts in different ways, while allowing the pieces to interact in larger patterns of interference and complementarity. The strategy is not only formal or aesthetic. A method of marking and crossing borders (here those of scholarly expression) is pursued throughout the book. Discursive domains, like cultures, are shown to be constituted at their policed and transgressed edges. Chapter 3, for example, portrays the historical making and remaking of "objective" anthropological research in relations of dialogue and conflict with the "subjective" practices of travel and travel writing. Scholarly genres are relational, negotiated, and in process.

In medias res, this book is manifestly unfinished. The personal explorations scattered throughout are not revelations from an autobiography but glimpses of a specific path among others. I include them in the belief that a degree of self-location is possible and valuable, particularly when it points beyond the individual toward ongoing webs of relationship. Hence, the struggle to perceive certain borders of my own perspective is not an end in itself but a precondition for efforts of attentiveness, translation, and alliance. I do not accept that anyone is permanently fixed by his or her "identity"; but neither can one shed specific structures of race and culture, class and caste, gender and sexuality, environment and history. I understand these, and other cross-cutting determinations, not as homelands, chosen or forced, but as sites of worldly travel: difficult encounters and occasions for dialogue. It follows that there is no cure for the troubles of cultural politics in some old or new vision of consensus or universal values. There is only more translation.

The essays gathered here grapple with this predicament. Is it possible to locate oneself historically, to tell a coherent global story, when historical reality is understood to be an unfinished series of encounters? What attitudes of tact, receptivity, and self-irony are conducive to nonreductive understandings? What are the conditions for serious translation between different routes in an interconnected but not homogeneous modernity? Can we recognize viable alternatives to "traveling West," old and new paths? In the face of questions such as these, the writings collected in *Routes* struggle to sustain a certain hope, and a lucid uncertainty.

TRAVELS

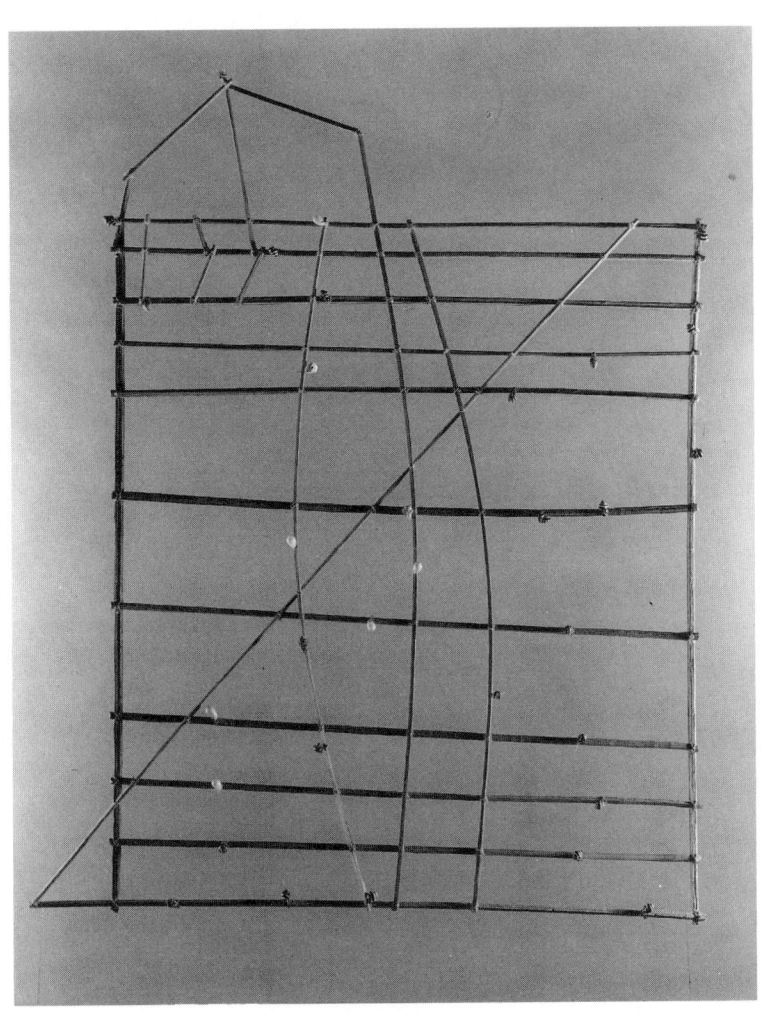

Stick chart, constructed of wood, fibers, shells, and coral, circa 1890. Such charts were used by Marshall Islanders in long-distance navigation. They show the location of islands and the wave patterns created by the interaction of land masses with ocean currents and swells. (*Courtesy of the Peabody Museum of Archaeology and Ethnology, Harvard University. Catalogue no. 00-8-70/55587.*)

1

Traveling Cultures

Remarks at a conference entitled "Cultural Studies, Now and in the Future," Champaign-Urbana, Illinois, April 6, 1990

To begin, a quotation from C. L. R. James in *Beyond a Boundary*: "Time would pass, old empires would fall and new ones take their place. The relations of classes had to change before I discovered that it's not quality of goods and utility that matter, but movement, not where you are or what you have, but where you come from, where you are going and the rate at which you are getting there."

Or begin again with hotels. Joseph Conrad, in the first pages of *Victory*: "The age in which we are encamped like bewildered travelers in a garish, unrestful hotel." In *Tristes Tropiques,* Lévi-Strauss evokes an out-of-scale concrete cube sitting in the midst of the new Brazilian city of Goiania in 1937. It's his symbol of civilization's barbarity, "a place of transit, not of residence." The hotel as station, airport terminal, hospital: a place you pass through, where the encounters are fleeting, arbitrary.

A more recent avatar: the hotel as figure of the postmodern in the new Los Angeles "downtown"—John Portman's Bonaventure Hotel, evoked by Fredric Jameson in an influential essay, "Postmodernism, or the Cultural Logic of Late Capitalism." The Bonaventure's glass cliffs refuse to interact, reflecting back their surroundings; there's no opening, no main entrance. Inside, a confusing maze of levels frustrates continuity, hinders the narrative stroll of a modernist *flâneur.*

Or begin with June Jordan's "Report from the Bahamas"—her stay in something called the Sheraton British Colonial Hotel. A black woman from the United States on vacation . . . confronting her privilege and wealth, uncomfortable encounters with people who make the beds and serve food in the hotel . . . reflections on conditions for human connection, alliances cutting across class, race, gender, and national locations.

Begin again with a London boardinghouse. The setting for V. S. Naipaul's *Mimic Men*—a different place of inauthenticity, exile, transience, rootlessness.

Or the Parisian hotels, homes away from home for the Surrealists, launching points for strange and wonderful urban voyages: *Nadia, Paysan de Paris*. Places of collection, juxtaposition, passionate encounter—"l'Hôtel des Grands Hommes."

Begin again with the hotel stationery and restaurant menus lining (with star charts) Joseph Cornell's magical boxes. Untitled: Hôtel du Midi, Hôtel du Sud, Hôtel de l'Etoile, English Hotel, Grand Hôtel de l'Univers. Enclosed beauty of chance encounters—a feather, ball bearings, Lauren Bacall. Hotel/*autel*, reminiscent of, but *not the same as* marvelous-real altars improvised from collected objects in Latin American popular religions, or the home "altars," *offrendas* constructed by contemporary Chicano artists. A local/global fault line opening in Cornell's basement, filled with souvenirs of Paris, the place he never visited. Paris, the Universe, basement of an ordinary house in Queens, New York, 3708 Utopia Parkway.

This, as we often say, is "work in progress," work *entering* a very large domain of comparative cultural studies: diverse, interconnected histories of travel and displacement in the late twentieth century. This entry is marked, empowered and constrained, by previous work—my own, among others. And so I'll be working, today, *out of* my historical research on ethnographic practice in its twentieth-century exoticist, anthropological forms. But the work I'm *going toward* does not so much build on my previous work as locate and displace it.

Perhaps I could start with a travel conjuncture that has, to my thinking at least, come to occupy a paradigmatic place. Call it the "Squanto effect." Squanto was the Indian who greeted the pilgrims in 1620 in Plymouth, Massachusetts, who helped them through a hard winter, and who spoke good English. To imagine the full effect of this meeting, you have to remember what the "New World" was like in 1620: you could smell the pines fifty miles out to sea. Think of coming into a new place like that and having the uncanny experience of running into a Patuxet just back from Europe.

A disconcertingly hybrid "native" met at the ends of the earth— strangely familiar, and different precisely in that unprocessed familiarity. The trope is increasingly common in travel writing: it virtually organizes "postmodern" reports like Pico Iyer's *Video Night in Kathmandu*. And it reminds me of my own historical research into specifically anthropological encounters, in which I'm always running up against a problematic figure, the "informant." A great many of these interlocutors, complex individuals routinely made to speak for "cultural" knowledge, turn out to have their own "ethnographic" proclivities and interesting histories of travel. Insider-outsiders, good translators and explicators, they've been around. The people studied by anthropologists have seldom been homebodies. Some of them, at least, have been travelers: workers, pilgrims, explorers, religious converts, or other traditional "long-distance specialists" (Helms, 1988). In the history of twentieth-century anthropology, "informants" first appear as natives; they emerge as travelers. In fact, as I will suggest, they are specific mixtures of the two.

Twentieth-century ethnography—an evolving practice of modern travel—has become increasingly wary of certain localizing strategies in the construction and representation of "cultures." I'm going to dwell on some of these localizing moves in the first part of my talk. But I should say right away that I'll be speaking here of an ideal type of mid-twentieth-century disciplinary anthropology. There have been exceptions, and these normative strategies have always been contested. My goal in criticizing a set of somewhat oversimplified practices is not primarily to say that they have been wrong, untruthful, or politically incorrect. Every focus excludes; there is no politically innocent methodology for intercultural interpretation. Some strategy of localization is inevitable if significantly different ways of life are to be represented. But "local" in whose terms? How is significant difference politically articulated, and challenged? Who determines where (and when) a community draws its lines, names its insiders and outsiders? These are far-reaching issues. My aim, initially, is to open up the question of how cultural analysis constitutes its objects—societies, traditions, communities, identities—in spatial terms and through specific spatial practices of research.[1]

Let's focus for a moment on two photographs near the beginning of Malinowski's *Argonauts of the Western Pacific,* arguably one of a few crucial texts that established the modern disciplinary norm of a certain kind of participant observation. This fieldwork rejected a certain style of research: living among fellow whites, calling up "informants" to talk culture in an encampment or on a veranda, sallying forth to "do the village." The fieldwork Malinowski dramatized required one to live full-time in the village, learn the language, and be a seriously involved participant-observer. The photographs at the beginning of *Argonauts,* Plates I and II, feature the "Ethnographer's tent" among Trobriand dwellings. One shows a small beach settlement, setting for the seafaring activities the book chronicles: the Kula trading cycle. The other shows the chief's personal hut in Omarakana village, with the researcher's tent pitched nearby. In the text, Malinowski defends this style of dwelling/research as a (relatively) unobtrusive way of sharing the life of those under study. "In fact, as they knew I would thrust my nose into everything, even where a well-mannered native would not dream of intruding, they finished by regarding me as part and parcel of their life, a necessary evil or nuisance, mitigated by donations of tobacco." He also claimed a kind of panopticism. There was no need to search out the important events in Trobriand life, rituals, rifts, cures, spells, deaths. "They took place under my very eyes, at my own doorstep, so to speak" (Malinowski, 1922: 8). (And in this regard, it would be interesting to discuss the image/technology of the research *tent:* its mobility; its thin flaps, providing an "inside" where notebooks, special foods, a typewriter could be kept; its function as a base of operations minimally separated from "the action.")[2]

Nowadays, when we see these pictures of tents in villages, we may find ourselves asking different questions: Who, exactly, is being observed? Who is localized when the ethnographer's tent is permitted in the center of a village? Cultural observers, anthropologists, are often themselves in the fishbowl, under surveillance (for example, by the omnipresent kids, who won't leave them alone). What are the political locations involved? It matters that Malinowski's tent is next to a chief's house. Which chief? What are the relations of power? What reverse appropriations may be going on? All of these are "postcolonial" questions that, we may assume, were not evoked by the photo in 1921. Then, the image represented a powerful localizing strategy: centering the *culture* around a particular locus, the *village,* and around a certain spatial practice of dwelling/research which itself depended on a complementary localization—that of the *field.*

Villages, inhabited by natives, are bounded sites particularly suitable for intensive visiting by anthropologists. They have long served as habitable, mappable centers for the community and, by extension, the culture. After Malinowski, fieldwork among natives tended to be construed as a practice of co-residence rather than of travel, or even of visiting. And what more natural place to live with people than in their village? (The village localization was, I might add, a portable one: in the great world's fairs—St. Louis, Paris, Chicago, San Francisco—native populations were exhibited as native villages, with live inhabitants.) The village was a manageable unit. It offered a way to centralize a research practice, and at the same time it served as synecdoche, as point of focus, or part, through which one could represent the cultural whole.[3]

Simple village/culture synecdoches have largely gone out of style in current anthropology. Anthropologists, as Geertz has written, don't study villages, they study *in* villages. And increasingly, they don't study in villages either, but rather in hospitals, labs, urban neighborhoods, tourist hotels, the Getty Center. This trend challenges a modernist/urban configuration of the "primitive" object of study as romantic, pure, threatened, archaic, and simple. But despite the move out of literal villages, the notion of fieldwork as a special kind of localized *dwelling* remains.

Of course, one is always a participant-observer some *where*. How is this place of work bounded in space and time? The question brings into view a more persistent localization: "the field." I'm concerned with how these specific disciplinary practices (spatial and temporal constraints) have tended to become confused with "the culture." How are complex, interactive, cultural conjunctures temporally and spatially bounded? In Boas' generation, the field was talked about with some seriousness as a "laboratory," a place of controlled observation and experiment. This sounds crudely positivist now. And contradictory: the field has also—since Boas' time—been seen as a "rite of passage," a place of personal/professional initiation, learning, growth, ordeal, and the like. One is struck by the powerfully ambiguous ways in which the field experience/experiment has been prefigured. (The French *experience* would serve us better here.) And, one wonders, what specific kinds of travel and dwelling (where? how long?) and interaction (with whom? in what languages?) have made a certain range of experiences count as *fieldwork*? The disciplinary criteria have changed since Malinowski's time, and are changing.

It may help if we view "the field" as both a methodological ideal and a concrete *place* of professional activity. The anthropologist's field is defined as a site of displaced dwelling and productive work, a practice of participant-observation which, since the 1920s, has been conceived as a sort of mini-immigration. The fieldworker is "adopted," "learns" the culture and the language. The field is a home away from home, an experience of dwelling which includes work and growth, the development of both personal and "cultural" competence (see Chapter 3). Ethnographers, typically, are travelers who like to stay and dig in (for a time). Unlike other travelers who prefer to pass through a series of locations, anthropologists tend to be homebodies abroad. The field as spatial practice is thus a specific style, quality, and duration of dwelling.[4]

The field is also a set of discursive practices. Dwelling implies real communicative competence: one no longer relies on translators, but speaks and listens for oneself. After Malinowski's generation, the discipline prescribed "learning the language" or at least "working in the local language." This opens a rather large can of worms. Can one speak of *the* language, singular, as if there were only one? What does it mean to learn or use a language? How well can one learn a language in a few years? What about "stranger talk," specific kinds of discourse used with outsiders? What about many anthropologists' continuing reliance on translators and explicators for complex events, idioms, and texts? The subject deserves a full study, which I am not yet able to offer. It's worth pointing out, however, the fallacy "culture (singular) equals language (singular)." This equation, implicit in nationalist culture ideas, has been thoroughly unraveled by Bakhtin, for whom a language is a diverging, contesting, dialoguing set of discourses that no "native"—let alone visitor—can ever control. An ethnographer thus works in or learns some *part* of "the language." And this does not even broach the question of multilingual/intercultural situations.[5]

I've been arguing that ethnography (in the normative practices of twentieth-century anthropology) has privileged relations of dwelling over relations of travel. I don't think I need to linger on the advantages, in focused "depth" of understanding, that can accrue to these fieldwork practices. Intensive participant-observation is probably anthropology's most enduring contribution to humanistic study, and it is, I think, adequately appreciated, even by those like me who find it deeply problematic while urging its reform and dissemination. Let me continue, then, to worry about the dangers of construing ethnography as *field*work.

Localizations of the anthropologist's objects of study in terms of a "field" tend to marginalize or erase several blurred boundary areas, historical realities that slip out of the ethnographic frame. Here is a partial list. (1) The means of transport is largely erased—the boat, the land rover, the mission airplane. These technologies suggest systematic prior and ongoing contacts and commerce with exterior places and forces which are not part of the field/object. The discourse of ethnography ("being there") is separated from that of travel ("getting there"). (2) The capital city, the national context, is erased. This is what Georges Condominas has called the *préterrain,* all those places you have to go through and be in relation with just to get to your village or to that place of work you will call your field. (3) Also erased: the university home of the researcher. Especially now that one can travel more easily to even the most remote sites and now that all sorts of places in the "First World" can be fields (churches, labs, offices, schools, shopping malls), movement in and out of the field by both natives and anthropologists may be very frequent. (4) The sites and relations of *translation* are minimized. When the field is a dwelling, a home away from home where one speaks the language and has a kind of vernacular competence, the cosmopolitan intermediaries—and complex, often political, negotiations involved—tend to disappear. We are left with participant-observation, a kind of hermeneutic freedom to circle inside and outside social situations.

Generally speaking, what's hidden is the wider global world of intercultural import-export in which the ethnographic encounter is always already enmeshed. But, as we shall see, things are changing. Moreover, in various critiques of anthropology—which are responses in part to anticolonial upheavals—we see the emergence of the informant as a complex, historical subject, neither a cultural *type* nor a unique *individual.* My own work, to take only one among many examples, has questioned the oral-to-literate narrative hidden in the very word "informant" (Clifford, 1986). The native speaks; the anthropologist writes. The writing/inscribing practices of indigenous collaborators are erased. My own attempt to multiply the hands and discourses involved in "writing culture" aims not to assert a naive democracy of plural authorship, but to loosen at least somewhat the monological control of the executive writer/anthropologist and to open for discussion ethnography's hierarchy and negotiation of discourses in power-charged, unequal situations.

If thinking of the so-called informant as writer/inscriber shakes things up a bit, so does thinking of her or him as *traveler.* Arjun Appadurai

(1988a, 1988b) challenges anthropological strategies for localizing non-Western people as "natives." He writes of their "confinement," even "imprisonment," through a process of representational essentializing that he calls "metonymic freezing," a process in which one part or aspect of peoples' lives come to epitomize them as a whole, constituting their theoretical niche in an anthropological taxonomy. India equals hierarchy, Melanesia equals exchange, and so forth. "Natives, people confined to and by the places to which they belong, groups unsullied by contact with a larger world, have probably never existed" (Appadurai, 1988a: 39).[6]

In much traditional ethnography, the ethnographer has localized what is actually a regional/national/global nexus, relegating to the margins the external relations and displacements of a "culture." This practice is now increasingly questioned. The title of Greg Dening's superb ethnographic history of the Marquesas is indicative: *Islands and Beaches*. Beaches, sites of travel interaction, are half the story. Eric Wolf's *Europe and the People without History*, though it may tip the local/global cultural dialectic a little too strongly toward "external" (global) determinations, is a dramatic and influential step away from an ethnographic focus on separate, integral cultures. "Rather than thinking of social alignments as self-determining," Wolf writes, "we need—from the start of our inquiries—to visualize them in their multiple external connections" (1982: 387). Or, in another current anthropological vein, consider a sentence from the opening of James Boon's intricate work of ethnological "crisscrossing," *Affinities and Extremes*: "What has come to be called Balinese culture is a multiply authored invention, a historical formation, an enactment, a political construct, a shifting paradox, an ongoing translation, an emblem, a trademark, a nonconsensual negotiation of contrastive identity, and more" (1990: ix). Anthropological "culture" is not what it used to be. And once the representational challenge is seen to be the portrayal and understanding of local/global historical encounters, co-productions, dominations, and resistances, one needs to focus on hybrid, cosmopolitan experiences as much as on rooted, native ones. In my current problematic, the goal is not to *replace* the cultural figure "native" with the intercultural figure "traveler." Rather, the task is to focus on concrete mediations of the two, in specific cases of historical tension and relationship. In varying degrees, both are constitutive of what will count as cultural experience. I am recommending not that we make the margin a new center ("we" are all travelers) but that specific dynamics of dwelling/traveling be understood comparatively.

In tipping the balance toward traveling, as I am doing here, the "chronotope" of culture (a setting or scene organizing time and space in representable whole form) comes to resemble as much a site of travel encounters as of residence; it is less like a tent in a village or a controlled laboratory or a site of initiation and inhabitation, and more like a hotel lobby, urban café, ship, or bus. If we rethink culture and its science, anthropology, in terms of travel, then the organic, naturalizing bias of the term "culture"—seen as a rooted body that grows, lives, dies, and so on—is questioned. Constructed and disputed *historicities*, sites of displacement, interference, and interaction, come more sharply into view.[7]

To press the point: Why not focus on any culture's farthest range of travel while *also* looking at its centers, its villages, its intensive fieldsites? How do groups negotiate themselves in external relationships, and how is a culture also a site of travel for others? How are spaces traversed from outside? To what extent is one group's core another's periphery? If we looked at the matter in this way, there would be no question of relegating to the margins a long list of actors: missionaries, converts, literate or educated informants, people of mixed blood, translators, government officers, police, merchants, explorers, prospectors, tourists, travelers, ethnographers, pilgrims, servants, entertainers, migrant laborers, recent immigrants. New representational strategies are needed, and are, under pressure, emerging. Let me evoke quickly several examples—notes for ways of looking at culture (along with tradition and identity) in terms of travel relations.

Ex-centric natives. The most extreme case I know of traveling "indigenous" culture-makers is a story I learned about through Bob Brosman, a musician and nonacademic historian of music, who for some years has been bringing traditional Hawaiian music into the continental United States. Brosman became very involved with the Moe (pronounced "Moay") family, a group of veteran performers who play Hawaiian guitar, sing, and dance. Their work represents the most authentic version of early twentieth-century Hawaiian slide guitar and vocal styles. But to approach "traditional" Hawaiian music through the Moes brings some unexpected results, because their experience has been one of almost uninterrupted travel. For various reasons, the Moes spent something like fifty-six years on the road, almost never going back to Hawaii. They played Hawaiian music in "exoticist" shows all over the Far East, South Asia, the Middle East, North Africa, eastern and western Europe, and the United States.

And they performed, too, the gamut of hotel-circuit pop music. Now in their eighties, the Moes have recently returned to Hawaii, where, encouraged by revivalists like Brosman, they are making "authentic" music from the teens and twenties.

Bob Brosman is working on a film about the Moes which promises to be quite remarkable, in part because Tal Moe made his own home movies everywhere he went. Thus, the film can present a traveling Hawaiian view of the world, while posing the question of how the Moe family maintained a sense of identity in Calcutta, Istanbul, Alexandria, Bucharest, Berlin, Paris, Hong Kong. How did they compartmentalize their Hawaiianness in constant interaction with different cultures, musics, and dance traditions—influences they worked into their act, as needed? How, for fifty-six years in transient, hybrid environments, did they preserve and invent a sense of Hawaiian "home"? And how, currently, is their music being recycled in the continuing invention of Hawaiian authenticity? This story of dwelling-in-travel is an extreme case, no doubt. But the Moes' experience is strangely resonant. (By the way, I also learned from Brosman's research that the National Steel Guitar, an instrument popular across the United States in the twenties and thirties and often called the "Hawaiian Guitar," was actually invented by a Czech immigrant living in California.)

Several more glimpses of an emergent culture-as-travel-relations ethnography. *Joe Leahy's Neighbors,* a film by Bob Connolly and Robin Anderson, is a good example. (Its better-known predecessor, *First Contact,* is set in early twentieth-century New Guinea.) Joe Leahy, a mixed-blood colonial product, is a successful entrepreneur—kids in Australian schools, satellite dish behind his house in the New Guinea highlands. Connolly and Anderson include Leahy's own travels to Port Moresby and to Australia, while focusing on his ambiguous relations with the highland locals, his relatives. The entrepreneur seems to be exploiting his "neighbors," who resent his wealth. Sometimes he appears as an uncontrolled individualist impervious to their demands; on other occasions he distributes gifts, acting as a "big man" within a traditional economy. Joe Leahy seems to move in and out of a recognizably Melanesian culture. This sort of focus simply could not have been entertained by Malinowski. Here, not only is the "native" a traveler in the world system, but the focus is on an atypical character, a person out of place but not entirely—a person *in history.* Joe Leahy is the sort of figure who turns up in travel books, though not in traditional ethnographies. Yet he is not simply an eccentric or acculturated individual.

Watching Connolly and Anderson's film, we remain uncertain whether Joe Leahy is a Melanesian capitalist or a capitalist Melanesian—a *new* kind of big man, still bound in complex ways to his jealous, more traditional neighbors. He is and is not of the local culture.

In the domain of ethnographic films, I might mention Jean Rouch as a precursor. His film *Jaguar*, for example, is a marvelous (real) travel story set in West Africa in the early 1950s. Rouch follows three young men as they walk from Mali to the cities of what was then called Gold Coast—in search of adventure, fun, prestige, bride-wealth. In a kind of *ethnographie vérité*, the three act themselves for the camera; and their recorded commentary / travel story / myth of the journey ends up as the film's soundtrack. Much could be said about *Jaguar*'s peculiarly seductive, and problematic, dialogical realism. Suffice it to say that the cultural "performance" of the film is an encounter among travelers, Rouch included. And the characters in this home movie "play" themselves, for the camera, as individuals *and* allegorical types.

Other examples: the very complex localization of Michael Taussig's book *Shamanism, Colonialism, and the Wild Man.* His "field" includes the Putumayo region of Columbia and Amazonia, the contiguous Andean Highlands, migrant Indian shamans, traveling mestizos in search of healing, a meandering anthropologist, the violent inroads of world commerce in the 1890s rubber boom and currently in the World Bank's development policies. Taussig's sprawling ethnography (of almost Melvillean ambitions) portrays a region in historical relations of travel—involving conquest, curing, commerce, and mutual ideological appropriation. As George Marcus and Michael Fischer have stressed, innovative forms of multi-locale ethnography will be necessary to do justice to transnational political, economic, and cultural forces that traverse and constitute local or regional worlds (1986: 94–95). So too, specific histories of population movement, exile, and labor migration require new approaches to the representation of "diaspora cultures." Michael Fischer and Mehdi Abedi's multiply centered work of ethnographic cultural critique, *Debating Muslims*, is a powerful case in point. Subtitled "Cultural Dialogues in Postmodernity and Tradition," the work (dis)locates Iranian Islamic culture in a history of national and transnational relations. One chapter is set in Houston, Texas.

Traveling cultures. One could cite many more examples, opening up an intricate comparative field. So far, I have been talking about the ways people leave home and return, enacting differently centered worlds, interconnected cosmopolitanisms. To this I should add: sites traversed—by tourists, by oil pipelines, by Western commodities, by radio and television signals. For example, Hugh Brody's ethnography *Maps and Dreams* focuses on conflicting spatial practices—ways of occupying, moving through, using, mapping—by Athapascan hunters and the oil companies that are driving pipelines across their lands. But here a certain normative concept and history built into the word "travel" begins to weigh heavily. (Can I, without serious hesitations, translate Athapascan hunting as travel? With what violence and what loss of specificity?)

The anthropologist Christina Turner has pressed me on this point. Squanto as emerging norm? Ethnographic informants as travelers? But informants are not all travelers, and they're not natives either. Many people choose to limit their mobility, and even more are kept "in their place" by repressive forces. Turner did ethnographic work among female Japanese factory workers, women who have not "traveled," by any standard definition. They do watch TV; they do have a local/global sense; they do contradict the anthropologist's typifications; and they don't simply enact a culture. But it's a mistake, she told me, to insist on literal "travel." This begs too many questions and overly restricts the important issue of how subjects are culturally "located." It would be better to stress different modalities of inside-outside connection, recalling that the travel, or displacement, can involve forces that pass powerfully *through*—television, radio, tourists, commodities, armies.[8]

Turner's point leads me to my last ethnographic example, Smadar Lavie's *The Poetics of Military Occupation*. Lavie's ethnography of Bedouins is set in the southern Sinai, a land long traversed by all sorts of people, most recently by an Israeli occupation immediately followed by Egyptian occupation. The ethnography shows Bedouins in their tents telling stories, joking, making fun of tourists, complaining about military rule, praying, and doing all sorts of "traditional" things . . . but with the radio on, the BBC World Service (Arabic version). In Lavie's ethnography, you hear the crackle of that radio.

> "Shgetef, could you pour some tea?" the Galid nonchalantly requests the local Fool. Shgetef enters the mag'ad and for the umpteenth time pours us yet more cups of hot sweet tea.
> "So what did the news say?" the Galid asks the man with his ear glued

to the transistor radio, but doesn't wait for an answer. "I'll tell you," he says with a half-bemused, half-serious expression. "No one will solve the problems between Russia and America. Only the Chinese will ever figure a way out. And when the day comes that they conquer the Sinai, that will be the end of that."

It's a good pun—the Arabic for "Sinai" is *Sina,* for "Chinese" is *Sini*—and we laugh heartily. But Shgetef, perhaps betraying his deep fool's wisdom, stares at us with eyes wide open.

The Galid continues, "The Greeks were here and left behind the Monastery [Santa Katarina], the Turks were here and left behind the Castle [in Nuweb'at Tarabin], and the British drew up maps, and the Egyptians brought the Russian army (and a few oil wells), and the Israelis brought the Americans who made the mountains into movies, and tourists from France and Japan, and scuba divers from Sweden and Australia, and, trust Allah to save you from the devil, we Mzeina are nothing but pawns in the hands of them all. We are like pebbles and the droppings of the shiza."

Everyone but Shgetef again roars with laughter. The Coordinator points to me with his long index finger, saying in a commanding voice, "Write it all down, The One Who writes Us!" (*Di Illi Tuktubna*—one of my two Mzeini nicknames). (1990: 291)

Before moving to the second part of my talk, I should say that I have deliberately restricted this discussion to examples of exotic ethnography/anthropology. Of course, the field of "ethnographic" practice is much wider and more diverse. The recent return of anthropology to the metropoles, the increasing practice of what's called in the trade "studying up" (studying elite institutions)—these and other developments have forged and reforged many connections: with sociological ethnography, with sociocultural history, with communications, and with cultural criticism. Anthropologists are in a much better position, now, to contribute to a genuinely comparative and nonteleological cultural studies, a field no longer limited to "advanced," "late capitalist" societies. Diverse ethnographic/historical approaches need to be able to work together on the complexities of cultural localization in post- or neocolonial situations, on migration, immigration, and diaspora, on different paths through "modernity" (see Chapter 3). These are some of the domains in which a reconstructed anthropological ethnography can participate, bringing to bear its inherently bifocal approach, its intensive research practices, its distinctive and changing forms of travel and enunciation.[9]

Begin again with that odd invocation of hotels. I wrote it in the course of returning to an earlier essay on Surrealism and the Paris of the 1920s and 1930s. I was struck by how many of the Surrealists lived in hotels, or hotel-like transient digs, and were moving in and out of Paris. I was beginning to see that the movement was not necessarily *centered* in Paris, or even in Europe. (Paris may have been Walter Benjamin's "capital of the nineteenth century"—but of the twentieth?) It all depended on how (and where) one saw the historical *outcomes* of the modernist moment.

Rereading that earlier essay, "On Ethnographic Surrealism," which was reprinted in my book the *Predicament of Culture,* I came, with some embarrassment, on a footnote that ended with a throwaway: "and Alejo Carpentier, who was a collaborator on the journal *Documents.*" The loose thread suddenly seemed crucial. Could I revise my account of Paris, pulling out and reweaving that thread, and many others like it? I began to imagine rewriting Paris of the twenties and thirties as travel encounters—including New World detours through the old—a place of departures, arrivals, transits (Clifford, 1990b). The great urban centers could be understood as specific, powerful sites of dwelling/traveling.

I found myself working with intersecting histories—discrepant detours and returns. The notions of *détour* and *retour* were proposed by Edouard Glissant in *Le Discours Antillais,* and developed productively in a theory of "postcolonial habitus" by Vivek Dhareshwar (1989a, 1989b). Paris as a site of cultural creation included the detour and return of people like Carpentier. He moved from Cuba to Paris and then back to the Caribbean and South America, to name *Lo real maravilloso,* magical realism, Surrealism with a difference. Surrealism traveled, and was translated in travel. Paris included also the detour and return of Leopold Senghor, Aimé Césaire, and Ousmane Socé, meeting at the Lycée Louis le Grand, returning to different places with the cultural politics of "Negritude." Paris was the Chilean Vincente Huidobro challenging modernist genealogies, proclaiming, "Contemporary poetry begins with me." In the thirties it was Luis Buñuel moving, somehow, between Montparnasse Surrealist meetings, civil war Spain, Mexico, and . . . Hollywood. Paris included the salon of the Martiniquan Paulette Nardal and her sisters. Nardal founded the

Revue du Monde Noir, a place of contact between the Harlem Renaissance and the Negritude writers.

In my invocation of different hotels, the relevant sites of cultural encounter and imagination began to slip away from metropolitan centers such as Paris. At the same time, levels of ambivalence appeared in the hotel chronotope. At first I saw my task as finding a frame for negative and positive visions of travel: travel, negatively viewed as transience, superficiality, tourism, exile, and rootlessness (Lévi-Strauss's invocation of Goiania's ugly structure, Naipaul's London boarding house); travel positively conceived as exploration, research, escape, transforming encounter (Breton's Hôtel des Grands Hommes, June Jordan's tourist epiphany). The exercise also pointed toward the broader agenda I've been getting at here: to rethink cultures as sites of dwelling *and* travel, to take travel knowledges seriously. Thus, the ambivalent setting of the hotel suggested itself as a supplement to the field (the tent and the village). It framed, at least, encounters between people to some degree away from home.

But almost immediately the organizing image, the chronotope, began to break up. And I now find myself embarked on a research project where any condensed epitome or place of survey is questionable. The comparative scope I'm struggling toward is not a form of overview. Rather, I'm working with a notion of comparative knowledge produced through an *itinerary,* always marked by a "way in," a history of locations and a location of histories: "partial and composite traveling theories," to borrow a phrase from Mary John (1989, 1996). The metaphor of travel, for me, has been a serious dream of mapping without going "off earth."

As recycled in this talk, then, the hotel epitomizes a specific *way into* complex histories of traveling cultures (and cultures of travel) in the late twentieth century. As I've said, it has become seriously problematic, in several major ways involving class, gender, race, cultural/historical location and privilege. The hotel image suggests an older form of gentlemanly occidental travel, when home and abroad, city and country, East and West, metropole and antipodes, were more clearly fixed. Indeed, the marking of "travel" by gender, class, race, and culture is all too clear.

"Good travel" (heroic, educational, scientific, adventurous, ennobling) is something men (should) do. Women are impeded from serious travel. Some of them go to distant places, but largely as companions or as "exceptions"—figures like Mary Kingsley, Freya Stark, or Flora Tristan, women now rediscovered in volumes with titles like *The Blessings of a Good*

Thick Skirt, or *Victorian Lady Travellers* (Russell, 1986; Middleton, 1982). "Lady" travelers (bourgeois, white) are unusual, marked as special in the dominant discourses and practices. Although recent research is showing that they were more common than formerly recognized, women travelers were forced to conform, masquerade, or rebel discreetly within a set of normatively male definitions and experiences.[10] One thinks of George Sand's famous account of dressing as a man in order to move freely in the city, to experience the gendered freedom of the *flâneur.* Or Lady Mary Montague's envy of the anonymous mobility of veiled women in Istanbul. And what forms of displacement, closely associated with women's lives, do not count as proper "travel"? Visiting? Pilgrimage? We need to know a great deal more about how women have traveled and currently travel, in different traditions and histories. This is a very large comparative topic that's only beginning to be opened up: for example, in the work of Sara Mills (1990, 1991), Caren Kaplan (1986, 1996), and Mary Louise Pratt (1992, chs. 5 and 7). The discursive/imaginary topographies of Western travel are being revealed as systematically gendered: symbolic stagings of self and other that are powerfully institutionalized, from scientific research work (Haraway, 1989a) to transnational tourism (Enloe, 1990). Although there are certainly exceptions, particularly in the area of pilgrimage, a wide predominance of male experiences in the institutions and discourses of "travel" is clear—in the West and, to differing degrees, elsewhere.

But it is hard to generalize with much confidence, since the serious, *cross-cultural* study of travel is not well developed. What I'm proposing here are research questions, not conclusions. I might note, in passing, two good sources: *Ulysses' Sail,* by Mary Helms, a broadly comparative study of the cultural uses of geographic distance and the power/knowledge gained in travel (a study focused on male experiences); and *Muslim Travelers,* edited by Dale Eickelman and James Piscatori, an interdisciplinary collection designed to bring out the complexity and diversity of religious/economic spatial practices.

Another problem with the hotel image: its nostalgic inclination. For in those *parts* of contemporary society that we can legitimately call postmodern (I do not think, *pace* Jameson, that postmodernism is yet a cultural dominant, even in the "First World"), the *motel* would surely offer a better chronotope. The motel has no real lobby, and it's tied into a highway network—a relay or node rather than a site of encounter between coherent cultural subjects. Meaghan Morris has used the motel chronotope effectively to organize her essay "At Henry Parkes Motel." I can't do justice to its suggestive discussions of nationality, gender, spaces, and possible narratives. I cite it here as a displacement of the hotel chronotope of travel, for, as Morris says, "Motels, unlike hotels, demolish sense regimes of place, locale, and history. They memorialize only movement, speed, and perpetual circulation" (1988a: 3).

Other major ways in which the hotel chronotope—and with it the whole travel metaphor—becomes problematic have to do with class, race, and sociocultural "location." What about all the travel that largely avoids the hotel, or motel, circuits? The travel encounters of someone moving from rural Guatemala or Mexico across the United States border are of a quite different order; and a West African can get to a Paris *banlieu* without ever staying in a hotel. What are the settings that could realistically configure the cultural relations of these "travelers"? As I abandon the bourgeois hotel setting for travel encounters, sites of intercultural knowledge, I struggle, never quite successfully, to free the related term "travel" from a history of European, literary, male, bourgeois, scientific, heroic, recreational meanings and practices (Wolff, 1993).

Victorian bourgeois travelers, men and women, were usually accompanied by servants, many of whom were people of color. These individuals have never achieved the status of "travelers." Their experiences, the cross-cultural links they made, their different access to the societies visited—such encounters seldom find serious representation in the literature of travel. Racism certainly has a great deal to do with this. For in the dominant discourses of travel, a nonwhite person cannot figure as a heroic explorer, aesthetic interpreter, or scientific authority. A good example is provided by the long struggle to bring Matthew Henson, the black American explorer who reached the North Pole with Robert Peary, equally into the story of this famous feat of discovery—as it was constructed by Peary, a host of historians, newspaper writers, statesmen, bureaucrats, and interested institutions such as *National Geographic* magazine (Counter, 1988). And this is still to say nothing of the Eskimo travelers who made the trip possible![11] A host of servants, helpers, companions, guides, and bearers have been excluded from the role of proper travelers because of their race and class, and because theirs seemed to be a dependent status in relation to the supposed independence of the individualist, bourgeois voyager. The independence was, in varying degrees, a myth. As Europeans moved through unfamiliar places, their relative comfort and safety were ensured by a well-developed infrastructure of guides, assistants, suppliers, translators, and carriers (Fabian, 1986).

Does the labor of these people count as "travel"? Clearly, a comparative cultural studies account would want to include them and their specific cosmopolitan viewpoints. But in order to do so, it would have to thoroughly transform travel as a discourse and genre. Obviously, many different kinds of people travel, acquiring complex knowledges, stories, political and intercultural understandings, without producing "travel writing." Some accounts of these experiences have found their way to publication in Western languages—for example, the nineteenth-century travel journals of the Rarotongan missionary Ta'unga, or the fourteenth-century records of Ibn Battouta (Crocombe and Crocombe, 1968; Ibn Battouta, 1972). But they are tips of lost icebergs.

Working in a historical vein, one might gain access to some of this diverse travel experience through letters, diaries, oral histories, music and performance traditions. Marcus Rediker provides a fine example of a reconstructed working-class traveling culture in his history of eighteenth-century Anglo-American merchant seamen (and pirates), *Between the Devil and the Deep Blue Sea*. A cosmopolitan, radical, political culture is revealed, fully justifying the several resonances of Rediker's final chapter title, "The Seaman as Worker of the World." Ongoing research by Rediker and Peter Linebaugh (1990) is bringing more sharply into view the role of African laborers and travelers in this North Atlantic maritime (often insurrectionary) capitalist world. The resonances with Paul Gilroy's current research on the black Atlantic diaspora are clear (Gilroy, 1993a).[12]

To call the mobile, maritime workers described by Rediker and Linebaugh "travelers" ascribes to their experience a certain autonomy and cosmopolitanness. It risks, however, downplaying the extent to which the mobility is coerced, organized within regimes of dependent, highly disciplined labor. In a contemporary register, to think of cosmopolitan workers, and especially migrant labor, in metaphors of "travel" raises a complex set of problems. The political disciplines and economic pressures that control migrant-labor regimes pull very strongly against any overly sanguine view of the mobility of poor, usually nonwhite, people who *must* leave home in order to survive. The traveler, by definition, is someone who has the security and privilege to move about in relatively unconstrained ways. This, at any rate, is the travel myth. In fact, as studies like those of Mary Louise Pratt are showing, most bourgeois, scientific, commercial, aesthetic, travelers moved within highly determined circuits. But even if these bour-geois travelers can be "located" on specific itineraries dictated by political, economic, and intercultural global relations (often colonial, postcolonial, or neocolonial in nature), such constraints do not offer any simple equiva-lence with other immigrant and migrant laborers. Alexander von Hum-boldt obviously did not arrive on the Orinoco coast for the same reasons as an Asian indentured laborer.

But although there is no ground of equivalence between the two "trav-elers," there is at least a basis for comparison and (problematic) transla-tion. Von Humboldt became a canonical travel writer. The knowledge (predominantly scientific and aesthetic) produced in his American explo-rations has been enormously influential. The Asian laborer's view of the "New World," knowledge derived from displacement, was certainly quite different. I do not now, and may never, have access to it. But a comparative cultural studies would be very interested in such knowledge and in the ways it could potentially complement or critique von Humboldt's. Given the prestige of travel experiences as sources of power and knowledge in a wide range of societies, Western and non-Western (Helms, 1988), the project of comparing and translating different traveling cultures need not be class- or ethnocentric. Justin-Daniel Gandoulou details a modern Afri-can traveling culture in his *Entre Paris et Bacongo,* a fascinating study of Congolese *aventuriers,* migrant workers in Paris. He compares their spe-cific culture (focused on the goal of being "well dressed") with the Euro-pean tradition of the dandy, as well as with that of the "Rastas," a different group of black visitors to Paris.

The project of comparison would have to grapple with the evident fact that travelers move about under strong cultural, political, and economic compulsions and that certain travelers are materially privileged, others oppressed. These specific circumstances are crucial determinations of the travel at issue—movements in specific colonial, neocolonial, and postcolo-nial circuits, different diasporas, borderlands, exiles, detours, and returns. Travel, in this view, denotes a range of material, spatial practices that produce knowledges, stories, traditions, comportments, musics, books, diaries, and other cultural expressions. Even the harshest conditions of travel, the most exploitative regimes, do not entirely quell resistance or the emergence of diasporic and migrant cultures. The history of transat-lantic enslavement, to mention only a particularly violent example, an experience including deportation, uprooting, marronnage, transplantation, and revival, has resulted in a range of interconnected black cultures: African American, Afro-Caribbean, British, and South American.

We need a better comparative awareness of these and a growing number of other "diaspora cultures" (Mercer, 1988). As Stuart Hall has argued in a provocative series of articles (1987b, 1988a, 1990b), diasporic conjunctures invite a reconception—both theoretical and political—of familiar notions of ethnicity and identity. Unresolved historical dialogues between continuity and disruption, essence and positionality, homogeneity and differences (cross-cutting "us" and "them") characterize diasporic articulations (see Chapter 10). Such cultures of displacement and transplantation are inseparable from specific, often violent, histories of economic, political, and cultural interaction—histories that generate what might be called *discrepant cosmopolitanisms*. In this emphasis we avoid, at least, the excessive localism of particularist cultural relativism, as well as the overly global vision of a capitalist or technocratic monoculture. And in this perspective the notion that certain classes of people are cosmopolitan (travelers) while the rest are local (natives) appears as the ideology of one (very powerful) traveling culture. My point, again, is not simply to invert the strategies of cultural localization, the making of "natives," which I criticized at the outset. I'm not saying there are no locales or homes, that everyone is—or should be—traveling, or cosmopolitan, or deterritorialized. This is not nomadology. Rather, what is at stake is a comparative cultural studies approach to specific histories, tactics, everyday practices of dwelling *and* traveling: traveling-in-dwelling, dwelling-in-traveling.

I'll conclude with a series of exhortations.

We need to think comparatively about the distinct routes/roots of tribes, barrios, favelas, immigrant neighborhoods—embattled histories with crucial community "insides" and regulated traveling "outsides." What does it take to define and defend a homeland? What are the political stakes in claiming (or sometimes being relegated to) a "home"? As I've said, we need to know about places traveled through, kept small, local, and powerless by forces of domination. *A Small Place,* Jamaica Kincaid's trenchant portrayal of tourism and economic dependency in Antigua, criticizes a local neocolonial history in ways that resonate globally. (An Antiguan critique written from Vermont!) How are national, ethnic, community "insides" and "outsides" sustained, policed, subverted, crossed—by distinct historical subjects—for their own ends, with different degrees of power and freedom?

We need to conjure with new localizations, such as the "border." A specific place of hybridity and struggle, policing and transgression, the U.S./Mexico frontier has recently attained "theoretical" status, thanks to the work of Chicano writers, activists, and scholars: Americo Paredes, Renato Rosaldo, Teresa McKenna, José David Saldívar, Gloria Anzaldúa, Guillermo Gómez-Peña, Emily Hicks, and the Border Arts Project of San Diego/Tijuana. The border experience is made to produce powerful political visions: a subversion of binarisms, the projection of a "multicultural public sphere (versus hegemonic pluralism)" (Flores and Yudice, 1990). How translatable is this place/metaphor of crossing? How are historical borderlands (sites of regulated and subversive travel, natural and social landscapes) like and unlike diasporas?

We conjure now with "cultures," such as Haiti, that can be ethnographically studied both in the Caribbean and in Brooklyn.[13] We often need to consider circuits, not a single place. Some of you may know an exuberant short story by Luis Rafael Sánchez, "The Airbus" (beautifully translated by Diana Vélez). Something like Puerto Rican "culture" erupts in a riot of laughter and overflowing conversation during a routine night flight from San Juan to New York. Everyone more or less permanently in transit . . . Not so much "Where are you from?" as "Where are you between?" Puerto Ricans who can't bear to think of staying in New York. Who treasure their return ticket. Puerto Ricans stifled "down there," newly alive "up here." "Puerto Ricans who are permanently installed in the wanderground between here and there and who must therefore informalize the trip, making it little more than a hop on a bus, though airborne, that floats over the creek to which the Atlantic Ocean has been reduced by the Puerto Ricans" (1984: 43).

In dealing with migration and immigration, serious attention to gender and race complicates a variety of classic approaches, particularly overly linear models of assimilation. Aihwa Ong, an anthropologist at Berkeley, is currently studying Cambodian immigrants in Northern California. Her research is attentive to different, and incomplete, ways of belonging in America, different ways Cambodian men and women negotiate identities in the new national culture. Sherri Grasmuck and Patricia Pessar's study of Dominican international migration, *Between Two Islands,* is concerned, among other things, with differences between male and female attitudes toward settlement, return, and workplace struggle. Julie Matthaeli and Teresa Amott (1990) have written perceptively on specific struggles and barriers, relating to race, gender, and work, facing Asian and Asian American women in the United States.

I've already mentioned the crucial role of political-economic push and pull in such movements of populations. (It's prominent in the Cambodian, Dominican, and Asian American studies just cited.) A comprehensive theory of migration and capitalist labor regimes is proposed by Robin Cohen in *The New Helots: Migrants in the International Division of Labor,* a work that leaves room for political/cultural resistance within a strongly determinist global account. In a regionally centered analysis, "The Emerging West Atlantic System," Orlando Patterson tracks the development of a "postnational" environment centered on Miami, Florida. "Three powerful currents," he writes, "are undermining the integrity of national boundaries." The first is a long history of military, economic, and political intervention by the United States beyond its frontiers. The second is the growing transnational character of capitalism, its need to organize markets at a regional level. "The third current undermining the nation state is that of migration": "Having spent the last century and a half violating, militarily, economically, politically, and culturally, the national boundaries of the region, the center now finds itself incapable of defending the violation of its own national borders. The costs of doing so are administratively, politically, and, most important, economically too high. Trade, and the international division of labor, follows the flag. But they also set in motion winds that tear it down" (1987: 260). The cultural consequences of a "Latinization" of significant regions within the political-economic "center" are, according to Patterson, likely to be unprecedented. They will certainly differ from more classic immigrant patterns (European and Asian) which do not build upon "geographic proximity and co-historical intimacy" (259). We are seeing the emergence of new maps: borderland culture areas, populated by strong, diasporic ethnicities unevenly assimilated to dominant nation-states.

And if contemporary migrant populations are not to appear as mute, passive straws in the political-economic winds, we need to listen to a wide range of "travel stories" (not "travel literature" in the bourgeois sense). I'm thinking, among others, of the oral histories of immigrant women that have been gathered and analyzed at the Centro de Estudios Puertorriqueños in New York City (Benmayor et al., 1987). And, of course, we cannot ignore the full range of expressive culture, particularly music—a rich history of traveling culture-makers and transnational influences (Gilroy, 1987, 1992, 1993a).

Enough. Too much. The notion of "travel," as I've been using it, cannot possibly cover all the different displacements and interactions I've just invoked. Yet it has brought me into these borderlands.

I hang on to "travel" as a term of cultural comparison precisely because of its historical taintedness, its associations with gendered, racial bodies, class privilege, specific means of conveyance, beaten paths, agents, frontiers, documents, and the like. I prefer it to more apparently neutral, and "theoretical," terms, such as "displacement," which can make the drawing of equivalences across different historical experiences too easy. (The postcolonial/postmodern equation, for example.) And I prefer it to terms such as "nomadism," often generalized without apparent resistance from non-Western experiences. (Nomadology: a form of postmodern primitivism?) "Pilgrimage" seems to me a more interesting comparative term to work with. It includes a broad range of Western and non-Western experiences and is less class- and gender-biased than "travel." Moreover, it has a nice way of subverting the constitutive modern opposition between traveler and tourist. But its "sacred" meanings tend to predominate—even though people go on pilgrimages for secular as well as religious reasons. And in the end, for whatever reasons of cultural bias, I find it harder to make "pilgrimage" stretch to include "travel" than to do the reverse. (The same is true of other terms such as "migration.") There are, in any event, no neutral, uncontaminated terms or concepts. A comparative cultural studies needs to work, self-critically, with compromised, historically encumbered tools.

Today I've been working, overworking, "travel" as a translation term. By "translation term" I mean a word of apparently general application used for comparison in a strategic and contingent way. "Travel" has an inextinguishable taint of location by class, gender, race, and a certain literariness. It offers a good reminder that all translation terms used in global comparisons—terms like "culture," "art," "society," "peasant," "mode of production," "man," "woman," "modernity," "ethnography"—get us some distance *and* fall apart. *Tradittore, traduttore.* In the kind of translation that interests me most, you learn a lot about peoples, cultures, and histories different from your own, enough to begin to know what you're missing.

Discussion

Jenny Sharpe: I'm sympathetic to what you say about the field of anthropology being a fiction constituted only as exclusions of movements of both the anthropologist and of cultures. But I'm wondering if that notion of the field itself exists in anthropology any longer. I'm thinking of the fact that anthropologists can no longer go out to the field in the way that they used to because of political upheavals. I'm thinking also of the recent shifts in the notion of the field itself (to include, for example, the work of anthropologists in Philadelphia's inner-city ghettos, work which constructs those ghettos as transplanted migrant communities from "Third World" countries), so that we no longer have a field that looks like what Malinowski and the others you mentioned were talking about.

Clifford: These are very important political issues connected to current attempts to redefine anthropology's "fields." As you said, a whole series of political upheavals has made it more and more difficult to do fieldwork in the way Malinowski, Mead, and their generation did. And, as you know, it's not that things have suddenly gotten "political," whereas previously the research was somehow neutral. One of the advantages of looking at ethnography as a form of travel is that you can't avoid certain concerns that always come up in travel accounts, but seldom come up in social scientific ones. I mentioned some of them. But one I didn't go into is the issue of physical safety. Here the gender and race of the traveler in foreign lands matter a lot. Ethnographers "in the field" have, of course, taken risks. Some have died from disease and accidents. But few, to my knowledge, have actually been killed by their "hosts." Why, to take a rather stark case, was Evans-Pritchard not killed, or at least hurt, by the Nuer when he set up his tent in their village on the heels of a military expedition? (He makes it perfectly clear in his book, *The Nuer,* that they didn't want him there.) Underlying his safety, and that of a host of other anthropologists, missionaries, and travelers, was a prior history of violent conflict. All over the world "natives" learned, the hard way, not to kill whites. The cost, often a punitive expedition against your people, was too high. Most anthropologists, certainly by Malinowski's time, came into their "fieldsites" *after* some version of this violent history. To be sure, a few daring researchers worked in unpacified areas, becoming, as they did so, part of the contact and pacification process. But by the twentieth century there were relatively few of these. My point is simply that the safety of the field as a place of dwelling and work, a place for neutral, unpolitical social science, was itself a historical and political creation.

Your question presupposes this, because the recent lack of safety (at least of political safety) for fieldworkers in many places marks the collapse of a historical "world" containing inhabitable research "fields." I'd just want to add that the collapse is a very uneven one, with a lot of room for local variation and negotiation. There are still many places anthropologists can go with impunity. In other places they can do fieldwork, sometimes, with restrictions. In others, it's basically off limits. Since I'm not among those who think postcolonial ethnographers should simply stay home (wherever *that* is!), I'm particularly interested in the situations where an ethnography of initiation is giving way to one of negotiation, where rapport is recast as alliance. Of course, this only makes explicitly political something that was going on already in the social relations of ethnographic "dwelling." (I touched on it in the questions about Malinowski's tent next to the chief's house, the matter of reverse appropriations.) But there is a new context, and the balance of power has shifted, in many places. Today, if ethnographers want to work among Native American communities, or in many regions of Latin America, the question "What's in it for us?" is right up front. The researcher may be required to hire, or train, local students. He or she may have to testify in a land-claims case, or work on a pedagogic grammar of the language, or help with local history projects, or support the repatriation of ancestral objects from metropolitan museums. Not all communities can make this kind of demand, of course. And there's a danger that an anthropology that wants to preserve its political neutrality (also its objectivity and authority) will simply turn away from such places and toward populations where fieldwork is less "compromised," where people can be construed in the old exoticist ways.

The issue of reconstituting disciplinary practices around a new "primitive," no longer in the so-called Third World, is very suggestive. You mentioned the transplanted Third World immigrant communities in Philadelphia. I don't think there's any question of going back to, say, the pre-1950 "primitive." But aspects of that figure are being reinvented in new conditions. For example, I said that we need to be very wary of a "postmodern primitivism" which, in an affirmative mode, discovers non-Western travelers ("nomads") with hybrid, syncretic cultures, and in the process projects onto their different histories of culture contact, migration, and inequality a homogeneous (historically "avant-garde") experience.

I do think "postmodernism" can serve as a translation term, to help make visible and valid something strange (as modernism did for the early twentieth-century primitivists discovering African and Oceanian "art");

but I want to insist on the crucial *traduttore* in the *tradittore,* the lack of an "equals" sign, the reality of what's missed and distorted in the very act of understanding, appreciating, describing. One keeps getting closer *and* farther away from the truth of different cultural/historical predicaments. This reflects a historical process by which the global is always localized, its range of equivalences cut down to size. It's a process that can be contained—temporarily, violently—but not stopped. New political subjects will, I assume, continue to emerge, demanding that their excluded history be recognized.

How the inescapably political dialectic of understanding and contestation is being played out in the Philadelphia neighborhoods you mentioned, I don't know. You suggested that the new immigrant Third World people there are being objectified. A taste of otherness, without having to travel very far? Anthropology might here be seen as rejoining one of its forgotten roots: the study of "primitive" communities in the urban centers of capitalism. I'm thinking of the nineteenth-century precursors Mayhew, Booth, and company doing research in "darkest England." The equivalence of savages "out there" and "in our midst," of travel out to the Empire and travel in to the city, was explicit in their work. You suggest we may be rearticulating that equivalence in a new historical moment. I'd want to know exactly how the ethnographers in question are working in the immigrant neighborhoods, how their "fields" are politically negotiated.

Homi Bhabha: I really want you to talk about the place of a lack of movement and fixity in a politics of movement and a theory of travel. Refugees and exiles are of course a part of this economy of displacement and travel; but also, once they are in a particular place, then almost for their survival they need to fix upon certain symbols. The process of hybridization which goes on can often represent itself by a kind of impossibility of movement and by a kind of survival identified in the holding on to something which actually then doesn't allow that circulation and movement to take place. Another site for this, which actually is not dealt with enough, are the proletariat and the lower middle classes in what is called the Third World who are recipients of the Urbana, Illinois, or Harvard T-shirts which you see on the streets of Bombay, or of particular kinds of sunglasses, or particular kinds of television programs, or indeed particular kinds of music. There is another problem of travel and fixity when they then, in something like Fanon's sense, hold on to certain symbols of the elsewhere, of travel, and elaborate around it a text which has to do not with movement and displacement but with a kind of fetishization of other cultures, of the elsewhere, or of the image and figure of travel. And it's just that element of people caught in that margin of nonmovement within an economy of movement that I would like you to address.

Clifford: What you've said is very interesting, and I must confess I haven't got a lot to say about it at this stage. I suppose I've steered away from a focus on "exile" because of the privilege it enjoys in a certain modernist culture: Joyce, Beckett, Pound, Conrad, Auerbach, their special uprootedness, pain, authority. And for me, Conrad is the prime example of the sort of "fixing" you mention: his deliberate limitation of horizons, the labored fiction of his "Englishness," that persona of "everyone's favorite old English author" he produced in the "author's notes" to his books (as Edward Said has shown), the fixation on certain symbols of Englishness because he needed to stay put, there was nowhere else for him. And paradoxically, as you know, Conrad's extraordinary experience of travel, of cosmopolitanness, finds expression only when it is limited, tied down to a language, a place, an audience—however violent and arbitrary the process. But perhaps this is the paradox you're getting at in foregrounding the exile's desire and need for fixity. Because in your question dwelling seems the artificial, achieved, hybrid "figure" against the "ground" of traveling, movement, and circulation. This reverses, it seems to me, the usual relation of stasis to movement, and it presupposes the problematic I was working my way into through a critique of exoticist anthropology and its culture ideas. A focus on comparative travel raises the question of dwelling, seen not as a ground or starting place but as an artificial, constrained practice of fixation. Is that what you're getting at?

In that optique, we could compare, for example, the experience/practice of "exile" with that of "diaspora," and with that of people fixing themselves in Bombay by means of University of Illinois T-shirts. But I'd want to ask: What dialectic or mediation (I don't know how to theorize the relation) of fixation and movement, of dwelling and traveling, of local and global, is articulated on those T-shirts? I recall, more than a decade ago, seeing UCLA T-shirts all over the Pacific. What did they mean? I don't know. Or the New Caledonian Kanak militant in a Tarzan T-shirt whom I also saw, or the Lebanese militiamen I recently heard about who were wearing the name "Rambo"? Is this a fetishization of other cultures, of the elsewhere, as you suggest, or is it a way of localizing global symbols, for the purposes of action? Again, I don't know. Both processes must somehow be at work. (And of course T-shirts are made in virtually every locale to advertise festivals, local bands, all manner of institutions and productions.) I'm eager for a comparative cultural studies account of the T-shirt, that blank sheet, mystical writing pad, so close to the body . . .

Stuart Hall: One of the things I appreciated in your paper was that you took the travel metaphor as far as it could go, and then showed us where it couldn't go. In that way, you separated yourself from the fashionable postmodernist notion of nomadology—the breakdown of everything into everything. But if you don't want it simply to be "everybody now goes everywhere," then you also have to conceptualize what "dwelling" means. Hence, the T-shirt is not a good example because the T-shirt is something which travels well. The question is: What stays the same even when you travel? And you gave us a wonderful illustration of that in the Hawaiian musicians who were never at home for most of their lives, who traveled round the world. But you said they carried something Hawaiian with them. What?

Clifford: I agree very strongly with what I hear you saying and with what I only half heard in Homi's question. Once traveling is foregrounded as a cultural practice, then dwelling, too, needs to be reconceived—no longer simply the ground from which traveling departs and to which it returns. I've not gone far enough yet in reconceptualizing the varieties, different histories, cultures, constraints, and practices of dwelling in the transnational contexts I've been sketching here. So far, I've been better on traveling-in-dwelling than on dwelling-in-travel. You ask: What stays the same even when you travel? A lot. But its significance may differ with each new conjuncture. How was the Moes' Hawaiianness maintained for fifty-six years on the road? (And how was it reconstituted as "authenticity" on their return?) Are we to think of a kind of kernel or core of identity they carried everywhere with them? Or is it a question of something more polythetic, something more like a habitus, a set of practices and dispositions, parts of which could be remembered, articulated in specific contexts? I lean toward the latter view, but I have to say I don't really know enough about the Moes to be at all sure. I've just begun to learn about them.

Obviously the issue is a crucial one in discussing diaspora cultures. What is brought from a prior place? And how is it both maintained and transformed by the new environment? Memory becomes a crucial element in the maintenance of a sense of integrity—memory which is always constructive. But one would not want to go too far along the invention-of-tradition tack, certainly not in all cases. Oral tradition can be very precise, transmitting a relatively continuous, if rearticulated, cultural substance over many generations. This is particularly true when there is a land base to organize recollection, as with Native American societies, Melanesians, or Aboriginals. But African American, Afro-Caribbean, and other diasporic experiences also show varying degrees of continuity, of something like a collective memory (which is not, of course, individual memory writ large). But you, especially, could tell me a lot more about this! I just want to affirm what I take to be the general direction of your question and repeat that, in my terms, cultural dwelling cannot be considered except in specific historical relations with cultural traveling, and vice versa.

Keya Ganguly: I'd like to preface by saying I find your idea of bifocality very interesting. I think it sort of resembles, in some ways, I hope, Stuart Hall's notion of the contrastive double vision of a familiar stranger of sorts. When you extend the metaphor of bifocality to call for a comparative study of, for example, Haitians in Haiti and Haitians in Brooklyn, New York, don't you make the kind of reifying move that Appadurai critiques, as the othering of others? By locating them as Haitians in a continuous space between Haiti and New York, Indian in India and Indian in New York, are you reinscribing an ideology of cultural difference? Being a child of Indian immigrants, I find it very difficult to identify myself with that sort of ideology of difference, especially since the identification may occur at another level. For instance, I choose to be identified with Philadelphians rather than with Indians from Bombay.

Clifford: A very far-reaching question. I can say a few things. First, the sort of comparative account I'm proposing would want to be sensitive to the differences between, say, Indians in New York and Haitians in New York, while claiming their comparability. The proximity, patterns of immigration and return, the sheer political-economic weight of the relationship between the two places may make it more useful to talk of a kind of intercultural axis in the Haitian case than in the Indian one. I'm not sure. But I do want to hesitate before generalizing what I first heard Vivek Dhareshwar call "immigritude." And having said that, I will admit to a specific localizing of "Haitian" difference when I speak of Haiti simultaneously in Brooklyn and the Caribbean. I would hope that this does not reinscribe an ideology of absolute cultural difference. I would also want to hold onto the notion that there are different cultures that are some where(s), not all over the map. It's a fine line to walk, as you suggest. Why Haiti/Brooklyn, and not Haiti/Paris, or other places Haitians travel and emigrate? Here I would return to the research of Orlando Patterson. Patterson sees the Caribbean as enmeshed in political-economic relations of "peripheral dualism," destructively tied to a United States "center."

This dualism would account for why the transnational relationship with the North overrides other possible historical connections—with France, for example. And it might justify localizing an intercultural "Haiti" along that axis. I would certainly not want to exoticize Haitians in this cultural space by pinning their identity on some sort of essence (vodou, for example, important though it is).

But your question nicely opens up the whole question of identity as a politics rather than an inheritance—the tense interaction between these two sources. When you speak about possibly choosing to be identified with Philadelphians rather than with Bombay Indians, I hear you rejecting all-or-nothing ethnic agendas. And I certainly agree with this questioning of a kind of automatic cultural or racial inscription as a diasporic "Indian." (Inscriptions made in hostile as well as friendly ways.) I would only add, as I'm sure you'd agree, that the "choice"—not voluntarist, but historically constrained—is *neither* a binary one (in assimilationist scenarios, a before/after) *nor* an open set of alternatives. Rather, cultural/political identity is a processual configuration of historically given elements—including race, culture, class, gender, and sexuality—different combinations of which may be featured in different conjunctures. These elements may, in some conjunctures, cross-cut and bring each other to crisis. What components of identity are "deep" and what "superficial"? What "central" and what "peripheral"? What elements are good for traveling and what for dwelling? What will be articulated within the "community"? What in coalition work? How do these elements interact historically, in tension and dialogue? Questions like these do not lend themselves to systematic or definitive answers; they are what cultural politics is all about.

2

A Ghost among Melanesians

Bernard Deacon was a brilliant young anthropologist who in 1926, after undergraduate studies at Cambridge, undertook difficult fieldwork on the island of Malekula in the New Hebrides (now Vanuatu). At the end of fourteen months, on the verge of departing for Australia, he was carried off by black water fever (a form of malignant malaria). Deacon was twenty-four years old when he died. He would certainly have made a mark, probably a profound one, on his discipline. As it stands, he is known for discovering a "six-class" marriage system on nearby Ambrym Island (a system of enduring fame in the arcane world of kinship studies) and for one book, *Malekula: A Vanishing People in the New Hebrides* (1934), heroically compiled from his fieldnotes by Camilla Wedgwood.

Everyone agreed that Bernard Deacon was special. He dazzled his teachers. But he was more than simply a fine student—winning first-class honors in natural sciences, medieval and modern languages, and anthropology. He possessed uncommon linguistic virtuosity joined to scientific rigor and a philosophical, poetic temperament. *Malekula,* as its editor well knew, was only a mock-up of the book Deacon might have written. We catch glimpses of that unwritten book in the "memoir" composed by his friend Margaret Gardiner, *Footprints on Malekula* (1984).

This affecting, small work contains not a word too many or too few. Margaret Gardiner selects passages from the letters Deacon wrote to her from the field. She surrounds them with an understated account of Cambridge life in the early twenties, of her first meetings with Deacon, his family background (a childhood in Russia, where his father held a consular post), and the strange metamorphosis of their friendship into love and finally a kind of commitment. (She intended to join him in Australia— although they had spent only a handful of days in each other's company and were never engaged.) We follow a subtle amorous intensification in Deacon's letters, which occupy center stage in the memoir. He seems to fall more deeply in love through writing; he longs to be with his correspondent; then the writing stops. Deacon's last letter arrived more than a month after Gardiner had heard by telegram of his death. She recounts the moment sparely, with almost no comment, leaving us—as she was left for half a century—with the wound, the silence and the possibility, open. (*Would* they have lived happily ever after?) The memoir concludes with an observant short narrative of Gardiner's own visit to Malekula in 1983. Fifty-five years later, Deacon is remembered and appropriately honored by local Melanesians (a people and culture that did not in fact "vanish," as seemed inevitable in 1926).

> Bernard's headstone was a plain rectangular slab with the words "A. B. Deacon Anthropologist 1903–1927" engraved upon it. Now it was surrounded by jars and tins of flowers and hung with little garlands—moving tributes from the villagers for this special occasion. I added my jar and, turning, looked down a hill on the other side where, through the trees, there was a glimpse of the sea. Suddenly, for some inexplicable reason and despite my belief that graves are irrelevant, I was glad that Bernard had been buried within sight of the sea.

Deacon was consumed by his ethnographic work. At times—like all fieldworkers—he felt isolated, trapped by the difficulty of his interpretive task (the sheer complexity of Melanesian custom) and by the island environment (its intense beauty and crushing, malarial climate). He writes to his distant companion—for that is her role in the letters—with a mixture of amorous yearning, lucid self-awareness, and at times a (literally) feverish search for some vision or grasp of an illusive "whole" reality. There is an irreducible oddness and originality to his turn of mind which the edited letters preserve. Supremely intelligent, he allows himself to be confused.

Deacon had come to Malekula schooled in Cambridge anthropology and particularly in the work of W. H. R. Rivers. Midway through his stay, the explanatory guides began to crumble. In the letters, he is overwhelmed by how much is left out of his teachers' overly neat formulas, and also by how incompatible earlier accounts of the New Hebrides are with one another and with his own research. Observant, he writes at a period in his fieldwork when he has learned enough to know what vast and formerly unsuspected levels of ignorance remain. Synthetic vision escapes; he lacks a theoretical overview or the distance needed to see broad patterns. Deacon confronts this experience honestly and without clutching at premature keys to the "culture" (as if it were a single thing). He makes some very acute and disabused observations about fieldwork "rapport," about the push and pull, sympathy and impatience, exposure and isolation of ethnographic work. "The only privacy, the only remnant of Europe here, is thought." And wrestling with his role as cultural observer, he notes: "my interest in natives is too general—in fact, in people as a whole—I don't react spontaneously to them as a person, except rarely. It is only the realization that something I know in myself is known by another that may suddenly—what?—waken me to him. I don't know. Otherwise I may know him but he is relevant only in relation to others. I'm sorry, all this is very dull . . ."

It is far from dull. It cuts deeply. But if in his letters Deacon seriously questioned interpersonal ethnographic relations and the possibility of deriving overarching anthropological theories, and if he sensed, at times, an enormous gulf separating him from the complex people immediately at hand, none of this should be taken to suggest that he was constantly estranged in the New Hebrides. There are moods of intense joy, of closeness to people and place. He was, apparently, well liked by his hosts. And there are moments of (Melanesian?) clarity about the whole situation: "Here come the men and I must talk about offerings to ghosts. I am a ghost." Nor should we assume that Deacon's questioning of anthropological attitudes and methods would have led him to abandon his scientific task. He was devoted to empirical research and to the search for rigorous explanations. The letters contain various proposals for more systematic forms of ethnographic description and cross-cultural comparison. He would certainly have wrestled his texts and observations into a "theory" of New Hebridean culture and history. But reading these deeply reflective and poetic letters, one wonders what shape that theory would have taken. Might it have avoided some of the pseudo-scientific reductions and ahistorical visions that beset the structural functionalism of his generation?

Would his ethnography have found room in its analytic structure for the kind of searching, lucid uncertainty we read in his letters?

But we should be wary of projecting too much method into these meandering, evocative texts. They are, after all, love letters, written in a desire for communion. They can be sensuous, as in this description of Norfolk Island:

> Feathery pines on the hills, like a frieze against the sky, and steep, fertile valleys, with lemon orchards hidden by blue convolvulus and hanging bougainvillaeas like lava flowing down the sides, blossomy frosted flame trees, sweet smelling oaks in flower (not our English oak), olives among the rocks, a creeper called Samson's hairs, & the Alsophilas, tree ferns, rising above the bed of the valley like starfish opening to the sun— teeming, silent growth everywhere. Out behind the house there are scarlet splashes of hibiscus, lovely flowers: I had breakfast there, and then lunch—or dinner—with baked sweet potatoes and yams, and pas-sion-fruit and peaches, endless peaches,—you squash them underfoot as you walk.

In these letters, Deacon's writing modulates freely between scientific, erotic, and spiritual registers. He is possessed by a "strange love"—for an impossible *intimacy* with truth. He sometimes feels cut off, torn between the need to be with his distant companion and to finish the research on Malekula. At other times, there is no conflict. Throughout the letters, scientific and amorous discourses unexpectedly and movingly intertwine. Just one example, from a moment when, reviewing his ethnographic work so far, he perceives "how lamentably inadequate it is":

> At one or two points there has been a sudden vision of what the whole might be like, a sense of the movement of everything as marvellously living and an uncontrollable joy in it—and then suddenly there is this now constantly recurring, overwhelming depression, a sudden draining of intellect and will, by which alone it is possible to live here. There is nothing in this forgotten world to which I can act as a whole, except this vision of a consummation and a unity—and yet it is what I must constantly doubt. It is so easy, in this strange heat, for very weariness of flesh to rest content with something imperfect and obscure, a prostitu-tion of the desire of the inmost spirit towards—what? the possibility of truth? It is a strange love. You are so much more than a possibility: perhaps it is just that.

Margaret Gardiner interposes her own comments sparingly among Deacon's letters. And she casts herself in 1926 as a rather insouciant, willful young woman. Deacon's letters give a rather different sense of her. During the Cambridge years, she writes, "I took it for granted that every young man I got to know would fall in love with me: it seemed inevitable, part of the natural order of things." Her friendship with Deacon was of a different order, a serious, deepening loyalty and shared intelligence that has endured. The present memoir, composed with tact, love, and gentle humor, reveals more than just a man. It portrays a beautiful, bitter relationship. And it infuses a tragic story—for Deacon's death haunts every line—with many affirmations. There is his amazing, courageous last letter, written from the "world of death." And there are happy photos of Deacon as a schoolboy, on a picnic with his parents, handsome and dandyish with cane and cigarette, or pensive on Malekula, . . . and Margaret Gardiner at Cambridge, in a gay pose, scarf at her throat, waving a flower or vine of some sort.

3

Spatial Practices: Fieldwork, Travel, and the Disciplining of Anthropology

The day after the Los Angeles earthquake of 1994, I watched a TV interview with an earth scientist. He said he had been "in the field" that morning looking for new fault lines. It was only after a minute or so of talk that I realized he had been flying around in a helicopter the whole time. Could this be fieldwork? I was intrigued by his invocation of the field, and somehow unsatisfied.

My dictionary begins its long list of definitions for "field" with one about open spaces and another that specifies cleared space. The eye is unimpeded, free to roam. In anthropology Marcel Griaule pioneered the use of aerial photography, a method continued, now and again, by others. But if overview, real or imagined, has long been part of fieldwork, there was still an oxymoronic bump in the earth scientist's airborne "field." Particularly in geology, indeed in all the sciences which value fieldwork, the practice of research "on the ground," observing minute particulars, has been a sine qua non. The French equivalent, *terrain,* is unequivocal. Gentlemen naturalists were supposed to have muddy boots. Fieldwork is earthbound—intimately involved in the natural and social landscape.

It was not always so. Henrika Kuklick (1997) reminds us that the move toward professional field research in a range of disciplines, including anthropology, took place at a particular historical moment: in the late nineteenth century. A presumption in favor of professional work that was down-close, empirical, and interactive was quickly naturalized. Fieldwork would put theory to the test; it would *ground* interpretation.

In this context, flying around in a helicopter seemed a bit abstract. Yet, on reflection, I had to allow the earth scientist his practice of going "into the field" while never setting foot there. In some crucial way, his use of the term qualified. What mattered was not simply the acquisition of fresh empirical data. A satellite photo could provide that. What made this fieldwork was the act of physically *going out* into a *cleared place of work.* "Going out" presupposes a spatial distinction between a home base and an exterior place of discovery. A cleared space of work assumes that one can keep out distracting influences. A field, by definition, is not over-grown. The earth scientist could not have done his helicopter "fieldwork" on a foggy day. An archeologist cannot excavate a site properly if it is inhabited or built over. An anthropologist may feel it necessary to clear his or her field, at least conceptually, of tourists, missionaries, or govern-ment troops. Going out into a cleared place of work presupposes specific practices of displacement and focused, disciplined attention.

In this essay I hope to clarify a crucial and ambivalent anthropological legacy: the role of travel, physical displacement, and temporary dwelling away from home in the constitution of fieldwork. I will discuss fieldwork and travel in three sections. The first sketches some recent developments in sociocultural anthropology, showing where classic research practices are under pressure. I suggest why fieldwork remains a central feature of disciplinary self-definition. The second section focuses on fieldwork as an embodied spatial practice, showing how, since the turn of the century, a disciplined professional body has been articulated along a changing border with literary and journalistic travel practices. In opposition to these pur-portedly superficial, subjective, and biased forms of knowledge, anthro-pological research was oriented toward the production of deep, *cultural* knowledge. I argue that the border is unstable, constantly renegotiated. The third section surveys current contestations of normative Euro-Ameri-can travel histories that have long structured anthropology's research prac-tices. Notions of community insides and outsides, homes and abroads, fields and metropoles, are increasingly challenged by postexotic, decolo-nizing trends. It is much less clear what counts, today, as acceptable fieldwork, the range of spatial practices "cleared" by the discipline.

I borrow the phrase "spatial practice" from Michel de Certeau's book

The Practice of Everyday Life (1984). For de Certeau, "space" is never ontologically given. It is discursively mapped and corporeally practiced. An urban neighborhood, for example, may be laid out physically according to a street plan. But it is not a space until it is practiced by people's active occupation, their movements through and around it. In this perspective, there is nothing given about a "field." It must be worked, turned into a discrete social space, by embodied practices of interactive travel. I will have more to say, en route, about the expanded sense, and limitations, of the term "travel" as I use it. And I will be concerned, primarily, with norms and ideal types. In the introduction to an important collection of essays on the "field" in anthropology, Gupta and Ferguson (1996) argue that current practice potentially draws on a broad range of ethnographic activities, some of them unorthodox by modern standards. But they confirm that, since the 1920s, a recognizable norm has held sway in the academic centers of Euro-America.[1] Anthropological fieldwork has represented something specific among overlapping sociological and ethnographic methods: an especially deep, extended, and interactive research encounter. That, of course, is the ideal. In practice, criteria of "depth" in fieldwork (length of stay, mode of interaction, repeated visits, grasp of languages) have varied widely, as have actual research experiences.

This multiplicity of practices blurs any sharp, referential meaning for "fieldwork." What are we talking about when we invoke anthropological fieldwork? Before proceeding, I must linger a moment on this problem of definition. Elementary semantics distinguishes several ways meanings are sustained: roughly, by reference, concept, and use. I will draw primarily on the latter two, commonly qualified as "mentalist" (Akmajian et al., 1993: 198–201). Conceptual definitions use a prototype, often a visual image, to define a core against which variants are evaluated. A famous photograph of Malinowski's tent pitched in the midst of a Trobriand village has long served as a potent mental *image* of anthropological fieldwork. (Everyone "knows" it, but how many could describe the actual scene?) There have been other images: visions of personal interaction—for example, photos of Margaret Mead leaning intently toward a Balinese mother and baby. Moreover, as I have already suggested, the word "field" itself conjures up mental images of cleared space, cultivation, work, ground. When one speaks of working *in* the field, or *going* into the field, one draws on mental images of a distinct place with an inside and outside, reached by practices of physical movement.

These mental images focus and constrain definitions. For example, they make it strange to say that an anthropologist in his or her office talking on the phone is doing fieldwork—even if what is actually happening is the disciplined, interactive collection of ethnographic data. Images materialize concepts, producing a semantic field that seems sharp at the "center" and blurred at the "edges." The same function is served by more abstract concepts. A range of phenomena are gathered around prototypes; I will, in deference to Kuhn (1970: 187), speak of *exemplars*. Just as a robin is taken to be a more typical bird than a penguin, thus helping to define the concept "bird," so certain exemplary cases of fieldwork anchor heterogeneous experiences. "Exotic" fieldwork pursued over a continuous period of at least a year has, for some time now, set the norm against which other practices are judged. Given this exemplar, different practices of cross-cultural research seem less like "real" fieldwork (Weston, 1997).

Real for whom? The meaning of an expression is ultimately determined by a language community. This *use* criterion opens space for a history and sociology of meanings. But it is complicated, in the present case, by the fact that those people recognized as anthropologists (the relevant community) are critically defined by having accepted and done something close (or close enough) to "real fieldwork." The boundaries of the relevant community have been (and are, increasingly) constituted by struggles over the term's proper range of meanings. This complication is present, to some extent, in all community-use criteria for meaning, especially when "essentially contested concepts" (Gallie, 1964) are at stake. But in the case of anthropologists and "fieldwork," the loop of mutual constitution is unusually tight. The community does not simply use (define) the term "fieldwork"; it is materially used (defined) by it. A different range of meanings would make a different community of anthropologists, and vice versa. The sociopolitical stakes in these definitions—issues of inclusion and exclusion, center and periphery—need to be kept explicit.

Disciplinary Borderlands

Consider the project of Karen McCarthy Brown, who studied a vodou priestess in Brooklyn (and accompanied her on a visit to Haiti). Brown traveled into the field by car, or on the New York subway, from her home in Manhattan. Her ethnography was less a practice of intensive dwelling (the "tent in the village") and more a matter of repeated visiting, collaborative work. Or perhaps her work involved what Renato Rosaldo once called, in a discussion of what makes anthropological ethnography distinctive, "deep hanging out."[2] Before working with Alourdes, the subject of her study, Brown had made research trips to Haiti. But when she visited Alourdes for the first time, she felt a new kind of displacement:

> Our nostrils filled with the smells of charcoal and roasting meat and our ears with overlapping episodes of salsa, reggae, and the bouncy monotony of what Haitians call jazz. Animated conversations could be heard in Haitian French Creole, Spanish, and more than one lyrical dialect of English. The street was a crazy quilt of shops: Chicka-Licka, the Ashanti Bazaar, a storefront Christian church with an improbably long and specific name, a Haitian restaurant, and Botanica Shango—one of the apothecaries of New World African religions offering fast-luck and get-rich-quick powders, High John the Conqueror root, and votive candles marked for the Seven African Powers. I was no more than a few miles from my home in lower Manhattan, but I felt as if I had taken a wrong turn, slipped through a crack between worlds, and emerged on the main street of a tropical city. (Brown, 1991: 1)

Compare this "arrival scene" (Pratt, 1986) with Malinowski's famous "Imagine yourself set down [on a Trobriand Island beach]" (Malinowski, 1961). Both rhetorically construct a sharply different, tropical "place," a topos and topic for the work to follow. But Brown's contemporary version is presented with a degree of irony: her tropical city in Brooklyn is sensuously real *and* imaginary—an "illusion," she goes on to call it, projected by an ethnographic traveler in a complexly hybrid world-city. Hers is not a neighborhood (urban village) study. If it has a microcosmic locus, it is Alourdes' three-story row house in the shadow of the Brooklyn-Queens Expressway—home of the only Haitian family in a black North American neighborhood. Diasporic "Haiti," in this ethnography, is multiply located. Brown's ethnography is situated less by a discrete place, a field she enters and inhabits for a time, than by an interpersonal relationship—a mixture of observation, dialogue, apprenticeship, and friendship—with Alourdes. With this relationship as its center, a cultural world of individuals, places, memories, and practices is evoked. Brown visits, frequents, this world both in Alourdes' house, where ceremonies and socializing take place, and elsewhere. Brown's "field" is wherever she is with Alourdes. She returns, typically, to sleep, reflect, write up her notes, lead her life at home in lower Manhattan.

Following established fieldwork practice, Brown's ethnography contains little detail about the everyday life in Manhattan interspersed with the visits to Brooklyn. Her field remains discrete, "out there." And while the relationship/culture under study cannot be neatly spatialized, a different place is visited intensively. There is a physical, interpersonal interaction with a distinct, often exotic, world, leading to an experience of initiation. While the spatial practice of dwelling, taking up residence in a community, is not observed, the ethnographer's movement "in" and "out," her coming and going, is systematic. One wonders what effects these proximities and distances have on the way Brown's research is conceived and represented. How, for example, does she pull back from her research relationship in order to write about it? This taking of distance has typically been conceived as a "departure" from the field, a place clearly removed from home (Crapanzano, 1977). What difference does it make when one's "informant" routinely calls one at home to demand help with a ceremony, support in a crisis, a favor? Spatial practices of travel and temporal practices of writing have been crucial to the definition and representation of a *topic*— the translation of ongoing experience and entangled relationship into something distanced and representable (Clifford, 1990). How did Brown negotiate this translation in a field whose boundaries were so fluid?

A similar but more extreme challenge for the definition of "real" fieldwork is raised by David Edwards in his article "Afghanistan, Ethnography, and the New World Order." Entering anthropology with hopes of returning to Afghanistan to conduct "a traditional sort of village study in some mountain community," Edwards confronted a war-torn, dispersed "field": "Since 1982, I have carried out fieldwork in a variety of places, including the city of Peshawar, Pakistan, and various refugee camps scattered around the Northwest Frontier Province. One summer, I also traveled inside Afghanistan to observe the operations of a group of *mujahadin,* and I have spent quite a bit of time among Afghan refugees in the Washington, D.C., area. Finally, I have been monitoring the activities of an Afghan computer newsgroup" (Edwards, 1994: 343).

Multi-locale ethnography (Marcus and Fischer, 1986) is increasingly familiar; multi-locale *fieldwork* is an oxymoron. How many sites can be studied intensively before criteria of "depth" are compromised?[3] Roger Rouse's fieldwork in two linked sites retains the notion of a single, albeit mobile, community (Rouse, 1991). Karen McCarthy Brown stays within the "world" of an individual. But David Edwards' practice is more scattered. Indeed, when he begins to link his dispersed instances of "Afghan culture," he must rely on fairly weak thematic resonances and the common feeling of "ambiguity" they produce—at least for him. Whatever the borders of Edwards' "multiply inflected" cultural object (Harding, 1994), the range of spatial practices he adopts to encounter it is exemplary. He writes that he has "carried out fieldwork" in a city and refugee camps; he has "traveled" to observe the *mujahadin;* he has "spent quite a lot of time" (hanging out, deeply?) with Afghans in Washington, D.C.; and he has been "monitoring" the exile computer newsgroup. This last ethnographic activity is the least comfortable for Edwards (349). At the time of writing, he has only been "lurking" not posting his own messages. His research on the Internet is not yet interactive. But it is very informative. Edwards intensively listens in on a group of exiled Afghans—male, relatively affluent—worrying together about politics, religious practices, the nature and boundaries of their community.

The experiences of Karen McCarthy Brown and David Edwards suggest some of the current pressures on anthropological fieldwork seen as a spatial practice of intensive dwelling. The "field" in sociocultural anthropology has been constituted by a "historically specific range of distances, boundaries, and modes of travel" (Clifford, 1990: 64). These are changing, as the geography of distance and difference alters in postcolonial/neocolonial situations, as power relations of research are reconfigured, as new technologies of transport and communication are deployed, and as "natives" are recognized for their specific worldly experiences and histories of dwelling and traveling (Appadurai, 1988a; Clifford, 1992; Teaiwa, 1993; Narayan, 1993). What remains of classic anthropological practices in these new situations? How are the notions of travel, boundary, co-residence, interaction, inside and outside that have defined the field and proper fieldwork being challenged and reworked in contemporary anthropology?

Before taking up these questions, we need a clear sense of what dominant practices of the "field" are at issue, what issues of disciplinary definition constrain current arguments. Fieldwork normally involves physically leaving "home" (however that is defined) to travel in and out of some distinctly *different* setting. Today, the setting can be Highland New Guinea; or it can be a neighborhood, house, office, hospital, church, or lab. It can be defined as a mobile society, that of long-distance truckers, for example—providing one spends long hours in the cab, talking (Agar, 1985). Intensive, "deep" interaction is required, something canonically guaranteed by the spatial practice of extended, if temporary, dwelling in a community. Fieldwork can also involve repeated short visits, as in the American tradition of reservation ethnology. Teamwork and long-term research (Foster et al., 1979) have been variously practiced in different local and national traditions. But common to these practices, anthropological fieldwork requires that one do something more than pass through. One must do more than conduct interviews, make surveys, or compose journalistic reports. This requirement continues today, embodied in a flexible range of activities, from co-residence to various forms of collaboration and advocacy. The legacy of intensive fieldwork defines *anthropological* styles of research, styles critically important for disciplinary (self-)recognition.[4]

There are no natural or intrinsic disciplines. All knowledge is interdisciplinary. Thus, disciplines define and redefine themselves interactively and competitively. They do this by inventing traditions and canons, by consecrating methodological norms and research practices, by appropriating, translating, silencing, and holding at bay adjacent perspectives. Active processes of *disciplining* operate at various levels, defining "hot" and "cold" domains of the disciplinary culture, certain areas that change rapidly and others that are relatively invariant. They articulate, in tactically shifting ways, the solid core and the negotiable edge of a recognizable domain of knowledge and research practice. Institutionalization channels and slows but cannot stop these processes of redefinition, except at peril of sclerosis.

Consider the choices faced today by someone planning the syllabus for an introductory graduate proseminar in sociocultural anthropology.[5] Given a limited number of weeks, how important is it that novice anthropologists read Radcliffe-Brown? Robert Lowie? Would it be better to include Meyer Fortes or Kenneth Burke? Lévi-Strauss, surely . . . but why not also Simone de Beauvoir? Franz Boas, of course . . . and Frantz Fanon? Margaret Mead or Marx . . . or E. P. Thompson, or Zora Neale Hurston, or Michel Foucault? Melville Herskovitz perhaps . . . and W. E. B. DuBois? St. Clair Drake? Work on photography and media? Kinship, once a disciplinary core, is now actively forgotten in some departments. Anthropological linguistics, still invoked as one of the canonical "four fields," is very unevenly covered. In some programs, one is more likely to read literary theory, colonial history, or cognitive science . . . Synthetic notions of *man,* the "culture-bearing animal," that once stitched together a discipline now seem antiquated, or perverse. Can the disciplinary center hold? In the introductory syllabus, a hybrid selection will eventually be made, tuned to local traditions and current demands, with recognizably "anthropological" authors at the center. (Sometimes the "pure" disciplinary lineage will be cordoned off in a History of Anthropology course, required or not.) Anthropology reproduces itself while selectively engaging with relevant interlocutors: from social history, from cultural studies, from biology, from cognitive science, from minority and feminist scholarship, from colonial discourse critique, from semiotics and media studies, from literary and discourse analysis, from sociology, from psychology, from linguistics, from ecology, from political economy, from . . .

Sociocultural anthropology has always been a fluid, relatively open discipline. It has prided itself on its ability to draw on, enrich, and synthesize other fields of study. Writing in 1964, Eric Wolf optimistically defined anthropology as a "discipline between disciplines" (Wolf, 1964: x). But this openness poses recurring problems of self-definition. And partly because its theoretical purview has remained so broad and interdisciplinary, despite recurring attempts to cut it down to size, the discipline has focused on research practices as defining, core elements. Fieldwork has played—and continues to play—a central disciplining function. In the current conjuncture, the range of topics anthropology can study and the array of theoretical perspectives it can deploy is immense. In these areas the discipline is "hot," constantly changing, hybridizing. In the "colder" domain of acceptable fieldwork, change is also occurring but more slowly. In most anthropological milieus, "real" fieldwork continues to be actively defended against other ethnographic styles.

The exotic exemplar—co-residence for extended periods away from home, the "tent in the village"—retains considerable authority. But it has, in practice, been decentered. The various spatial practices it authorized, as well as the relevant criteria for evaluating "depth" and "intensity," have changed and continue to change. Contemporary political, cultural, and economic conditions bring new pressures and opportunities to anthropology. The range of possible venues for ethnographic study has expanded dramatically, and the discipline's potential membership is more diverse. Its geopolitical location (no longer so securely in the Euro-American "center") is challenged. In this context of change and contestation, academic anthropology struggles to reinvent its traditions in new circumstances. Like the changing societies it studies, the discipline sustains itself in blurred and policed borderlands, using strategies of hybridization and reauthentification, assimilation and exclusion.

Suggestive boundary problems emerge from David Edwards' awkward time on the Afghan Internet. What if someone studied the culture of computer hackers (a perfectly acceptable anthropology project in many, if not all, departments) and in the process never "interfaced" in the flesh with a single hacker. Would the months, even years, spent on the Net be fieldwork? The research might well pass both the length-of-stay and the "depth"/interactivity tests. (We know that some strange and intense conversations can occur over the Net.) And electronic travel is, after all, a kind of *dépaysement*. It could add up to intensive participant observation in a different community without ever physically leaving home. When I've asked anthropologists whether this could be fieldwork, they have generally responded "maybe," even, in one case, "of course." But when I press the point, asking whether they would supervise a Ph.D. dissertation based primarily on this kind of disembodied research, they hesitate or say no: it would not be currently acceptable fieldwork. Given the traditions of the discipline, a graduate student would be ill-advised to follow such a course. We come up against the institutional-historical constraints that enforce the distinction between fieldwork and a broader range of ethnographic activities. Fieldwork in anthropology is sedimented with a disciplinary history, and it continues to function as a rite of passage and marker of professionalism.

A boundary that currently preoccupies sociocultural anthropology is that which separates it from a heterogeneous collection of academic practices often called "cultural studies."[6] This border renegotiates, in a new context, some of the long-established divisions and crossings of sociology and anthropology. Qualitative sociology, as least, has its own ethnographic traditions, increasingly relevant to a postexoticist anthropology.[7] But given fairly firm institutional identities, in the United States at least, the border with sociology seems less unruly than that with "cultural studies." This new site of border crossing and policing partly repeats an ongoing, fraught relationship with "textualism" or "lit. crit." The move to "recapture" anthropology—manifested in dismissals of the collection *Writing Culture* (Clifford and Marcus, 1986) and more recently, often incoherently, in sweeping rejections of "postmodern anthropology"—is by now routine in some quarters. But the border with cultural studies may be less manageable; for it is easier to maintain a clear separation when the disciplinary other, literary-rhetorical theory or textualist semiotics, has no fieldwork component and at best an anecdotal "ethnographic" approach to cultural phenomena. "Cultural studies," in its Birmingham tradition as well as in some of its sociological veins, possesses a developed ethnographic tradition much closer to anthropological fieldwork. The distinction, "We do fieldwork, they do discourse analysis," is more difficult to sustain. Some anthropologists have turned to cultural studies ethnography for inspiration (Lave et al., 1992), and indeed there is much to learn from its increasingly complex articulations of class, gender, race, and sexuality. Moreover, what Paul Willis did with the working-class "lads" of *Learning to Labour* (1977)—hanging out with them at school, talking with parents, working alongside them on the shop floor—is comparable to good fieldwork. Its depth of social interaction was surely greater than, say, that achieved by Evans-Pritchard during his ten months with hostile and reluctant Nuer.

Many contemporary anthropological projects are difficult to distinguish from cultural studies work. For example, Susan Harding is writing an ethnography of Christian fundamentalism in the United States. She has done extensive participant observation in Lynchburg, Virginia, in and around Jerry Falwell's church. And of course the television ministry of Falwell and others like him is very much her concern—her "field." Indeed, she is interested not primarily in a spatially defined community but in what she calls the "discourse" of the new fundamentalisms.[8] She is concerned with TV programs, sermons, novels, media of all kinds, as well as with conversations and everyday behavior. Harding's mixture of participant-observation, cultural criticism, and media and discourse analysis is characteristic of work in the current ethnographic border zones. How "anthropological" is it? How different is Susan Harding's frequenting of evangelicals in Lynchburg from Willis' or Angela McRobbie's studies of youth cultures in Britain or the earlier work of the Chicago School sociologists? There are certainly differences, but they do not coalesce as a discrete method, and there is considerable overlap.

One important difference is Harding's insistence that a crucial portion of her ethnographic work must involve *living with* an evangelical Christian family. Indeed, she reports that this was when she felt she had really "entered the field." Previously she had stayed in a motel. One might think of this as a classic articulation of fieldwork, deployed in a new setting. In a sense it is. But it is part of a potentially radical decentering. For there can be no question of calling the period of intensive co-residence in Lynchburg the essence or core of the project to which the TV viewing and reading were ancillary. In Harding's project, "fieldwork" was an important way of finding out how the new fundamentalism was lived in everyday terms. And while it certainly helped define her hybrid project as anthropological, it was not a privileged site of interactive depth or initiation.

Harding's work is an example of research which draws on cultural studies, discourse analysis, and gender and media studies while maintaining crucial anthropological features. It marks a current direction for the discipline, one in which fieldwork remains a necessary but no longer privileged method. Does this mean that the institutional border between anthropology, cultural studies, and allied traditions is open? Far from it. Precisely because the crossings are so promiscuous, the overlaps so frequent, actions to reassert identity are mounted at strategic sites and moments. These include the initiatory process of graduate certification, and moments when people need to be denied a job, funding, or authority. In the everyday disciplining that makes anthropologists and not cultural studies scholars, the boundary is reasserted, routinely. Most publicly perhaps, when graduate students' "field" projects are approved, the distinctive spatial practices that have defined anthropology tend to be reasserted—often in nonnegotiable ways.

The concept of the field and the disciplinary practices associated with it constitute a central, ambiguous legacy for anthropology. Fieldwork has become a "problem" because of its positivist and colonialist historical associations (the field as "laboratory," the field as place of "discovery" for privileged sojourners). It has also become more difficult to circumscribe, given the proliferation of ethnographic topics and the time-space compressions (Harvey, 1989) characteristic of postmodern, postcolonial/ neocolonial situations. What will anthropology make of this problem? Time will tell. Fieldwork, a research practice predicated on interactive depth and spatialized difference, is being "reworked" (Gupta and Ferguson's term), for it is one of the few relatively clear marks of disciplinary distinction left. But how wide can the range of sanctioned practices be? And how "decentered" (Gupta and Ferguson) can fieldwork become before it is just one of a range of ethnographic and historical methods used by the discipline, in concert with other disciplines?

Anthropology has always been more than fieldwork, but fieldwork has been something an anthropologist *should* have done, more or less well, at least once.[9] Will this change? Perhaps it should. Perhaps fieldwork will become merely a research tool rather than an essential disposition or professional marker. Time will tell. At present, however, fieldwork remains critically important—a disciplining process and an ambiguous legacy.

The Fieldwork Habitus

The institutionalization of fieldwork in the late nineteenth and early twentieth centuries can be understood within a larger history of "travel." (I use the term in an expanded sense, of which more in a moment.) Among Westerners traveling and dwelling abroad, the anthropological fieldworker was a latecomer. Explorers, missionaries, colonial officers, traders, colonists, and natural scientific researchers were well-established figures before the emergence of the on-the-ground anthropological professional. Prior to Boas, Malinowski, Mead, Firth, et al., the anthropological scholar usually remained at home, processing ethnographic information sent by "men on the spot" who were drawn from among the sojourners just mentioned. If metropolitan scholars ventured out, it was on survey and museum-collection expeditions. Whatever exceptions there may have been to this pattern, interactive depth and co-residence were not yet professional requirements.

When intensive fieldwork began to be championed by the Boasians and Malinowskians, an effort was required to distinguish the kind of knowledge produced by this method from that acquired by other long-term residents in the areas studied. At least three "disciplinary others" were held at arm's length: the missionary, the colonial officer, and the travel writer (journalist or literary exoticist). Much could be said about anthropology's fraught relations with these three professional alter egos whose purportedly amateur, interventionist, subjective accounts of indigenous life would be "killed by science," as Malinowski put it.[10] My focus here is limited to the border with literary and journalistic travel. As a methodological principle I do not presuppose the discipline's self-definitions, whether positive ("we have a special research practice and understanding of human culture") or negative ("we are *not* missionaries, colonial officers, or travel writers"). Rather, I assume that these definitions must be actively produced, negotiated, and renegotiated through changing historical relationships. It is often easier to say clearly what one is not than what one is. In the early years of modern anthropology, while the discipline was still establishing its distinctive research tradition and authoritative exemplars, negative definitions were critical. And in times of uncertain identity (such as the present), definition may be achieved most effectively by naming clear *outsides* rather than by attempting to reduce always diverse and hybrid *insides* to a stable unity. A more or less permanent process of disciplining at the edges sustains recognizable borders in entangled borderlands.

Anthropological research travelers have, of course, regularly depended on missionaries (for grammars, transportation, introductions, and in certain cases for a deeper translation of language and custom than can be acquired in a one- or two-year visit). The fieldworker's professional difference from the missionary, based on real discrepancies of agenda and attitude, has had to be asserted against equally real areas of overlap and dependency. So, too, with colonial (and neocolonial) regimes: ethnographers typically have asserted their aim to understand not govern, to collaborate not exploit. But they have navigated in the dominant society, often enjoying white skin privilege and a physical safety in the field guaranteed by a history of prior punitive expeditions and policing (Schneider, 1995: 139). Scientific fieldwork separated itself from colonial regimes by claiming to be apolitical. This distinction is currently being questioned and renegotiated in the wake of anticolonial movements which have tended not to recognize the distance claimed by anthropologists from contexts of domination and privilege.

The travel writer's transient and literary approach, sharply rejected in the disciplining of fieldwork, has continued to tempt and contaminate the scientific practices of cultural description. Anthropologists are, typically, people who leave and write. Seen in a long historical perspective, fieldwork is a distinctive cluster of travel practices (largely but not exclusively Western). Travel and travel discourse should not be reduced to the relatively recent tradition of literary travel, a narrowed conception which emerged in the late nineteenth and early twentieth centuries. This notion of "travel" was articulated against an emerging ethnography (and other forms of "scientific" field research) on the one hand, and against tourism (a practice defined as incapable of producing serious knowledge) on the other. The spatial and textual practices of what might now be called "sophisticated travel"—a phrase taken from *New York Times* supplements catering to the "independent" traveler[11]—function within an elite, and highly differentiated, tourist sector defined by the statement, "We are *not* tourists." (Jean-Didier Urbain, in *L'idiot du voyage* (1991), has thoroughly analyzed this discursive formation. See also Buzzard, 1993, and Chapter 8 below.) The literary tradition of "sophisticated travel," whose disappearance has been lamented by critics such as Daniel Boorstin and Paul Fussell, is reinvented by a long list of contemporary writers—Paul Theroux, Shirley Hazzard, Bruce Chatwin, Jan Morris, Ronald Wright, et al.[12]

"Travel," as I use it, is an inclusive term embracing a range of more or less voluntarist practices of leaving "home" to go to some "other" place. The displacement takes place for the purpose of gain—material, spiritual, scientific. It involves obtaining knowledge and/or having an "experience" (exciting, edifying, pleasurable, estranging, broadening). The long history of travel that includes the spatial practices of "fieldwork" is predominantly Western-dominated, strongly male, and upper-middle class. Good critical and historical work is now appearing in this comparative domain, paying attention to political, economic, and regional contexts, as well as to the determinations and subversions of gender, class, culture, race, and individual psychology (Hulme, 1986; Porter, 1991; Mills, 1991; Pratt, 1992).

Before the separation of genres associated with the emergence of modern fieldwork, travel and travel writing covered a broad spectrum. In eighteenth-century Europe, a *récit de voyage* or "travel book" might include exploration, adventure, natural science, espionage, commercial prospecting, evangelism, cosmology, philosophy, and ethnography. By the 1920s, however, the research practices and written reports of anthropologists had been much more clearly set apart. No longer scientific travelers or explorers, they were defined as fieldworkers, a change shared with other sciences (Kuklick, 1996). The field was a distinctive cluster of academic research practices, traditions, and representational rules. But while competing practices and rhetorics were actively held at bay in the process, the newly cleared disciplinary space could never be entirely free of contamination. Its borders would have to be rebuilt, shifted, and reworked. Indeed, one way to understand the current "experimentalism" of ethnographic writing is as a renegotiation of the boundary, agonistically defined in the late nineteenth century, with "travel writing."

"Literariness," held at a distance in the figure of the travel writer, has returned to ethnography in the form of strong claims about the prefiguration and rhetorical communication of "data." The facts do not speak for themselves; they are emplotted rather than collected, produced in worldly relationships rather than observed in controlled environments.[13] This growing awareness of the poetical and political contingency of field-work—an awareness forced on anthropologists by postwar anticolonial challenges to Euro-American centrality—is reflected in a more concrete textual sense of the ethnographer's location. Elements of the "literary" travel narrative that were excluded from ethnographies (or marginalized in their prefaces) now appear more prominently. These include the re-searcher's routes into and through "the field"; time in the capital city, registering the surrounding national/transnational context; technologies of transport (getting there as well as being there); interactions with named, idiosyncratic individuals rather than anonymous, representative inform-ants.

In Chapter 1, I worked to decenter the field as a naturalized practice of *dwelling* by proposing a cross-cutting metaphor: fieldwork as *travel encounters*. To decenter or interrupt fieldwork-as-dwelling is not to reject or refute it. Fieldwork has always been a mix of institutionalized practices of dwelling and traveling. But in the disciplinary idealization of the "field," spatial practices of moving to and from, in and out, passing through, have tended to be subsumed by those of dwelling (rapport, initiation, familiar-ity). This is changing. Ironically, now that much anthropological fieldwork is conducted (like Karen McCarthy Brown's) close to home, the materiality of travel, in and out of the field, becomes more apparent, indeed consti-tutive of the object/site of study. Fieldwork in cities must distinguish itself from other forms of interclass, interracial travel and appreciation, marking a difference from established traditions of urban social work and liberal "slumming." The home of the research traveler exists in a politicized prior relation to that of the people under study (or, in contemporary parlance, the people "worked with"). These latter may themselves travel regularly to and from the home base of the researcher, if only for employment. (The "ethnographic," cross-cultural knowledge of a maid or service worker is considerable.) These parallel, sometimes intersecting, spatiopolitical rela-tions have also been present in "exotic" anthropological research, particu-larly when colonial or neocolonial flows of armies, commodities, labor, or education materially link the poles of fieldwork travel. But images of distance, rather than of interconnection and contact, have tended to naturalize the field as an other *place*. The socially established routes constitutive of field *relations* are harder to ignore when the research is conducted nearby, or when airplanes and telephones compress space.

Fieldwork thus "takes place" in worldly, contingent relations of travel, not in controlled sites of research. Saying this does not simply dissolve the boundary between contemporary fieldwork and travel (or journalistic) work. There are important generic and institutional distinctions. The injunction to dwell intensively, to learn local languages, to produce a "deep" interpretation is a difference that makes a difference. But the border between the two relatively recent traditions of literary travel and academic fieldwork is being renegotiated. Indeed, the example offered above by David Edwards' multiple sites of encounter brings fieldwork (dangerously, some may feel) close to travel. This rapprochement takes a different form in Anna Tsing's innovative ethnography *In the Realm of the Diamond Queen* (1993). Tsing conducts fieldwork in a classic "exotic" site, the Meratus Mountains of South Kilimantan, Indonesia. While preserving disciplinary practices of intensive local interaction, her writing systematically crosses the border of ethnographic analysis and travel narration. Her account historicizes both her own and her subjects' practices of dwelling and traveling, deriving her knowledge from specific encounters between differently cosmopolitan, gendered individuals, not cultural types. (See, particularly, Part Two: "A Science of Travel.") Her field site in what she calls an "out of the way place" is never taken for granted as a natural or traditional environment. It is produced, a contact space, by local, national, and transnational forces of which her research travel is a part.

Edwards and Tsing exemplify exotic fieldwork at the edges of changing academic practice. In both, differently spatialized, we see the increased prominence of practices and tropes commonly associated with travel and travel writing.[14] These are currently visible in much anthropological ethnography, figuring different versions of the routed/rooted researcher, the "positioned subject" (Rosaldo, 1989: 7). Signs of the times include a trend toward use of the first-person singular pronoun in accounts of fieldwork, presented as stories rather than as observations and interpretations. Often the field journal (private, and closer to the "subjective" accounts of travel writing) leaks into the "objective" field data. I am not describing a linear movement from collection to narration, objective to subjective, impersonal to personal, co-residence to travel encounter. It is a question not of a progression from ethnography to travel writing but rather of a shifting balance and a renegotiation of key *relations* that have constituted the two practices and discourses.

In tracking anthropology's changing relations with travel, we may find it useful to think of the "field" as a habitus rather than as a place, a cluster of *embodied* dispositions and practices. The work of feminist scholars has played a crucial role in specifying the social body of the ethnographer, while criticizing the limitations of androcentric "gender-neutral" work and opening up major new areas of understanding.[15] Similarly, anticolonial pressures, colonial discourse analysis, and critical race theory have decentered the predominantly Western, and white, traditional fieldworker. Seen in light of these interventions, the fieldwork habitus of the Malinowskian generation appears as the articulation of specific, disciplined practices.

This normative "body" was *not* that of a traveler. As it drew on older traditions of scientific travel, it did so in sharpened opposition to romantic, "literary," or subjective strands. The body legitimated by modern fieldwork was not a sensorium moving through extended space, across borders. It was not on an expedition or a survey. Rather, it was a body circulating and working (one might almost say "commuting") within a delimited space. The local map predominated over the tour or itinerary as a technology of physical location. Being there was more important than getting there (and leaving there). The fieldworker was a homebody abroad, not a cosmopolitan visitor. I am, of course, speaking broadly of disciplinary norms and textual figures, not of the actual historical experiences of field anthropologists. In varying degrees, these diverged from the norms while being constrained by them.

Emotions, a necessary part of the controlled empathy of participant-observation, were not accorded primary expression. They could not be the chief source of public judgments about the communities under study. This was particularly true of negative assessments. The moral judgments and curses of the travel writer, based on social frustrations, physical discomforts, and prejudices as well as on principled criticism, were excluded or downplayed. An understanding rapport and measured affection were favored. Expressions of overt enthusiasm and love were circumscribed. Anger, frustration, judgments on individuals, desire, and ambivalence went into private diaries. The scandal provoked, in some quarters, by the publication of Malinowski's intimate diary (1967) was related to the glimpse it gave of a less temperate, race- and sex-conscious subject/body in the field. Early public transgressions of the professional habitus include works by Leiris (1934, written as a field journal), Bowen (1954, in novel form), and Jean Briggs (1970, in which personal emotions perhaps for the first time were central to an ethnographic monograph).

If emotions tended to be marginalized, so, for the most part, did the researcher's experiences of gender, race, and sex. Gender, while occasionally featured (particularly in the "marked," female case), was not publicly recognized as constituting the research process in a systematic way. Margaret Mead, for example, did at times conduct research and write "as a woman," crossing defined women's and men's spheres, but her disciplinary persona was that of a scientifically authoritative cultural observer, of unmarked gender and by default "male." Her more "subjective," "soft" stylistic experiments and popular writings did not bring her credit within the disciplinary fraternity, where she adopted a more "objective," "hard" voice. Lutkehaus (1995) provides a contextual account of these historically gendered locations and Mead's shifting persona. Male researchers of Mead's generation did not conduct research "as men" among locally defined women and men. Many purportedly holistic "cultural" accounts were, in fact, based on intensive work with men only. Overall, the constraints and possibilities attached to the researcher's gender were not salient features of the field habitus.

The same went for race. Here sociocultural anthropology's important theoretical and empirical critique of racialist essences doubtless influenced the professional habitus. "Race" was not the social/historical formation of contemporary critical race theorists (for example, Omi and Winant, 1986; Gilroy, 1987) but a biological essence whose "natural" determinations were contested by the contextual determinations of "culture." Anthropologists, the culture-bearing scholars, needed to decenter and cross over putatively essential racial lines. Their interactive and intensive understanding of cultural formations gave them a powerful tool against racial reductions. But in attacking a *natural* phenomenon, they did not confront race as a *historical* formation that located their subjects politically and that simultaneously constrained and empowered their own research (Harrison, 1991: 3).[16] Occasionally this positioning could be glimpsed—for example, in Evans-Pritchard's introduction to *The Nuer* (1940); but it was not part of the explicit body, the professional habitus, of the fieldworker.

By contrast, travel writers often noticed color and spoke from a racialized position. Of course, they were not necessarily critical of the relations involved—often quite the reverse! The point is not to celebrate a relatively greater awareness of race—and gender—in travel writing but to show how, by contrast, the habitus of the ethnographer downplayed these historical determinations. However marked it was by gender, race, caste, or class privilege, ethnography needed to transcend such locations in order to articulate a deeper, *cultural* understanding. This articulation was based on powerful techniques, including at least the following: extended co-residence; systematic observation and recording of data; effective interlocution in at least one local language; a specific mix of alliance, complicity, friendship, respect, coercion, and ironic toleration leading to "rapport"; a hermeneutic attention to deep or implicit structures and meanings. These techniques were designed to produce (and often did produce, within the horizons I am trying to delimit) more contextual, less reductive understandings of local lifeways than did the passing observations of the traveler.

Some writers who could be classified as travelers stayed for extended periods abroad, spoke local languages, and had complex views of indigenous (as well as of creole/colonial) life. Some classified as ethnographers stayed relatively short times, spoke languages badly, and did not interact intensively. The range of actual social relations, communicative techniques, and spatial practices deployed between the poles of fieldwork and travel is a continuum, not a sharp border. There has been considerable overlap.[17] But in spite of, or rather because of, this border complexity, the discursive/institutional lines had to be clearly drawn. This need sustained pressures which, over time, gathered empirical experiences closer to the two poles. In this process, the "superficiality" of the traveler and travel writer was opposed to the "depth" of the fieldworker. But one might also say, provocatively, that the former's "promiscuity" was disciplined in favor of the "family values" often invoked in ethnographic prefaces: fieldwork as a process of getting along with others, of adoption, initiation, learning local norms—much as a child learns.

The habitus of modern fieldwork, defined against that of travel, has proscribed interactive modes long associated with travel experience. Perhaps the most absolute continuing taboo is on sexual liaisons. Fieldworkers could love but not desire the "objects" of their attention. On the continuum of possible relations, sexual entanglements were defined as dangerous, too close. Participant-observation, a delicate management of distance and proximity, should not include entanglements in which the ability to maintain perspective might be lost. Sexual relations could not be avowed sources of research knowledge. Nor could going into trance or taking hallucinogens, though the taboo there has been somewhat less strict, a certain amount of "experimentation" sometimes being justifiable in the name of participant-observation. Sexual experimentation was, however, out of bounds. A disciplined, participant-observing body "went along" with indigenous life, selectively.

At its inception, though, the taboo on sex may have been less against "going native" or losing critical distance than against "going traveling," violating a professional habitus. In travel practices and texts, having sex, heterosexual and homosexual, with local people was common. Indeed in certain travel circuits, such as the nineteenth-century *voyage en Orient,* it was quasi-obligatory.[18] A popular writer such as Pierre Loti consecrated his authority, his access to the mysterious and feminized Other, through stories of sexual encounter. In fieldwork accounts, however, such stories have been virtually nonexistent. Only recently, and still rarely, has the taboo been broken (Rabinow, 1977; Cesara, 1982). Why should sharing beds be a less appropriate source of fieldwork knowledge than sharing food? There may, of course, be many practical reasons for sexual restraint in the field, just as certain places and activities may be off limits to the tactful (and locally dependent) sojourner. But they are not off limits in all places and at all times. Practical constraints, which vary widely, cannot account for the disciplinary taboo on sex in fieldwork.[19]

Enough has been said, perhaps, to make the central point: a disciplinary habitus has been sustained around the embodied activity of fieldwork: an ungendered, unraced, sexually inactive subject interacts intensively (on hermeneutic/scientific levels, at the very least) with its interlocutors. If actual experiences in the field have diverged from the norm, if the taboos have sometimes been broken, and if the disciplinary habitus is now publicly contested, its normative power remains.

Another common travel practice before 1900, cross-dressing, was suppressed or channeled in the disciplining of modern fieldwork's professional "body." This is a far-reaching topic, and I must limit myself to preliminary remarks. Daniel Defert (1984) has written suggestively on the history of "clothing" in codes of European travel observation prior to the nineteenth century. A substantial, integral link was once assumed between the person and his/her outward appearance—*habitus,* in Defert's premodern usage.[20] In a deep sense it was understood that "clothes make the man" ("L'habit fait le moine"). Interpretations of *habitus,* not to be confused with *habits* ("clothes") or with the later concept of culture, were a necessary part of travel interactions. This included the communicative manipulation of appearances—what might be called, somewhat anachronistically, cultural cross-dressing. By the nineteenth century, in Defert's account, *habitus* had been reduced to *habits,* to surface coverings and adornments; *costume* had emerged as a deformation of the richer *coustume* (a term which combined the ideas of costume and custom).

Clothes would become just one of many elements in a taxonomy of observations made by scientific travelers, components of an emerging *cultural* explanation. Defert perceives this transition in Gérando's scientific advice to travelers and explorers, published in 1800. Explorers have often merely described the clothes of indigenous peoples, he wrote. You should go farther and inquire why they may or may not be willing to give up their traditional clothing for ours, and how they conceive of their origin (Defert, 1984: 39). Here the interpretive grid of *habitus* is replaced (and made to seem superficial) by a deeper conception of identity and difference. Travel relations had long been organized by complex and highly codified protocols, "surface" semiotics and transactions. The interpretation and manipulation of clothing, gesture, and appearance were integral to these practices. Seen as the outcome of this tradition, nineteenth-century cultural cross-dressing was more than just dress-up. A serious, communicative play with appearances and a site of crossover, it articulated a less absolute or essential notion of difference than that instituted by relativist notions of culture with their concepts of nativeness inscribed in language, tradition, place, ecology, and—more or less implicitly—race. The experiences of a Richard Burton or an Isabelle Eberhardt passing as "Orientals," and even the more blatantly theatrical costuming of Flaubert in Egypt or Loti on shore leave, partake of a complex tradition of travel practices held at arm's length by a modernizing ethnography.[21]

Seen from the perspective of fieldwork (intensive, interactive, based in language learning), cross-dressing could appear only as superficial dress-up, a kind of touristic slumming. In this optique, the practices of an ethnographer like Frank Hamilton Cushing, who adopted Zuni dress (and even, it has been suggested, produced "authentic" indigenous artifacts), would be somewhat embarrassing. His intensive, interactive research was not quite "modern fieldwork." A similar sense of embarrassment is experienced today by many viewers of Timothy Asche's film *A Man Called Bee,* devoted to Napoleon Chagnon's research among the Yanomami. I am thinking particularly of the opening shot, which zooms in slowly on a painted, scantily clad figure in a fighting pose who turns out, finally, to be the anthropologist. Whatever the intent of this opening, satiric or otherwise (it's not entirely clear), the impression remains that this is not a "professional" way to appear. A certain excess is registered, perhaps too easily written off as egotism. Liza Dalby's book *Geisha* (1983), which includes photographs of the anthropologist being transformed through makeup and wearing full geisha attire, is more acceptable, since the adoption of a geisha "habitus" (in Defert's older sense—a mode of being, manifested through clothes, gesture, and appearance) is a central issue in her participant observation and written ethnography. Yet the photographs of Dalby looking almost exactly like a "real" geisha break with established ethnographic conventions.

At another pole are the photographs published by Malinowski (in *Coral Gardens and Their Magic,* 1935) of himself in the field. He is dressed entirely in white, surrounded by black bodies, sharply distinguished by posture and attitude. This is insistently not a man about to "go native." Such a self-presentation is akin to the gestures of colonial Europeans who dressed formally for dinner in sweltering climates so as not to feel they were slipping "over the edge." (The miraculous starched collars of Conrad's accountant in *Heart of Darkness* are a paradigm case in colonial literature.) But ethnographers have not, typically, been so formal, and I would suggest that their fieldwork habitus was more of an intermediate formation, predicated on not theatrically standing out from local life (not asserting their difference or authority by wearing military uniforms, pith helmets, and the like) while remaining clearly marked by white skin, proximity to cameras, note pads, and other nonnative accoutrements.[22] Most professional fieldworkers did not try to disappear into the field by indulging in "superficial" travel practices of masquerade. Their embodied distinction suggested connections at deeper, hermeneutic levels, understandings forged through language, co-residence, and *cultural* knowledge.

More than a few telling glimpses of the anthropologist's habitus, overlapping and distinct from that of the traveler, are provided by Lévi-Strauss in *Tristes Tropiques* (1973). "In September 1950," he writes, "I happened to find myself in a Mogh village in the Chittagong hill tracts." After several days, he ascends to the local temple, whose gong has punctuated his days, along with the sound of "childish voices intoning the Burmese alphabet." All is innocence and order. "We had taken off our shoes to climb the hillock, and the fine, damp clay felt soft under our bare feet." At the entry to the simple, beautiful temple, built on stilts like the village houses, the visitors perform "prescribed ablutions," which after the climb through the mud seem "quite natural and devoid of any religious significance."

> A peaceful, barn-like atmosphere pervaded the place and there was a smell of hay in the air. The simple and spacious room which was like a hollowed-out haystack, the courteous behaviour of the two priests standing next to their beds with straw mattresses, the touching care with which they had brought together or made the instruments of worship— all these things helped to bring me closer than I had ever been before to my idea of what a shrine should be like. "You need not do what I am doing," my companion said to me as he prostrated himself on the ground four times before the altar, and I followed his advice. However, I did so less through self-consciousness than discretion: he knew that I did not share his beliefs, and I would have been afraid of debasing the ritual gestures by letting him think I considered them as mere conventions: but for once, I would have felt no embarrassment in performing them. Between this form of religion and myself, there was no likelihood of misunderstanding. It was not a question of bowing down in front of idols or of adoring a supposed supernatural order, but only of paying homage to the decisive wisdom that a thinker, or the society that created his legend, had evolved twenty-five centuries before and to which my civilization could contribute only by confirming it. (410–411)

Going barefoot could hardly be a casual gesture for Lévi-Strauss; but here, along with ritual cleansing prior to entering the shrine, it seems simply natural. Everything draws him into sympathy and participation. But he marks a line at the physical act of prostration. The line expresses a specific *discretion,* that of a visitor who looks beyond "mere conventions" or going along with appearances to a deeper level of respect based on historical knowledge and cultural comprehension. The anthropologist's authentic bow to Buddhism is a mental one.

Lévi-Strauss is tempted, retrospectively at least, to prostrate himself in the hill temple. Another anthropologist might well have done so. My point in noticing this line between physical and hermeneutic acts of connection is not to claim that Lévi-Strauss draws it in a place typical of anthropologists. I do want to suggest, however, that a similar line will be drawn somewhere, sometime, in the maintenance of a professional fieldwork habitus. Lévi-Strauss is clearly not one of those Western spiritual travelers who sojourn in Buddhist temples, shaving their heads and wearing saffron robes. And in this he represents the traditional ethnographic norm. One could, of course, imagine a Buddhist anthropologist becoming almost indistinguishable, in both practice and appearance, from other adepts during a period of fieldwork in a temple. And this would be a limit case for the discipline. It would be treated with suspicion, in the absence of other clearly visible signs of professional *discretion* (etymologically: a separation).[23]

Today, in many locations, indigenous people, ethnographers, and tourists all wear T-shirts and shorts. Elsewhere, distinctions of dress are more salient. In highland Guatemala it may be a necessity of decorum, a sign of respect or solidarity, to wear a long skirt or an embroidered shirt in public. But this is hardly cross-dressing. Can, should, an anthropologist wear a turban, yarmulke, *jallabeyya, huipil,* or veil? Local conventions vary. But whatever tactics are adopted, they are employed from a position of assumed *cultural* discretion. Moreover, as ethnographers work increasingly in their own societies, the issues I have been discussing in an exoticist frame become confused, the lines of separation less self-evident. Embodied professional practices of the "field"—gendered, raced, sexualized locations and crossovers, forms of self-presentation, and regulated patterns of access, departure, and return—are renegotiated.

Rerouting the Field

I have tried to identify some of the sedimented practices through and against which newly diverse ethnographic projects struggle for recognition within anthropology. Established practices come under pressure as the range of sites that can be treated ethnographically multiplies (the academic border with "cultural studies") and as differently positioned, politically invested scholars enter the field (the challenge of a "postcolonial anthropology"). The latter development has far-reaching implications for disciplinary reinvention. Fieldwork defined through spatial practices of travel and dwelling, through the disciplined, embodied interactions of participant-observation, is being rerouted by "indigenous," "postcolonial," "diasporic," "border," "minority," "activist," and "community-based" scholars. The terms overlap, designating complex sites of identification, not discrete identities.

Kirin Narayan (1993) questions the opposition of native and nonnative, insider and outsider anthropologists. This binary, she argues, stems from a discredited, hierarchical colonial structure. Drawing on her own ethnography in different parts of India, where she feels different degrees of affiliation and distance, Narayan shows how "native" researchers are complexly and multiply located vis-à-vis their worksites and interlocutors. Identifications cross-cut, complement, and trouble one another. "Native" anthropologists—like all anthropologists, Narayan argues—"belong to several communities simultaneously (not least of all the community we were born into and the community of professional academics)" (Narayan 1993: 24). Once the structuring opposition between "native" and "outside" anthropologist is displaced, the relations of cultural inside and outside, home and away, same and different that have organized the spatial practices of fieldwork must be rethought. How does the disciplinary injunction that fieldwork involve some sort of "travel"—a practice of physical displacement that defines a site or object of intensive research—constrain the range of practices opened up by Narayan and others?

In Narayan's analysis, fieldwork begins and ends in displacement, enacted across constitutive borders—fraught, amorous edges. There is no simple, undivided, "native" position. Once this is recognized, however, the hybridity she embraces needs specification: What are its limits and conditions of movement? One can be more or less hybrid, native, or "diasporic" (a term that perhaps best captures Narayan's own complex locations) for determinate historical reasons. Indeed, the title of "native" or "indigenous" anthropologist might be retained to designate a person whose research travel leads out and back from a home base, "travel" understood as a detour through a university or other site which provides analytic or comparative perspective on the place of dwelling/research. Here the usual spatialization of home and abroad would be reversed. Moreover, for many fieldworkers neither the university nor the field provides a stable base; rather, both serve as juxtaposed sites in a mobile comparative project. A continuum, not an opposition, separates the explorations, detours, and returns of the indigenous or native scholar from those of the diasporic or postcolonial.[24] Thus, the requirement that anthropological fieldwork involve *some* kind of travel need not marginalize those formerly called "natives." The roots and routes, the varieties of "travel," need to be more broadly understood.

Recent work by Mary Helms (1988), David Scott (1989), Amitav Ghosh (1992), Epeli Hau'ofa et al. (1993), Teresia Teaiwa (1993), Ben Finney (1994), and Aihwa Ong (1995), among others, has reinforced a growing awareness of discrepant travel routes—traditions of movement and interconnection not definitively oriented by the "West" and an expanding cultural-economic world system. These routes follow "traditional" and "modern" paths, within and across contemporary transnational and interregional circuits. A recognition of these paths makes space for travel (and fieldwork) that does not originate in the metropoles of Euro-America or their outposts. If, as is likely, some form of travel or displacement remains a constituting element in professional fieldwork, reworking the "field" must mean multiplying the range of acceptable routes and practices.

An attention to the varieties of "travel" also helps clarify how, in the past, cleared spaces of scientific work have been constituted through the suppression of cosmopolitan experiences, especially those of the people under study. Generally speaking, the localization of "natives" meant that intensive interactive research was done in spatially delimited fields and not, for example, in hotels or capital cities, on ships, in mission schools or universities, in kitchens and factories, in refugee camps, in diasporic neighborhoods, on pilgrimage buses, or at a variety of cross-cultural sites of encounter.[25] As a Western travel practice, fieldwork was grounded by a historical vision, what Gayatri Spivak calls a "worlding," in which one section of humanity was restless and expansive, the rest rooted and immobile. Indigenous authorities were reduced to native informants. The marginalization of travel practices, those of researchers and hosts, contributed to a *domestication* of fieldwork, an ideal of interactive dwelling which, however temporary, could not be seen as merely passing through. That anthropology's interlocutors often saw things differently did not, until recently, disturb the discipline's self-image.[26]

Alternate forms of travel/fieldwork, whether indigenous or diasporic, grapple with many problems similar to those of conventional research: problems of strangeness, privilege, miscomprehension, stereotyping, and political negotiation of the encounter. Ghosh is especially trenchant on the potentially violent miscomprehensions and stereotypes integral to his research as a *doktor al Hindi* among Muslims. Epeli Hau'ofa speaks for an interconnected "Oceania," but he does so as a Tongan living in Fiji, a location not forgotten by his diverse Islander audiences. At the same time, the routes and encounters of ethnographers such as Ghosh or Hau'ofa are different from those of traditional fieldwork sojourners. Their cultural comparisons need not presuppose a Western/university home, a "central" site of theoretical accumulation. And while their research encounters may involve hierarchical relations, they need not presuppose "white" privilege. Their work may or may not crucially depend on colonial and neocolonial circuits of information, access, and power. For example, Hau'ofa publishes in Tonga and Fiji and wants to articulate an old/new "Oceania." In this he differs from Ghosh, who publishes, crucially though not exclusively, in the West. The language(s) the ethnography uses, the audiences it addresses, the circuits of academic/media prestige it appeals to, may be discrepant from, though seldom unconnected with, the communicative structures of global political economy. A case in point: *A New Oceania,* by Hau'ofa et al., was delivered to me by hand.[27] Published in Suva, the book would not have reached me through my normal reading networks. Can a work centered and routed like this one intervene in Euro-American anthropological contexts? What are the institutional barriers? The power to determine audiences, publications, and translations is very unevenly distributed, as Talal Asad has often reminded us (Asad, 1986).

The oxymoronic term "indigenous anthropologist," coined at the beginning of the ongoing postcolonial/neocolonial recentering of the discipline, is no longer adequate to characterize a wide range of scholars studying in their home societies. Difficult issues arise. How exactly will "home" be defined? If, as I assume, no *inherent* authority can be accorded to "native" ethnographies and histories, what constitutes their *differential* authority? How do they supplement and criticize long-established perspectives? And under what conditions will local knowledge enunciated by locals be recognized as "anthropological knowledge"? What kinds of displacement, comparison, or taking of "distance" are required for family knowledge and folk history to be recognized as serious ethnography or cultural theory by the disciplinary center?

Anthropology potentially includes a cast of diverse dwellers and travelers whose displacement or travel in "fieldwork" differs from the traditional spatial practice of the field. The West itself becomes an object of study from variously distanced and entangled locations. Going "out" to the field now sometimes means going "back," the ethnography becoming a "notebook of a return to the native land." In the case of a diasporic scholar, the "return" may be to a place never known personally but to which she or he ambivalently, powerfully "belongs." *Returning* to a field will not be the same as *going out* to a field. Different subjective distances and affiliations are at stake.

A growing awareness of these differences has emerged within Euro-American anthropology during recent decades. In an important discussion, David Scott named some of the historical locations constraining an emergent "postcoloniality" in anthropology.

> By raising in different ways the problem of "place" and the non-Western anthropologist, both Talal Asad [1982] and Arjun Appadurai [1988b] have suggested that to undermine the asymmetry in anthropological practice many more such anthropologists should study Western societies. This, to be sure, is a step in the right direction inasmuch as it subverts the pervasive notion that the non-Western subject can speak only within the terms of his/her own culture. Moreover, it privileges in some degree the possibility of tacking back and forth between cultural spaces. At the same time, it would seem to fix and repeat the colonially established territorial boundaries within which the postcolonial is encouraged to move: center/periphery—and typically, the center of neocolonial governance and the periphery of origin. European and American anthropologists continue to go where they please, while the postcolonial stays home or else goes West. One wonders whether there might not be a more engaging problematic to be encountered where the postcolonial intellectual from Papua New Guinea goes not to Philadelphia but to Bombay or Kingston or Accra. (Scott, 1989: 80)

Escape from the polarizing historical force field of the "West" is no easy matter, as Scott's subsequent discussion of Ghosh makes clear. But Scott also argues that the cross-cultural "tacking" of anthropologists should not be reduced to movements between centers and peripheries in a world system. Contemporary ethnography, including Scott's own from Jamaica via New York to Sri Lanka, is necessarily "traveling in the West" (Ghosh, quoted by Scott, 82). It is also traveling in and against, through the West.

Ethnography is no longer a normative practice of outsiders visiting/studying insiders but, in Narayan's words, a practice of attending to "shifting identities in relationship with the people and issues an anthropologist seeks to represent" (Narayan, 1993: 30). How identities are negotiated relationally, in determined historical contexts, is thus a process constituting both the subjects and objects of ethnography. Much emerging work now makes these complex relational processes explicit. Paula Ebron (1994, 1996), for example, conducts research on Mandinka praise-singers both in West Africa and in the United States, where they find appreciative audiences. Her ethnography is multiply located and—as she clearly shows—entangled in the traveling culture circuits of world music and tourism. It also works in tension with a history of dominant Western inventions of Africa—she cites Mudimbe (1988)—and more or less romanticized African American projections formed in reaction to histories of racism. Ebron moves among these intersecting contexts. "Africa" cannot be held "out there." It is an empowering and problematic part of her own African American tradition as well as a relay—not an origin—in a continuing diasporic history of transits and returns (see Chapter 10). This history implicates her academic ethnography, whose site is the relational negotiation of "subjects in difference," a space where praise-singers, tourists, and anthropologists claim and negotiate cultural meanings. Her field includes the airports where these travelers cross.

"Indigenous," "postcolonial," "diasporic," or "minority" attachments are frequently at issue in the way anthropological "fields" are negotiated. Scholars such as Rosaldo (1989), Kondo (1990), Behar (1993), and Limón (1994), to cite only a few, define the spatial practices of their fieldwork in terms of a politics of locations, of tactically shifting insides and outsides, affiliations and distances. Their anthropological "distance" is challenged, blurred, relationally reconstructed. Often they express their complex situated knowledges by textual strategies in which the embodied, narrating, traveling scholar/theorist is prominent. But this choice should be seen as a critical intervention against disembodied, neutral authority, not as an emerging norm. There is no narrative form or way of writing inherently suited to a politics of location. Others working within and against a still predominantly Western anthropology may choose to adopt a more impersonal, demystifying, indeed objective rhetoric. David Scott and Talal Asad are strong examples. Their discourses are, nevertheless, openly that of politically committed, situated scholars, not neutral observers. A very wide range of rhetorics and narratives—personal and impersonal, objective and subjective, embodied and disembodied—are available to the located scholar-traveler. The only tactic excluded, as Donna Haraway has said, is the "God Trick" (Haraway, 1988).

Most of the anthropologists cited in the previous section have done something *like* traditional fieldwork: studying "out" or "down." This has contributed to their survival, indeed success, within the academy, even as they work to criticize and open it up. The licensing function of having done "real" fieldwork—intensive and displaced from the university—remains strong. Indeed, ethnography that takes place within *diasporic* affiliations may be more easily accepted than research whose attachments, however ambivalent, are indigenous or *native*. (Recall that these locations fall on an overlapping continuum, not on either side of a binary opposition.) Diasporic (dis)locations have travel and distance built into them, usually including metropolitan spaces. Native (re)locations, while they include travel, are centered in a way that makes the metropole and the university peripheral. I have suggested that displacement, Scott's "tacking" between cultural spaces, remains a constitutive feature of anthropological fieldwork. Can this displacement be extended to include travel to and through the university? Can the university itself be seen as a kind of fieldsite—a place of cultural juxtaposition, estrangement, rite of passage, a place of transit and learning? Mary John (1989) opens such a possibility in her prescient discussion of a compromised, emergent "anthropology in reverse" for postcolonial feminists: a coerced and desired travel "West," and an unstable coexistence of roles, anthropologist and native informant. How does travel through the university reposition the "native" place, where the anthropologist maintains connections of residence, kinship, or political affiliation that go beyond visiting, however intensive? Angie Chabram explores this repositioning in her provocative sketch of a Chicana/o "oppositional ethnography" (Chabram, 1990). Here, "minority" and "native" trajectories may overlap: rooted in the "community" (however defined) and routed through academia.

When ethnography has primarily served the interests of community memory and mobilization and only secondarily the needs of comparative knowledge or science, it has tended to be relegated to the less prestigious categories of "applied anthropology," "oral history," "folklore," "political journalism," or "local history." But as fieldwork becomes differently rooted and routed in some of the ways I have been tracking, many scholars may take a renewed interest in applied research, oral history, and folklore, stripped now of their sometimes paternalistic traditions. The oral history/community mobilization work of the El Barrio Project at the New York Centro de Estudios Puertoriqueños is a frequently cited example (see Benmayor, 1991; Gordon, 1993). Dara Culhane Speck's *An Error in Judgment* (1987) carefully fuses community memory, historical scholarship, and current political advocacy. Esther Newton's subtle articulation of margins, as loyal lesbian participant-observer, outsider/insider in a predominantly gay male community, produces an exemplary fusion of local history and cultural criticism (Newton, 1993a). Epeli Hau'ofa's research in Tonga is another case in point (as distinct from his exoticist work in Trinidad or his studies in Papua New Guinea, where he was a different kind of "Pacific" outsider). Returning to do research in his native Tonga, Hau'ofa writes in more than one language and style to both analyze and influence local responses to Westernization. He maintains a stylistic distinction between writing for the discipline and writing as political intervention and as satiric fiction (Hau'ofa, 1982). But the discourses are clearly connected in his view, and others might be more inclined than he to blur them.

To do "professional" anthropology, one must maintain connections with university centers and their circuits of publication and sociality. How close must these connections be? How central? When does one begin to lose disciplinary identity at the margins? These questions have always faced scholars working for governments, corporations, activist social organizations, and local communities. They continue to trouble, and discipline, the work of the differently located anthropologists I have been discussing. Moreover, the university itself is not a single site. Though it may have Western roots, it is hybridized and transculturated in non-Western places. Its ties to nation, to "development," to region, to post-, neo-, and anticolonial politics can make it a significantly different base of anthropological operations, as Hussein Fahim's pioneering collection, *Indigenous Anthropology in Non-Western Countries* (1982), makes clear. In principle at least, universities are sites of comparative theory, of communication and critical argument among scholars. The ethnographic or ethnohistorical interpretations of nonuniversity authorities are seldom recognized as fully scholarly discourse; rather, they tend to be seen as local, amateur knowledge. In anthropology the research that produces such knowledge, however intensive and interactive, is not *fieldwork*.

The disciplinary "Other" who perhaps most epitomizes the border at issue here is the figure of the *local historian*. This supposedly partisan chronicler and keeper of the community's records is even harder to integrate with conventional fieldwork than the emerging figure of the diasporic postcolonial, the oppositional minority scholar, or even the traveling native. Tainted by a presumed immobility and by assumptions of amateurism and boosterism, the local historian, like the activist or culture-worker, lacks the required professional "distance." As we have seen, this distance has been naturalized in spatial practices of the "field," a circumscribed place one enters and leaves. Movement in and out has been considered essential to the interpretive process, the management of depth and discretion, absorption and the "view from afar" (Lévi-Strauss, 1985).

The disciplinary border that keeps locally based authorities in the position of informants is, however, being renegotiated. Where and how the boundary is redrawn—which spatial practices will be accommodated by the evolving tradition of anthropological fieldwork and which will be excluded—remains to be seen. But in this context it may be useful to ask how the legacy of fieldwork-as-travel helps account for an issue raised during recent presidential sessions on diversity at the American Anthropological Association: the fact that North American minorities are entering the field in relatively small numbers. Anthropology has difficulty reconciling goals of analytic distance with the aspirations of Gramscian "organic intellectuals." Has the discipline adequately confronted the problem of doing sanctioned, "real" fieldwork in a community one wants *not* to leave? Departure, taking distance, has long been crucial to the spatial practice of fieldwork. How can the discipline make room for research that is importantly about return, reterritorialization, belonging—attachments that go beyond gaining rapport as a research strategy? Robert Alvarez (1994) provides a revealing discussion of these issues, showing how different kinds of community involvement in the course of research are valued and devalued by the discipline in ways that tend to reproduce a white hegemony.

The definition of "home" is fundamentally at issue here. In local/global situations where displacement appears increasingly to be the norm, how is collective dwelling sustained and reinvented? (See Bammer, 1992.) Binary oppositions between home and abroad, staying and moving, need to be thoroughly questioned (Kaplan, 1994). These oppositions have often been naturalized along lines of gender (female, domestic space versus male travel), class (the active, alienated bourgeoisie versus the stagnant, soulful poor), and race/culture (modern, rootless Westerners versus traditional, rooted "natives"). The fieldwork injunction to go elsewhere construes "home" as a site of origin, of sameness. Feminist theory and gay/lesbian studies have, perhaps most sharply, showed home to be a site of unrestful differences. Moreover, in the face of global forces that coerce displacement and travel, staying (or making) home can be a political act, a form of resistance. Home is not, in any event, a site of immobility. These few indications, of which much more could be said, should be enough to question anthropological assumptions of fieldwork as travel, going *out* in search of *difference*. To a degree these assumptions continue to apply in practices of "repatriated" fieldwork (Marcus and Fischer, 1986) and of "studying up" (Nadar, 1972). The field remains *somewhere else*, albeit within one's own linguistic or national context.

An unsettling discussion of "home" with reference to anthropological practice is provided by Kamela Visweswaran (1994). She argues that feminist ethnography, part of an ongoing struggle to decolonize anthropology, needs to recognize the "failure" that is inevitably bound up with the project of cross-cultural translation in power-charged situations. Precisely at "those moments when a project is faced with its own impossibility" (98), ethnography can struggle for accountability, a sense of its own positioning. Building on Gayatri Spivak's formulation of every cultural/political subject's "sanctioned ignorances," Visweswaran argues that by openly confronting failure, feminist ethnography discovers both limits and possibilities. Among the latter are critical movements "homeward." In a section titled "Homework, Not Fieldwork," she develops a concept of ethnographic work not based on the home/field dichotomy. "Homework" is not defined as the opposite of exoticist fieldwork; it is not a matter of literally staying home or studying one's own community. "Home," for Visweswaran, is a person's location in determining discourses and institutions—cutting across locations of race, gender, class, sexuality, culture. "Homework" is a critical confrontation with the often invisible processes of learning (the French word *formation* is apt here) that shape us as subjects. Playing on the pedagogical senses of the term, Visweswaran proposes "homework" as a discipline of unlearning as much as of learning. "Home" is a locus of critical struggle that both empowers and limits the subject wherever she or he conducts formal research. By deconstructing the home/field opposition, Visweswaran clears space for unorthodox routings and rootings of ethnographic work.

In a related but not identical vein, Gupta and Ferguson (1997) urge an anthropology focused on *"shifting locations* rather than *bounded fields."* Theirs is a reformist rather than a deconstructive project. While rejecting the tradition of spatially restricted research, they preserve certain practices long associated with fieldwork. Anthropology still studies "Others" intensively and interactively. It provides, they remind us, one of the few Western academic sites where unfamiliar, marginalized, nonelite peoples are seriously attended to. Long-term immersion, interest in informal knowledge and embodied practices, and an injunction to *listen* are all elements of the fieldwork tradition they value and hope to preserve. Moreover, Gupta and Ferguson's notion of *shifting locations* suggests that even when the ethnographer is positioned as an insider, a "native" in her or his community, some taking of distance and translating differences will be part of the research, analysis, and writing. No one can be an insider to all sectors of a community. How the shifting locations are managed, how affiliation, discretion, and critical perspective are sustained, have been and will remain matters of tactical improvisation as much as of formal methodology. Thus, whatever comes to be recognized as a reformed fieldwork will entail David Scott's "tacking between cultural spaces," though not necessarily or solely along colonial or neocolonial axes of center and periphery.

Moreover, the constitutive displacements need not be between "cultural" spaces, at least not as the term is conventionally defined, in spatial terms. An ethnography focused on shifting *locations* would assume only that the borders negotiated and crossed were salient to a co-constructed project in a specific "contact zone" (Pratt, 1992). This would mean not that the borders in question were invented or unreal, but only that they were not absolute and could be cross-cut by other borders or affiliations also potentially relevant to the project. These other constitutive locations might become central in other historical and political conjunctures or in a differently focused project. One cannot represent "in depth" all salient differences and affinities. For example, a middle-class researcher studying among working people may find class to be a critical location, even if his or her research topic is explicitly focused elsewhere—say, on gender relations in secondary schools. In this case, race might or might not be a site of crucial difference or affinity.

A project will always "succeed" on certain axes and "fail" (in Visweswaran's constitutive sense) on others. Thus, we should not confuse a more or less conscious research strategy of *shifting locations* with *being located* (often antagonistically) in the ethnographic encounter. For an

Indian Hindu working in Egypt, religion may be imposed as a prime differentiating factor, asserting its salience for a research project on agricultural techniques, in spite of the author's desires (Ghosh, 1992). Moreover, the process need not be antagonistic. A student of his or her own community may be located, firmly and lovingly, as "family," thus putting real restrictions on what can be probed and revealed. A gay or lesbian ethnographer may be constrained to highlight or downplay sexual location, depending on the political context of research. Or an anthropologist from Peru may find him- or herself negotiating a national boundary when working in Mexico, but a racial one in the United States. The examples could be multiplied.

None of these locations is optional. They are imposed by historical and political circumstances. And because locations are multiple, conjunctural, and cross-cutting, there can be no guarantee of shared perspective, experience, or solidarity. I build here on a nondismissive critique of identity politics that has been compellingly stated by June Jordan (1985) and developed by many others (for example, Reagon, 1983; Mohanty, 1987). In ethnography, what was previously understood in terms of *rapport*—a kind of achieved friendship, kinship, empathy—now appears as something closer to *alliance building*. The relevant question is less "What fundamentally unites or separates us?" and more "What can we do for one another in the present conjuncture?" What, from our similarities and differences, can we bend together, hook up, articulate? (See Hall, 1986: 52–55; Haraway, 1992: 306–315.) And when identification becomes too close, how can a disarticulation of agendas be managed, in the context of alliance, without resorting to claims to objective distance and tactics of definitive departure? (For a sensitive account of these issues in the context of lesbian ethnography, see Lewin, 1995.)

A stress on shifting locations and tactical affiliations explicitly recognizes ethnography's political dimensions, dimensions that can be hidden by presumptions of scientific neutrality and human rapport. But "political" in what senses? There are no guaranteed or morally unassailable positions. In the present context—a shift from rapport to alliance, from representation to articulation—rigid prescriptions of advocacy have a tendency to emerge. An older politics of neutrality with its goal of ultimate disengagement may simply be reversed—a binary starkly evident in the juxtaposition of eloquent, opposing essays by Roy d'Andrade and Nancy Schepper-Hughes in a 1995 forum of *Current Anthropology*. The place for a politics of skepticism and critique (not to be confused with dispassion or neutrality), for engaged disloyalty, or for what Richard Handler (1985, following Sapir) calls "destructive analysis" seems endangered. An alliance model leaves little room for work in a politicized situation that pleases none of the contestants. I am not suggesting that such research is superior or more objective. It, too, is partial and located. And it should not be excluded from the range of situated research practices now contending for the name "anthropology."

These are just some of the dilemmas facing anthropological ethnography as its roots and routes, its different patterns of affiliation and displacement, are reworked in late twentieth-century contexts. What remains of *fieldwork?* What, if anything, is left of the injunction to travel, to get out of the house, to "enter the field," to dwell, interact intensively in a (relatively) unfamiliar context? A research practice defined by "shifting locations," without the prescription of physical displacement, extended face-to-face encounter, could, after all, describe the work of a literary critic, attentive, as many are today, to the politics and cultural contexts of different textual readings. Or, once freed of the notion of a "field" as a spatialized site of research, could an anthropologist investigate the shifting locations of her or his own life? Could "homework" be autobiography?

Here we cross a blurred border that the discipline is struggling to define. Autobiography can, of course, be quite "sociological"; it can move systematically between personal experience and general concerns. A certain degree of autobiography is now widely accepted as relevant to self-critical projects of cultural analysis. But how much? Where is the line to be drawn? When is self-analysis dismissed as "mere" autobiography? (One sometimes hears rather modest amounts of personal revelation in ethnographies described as solipsism or "navel gazing.") Writing an ethnography of one's subjective space as a kind of complex community, a site of shifting locations, could be defended as a valid contribution to anthropological work. It would not, I think, be widely recognized as fully or characteristically *anthropological* in the way that work in an externalized *field* still is. One could hardly count on being awarded a Ph.D., or finding a job in an anthropology department, for autobiographical research. The legacy of the field in anthropology requires, at least, that "first-hand" research involve extended face-to-face interactions with members of a community.

Practices of displacement and encounter still play a defining role. Without these, what are under discussion are not new versions of fieldwork but a range of quite different practices.

In this essay, I have tried to show how definite spatial practices, patterns of dwelling and traveling, have constituted fieldwork in anthropology. I have argued that the disciplining of fieldwork, of its sites, routes, temporalities, and embodied practices, has been critical in maintaining the identity of sociocultural anthropology. Currently contested and under renegotiation, fieldwork remains a mark of disciplinary distinction. The most disputed elements of traditional fieldwork are, perhaps, its injunction to leave home and its inscription within relations of travel that have depended on colonial, race-, class-, and gender-based definitions of center and periphery, cosmopolitan and local. The linked requirement that anthropological fieldwork be intensive and interactive is less controversial, although criteria for measuring "depth" are more debatable than ever. Why not simply purge the discipline's exoticist travel legacy while sustaining its intensive/interactive styles of research? In a utopian mode one might argue for such a solution, and indeed things seem to be moving in this general direction. A radical course is urged by Deborah D'Amico-Samuels, in an essay that anticipates many of the critiques previously referred to. She questions traditional spatial and methodological definitions of the "field," concluding rigorously: "the field is everywhere" (1991: 83). But if the field is everywhere, it is nowhere. We should not be surprised if institutional traditions and interests resist such radical dissolutions of fieldwork. Thus, some forms of travel, of disciplined displacement in and out of one's "community" (seldom a single place, in any event), will probably remain the norm. And this disciplinary "travel" will require at least a serious sojourn in the university. I conclude, provocatively, in this hazardous future tense.

Travel, redefined and broadened, will remain constitutive of fieldwork, at least in the near term. This will be necessary for institutional and material reasons. Anthropology must preserve not only its disciplinary identity but also its credibility with scientific institutions and funding sources. Given a shared genealogy with other natural- and social-science research practices, it is no accident that the field has, at times, been called anthropology's "laboratory." Criteria of objectivity associated with a detached, outside perspective are strongly represented in the academic and government milieus that control resources. Thus, sociocultural anthropology will remain under pressure to certify the scientific credentials of an interactive, intersubjective methodology. Researchers will be constrained to take a certain "distance" from the communities they study. Of course, critical distance can be defended without appealing to ultimate grounds of authority in scientific objectivity. At issue is how distance is manifested in research practices. In the past, physically leaving the "field"—to "write up" research results in the presumably more critical, objective, or at least comparative environment of the university—was seen to be an important guarantee of academic independence. As we have seen, this spatialization of "inside" and "outside" locations no longer enjoys the credibility it once did. Will anthropology find ways to take seriously new forms of "field" research that diverge from earlier models of university-centered travel, spatial discontinuity, and ultimate disengagement?

As anthropology moves, haltingly, in postexoticist, postcolonial directions, a diversification of professional norms is under way. The process, accelerated by political and intellectual critiques, is reinforced by material constraints. In many contexts, given falling levels of funding, sociocultural fieldwork will increasingly have to be conducted "on the cheap." For graduate students, relatively expensive long-term sojourns abroad may be out of the question, and even a year of full-time research in a U.S. community can be too expensive. While traditional fieldwork will certainly maintain its prestige, the discipline may come to resemble more closely the "national" anthropologies of many European and non-Western countries, with short, repeated visits the norm and fully supported research years rare. It is important to recall that professional fieldwork in the Malinowskian mold depended materially on the mobilization of funding for a new "scientific" practice (Stocking, 1984a). "Subway ethnography," like Karen McCarthy Brown's (discussed above), will be increasingly common. But even as visiting and "deep hanging out" replace extended co-residence and the tent-in-the-village model, legacies of exoticist fieldwork influence the professional habitus of the "field"—now conceived less as a discrete, other place than as a set of embodied research practices, patterns of discretion, of professional distance, of coming and going.

I have located fieldwork in a long, increasingly contested tradition of Western travel practices. I have suggested, too, that other travel traditions and diasporic routes can help renovate methodologies of displacement, leading to metamorphoses of the "field." "Travel" denotes more or less voluntary practices of leaving familiar ground in search of difference, wisdom, power, adventure, an altered perspective. These experiences and desires cannot be limited to privileged male Westerners—although that elite has powerfully defined the terms of travel orienting modern anthropology. Travel needs to be rethought in different traditions and historical predicaments. Moreover, when criticizing specific legacies of travel, one should not come to rest in an uncritical localism, the inverse of exoticism. There is truth in the cliché, "Travel broadens."[28] Of course, the experience offers no guaranteed results. But, often, getting away lets uncontrollable, unexpected things happen (Tsing, 1994). An anthropologist friend, Joan Larcom, once told me, ruefully and gratefully: "Fieldwork gave me some experiences I didn't think I deserved." I remember thinking that a discipline requiring this of its adepts must be on to something. Is it possible to validate such experiences of displacement without reference to a mystified, professional "rite of passage"?

Sojourning somewhere else, learning a language, putting oneself in odd situations and trying to figure them out can be a good way to learn something new, simultaneously about oneself and about the people and places one visits. This commonplace truth has long encouraged people to engage with cultures beyond their own. It underlies what still seems most valuable in the linked/distinct traditions of travel and ethnography. Intensive fieldwork does not produce privileged or complete understandings. Nor does the cultural knowledge of indigenous authorities, of "insiders." We are differently situated as dwellers and travelers in our cleared "fields" of knowledge. Is this multiplicity of locations merely another symptom of postmodern fragmentation? Can it be collectively fashioned into something more substantial? Can anthropology be reinvented as a forum for variously routed fieldworks—a site where different contextual knowledges engage in critical dialogue and respectful polemic? Can anthropology foster a critique of cultural dominance which extends to its own protocols of research? The answer is unclear: powerful, newly flexible, centralizing forces remain. The legacies of the "field" are strong in the discipline and deeply, perhaps productively, ambiguous. I have focused on some defining spatial practices that must be turned to new ends if a multiply-centered anthropology is to emerge.

4

White Ethnicity

Entering Flaming Gorge, we quickly run through it on a swift current, and emerge into a little park. Half a mile below, the river wheels sharply to the left, and we turn into another canyon cut into the mountain. We enter the narrow passage. On either side, the walls rapidly increase in altitude. On the left are overhanging ledges and cliffs five hundred—a thousand—fifteen hundred feet high.*

He entered the IRT 7th Avenue subway at West 116th Street (Columbia University) and headed downtown on the local. Uptown would take him to 125th Street (Harlem) and to unknown parts of the Upper West Side. First stop downtown: 110th Street (OK to get out, and walk uptown or west); next 103rd Street (not OK to get out); then 96th Street (change for the express). The downtown express to Brooklyn rumbled into the station from Harlem. The passengers from the two subways mixed quickly. Express stops, downtown: 72nd Street (with its narrow platforms and stairs), 42nd (screeching wheels on the many switches, mobs of people pushing at the doors), 34th Street, Pennsylvania Station (entry and exit of suitcases), 14th Street (get off here, or take the local, one stop to Sheridan

*John Wesley Powell, *The Exploration of the Colorado River* (Chicago: University of Chicago Press, 1957; orig. pub. 1875). Further quotes from this source are marked with an asterisk.

Square). He pushed against a heavy revolving gate and climbed out into the "Village."

We trudged up the hill past the Stardust Lounge, Micky's Hair-Styling— Hot and Cold Press, the Harlem Bop Lounge, the Dream Cafe, the Freedom Barber Shop, and the Optimo Cigar Shop which seemed to decorate every important street corner of those years. There was the Aunt May Eat Shoppe, and Sadie's Ladies and Children's Wear. There was Lum's Chop Suey Bar, and the Shiloh Baptist Mission Church painted white with colored storefront windows, the Record store with its big radio chained outside setting a beat to the warming morning sidewalk. And on the corner of Seventh Avenue, as we waited for the green light arm in arm, the yeasty and suggestively mysterious smell issuing from the cool dark beyond the swinging half-doors of the Noon Saloon.**

In Greenwich Village he discovered folk music, and the Left. There was Gerde's Folk City and the Village Gate. There were scratchy folkways records of Woody Guthrie, Leadbelly, and Pete Seeger, Vanguard recordings of Odetta, Joan Baez. In the Eighth Street bookstore: Genet, Sartre, Pirandello, Brecht, Beckett, Albee: the "Theater of the Absurd." And every Sunday he unpacked a long-neck banjo at the fountain in Washington Square: "This Little Light of Mine," "Will the Circle Be Unbroken?" "Ain't Gonna Study War No More." He was a folkie. First (a dark secret) came the Kingston Trio, then Joan Baez and the Weavers. A sequence of Seegers (Pete, Peggy, Penny, and Mike) led him to old-time country music and, inexorably it seemed, to bluegrass. He went into the subway at 116th Street and traveled, a hundred blocks south, to Kentucky.

We take with us rations deemed sufficient to last ten months; for we expect, when winter comes on and the river is filled with ice, to lie over at some point until spring arrives; so we take with us abundant supplies of clothing. We have also a large quantity of ammunition and two or three dozen traps. For the purpose of building cabins, repairing boats, and meeting other exigencies, we are supplied with axes, hammers, saws, augurs, and other tools, and a quantity of nails and screws. For scientific

**Audre Lorde, *Zami: A New Spelling of My Name* (Trumansburg, N.Y.: Crossing Press, 1992). Further quotes from this source are marked with a double asterisk.

work, we have two sextants, four chronometers, a number of barometers, thermometers, compasses, and other instruments.*

We talked about leaving New York, about homesteading somewhere in the West where a Black woman and a white woman could live together in peace. Muriel's dream was to live on a farm and it felt like a good life to me. I borrowed pamphlets from the library, and we wrote to all the appropriate government offices to find out if there were any homestead lands still available anywhere in the continental United States.**

On his way home from Greenwich Village (and often from school) he passed through the 96th Street station, uptown platform. Here the 7th Avenue local and express trains diverged. The local continued to the Columbia University stop on Morningside Heights. The express veered off. Visitors from downtown had to be warned: if you make a mistake you'll emerge at the "wrong 116th Street." He was always troubled by the existence of another station with that number, across Morningside Park in the dangerous, off-limits world he never saw called Harlem. He recalled once (or was it fantasy?) forgetting to leave the express at 96th and getting off where everyone and everything, including the "116" set in tiles on each pillar (exactly like "our stop"), was unfamiliar. Eyes down, he hurried to the opposite platform and waited, exposed in his whiteness, for the train back. Later he recognized 96th Street in the film *Brother from Another Planet*. The subway pulls into a station and a white kid tells the black alien that he is going to perform a magic trick. "I'm going to make all the white people disappear!" The doors open and all the whites exit, including the magician who waves goodbye as the doors of the Harlem express close.

American racism was a new and crushing reality that my parents had to deal with every day of their lives once they came to this country. They handled it as a private woe. My mother and father believed that they could best protect their children from the realities of race in America and the fact of American racism by never giving them a name, much less discussing their nature. We were told we must never trust white people, but *why* was never explained, nor the nature of their ill will. Like so many other vital pieces of information in my childhood, I was supposed to know without being told.**

On weekdays, when he was old enough, he took the subway or the Amsterdam bus downtown to school. He enjoyed the independence; and on the way home he would linger with his best friend, Chung, stopping on Broadway for a slice of pizza. But he always walked the two blocks around school, Amsterdam and 94th Street, quickly. In spring and fall people were visible at the brownstones' open windows, or out on the stoops, talking, laughing, arguing—looking him over. There was a smell of garbage, and of pungent cooking. In winter the sidewalks were treacherous. He had to watch for snowballs. Spanish voices: "Mira! Mira!" (He heard "Meeda! Meeda!" . . . and didn't look up.) His only wish was to get through the two blocks without attracting attention. Were they talking to him? Did he hear the Caribbean music that would later become so interesting? He heard no music at all. Each morning the school doors closed behind him; it was quiet inside. He read at old tables among plants in brass pots.

I sat on the floor with my back against the wooden cabinet radio, *The Blue Fairy Book* on my lap. I loved to read and listen to the radio at the same time, feeling the vibrations of sound through my back like an activating background to the pictures that streamed through my head, spun by the fairy tales. I looked up, momentarily confused and disoriented as I usually was when I stopped reading suddenly. Had the trolls really attacked a harbor where some hidden treasure of pearls was buried?**

The river is very deep, the canyon very narrow, and still obstructed, so that there is no steady flow of the stream; but the waters wheel, and roll, and boil, and we are scarcely able to determine where we can go. Now the boat is carried to the right, perhaps close to the wall; again, she is shot into the stream, and perhaps is dragged over to the other side, where, caught in a whirlpool, she spins about. We can neither land nor run as we please. The boats are entirely unmanageable; no order in their running can be preserved; now one, now another, is ahead, each crew laboring for its own preservation.*

As a boy, he always wanted to be in the first car. There he could press against the glass of the forward door, cupping his hands on either side of his face to block the reflected light from inside the train. This gave him a view of the track like that of the motorman (whom he could hear shuffling behind the locked door to his right). As the subway rushed through the dark, there were exciting glimpses of ladders and passageways. Who went there? And occasionally, with blaring horn and screeching wheels, they would pass work crews pressed against the walls, or leaning casually on pickaxes . . . almost touching the deadly third rail. At times a red light stopped them for long minutes in the dark. Then, the surge of power. Dirty lightbulbs flashed by; the subway rocked noisily on its tracks. When a station approached (the bright ring of lights rushing toward them) he feared, for an instant, that the motorman had forgotten to brake, or had died between stations. He pressed his body against the glass with a mixed feeling of arousal and fear.

In such a place we come to another rapid. Two of the boats run it perforce. One succeeds in landing, but there is no foothold by which to make a portage, and she is pushed out again into the stream. The next minute a great reflex wave fills the open compartment; she is waterlogged, and drifts unmanageable. Breaker after breaker rolls over her, and one capsizes her. The men are thrown out; but they cling to the boat, and she drifts down some distance, alongside of us, and we are able to catch her.*

As I continued to pound the spice, a vital connection seemed to establish itself between the muscles of my fingers curved tightly around the smooth pestle in its insistent downward motion, and the molten core of my body whose source emanated from a new ripe fullness just beneath the pit of my stomach. That invisible thread, taut and sensitive as a clitoris exposed, stretched through my curled fingers up my round brown arm into the moist reality of my armpits, whose warm sharp odor with a strange new overlay mixed with the ripe garlic smells from the mortar and the general sweat-heavy aromas of high summer.**

His subway pass gave him the freedom of the city. He could get on and ride . . . Three basic routes: one of exploration, one of everyday anxiety, one forbidden. The first, "downtown," was defined by the IRT 7th Avenue line. (Certain stops: subway freedom is the power to duck under unpleasant places.) The end of the trip was usually the Village. On weekdays he followed the second path, to his school in a "changing neighborhood." This route was safe and familiar, though tinged with anxiety on the two blocks between Broadway and Columbus. (It was the 1950s, when a third—the largest—wave of Puerto Rican immigration transformed sections of the city.) His third route was marked by the magic trick performed on the uptown platform at 96th Street: it was the express train to Harlem, never taken. His freedom, his city. Routes and roots.

But there was no black-elm in Harlem, no black-oak leaves to be had in New York City. Ma-Mariah, her root-woman grandmother, had taught her well under the trees of Noel's Hill in Grenville, Grenada, overlooking the sea. Aunt Anni and Ma-Liz, Linda's mother, had carried it on. But there was no call for this knowledge now; and her husband Byron did not like to talk about home because it made him sad, and weakened his resolve to make a kingdom for himself in this new world. . . . She did not know if the stories about white slavers she read in the *Daily News* were true or not, but she knew to forbid her children ever to set foot in any candystore. We were not even allowed to buy penny gumballs from the machines in the subway. Besides being a waste of precious money, the machines were slot machines and therefore evil, or at least suspect as connected with white slavery—the most vicious kind, she'd say ominously.**

His uncle, who had been a hobo, strummed and sang "Mountain Dew" or "Mama Don't Allow No Guitar Playin'." His father, a professor of English literature, sang sentimental cowboy ballads. He was raised on Verdi and on Gilbert and Sullivan. On the weekend trips downtown, he became a fan of the Weavers. Pete Seeger's wavering voice and twangy banjo, especially, excited him. He learned to play and sing like Pete. The Weavers performed medleys: "Songs around the World." An Irish fiddle tune, a Virginia reel, an African chant, a Negro spiritual, an Israeli hora, a Japanese song about the Hiroshima bomb. Every song and tradition was accessible, noble, progressive. All "folk music."

It was in Mexico City those first few weeks that I started to break my lifelong habit of looking down at my feet as I walked along the street. There was always so much to see, and so many interesting and open faces to read, that I practiced holding my head up as I walked, and the sun felt hot and good on my face. Wherever I went, there were brown faces of every hue meeting mine, and seeing my own color reflected upon the streets in such great numbers was an affirmation for me that was brand-new and very exciting. I had never felt visible before, nor even known I lacked it.**

In the city he was surrounded by black rhythm and blues, gospel, and soul, by music from the Caribbean, by rock 'n' roll. He learned to dance to these beats later, in college. Entering the subway at Columbia University, he emerged, a hundred blocks south, in a global village. Folk music included every people and culture—so long as they hadn't been "commercialized." ("To everyone in all the world, I reach my hand. I shake their hand.") In his village, there were no uncomfortable antagonisms. ("He's got the whole world in his hands.") Race meant we shall overcome; class meant solidarity forever; gender meant love oh careless love; sexuality . . . ? He disapproved when Bob Dylan "sold out" by playing an electric guitar. Chuck Berry and Little Richard were alien bodies.

This fissure is narrow, and I try to climb up to the bench, which is about forty feet overhead. I have a barometer on my back, which rather impedes my climbing. The walls of the fissure are of smooth limestone, offering neither foot nor hand hold. So I support myself by pressing my back against one wall and my knees against the other, and, in this way, lift my body, in a shuffling manner, a few inches at a time, until I have, perhaps, made twenty-five feet of the distance, when the crevice widens a little, I cannot press my knees against the rock in front with sufficient power to give me support in lifting my body, and I try to go back. This I cannot do without falling.*

He had one recurring nightmare about the city. It was dark, and he was sprinting along his home block . . . chased by "gangs." They had switchblades and wide, garrison belts with sharp buckles. The dream would end with him frantically fumbling for his keys at the apartment-house door. Gang members wore black leather jackets. The beats, in the Village, wore black. The white girls with long hair who emerged from the subway at Sheridan Square wore black tights and turtlenecks. (He wore bluejeans and checked shirts.) What did blackness mean? He wished he had dark hair, like a "real" New Yorker (did he mean Jew?). He wished he could slick back his dark hair, a long comb in his back pocket (did he mean Elvis?). Rock 'n' roll was for the ones in black leather. What did blackness mean to him? He wished he could play better blues guitar (but he never got around to learning).

That summer all of New York, including its museums and parks and avenues, was our backyard. . . . When we decided to be workers, we wore loose pants and packed our shoe-dyed lunchboxes, and tied red bandannas around our throats. We rode up and down fifth avenue on the old open double-decker omnibuses, shouting and singing union songs at the top of our lungs. . . . When we decided to be hussies we wore tight skirts and high heels that hurt, and followed handsome respectable-looking lawyer types down Fifth and Park Avenues, making what we thought were salacious worldly comments about their anatomies in loud voices. . . . When we were African we wrapped our heads in gaily printed skirts and talked our own made-up language in the subway on the way down to the Village. When we were Mexican, we wore full skirts and peasant blouses and huaraches and ate tacos, which we bought at a little stall in front of Fred Leighton's on MacDougal Street. Once we exchanged the word "fucker" for "mother" in a whole day's conversation, and got put off the Number 5 bus by an irate driver.**

His parents, born and raised in Evansville, Indiana, moved to New York when he was three months old. His father once spent several years in Arizona, teaching at a ranch school for boys, where he learned to twirl a rope and jump through it. His ten-gallon hat smelled of sweat and was incredibly heavy. Once near Tucson, so the story went, his father climbed the Enchanted Mesa, at hair-raising risk, dangling out over sheer cliffs. His grandparents in Evansville were pillars of the community, church people, founders of Evansville College. Some of them were members of a teetotalers' club, the "Pink Poppers," who picnicked, Sunday afternoons, on sandbars in the Ohio River. (The Mason-Dixon Line ran along the river at that spot.) They didn't cross much into Kentucky, except for a trip to Mammoth Cave. Their grandson went into the 7th Avenue subway at 116th Street, and came home singing music from across the river, the hillbilly music they heard on their radios and turned off.

On Saturday afternoons, sometimes, after my mother finished cleaning the house, we would go looking for some park to sit in and watch the trees. Sometimes we went to the edge of the Harlem river at 142nd Street to watch the water. Sometimes we took the D train and went to the sea. Whenever we were close to water, my mother grew quiet and soft and absent-minded. Then she would tell us wonderful stories about Carriacou, where she had been born, amid the heavy smell of limes. She told us stories about plants that healed and about plants that drove you crazy, and none of it made much sense to us children because we had never seen any of them.**

His grandmother had a room in their New York apartment, when she was past eighty and he was five. She had come there to die. White-haired and going blind, she walked with a cane; he was her eyes, crossing the street with her on her daily walk. She spoke to him as if he were an adult, about the Korean War (she was a pacifist) and about her fantastic trip around the world. When she was twenty, she had accompanied a friend from college, daughter of a famous diplomat, on a semi-official mission to Europe, Egypt, India, and China. Her room in the apartment was different, furnished with favorite antiques brought from Indiana. There was a big four-poster bed, where she entertained her grandchildren with early-morning stories. There was an oriental rug, a massive, polished bureau, a writing desk with many pigeonholes, a globe, and a trunk holding papers and large brown photos: the pyramids, the Ganges, the Taj Mahal. In his grandmother's room he saw a picture of Mount Everest. (She told how she had watched the clouds miraculously lift to reveal the summit.) And a giant brick from the Great Wall of China.

Carriacou was not listed in the index of the *Goode's School Atlas* or in the *Junior Americana World Gazette,* nor appeared on any map that I could find, and so when I hunted for the magic place during geography lessons or in free library time, I never found it, and came to believe my mother's geography was a phantasy or crazy or at least too old-fashioned, and in reality maybe she was talking about the place other people called Curaçao, a Dutch possession on the other side of the Antilles. But underneath it all as I was growing up, *home* was still a sweet place somewhere else which they had not managed to capture yet on paper . . .**

The walls, now, are more than a mile in height—a vertical distance difficult to appreciate. Stand on the south steps of the Treasury building, in Washington, and look down Pennsylvania Avenue to the Capitol Park, and measure this distance overhead, and imagine cliffs to extend to that altitude, and you will understand what I mean; or, stand at Canal street, in New York, and look up Broadway to Grace Church, and you have about the distance; or, stand at Lake street bridge in Chicago, and look down to the Central Depot, and you have it again.*

The Carter Family, Flatt and Scruggs, Bill Monroe—his grandmother's people turned them out. Lower-class, "white-trash" music from across the river. He felt the same about Elvis. But bluegrass, with its roots in traditional country music, moved him. (Later he would discover that bluegrass was never simply from across the river, from the "country." It thrived in industrial centers like Gary or Detroit, and was carried to displaced proletarians not by acoustic banjos and mandolins but by radio waves.) The world he grew up in was built on a country-city opposition: school in New York, long summer months in Vermont. His playmates there were farm kids. The country was supposed to be different from the city; you had to "escape" New York in the summer. (But other friends in Vermont were the kids of similar "summer people," mostly ex-Communists from the Village.) He traveled to the country in the city, and vice versa.

The Colorado is never a clear stream, but for the past three or four days it has been raining much of the time, and the floods, which are poured over the walls, have brought down great quantities of mud, making it exceedingly turbid now. The little affluent, which we have discovered here, is a clear, beautiful creek, or river, as it would be termed in this western country, where streams are not abundant. We have named one stream, away above, in honor of the great chief of the "Bad Angels," and, as this is in beautiful contrast to that, we conclude to name it "Bright Angel."*

Pearl Primus, the African American dancer, had come to my high school one day and talked about African women after class, and how beautiful and natural their hair looked curling out into the sun, and as I sat there listening (one of fourteen Black girls in Hunter High School) I thought, that's the way god's mother must have looked and I want to look that way too so help me god. In those days I called it a natural, and kept calling it natural when everyone else called it crazy. It was a strictly homemade job done by a Sufi Muslim on 125th Street, trimmed with the office scissors and looking pretty raggedy. When I came home from school that day my mother beat my behind and cried for a week.**

Surrounded by black and Latin cultures, he traveled to the Village, where he discovered a pure white music. (He read much later about the interconnections of bluegrass and black minstrelsy.) Around him, New York was changing, a place of crossed roots. Rock music—white, black, and Latin—was breaking out all over. Around him, the city was being "Caribbeanized." But he hardly knew Barbados or Jamaica from Haiti. And "Puerto Rico" meant only a gang of juvenile delinquents in *West Side Story*. He read about all this history later.

I climb so high that the men and boats are lost in the black depths below, and the dashing river is a rippling brook; and still there is more canyon above than below. All about me are interesting geological records. The book is open, and I can read as I run. All about me are grand views, for the clouds are playing again in the gorges. But somehow I think of the nine days' rations, and the bad river, and the lesson of the rocks, and the glory of the scene is but half seen. I push on to an angle, where I hope to get a view of the country beyond, to see, if possible, what the prospect may be of our soon running through this plateau, or, at least, of meeting with some geological change that will let us out of the granite; but, arriving at the point, I can see below only a labyrinth of deep gorges.*

Lying in bed he listened to noises from the court. He could just hear his mother talking on the phone at the far end of the corridor, while Burl Ives 78s spun in a room nearby. The court . . . the court was an accumulator of city sounds, a great conch outside his sixth-floor bedroom. Through the half-opened window he heard snatches of talk, a slammed door, sirens, an airplane, jazz, a car starting, bass notes, a scraping noise, laughter, something crashing, echoing on the pavement far below. His drowsy ear collected all the separate parts of a complex hum that never ceased, day or night. Known and unknown New Yorks.

When we came down from the roof later, it was into the sweltering midnight of a west Harlem summer, with canned music in the streets and the disagreeable whines of overtired and overheated children. Nearby, mothers and fathers sat on stoops or milk crates and striped camp chairs, fanning themselves absently and talking or thinking about work as usual tomorrow and not enough sleep. . . . It was not onto the pale sands of Whydah, nor the beaches of Winneba or Annamabu, with cocopalms softly applauding and crickets keeping time with the pounding of a tar-laden, treacherous, beautiful sea. It was onto 113th Street that we descended after our meeting under the Midsummer Eve's Moon, but the mothers and fathers smiled at us as we strolled down to Eighth Avenue, hand in hand.**

Blanche—he recalled very black skin, glasses, and a voice. For several years, when he was five or six, she was in their apartment twice a week, doing laundry and housecleaning. She was distant, deliberate, a little intimidating. (Much later, he thought he recognized Blanche in an essay by Paule Marshall about the Barbadian women who came to New York during the interwar years—women who worked hard to make a home in "this man's country" while maintaining a certain "aloofness.") Her speech, the thick Caribbean English, bothered him. Blanche was old. He remembered her worn, pressed workdress, her loose brown stockings, glasses (rimless?), and thin, strong black arms and fingers. Their dog barked and barked each time she came in the front door. She would hurry to a private corner of the pantry, where she hung her coat and changed for work.

Our rations are still spoiling; the bacon is so badly injured that we are compelled to throw it away. By an accident this morning, the saleratus is lost overboard. We have now only musty flour sufficient for ten days, a few dried apples, but plenty of coffee. We must make all haste possible. If we meet with difficulties, as we have done in the canyon above, we may be compelled to give up the expedition, and try to reach the Mormon settlements to the north. Our hopes are that the worst places are passed, but our barometers are all so much injured as to be useless, so we have lost our reckoning in altitude, and know not how much descent the river has yet to make.*

From Barbados by way of Canada, she lived alone somewhere in Harlem. Later, he learned more from his mother, who admired Blanche and regretted not having done more than pay the low, going wage and send in regular Social Security contributions. ("She spent her whole life cleaning other people's dirty houses. And when she retired and went back to

Barbados, she was proud to have saved enough for a burial. That's so important for people like her.") Blanche helped his mother, who struggled to manage a large household, with advice about housework. And she got on well with his grandmother. They were close in age, and shared an old-fashioned courtesy and a Christian outlook. His grandmother always had "colored" help, back in Evansville. Blanche asked for respect and got it from the white-haired lady. (Perhaps they shared, too, a feeling of marginality in the New York apartment, of coming from another time and place.) The same couldn't be said for the kids. He and his sister were sometimes disrespectful, even cruel, in ways (like the dog's prolonged barking) that Blanche knew had to do with her race. She became indignant, lecturing them on their bad behavior.

And I remember Afrikete, who came out of a dream to me always being hard and real as the fire hairs along the under-edge of my navel. She brought me live things from the bush, and from her farm set out in cocoyams and cassava— those magical fruit which Kitty bought in the West Indian markets along Lenox Avenue in the 140s or in the Puerto Rican bodegas within the bustling market over on Park Avenue and 116th Street under the Central Railroad structures.**

Blanche worked slowly through the apartment. Sometimes she talked to herself. And she asked for just one special thing: that she always have a hot lunch, with meat—a hamburger, whitefish, a chicken pot pie, something. Only after seeing her cold room, which contained a single hotplate, did his mother realize how crucial these "proper" lunches were. She made the journey into Harlem only once, when Blanche was ill and confined to bed. Did she take the express at 96th Street, or was it the 125th Street crosstown bus? His mother couldn't remember much about the trip except dirty streets, a squalid building, and Blanche's clean, small place.

The canyon walls, for two thousand five hundred or three thousand feet, are very regular, rising almost perpendicularly, but here and there set with narrow steps, and occasionally we can see away above the broad terrace, to distant cliffs.*

CONTACTS

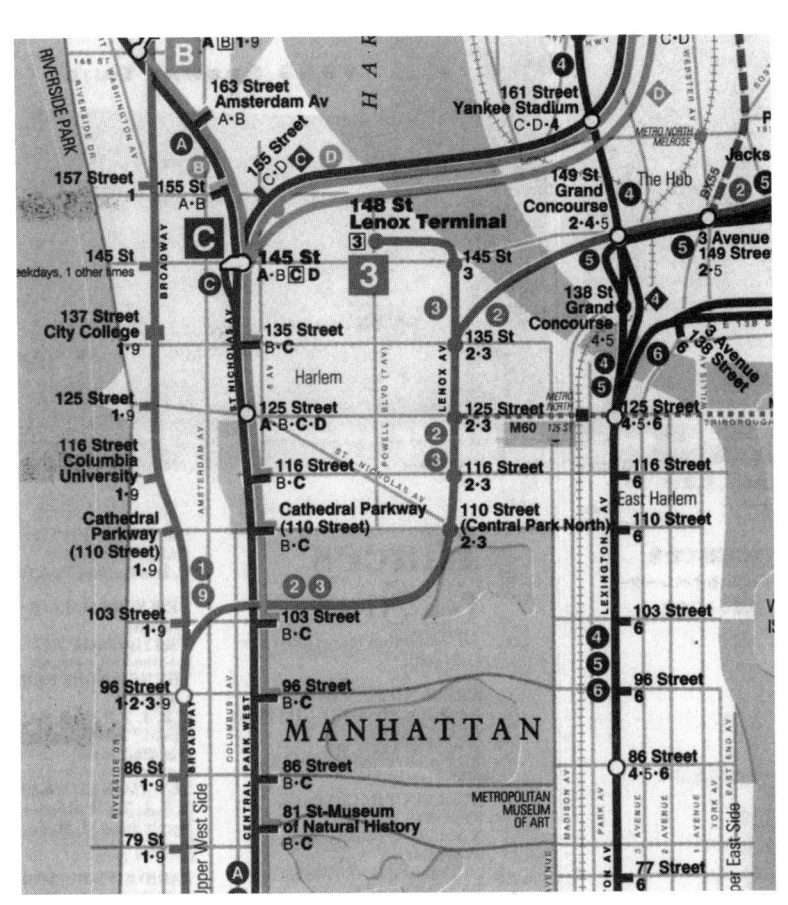

New York City subway map, detail. (*Copyright 1993, New York City Transit Authority. Used by permission.*)

5

Four Northwest Coast Museums: Travel Reflections

The University of British Columbia Museum of Anthropology is itself a famous artifact. Arthur Erickson's glass-and-concrete adaptation of Northwest Coast Indian styles simultaneously soars and crouches on a dramatic clifftop, looking out toward Vancouver Island and the setting sun. In early evening the reflected light makes visible a towering wall of windows between crowds of old totem poles within the building and new ones scattered outside.

The Kwagiulth[1] Museum and Cultural Centre, on Quadra Island, just off the east coast of Vancouver Island, is built in the spiral shape of a sea snail, symbolizing the importance of the sea in the lives of this Native American fishing community. It stands beside an elementary school and a church in Cape Mudge Village, a line of houses facing Discovery Passage, through which on summer nights cruise ships glide on the inland route to Alaska. Behind the museum, the remains of a totem pole, covered with wire mesh, decompose in the grass.

The Royal British Columbia Museum is a large white box. It shares civic space in downtown Victoria with government buildings, hotels, and tourist shops featuring English and Scottish collectibles. The museum's entrance is dominated by a large gift shop selling Native American jewelry, artifacts, books, and curios. Outside, in an open shed, a Hesquiaht/Nuu-Cha-Nulth artist from western Vancouver Island, Tim Paul, who has been senior carver at the museum since 1976, works on a replacement for an old totem pole in Vancouver's Stanley Park.

The U'mista Cultural Centre is located in Alert Bay, on Cormorant Island, near the northern tip of Vancouver Island. It adjoins a looming brick structure, formerly the St. Michael's Residential School for Indian Children, which now houses the Nimpkish band's administrative offices. The center extends downhill toward the harbor, ending with an exhibition space in the style of a traditional big house. Up the hill, beside a much larger ceremonial house, stands the world's tallest totem pole, enshrined in the *Guinness Book of World Records* and supported with guy wires, like an enormous radio antenna.

I went to Vancouver in August 1988 to teach in a summer institute. On long weekends I visited the four museums. What follows are reflections by an outsider, a white American visitor, lingering on the two institutions where I was able to spend the most time: the UBC Museum of Anthropology and the U'mista Cultural Centre. While I draw on conversations with curators and local people and on printed information, what follows are primarily personal impressions of locales, buildings, and styles of exhibition. I barely hint at the four museums' complex local histories, specific audiences, and internal debates. These reflections are closer to travel writing than to ethnography or historical research.

I had become interested in the four museums while writing an essay on collecting in Western museums and in anthropology (Clifford, 1988). The essay analyzed the "art-culture system," which has determined the classification and authentication of artistic or cultural artifacts in Europe and North America since the late nineteenth century. Why do certain non-Western objects end up in fine-art museums, others in anthropology collections? What systems of value regulate the traffic among diverse collections? The essay ended by evoking several contestations of the art-culture system by resurgent native groups that have not, as predicted, disappeared into modernity's homogenizing stream or into the national melting pot. Their current productions did not fit easily into prevailing definitions of either art or culture. I suggested that these groups had been both playing and subverting the dominant art-culture game. Theirs were different, not separate, paths through modernity (no one escapes the market, technology, and the nation-state). The repatriation of objects from national museums to new tribal institutions such as the U'mista Cultural Centre and the Kwagiulth Museum seemed to be a striking example of how a dominant practice of collection and display has been turned to unanticipated ends. Master narratives of cultural disappearance and salvage could be replaced by stories of revival, remembrance, and struggle.

Many Northwest Coast communities have survived and resisted the violence visited on them since the mid-nineteenth century: devastating diseases, commercial and political domination, suppression of the potlatch, forced education in residential schools and by missionaries.[2] Despite enormous damage to indigenous cultures and continuing economic and political inequality, many tribal groups and individuals have found ways to live separate from and in negotiation with the modern state. In the anthropological and museum milieus I frequented, the political climate was charged in ways I had never felt in other metropolitan settings: New York, Chicago, Washington, Paris, London. On the Northwest Coast today, struggles over land claims, the repatriation of museum collections, and

Figure 5.1. Tim Paul, senior carver, working on a totem pole in the public carving shed of the Royal British Columbia Museum, Victoria. Photo courtesy of the Royal B.C. Museum.

community constraints on scientific research are increasingly common. Indigenous art (carving, building, painting, printmaking, jewelry and blanket design), work that participates simultaneously in market and museum networks and in tribal ceremonial and political contexts, is a leading public manifestation of cultural vitality. A recurring pressure and critique—the threat at least of public embarrassment, and even of legal intervention—is felt by anthropologists and museum curators concerned with ancient and modern Northwest Coast Indian traditions.[3]

I had come to British Columbia expecting to focus on the two Kwagiulth tribal museums, but I found I could not ignore the province's "major" displays of Northwest Coast work in the museums at UBC and Victoria, which are responding in their own ways to the evolving context. They offer revealing counterpoints to the innovations at Alert Bay and Cape Mudge Village and help make clear that no museum in the 1990s, tribal or metropolitan, can claim any longer to tell the whole or essential story about Northwest Coast Indian artistic or cultural productions. Indeed, all four museums display the same kinds of objects—ceremonial masks, rattles, robes, and sculpture, as well as work produced for the curio and art markets. In four different contexts, these objects tell discrepant stories of cultural vitality and struggle. All four museums register the irruption of history and politics in aesthetic and ethnographic contexts, thus challenging the art-culture system still dominant in most major exhibitions of tribal or non-Western work. All mix the discourses of art, culture, politics, and history in specific, hierarchical ways. They contest and complement one another in response to a changing historical situation and an unequal balance of cultural and economic power.

It should be noted, however, that my overall comparative approach tends to limit what can be said about the four museums. They are seen less as specific articulations of local, regional, or national histories and more as variants within a unified field of representations. Such foreshortening is particularly questionable with respect to the tribal museums and cultural centers, institutions that both do and do not function on the terms of the dominant, majority culture. They are, in important aspects of their existence, minority or oppositional projects within a comparative museological context.[4] But in other crucial aspects they are not museums at all: they are continuations of indigenous traditions of storytelling, collection, and display. Some of these Kwagiulth traditions are touched on in what follows. Overall, however, my comparative approach tends to stress entanglement and relationship rather than independence or an experience significantly outside the national culture. Moreover, the latter dimensions of tribal life are not adequately captured by terms such as "minority" (denoting a location defined in relation to majority power). The missing tribal perspectives will have to be supplied in depth by other writers better placed and more knowledgeable than I am. This essay is strongly oriented, and limited, by the comparative museological context in which it seeks to intervene.[5]

The Royal British Columbia Museum in Victoria spreads its permanent installation over two large floors. The route through the exhibit is linear, chronological, and didactic, making extensive use of written and recorded explanations, period photographs, and documents. The first half of the installation, upstairs, focuses on precontact Northwest Coast aboriginal ecology and society. It explains adaptations to the environment, technology (weaving, canoes, costumes, houses, utensils), masks, and mythology. Elaborate traditional costumes are displayed on life-size mannequins. A silent video projection (from Edward Curtis' early film *In the Land of the Headhunters*) shows traditional canoes with masked dancers in the bows. (It is mesmerizing to see these familiar masks and canoes in motion.) Early prints and wall-size photographs suggest the aboriginal world in the early years of contact. In a dark space, masks are illuminated sequentially, with recorded voices recounting their different myths.

White culture, commerce, and power arrive *in medias res* as one descends to the lower floor. At the bottom of the stairs, Haida shaman figures, carved for the first time in the 1880s and 1890s, reflect the decline of the traditional shaman's authority. A Tlingit sculpture of a Christian priest signals the new forces with which native populations would have to negotiate. Their initial success, a change and diversification of cultural and artistic production in response to outside stimuli, is illustrated with exhibits from the flourishing curio trade. However, this portrayal of non-catastrophic cultural contact is soon interrupted by dramatic evocation of the smallpox epidemic of the 1860s. The visitor walks through a passageway where the walls are covered with large, haunting Native American faces (portraits by Edward Curtis) and where a recorded voice details the drastic population decline, cultural crisis, and subsequent struggle simply to survive. This harrowing passage is followed by an evocation of missionary influence (photos of students in uniform, a broken mask—but nothing on the complexity of conversion and what it may have meant from an Indian viewpoint). A section documenting the potlatch follows, with photographic and documentary evidence of its suppression by the Canadian government. This central ceremony in Northwest Coast cultures was thought to be a "savage" custom because of its dramatic dances and "excessive" redistributions of wealth. The exhibit includes hostile newspaper accounts, and defenses of the potlatch by Franz Boas. In this historical exhibit one can spend a good deal of time reading texts, both modern explanations and contemporary documents.

The trail then leads into the largest room of the installation, containing a reconstructed chief's house, a cluster of totems, and, in surrounding

Figure 5.2. Inside the Chief's House (Jonathan Hunt House), Royal British Columbia Museum, Victoria. Photo courtesy of the Royal B.C. Museum.

cases, masks and other ceremonial and artistic objects arranged by tribe—Tsimshian, Bella Coola, Tlingit. The exhibition continues through the dimly lit long house, atmospheric with simulated fire and recorded chants, into the final section, entitled "The Land: 1763–1976." Here photographs and texts evoke the long struggle over land use and possession, including a Coast Salish delegation to London in 1906 and recent land claims (a large photo of Athabaskan Indians blockading a rail line in 1975).

Overall, the exhibit's historical treatment is unusual in its complexity and especially in its introduction of white power so early in the sequence. Change is not compartmentalized or added on at the end.[6] The large culminating room with its chief's house and old artifacts is preceded by missions and the potlatch suppression and is followed by land struggles. Thus, it cannot appear simply as an archaic traditional space but is presented, rather, as a powerful site of cultural authenticity surrounded by conflict and change. The historical sequence suggests that the traditional objects on display were not necessarily made prior to white power but in relation to and sometimes in defiance of it.[7] The general historical approach of the Royal British Columbia Museum is linear and synthetic. It tells a story of cultural adaptation, crisis, and conflict on a broad regional scale. History as experienced by specific groups and the contributions of mythic traditions and local political agendas to different historical narratives are subsumed in the overarching sequence. As we shall see, history has a different inflection at the U'mista Cultural Centre.

At the University of British Columbia Museum of Anthropology, the objects on display sometimes seem to take second place to Arthur Erickson's building and its clifftop setting—something that cannot be said of the big windowless box in Victoria. Of the four museums, UBC is the only one that begins to do justice to the monumental aspects of Northwest Coast carving and spatial design. The structure provides large and small spaces, but is dominated by its Great Hall, a soaring room whose massive concrete beams evoke the features of a traditional big house. But unlike the traditional space, all shadow and flickering firelight, the UBC Great Hall is bathed in daylight, with one towering wall entirely of glass. In this space objects are guaranteed maximal visibility, often from several sides. The first sentence of the guide-brochure announces: "The Museum of Anthropol-

Figure 5.3. Great Hall of the University of British Columbia Museum of Anthropology, Vancouver. Photo by W. McLennan; courtesy of the University of British Columbia Museum of Anthropology.

ogy displays Northwest Coast Indian artifacts in ways that emphasize their visual qualities, treating them as works of fine art."

On entering the museum, one descends a ramp directly into the Great Hall, which contains old totem poles, house posts, boxes, and feast dishes. Among them one discovers two marvelous large sculptures by Bill Reid (the contemporary Haida artist who is a kind of presiding spirit in the museum), representing a sea wolf with killer whales and a crouching bear. The label for *Bear* reads as follows:

Cultural group	Haida
Place	Vancouver, B.C.
Date	1963
ObjectContemporary carving	
Description	
A50045	*Bear*
	Carved by Bill Reid
	This sculpture can be gently touched.

Most labels in the Great Hall, equally terse, include small drawings of each work in its original setting. These unobtrusive, somewhat idealized contexts are designed not to compete with the visual impact of the artifacts. (There are no such drawings of the Reid sculptures, for an obvious reason: their original setting is the museum.)

In the Great Hall everything is larger than life, but accessible, translating to some degree the *presence* of these carvings which are simultaneously monumental and intimate. (At Victoria, the largest old poles are behind glass.) In their original settings the poles, posts, and entryways were often attached to dwellings, and lined public sidewalks. People passed among them every day. The Great Hall, with no glass separating visitors from the artifacts, with ways to walk around them, and with inviting places to sit nearby, reproduces something of this intimate monumentality.

A certain ambiguity of indoors and outdoors is also created. The Great Hall is designed so that totem poles and houses in the traditional style recently constructed behind the museum are visible from within, becoming part of the display. Two Haida houses and several poles were made between 1958 and 1962 by the Haida artist Bill Reid, helped by the Nimpkish (Kwagiulth) artist Doug Cranmer. (Their cooperation signals the fact that in the emerging general context, and especially in a major urban museum, the category of Northwest Coast art and culture often takes precedence over specificities of clan, language, or village.) Poles by other contemporary artists representing different traditions are scattered on the grounds. The proximity of these new works to the old artifacts gathered behind the wall of glass makes very clear the museum's most important message: tribal works are part of an ongoing, dynamic tradition. The museum displays its works of art as part of an inventive process, not as treasures salvaged from a vanished past.

Leaving the Great Hall, one passes from the monumental to the miniature. The Masterpiece Gallery contains small objects, chosen for their

Figure 5.4. *The Bear,* contemporary carving by Bill Reid. Collection of the University of British Columbia Museum of Anthropology, Vancouver. Photo by W. McLennan; courtesy of the University of British Columbia Museum of Anthropology.

quality of workmanship: carvings in wood, bone, ivory, argillite; curios, combs, pipes, rattles, and jewelry. Again, the mix of old and new portrays traditional art in process. Elaborately engraved bracelets in the trade metals gold and silver, by the late nineteenth-century artist Charles Edenshaw, are placed beside comparable work by contemporary innovators Bill Reid and Robert Davidson. The gallery is dark; objects are displayed with boutique-style lighting and minimal labels, all emphasizing the message that these are fine-art treasures.

The theater, behind the Masterpiece Gallery, is used for small displays, lectures, film screenings, storytelling sessions, and demonstrations of Native American crafts. It adjoins a small temporary exhibit space and the UBC museum's best-known museographic innovation: its research collec-

Figure 5.5. Foreground: Haida house and totem poles made in 1962 by Bill Reid and Doug Cranmer. To the right is the University of British Columbia Museum of Anthropology, Victoria. Photo by James Clifford.

tions organized as visible storage. Works from various North American native cultures as well as from China, Japan, Melanesia, Indonesia, India, and Africa are stored in glass cases or in drawers that can be freely opened by the public. Extensive documentation on each piece is available in printed volumes. Here the presentation runs opposite to the aestheticizing approach pervasive elsewhere in the museum. Massed, stored objects do not appear as art masterpieces. Instead, taxonomy is featured: a large case of containers holds boxes and baskets of all shapes and sizes from around the world.

The drawers full of small pieces provoke an intimate sense of discovery, the excitement of an attic rather than the staged sublimity of great art. The visible-storage section compensates for the selectivity and minimal explanation of the permanent installation with a surfeit of artifacts and information. What is excluded by the two strategies, an elaborated historical narrative, is signaled by the marginal inclusion of one object, tucked in a corner on the way out of the permanent installation. An angel carved in 1886 by the Tsimshian artist Freddy Alexei for a Methodist baptismal font points to the elaborate story of culture contact, missions, colonization, and resistance that is told in Victoria.

The Royal British Columbia Museum's "black-box" installation creates a dark, wholly interior environment where sequence and viewpoint are controlled for explicitly didactic purposes. The UBC Museum of Anthropology offers a large open space, bathed in light, linked to smaller galleries, and accessible from more than one direction. While there is a preferred general route through the Museum of Anthropology, it is not a linear progress, and the permanent installation's message does not depend significantly on sequential passage. Attention is directed to the individual objects rather than to any narrative in which they are embedded. Developed historical contextualization is largely absent.

One of the indices of a historical approach, in contrast to an aesthetic one, is the systematic use of photographs, particularly in black-and-white or sepia. (Color photographs signal contemporaneity, black-and-white the past.) Historical photographs show the exhibited objects, or objects like them, in use, often including "impure" or "irrelevant" surroundings. Impressive shots of Northwest Coast Indian villages around the turn of the century reveal what are now often considered to be sculptures or artworks attached to and holding up houses. Sometimes a person in suspenders or high-button shoes can be seen on the boardwalk. Three of the four museums I am discussing make prominent use of old photos, sometimes dramatically enlarged. The UBC Museum of Anthropology, however, does not display any photographs at all in its permanent installation. This fact signals its distinctive strategy.

Although both the UBC and Victoria museums contextualize tribal objects in multiple ways, the dominant approaches of their permanent installations are strikingly different and complementary, one showing historical, the other aesthetic, process. The latter emphasis, at UBC, culminates in the rotunda area facing the visible-storage section, a space designed for Bill Reid's monumental carving *Raven and the First Men,* which depicts a Haida creation myth. Video programs document the production of this commissioned masterpiece; they also show the raising of a totem pole carved by Reid in the Queen Charlotte Islands and Nishga artist Norman Tait teaching young Native Americans to fashion a canoe.

Over the past decade, the UBC Museum of Anthropology and the Royal

Figure 5.6. Angel carved by Tsimshian artist Freddy Alexei in 1886 for a Methodist baptismal font. University of British Columbia Museum of Anthropology. Photo by James Clifford.

British Columbia Museum have opened their collections and educational programs to Native American artists and cultural activists. Both their permanent and temporary Northwest Coast exhibitions reflect the currency of tribal art, culture, and politics. Although the extent of their response is limited and their modes of display and contextualization do not break sharply with traditional museum practices, the two museums are unusual in their sensitivity to the vitality and contestation of the traditions they document.

The Royal British Columbia Museum has for some time encouraged Native American artists to use its objects as models and has hired artists as staff members. It has commissioned new traditional works and loaned them out for ceremonial use. An open, functioning workshop greets visitors on their way into the museum, while the conclusion of the permanent Northwest Coast installation gives historical depth to current land-claim movements, a struggle spanning more than a century. The installation ends with a gallery of Haida argillite carving, explaining that the art form originated in contacts with white traders and that it has been lately revived. After documenting the loss and suppression of very sophisticated carving techniques and principles of composition, the exhibit ends with the statement: "Only recently have these principles been rediscovered and mastered. Contemporary Haida art is experiencing an inspired resurgence, and it is hoped that this exhibit will contribute to its rebirth."

The UBC Museum of Anthropology makes room for work by prominent twentieth-century artists—Reid and Davidson. In the museum theater, women from the nearby Musqueam band demonstrate their revived weaving techniques. Major shows are being planned in collaboration with Native American artists, and indigenous curators have been instrumental in past exhibitions.[8] White staff members at UBC speak of moving from a "colonial" to a "cooperative" museology. Whatever one's feeling about the obstacles to such a transition—the risks of liberal paternalism, the stubborn custodial power of the museum, an unwillingness to look critically at the history of specific acquisitions—it is rare to hear such priorities so clearly articulated by North American museum professionals.[9]

The Victoria and UBC exhibits show how a sense of cultural and political process can be introduced into two important current contexts for displaying tribal works: the historical and the aesthetic. But in roughly characterizing the two institutions, I have focused on their permanent installations, both planned in the early seventies, and not on their more diverse temporary exhibitions or their archival, research, and outreach activities. In these more flexible areas, we can see a tendency to multiply explicit interpretive strategies, a trend characteristic of the changing and contested political context. For example, the familiar argument in major art and anthropology museums over the relative value of aesthetic versus scientific, formalist versus culturalist, presentations seems to be giving way to tactically mixed approaches. Some degree of cultural contextualization is present in all the museums I visited. So is an aesthetic appreciation. Indeed, the most formalist treatment in my sample occurs in an anthropology museum, with a resulting impression of art as cultural process.

Treatment of artifacts as fine art is currently one of the most effective ways to communicate cross-culturally a sense of quality, meaning, and importance.[10] This need not be done in ways that simply equate non-Western and Western aesthetic criteria. Each of the four museums, with its distinct mix of contextualization and narration, leaves open a possible aesthetic appreciation of the objects on display. Each evokes both local and global meanings for the interpretive categories (or translation devices) of art, culture, politics, and history.[11]

The two tribal museums in my collection suggest another comparative axis. Along this axis, the aesthetics-oriented UBC museum and the history-oriented Victoria museum are more alike than different, both sharing an aspiration to majority status and aiming at a cosmopolitan audience. By contrast, the U'mista Cultural Centre and the Kwagiulth Museum are tribal institutions, aiming at local audiences and enmeshed in local meanings, histories, and traditions.

Viewed schematically, majority museums articulate cosmopolitan culture, science, art, and humanism—often with a national slant. Tribal museums express local culture, oppositional politics, kinship, ethnicity, and tradition. The general characteristics of the majority museum are, I think, pretty well known, since any art or ethnography collection that strives to be important must partake of them: (1) the search for the "best" art or most "authentic" cultural forms; (2) the interest in exemplary or representative objects; (3) the sense of owning a collection that is a treasure for the city, for the national patrimony, and for humanity; and (4) the tendency to separate (fine) art from (ethnographic) culture. Carol Duncan's (1991) study of the Louvre as the prototypical national museum provides some of the relevant genealogy (Horn, 1984; Coombes, 1988). The majority museum's attitude to what it considers the local museum's "provincialism" and "limited" collection is familiar. The other side appears in a pointed comment about the UBC Museum of Anthropology by a staff member at one of the Kwagiulth tribal centers: "They've got a lot of stuff there, but they don't know much about it."

The tribal museum has different agendas: (1) its stance is to some degree oppositional, with exhibits reflecting excluded experiences, colonial pasts, and current struggles; (2) the art/culture distinction is often irrelevant, or positively subverted; (3) the notion of a unified or linear History (whether of the nation, of humanity, or of art) is challenged by local, community histories; and (4) the collections do not aspire to be included in the patrimony (of the nation, of great art, and so on) but aim to be inscribed within different traditions and practices, free of national, cosmopolitan patrimonies.

The oppositional predicament of tribal institutions is, however, more complex than this, and here the tribal experiences recall those of other minorities. The tribal or minority museum and artist, while locally based, may also aspire to wider recognition, to a certain national or global participation. Thus, a constant tactical movement is required: from margin to center and back again, in and out of dominant contexts, markets, patterns of success. Minority institutions and artists participate in the art-culture system, but with a difference. For example, the U'mista Cultural Centre produces and exploits familiar "museum effects" (Alpers, 1991). But as we shall see, it also questions them, historicizing and politicizing positions of viewing. On the one hand, then, no purely local or oppositional stance is possible or desirable for minority institutions. On the other, majority status is resisted, undercut by local, traditional, community attachments and aspirations. The result is a complex, dialectical hybridity, as Tomas Ybarra-Frausto (1991) shows for much contemporary Chicano art and culture. This mix of local and global agendas, of community, national, and international involvements, varies among tribal institutions, as will become apparent in the contrast between Cape Mudge Village and Alert Bay.

The Kwagiulth Museum and Cultural Centre is conventional in appearance. Beyond the reception area and gift shop, one large semicircular room with a loft displays traditional artifacts in glass cases, along with carved house posts, a totem pole, and a suspended canoe. Downstairs, a basement room is used for audiovisual presentations and school and community events. The overall aesthetic is modernist—clean-lined, brightly lit, uncluttered. Enlarged historical photographs of the region are distributed along the curving wall. A visitor from the city would not be immediately struck by anything unusual in this museum's style of display.

On closer inspection, anomalies appear. The masks in glass cases are labeled with a descriptive phrase or two, sometimes including the information: "Used in such-and-such a ceremony." As I pondered the museum's role in a living Native American community, the verb's tense became ambiguous. A question arose about the objects' current cultural or ceremonial use, a question I had never felt obliged to ask when viewing tribal artifacts in a metropolitan museum. Moreover, each label at the museum concludes with the phrase "owned by" and an individual's proper name. Are all the objects on loan to the museum? A question of property, never highlighted in such displays, is raised. In fact, the named owners are individual chiefs. The objects belong to specific families since, traditionally, there is no such thing as tribal property. Their current home in a tribal museum is the result of a political arrangement.

The objects displayed at the Kwagiulth Museum and at the U'mista Cultural Centre were forcibly acquired by the Canadian government in 1922 following a major "illegal" potlatch, the largest ever recorded in the region. The potlatch was hosted in late 1921 by Dan Cranmer (a Nimpkish from Alert Bay) in collaboration with his wife, Emma Cranmer, and her family (Mamalillikulla from Village Island, where the potlatch was held), assisted by Chief Billy Assu (a Lekwiltok of Cape Mudge Village). Over six days, Dan Cranmer distributed an impressive collection of goods to a large group of guests participating at the ceremony. Because the potlatch was held in winter at a remote location (Village Island is now uninhabited), it was hoped that even an occasion of this size could be hidden from the authorities. But the Indian agent at Alert Bay, William Halliday, a former Indian residential-school administrator imbued with civilizing zeal, learned of the event and decided that this would be a good opportunity to eradicate the "primitive," "excessive" potlatches in the region. Mobilizing the Royal Canadian Mounted Police, he had the participants arrested, tried, and condemned to prison.

A deal was then offered. If those condemned and their relatives would formally renounce the potlatch and surrender their regalia—coppers, masks, rattles, whistles, headdresses, blankets, boxes—there would be no imprisonment. Some resisted and served their time. But many, demoralized and fearful that their kin would suffer, gave up the cherished artifacts,

Figure 5.7. Main gallery of the Kwagiulth Museum and Cultural Centre, Cape Mudge Village. Photo by James Clifford.

a priceless collection of more than 450 items that ended up in major museums in Ottawa and Hull, as well as in the Museum of the American Indian in New York. The authorities offered token payments, amounts bearing no relation to the objects' value in the native economy. (Coppers, for example—highly prized plaques worth many thousands of dollars because of their prestigious histories of exchange—were "bought" for less than fifty dollars.) The punishments and loss of regalia dealt a severe blow to the traditional community: large-scale exchanges disappeared, and ceremonial life and social ties were maintained with difficulty in the face of socioeconomic change and hostility from government, missions, and residential schools.[12]

But the lost treasures were remembered, and with legalization of the potlatch and a general cultural resurgence in the 1950s and 1960s a movement for repatriation emerged. It was all too clear that the artifacts had been acquired by coercion. Thus, after considerable discussion, the Museum of Man in Hull (now the Canadian Museum of Civilization) agreed to their repatriation. The Royal Ontario Museum followed suit later. But certain conditions were imposed. The objects could not be given to individual chiefs and families, since it was feared that they would not be properly cared for or would be sold for large sums to private collectors. The regalia had to be housed in a fireproof tribal museum. There was disagreement, however, over where the museum should be built. In the years since 1922, the survivors of the great potlatch and their descendants had gathered in two Kwagiulth communities, Cape Mudge Village and Alert Bay. Eventually, with government and private funding, two museums were built and the repatriated objects divided between them. Family authorities who had a claim to specific objects decided where they would go. In case of dispute or uncertainty, the regalia was distributed following a principle of equal quantities to each locale.

The two museums are different in many respects: architecture, form of display, local political significance, range of activities, and reputation. The U'mista Cultural Centre is part of a larger, more mobilized Kwagiulth community, and the area around Alert Bay is home to a number of widely known Native American artists. The Centre functions as an artistic and cultural catalyst for the region and is also connected with the wider museum world of Vancouver, Victoria, and beyond. Its director, Gloria Cranmer Webster, daughter of Dan Cranmer, academically trained and an active participant in national and international forums, gives the center an outward-looking dynamism. By contrast, the Kwagiulth Museum and

Cultural Centre on Quadra Island has an intimate, somewhat sleepy feel about it. Its cultural activities are more circumscribed and village-centered. It has not, like U'mista, produced widely circulated videos on the suppression of the potlatch or the return of the lost regalia.[13] The Kwagiulth Museum presents its treasured heritage simply, with brief explanations of the pieces' history and traditional meaning. It shows the people they belong to. Here the objects are not cultural property (as in the majority museums) or tribal property (as in the U'mista Cultural Centre) but rather individual (family) property. The objects are displayed in ways that emphasize their specificity and visual appearance. A visitor can, without much distraction, engage them as great art. In its general style of contextualization the Quadra Island museum is compatible with the UBC Museum of Anthropology, though its use of historic photographs adds a different dimension. And unlike either the Royal British Columbia installation or, as we shall see, that of the U'mista Cultural Centre, the display does not subsume individual objects in a larger historical narrative.

Objects here are family and community memorabilia. To an outsider, at least, a great part of their evocative power—beyond their formal, aesthetic values—is the simple fact of their being *here,* in Cape Mudge Village. In a local museum, "here" matters. Either one has traveled to get here, or one already lives here and recognizes an intimate heritage. Of course, every museum is a local museum: the Louvre is Parisian, and the Metropolitan Museum of Art is a characteristically New York establishment. But while major museums reflect their city and region, they aspire to transcend this specificity, to represent a national, international, or human heritage. At places like Cape Mudge Village and Alert Bay, the surrounding community and history is inextricably part of the museum's impact. An outsider wonders about local involvement with the institution, what it means to band members. In Cape Mudge Village, kids ride up to the door on bikes; one wonders how often they go inside (to see a relative working behind the desk?). What do they think of the contents? What have they been taught about them? Questions like this do not immediately arise with regard to large metropolitan museums and their public. (Why? Taking tribal museums seriously forces the question. Why is it hard to see majority museums in terms of the imagined communities they serve and the local knowledges, aspiring to universality, that they express?)

Cape Mudge Village is a relatively prosperous fishing village. The wooden houses are strung out, one or two deep, facing the water, reminiscent of the Kwagiulth communities in the old photos. The museum lines up beside the school, the cemetery, a church. A woman working in the gift shop responds to my comment about the band members' reactions to the regalia's return by saying, "Yes, it's nice for them to have the artifacts nearby." ("Nearby" . . . A daily presence and feeling of kinship? A message of pride and local control? A remembered history of loss? What are the local meanings of her word "nearby"?) This specificity of meanings alters the perceptions of a visitor accustomed to majority museums' exhibits of tribal art and culture.

I become conscious of the change while in the gift shop of the Kwagiulth Museum. I notice that postcard photos by Edward Curtis are for sale there, sepia portraits of Kwagiulth men and women from the early part of the century. They are all too familiar to me. I know them from coffee-table books, from calendars (with titles like "Shadows"), from posters on dormitory walls. My first reaction is disappointment. Have I traveled all the way to Quadra Island to encounter these well-known, even stereotypical, faces? I know how staged many of the Curtis portraits are (Holm and Quimby, 1982; Lyman, 1982). Perhaps some of these people are wearing the wigs and costumes he carried with him and used to create a purified image. In any event, I strongly doubt that this man on a postcard—with a ring through his nose, wearing bark clothing, holding a copper—appeared that way in everyday life. Picking up a different postcard, I see a color portrait of a man wearing a vest decorated with buttons and a fur headdress with a carved face inlaid in abalone. On the back of the postcard the man is identified as "Kwakiutl chief Henry George of the Na-Kwa-Tok tribe in a Kla-sa-la (Peace) headgear at the opening of the Kwakiutl Museum, June 1979." This is not Henry George's everyday appearance. I look again at the Curtis postcard and turn it over, expecting a caption like the one Curtis gave it: "Nakoaktok Chief and Copper." That caption appears, in quotation marks, and is surrounded by other specifications: the Nakoaktok are identified as Kwakwaka'wakw (Kwakiutl); and the caption continues, "Hakalaht ('Overall'), the head chief, is holding the copper Wamistakila ('Takes Everything Out of the House'). The name of the copper refers to its great expense, which is valued at five thousand blankets." Holding the Curtis portrait in Cape Mudge Village, I realize that it represents an individual, a named ancestor. What the image communicates here may be quite different from the exoticism and pathos registered by an audience of strangers.

Figure 5.8. Two postcards on sale in the gift shop of the Kwagiulth Museum and Cultural Centre, Cape Mudge Village. Courtesy of the Kwagiulth Museum and Cultural Centre.

Later I come across a similar revelation in Ruth Kirk's book *Tradition and Change on the Northwest Coast*. A Hesquiaht/Nuu-Cha-Nulth elder, Alice Paul, looks at one of Edward Curtis' most striking images—a woman, in traditional bark clothing and basket with headband, staring out to sea—and sees her mother. Alice Paul's mother worked in a cannery while her husband shipped out on a sealing schooner. She was picked by Curtis because she was good at making the necessary bark clothes and baskets quickly. "I always see her picture . . . Every time I look at the books, she's there. But they never use her name, just 'Hesquiaht woman.' But I know her name. It's Virginia Tom."[14] (Kirk relocates the old image in a narrative of Hesquiaht/Nuu-Cha-Nulth women's accomplishments, juxtaposed with a contemporary photo of Virginia Tom's granddaughter, a graduate of the University of British Columbia law school. This is emphatically not Curtis' story.)

I'm unexpectedly reminded of Cape Mudge Village in the gift shop of the UBC Museum of Anthropology. An elderly man and a teenager are commenting on a catalogue about Musqueam weaving, searching in it for a picture of the girl's aunt. The Musqueam (Coast Salish) reserve is just a few kilometers away. They find the picture. After visiting the Kwagiulth Museum I can no longer forget the questions of kinship and ownership that must always surround objects, images, and stories collected from living traditions—questions elided in majority displays, where family relationships and local history are subsumed in the patrimony of Art or the synthetic narrative of History. But what is the ongoing significance of collected objects, images, and stories for Native American communities? For specific clans?

I'm not suggesting that the local connection is always present or meaningful, just that I can no longer ignore the issues of ownership and the histories of collecting that lie behind institutions such as the UBC Museum of Anthropology. Nor can I accept without pause the sweeping Northwest Coast emphasis at either the UBC or Victoria installations. It is true that something important is represented: a regional history and aesthetic achievement in process, on a scale sufficient to vie for importance and power in the national, cosmopolitan milieu of the majority museum. But something is missed: a density of local meanings, memories, reinvented histories.

Revisiting the Museum of Anthropology, I recognize local meanings in a temporary show installed in the theater, "Proud to be Musqueam."[15] Its opening case contains an enlarged photo of band elders and small children

Figure 5.9. Section of the "Proud to be Musqueam" exhibition, August 1988, University of British Columbia Museum of Anthropology. The text reads:

1. Joe Dan, Howard Grant, May Roberts, Wendy (Sparrow) Grant, Eileen (Charles) Williams. Courtesy of Mr. and Mrs. Vernon Dan. "This is a really nice picture. It's one of my favorites. This is a picture of confirmation. In a lot of the families they had to go to first communion. Church was a big thing then."

2. Bill Guerin, Johnny Sparrow, Andrew Charles. Courtesy the *Vancouver Sun.* "They were the first elected chief and council at Musqueam and the youngest in Canada. The picture was in the *Vancouver Sun.*"

3. Matilda Cole, mother of Ed Sparrow; Lloyd Dan, son of Vernon and Elizabeth Dan; Alice Louie, grandmother of Lloyd and Joe Dan.

4. James Point, father of Tony Point and Johnny Sparrow, son of Rose and Ed Sparrow. Courtesy the *Vancouver Sun.* "James Point is signing over the chieftainship. Johnny Sparrow's the next chief. The photo was also in the *Vancouver Sun.*"

Photo by James Clifford.

in 1988, a blanket woven by Barbara Cayou in 1987, and a piece of basket three thousand years old. The main exhibit is a sequence of photos documenting the band's history from the late nineteenth century to the present. The exhibit's Musqueam curators, Verna Kenoras and Leila Stogan, consulted with band elders and amassed more than 150 photographs. They have displayed their selection chronologically, making sure that each extended family on the reserve is represented. Labels are composed in the first person, and individuals in the photos are identified by name and family relation ("son of," "daughter of"). For a pre-1900 image, the curators write: "We weren't so lucky with this picture, because we didn't have the names of any of the ladies. That was really sad." According to museum staff, the exhibit's comment book registers an unusual level of interest from an international public, with reactions often addressed directly to the curators. When it leaves the Museum of Anthropology, the exhibit will be housed permanently in the Musqueam Elders' Center.

Photographs and texts also construct history at the entrance to the U'mista Cultural Centre in Alert Bay:

> The Kwagu'l chiefs were discussing the creation of their ancestors while waiting for the second course of a feast given by one of the chiefs of Tsaxis. At first no one spoke for a while. Then Malid spoke, saying, "It is the Sun, our chief, who created our ancestors of all the tribes." And when the others asked him how this was possible, for the Sun never made even one man, the chief was silent. Others said, it is the Mink, Tlisalagi'lakw, who made our first ancestors. Then spoke great-inviter, saying, "Listen Kwagu'l, and let me speak a really true word. I see it altogether mistaken what the others say, for it was the Seagull who first became man by taking off his mask and turning into a man. This was the beginning of one of the groups of our tribe. And the others were caused when the Sun, and Grizzly Bear, and Thunderbird also took off their masks. That is the reason that we Kwagu'l are many groups, for each group had its own original ancestor."
> A chief visiting from Nawitti disagreed, and the Kwagu'l of all four groups became angry. For the Nawitti believe that the Transformer (or Creator) went about creating the first ancestors of all the tribes from people who already existed. But the chiefs of the Kwagu'l scoffed at this, saying, "Do not say that the Transformer was the creator of all the tribes. Indeed, he just came and did mischief to men, when he made him into a raccoon, land otter, and deer, for he only transformed them into

animals. We of the Kwagu'l know that our ancestors were the Seagull, Sun, Grizzly Bear, and Thunderbird." (Adapted from a discussion recorded by George Hunt, 1903)

This text is one of a dozen displayed along the entry corridor, where creation stories are paired with old village photographs (in this case "Tsaxis, Fort Rupert, Kwagu'l," by Edward Dossetter, 1881). The pairings represent each of the principal native communities of the region, whether currently inhabited or not. The impression, as in the text just cited, is of difference and debate, diversity within a shared social and linguistic context (the feast and discussion). Introducing the paired photos and texts, the center's opening statement directly challenges the way these different but related peoples have been identified by outsiders: "Ever since the white people first came to our lands, we have been known as the Kwawkewlths by Indian Affairs or as the Kwakiutl by anthropologists. In fact, we are the Kwakwaka'wakw, people who speak the same language, but who live in different places and have different names for our separate groups." And introducing the origin stories, the statement ends with a strong claim:

> Each group of people on earth has its own story of how it came to be. As Bill Reid says in his prologue to *Indian Art of the Northwest Coast:* "In the world today, there is a commonly held belief that, thousands of years ago, as the world counts time, Mongolian nomads crossed a land bridge to enter the western hemisphere, and became the people now known as the American Indians. There is, it can be said, some scant evidence to support the myth of the land bridge. But there is an enormous wealth of proof to confirm that the other truths are all valid." These are some of our truths.

From the outset the U'mista Cultural Centre strikes an oppositional note, highlighting the politics of identity (conflict over the right to name, circumscribe, and essentialize specific groups) and of history (discordant true stories about where a people has come from and is going; the conflict of scientific history and local myth or political genealogy). From the outset, the power to reclaim and recontextualize texts and objects "collected" by outside authorities is demonstrated. Many of the creation stories quoted in the entryway are "adapted from Boas and Hunt, *Kwakiutl Texts,* 1903–1906." The gleanings of "salvage ethnography" are recycled, part of a renewed articulation of Kwakwaka'wakw identity and authority.

At the end of the long entry corridor, the visitor enters the "Potlatch

Figure 5.10. The potlatch collection along one wall of the big-house gallery, U'mista Cultural Centre, Alert Bay. Photo by James Clifford.

Collection" in its big-house setting. Here the regalia from Dan Cranmer's great potlatch are displayed around the walls of a large room in the approximate order of their appearance at the ceremony. At the door, one reads two recollections by elders who were present at the surrender of the objects in 1922:

> And my uncle took me to the Parish Hall, where the chiefs were gathered. Odan picked up a rattle and spoke. "We have come to say goodbye to our life"; then he began to sing his sacred song. All of the chiefs, standing in a circle around their regalia, were weeping, as if someone had died. (James Charles King, Alert Bay, 1977)

> My father took a large copper, it is still there. He took a large copper and paid our way out of gaol. For the white people didn't know that it was worth a lot of money. They didn't believe that it was expensive.
> Every one alive on earth has a story of their people; this is now part of our story, that we went to gaol for nothing.

There was no end to the things that Dan Cranmer did; even if people wanted it to end, it will be remembered. (George Glendale, Alert Bay, October 19, 1975)

In the dark big-house room, spotlights illuminate the regalia. The smell of wood is pervasive. Massive cedar beams and posts support a high ceiling. The objects on display are bolted to iron stands on raised platforms against the walls—which is where, at an actual potlatch, the audience would sit. (Patrick Houlihan [1991] remarks that sometimes it seems as if the artifacts are observing us.) Two large doors at the far end of the room can be opened on ceremonial occasions, giving direct access to the beach. Although the big house is primarily a museum (there's no smoke hole, and security cameras are mounted atop the great beams), the room can be used for other purposes. Elders teach young children songs and stories. Dance groups meet here (one notes a large log for rhythm pounding that is mounted on casters). And an elaborate Maori carving lying on a bench recalls a recent transpacific encounter in which a Maori delegation was received at the center.

Inside the big-house gallery the atmosphere is intimate; no glass separates observer from observed. The regalia, massed in a ritual procession, function as a group with a collective tale to tell. While it is possible to admire their individual formal properties, aesthetic attention is interrupted by historical and political discourses. (Indeed, some critics of the display find that its crowded presentation and lighting style do not bring out either the objects' formal strengths or the way they would appear at a potlatch, dramatic in the firelight.) Here coppers, masks, and rattles represent a very specific potlatch. Any other uses and meanings the objects may have had for their owners are subsumed (as are their owners' individual names) by the history of Dan Cranmer's ceremony and the regalia's return. *U'mista* is a Kwak'wala term denoting a state of luck or good fortune enjoyed by those captured in war who manage to return home safely.

Visitors to the exhibit learn about the 1921 potlatch, the surrounding climate of repression, and local memories of this history. The information is conveyed by interspersed quotations from oral testimonies and the historical archive. Contrary to a guiding rule of aesthetically oriented presentation, visitors are offered a good deal to read in close proximity to the objects. And in contrast to familiar ethnographic contextualizations, the objects are not specifically labeled or located by function (as they are at the other three museums). Indeed, they are not labeled at all, in the

Figure 5.11. Masks from the potlatch collection with historical texts, U'mista Cultural Centre, Alert Bay. Photo by James Clifford.

usual referential sense. Instead, large white cards are propped on the platform among the regalia, bearing texts and quotations selected by Kwagiulth community members. The cards include recent reminiscences by elders; quotations from the Indian agent Halliday's reports, paternalistic in tone; descriptions by other agents and missionaries of "heathen" customs; a 1919 petition by chiefs protesting the suppression of the potlatch (they note the economic loss to those possessing important coppers, listed by name and dollar value, and ask to be left alone); a message to Franz Boas from a Kwagiulth chief (essentially, "if you come to change our customs then leave; if not, you're welcome"); a quotation from a 1922 letter by the Chief Inspector of Indian Agencies (pointing out that Dr. Boas is an American; he should mind his own business and not get mixed up with defending potlatches); and so forth. The texts are powerfully evocative: voices from a troubled past that provoke curiosity, admiration, dismay, regret, anger . . . One of the briefer cards deserves quotation in full:

> I am returning to you cheque N. 3799 for $22.00 in favor of Abraham which he refuses to accept for his paraphernalia as he says the sum is absolutely too small for the paraphernalia he surrendered. He wants me

to tell you that he would rather give them to you for nothing than accept $22.00 for them.

Most of the other cheques have been paid out to the Indians and while some have thought the price very small, they have accepted them. (W. M. Halliday, Indian Agent, Kwawkewlth Agency, Alert Bay, May 1, 1923)

With regard to the cheque for $22.00 in favor of Abraham, I am returning it herewith and would ask you to request him to accept this amount. All these articles are now in the museum and the valuation was fixed by officials of that institution. (Duncan C. Scott, Deputy Superintendent General, Department of Indian Affairs, Ottawa, May 16, 1923)

Michael Baxandall (1991) reminds us that labels are not, properly speaking, descriptions of the objects to which they refer. Rather, they are interpretations that serve to open a meaningful space between the object's maker, its exhibitor, and its viewer, with the last-named given the task of intentionally, actively, building cultural translations and critical meanings. In the U'mista Cultural Centre's big house, the space between label and object has been widened dramatically, thus openly soliciting the viewer's constructive role. No relationship of direct reference remains between text and artifact. Evidence of an important story about the objects has simply been brought nearby. While reacting to the visually evocative carvings, the visitor pieces together a history. Since the objects' very visibility and presence here are inextricably tangled in that history, the objects themselves can never be treated as icons of pure art or culture. The display's effect, on me at least, was of powerful storytelling, a practice *implicating* its audience. Here the implication was political and historical. I was not permitted simply to admire or comprehend the regalia. They embarrassed, saddened, inspired, and angered me—responses that emerged in the evocative space between objects and texts.

There are, of course, at least two principal audiences for the exhibit. For local Native people, the display tells their history from their standpoint, drawing on oral memory as well as archival sources. (The resulting history may be contestable in some particulars by other groups of Kwakwaka'wakw, as we shall see.) Overall, a message of hope and pride is salvaged from tragedy. The simple presence of the regalia in Alert Bay is a sign of cultural resilience and an open-ended future, confirming George Glendale's feeling that "there was no end to the things that Dan Cranmer did." But a casual visitor can only guess at Native responses. I wonder what effects are felt when the printed cards propped in the big-house gallery are removed. And what about those visitors who have not internalized what Baxandall calls the "museum set"? How does the museum as Kwakwaka'wakw "box of treasures" continue and transform traditional forms of wealth, accumulation, collecting, and display?[16] What stories do these objects tell and retell? I know very little about how this exhibition instructs and implicates diverse indigenous audiences. What is being communicated? What specific tribal authority is displayed here?

For outsiders such as myself and white Canadians of the region, the exhibit tells our history, too. It is a history of colonization and exploitation for which we, to the extent we participate in the dominant culture and an ongoing history of inequality, bear responsibility. We encounter an informing and a shaming discourse. Any purely contemplative stance is challenged by the unsettling mélange of aesthetic, cultural, political, and historical messages. This history forces a sense of location on those who engage with it, contributing to the white person's feeling of being looked at. The historical display at the U'mista Cultural Centre is thus markedly different from the historical installation at the Royal British Columbia Museum in Victoria, which has the sweep, the nonoppositional completeness, characteristic of majority History. To identify an object as "used in the potlatch" is not the same as showing it to be property from a specific potlatch and part of an ongoing cultural struggle. The narratives of (objective) History and (political) genealogy do not coincide.

The difference between the guiding emphasis at UBC (majority, aesthetic) and at U'mista (tribal, historical) should be equally clear. To portray an object as fine art in an ongoing Northwest Coast tradition downplays its role as contested value in a local history of appropriation and reclamation. The objects in the U'mista collection of potlatch items are community treasures, not works of art. But while the two emphases do not coincide, neither do they entirely exclude each other. I have said that one of the most effective current ways to give cross-cultural value (moral and commercial) to a cultural production is to treat it as art. In the temporary galleries following the big-house room at the U'mista Cultural Centre, old and especially new art is displayed, including transitional work from the 1940s and 1950s by master carver Chief Willie Seaweed of Blunden Harbour.[17] (At the UBC Museum, although both old and new art are featured, the historical links between them are downplayed: there is no work by Willie Seaweed or Mungo Martin, a bit by Charles Edenshaw.) All of the art represented at Alert Bay retains a strong historical cast. And it is difficult to separate art from culture in a print of a killer whale by

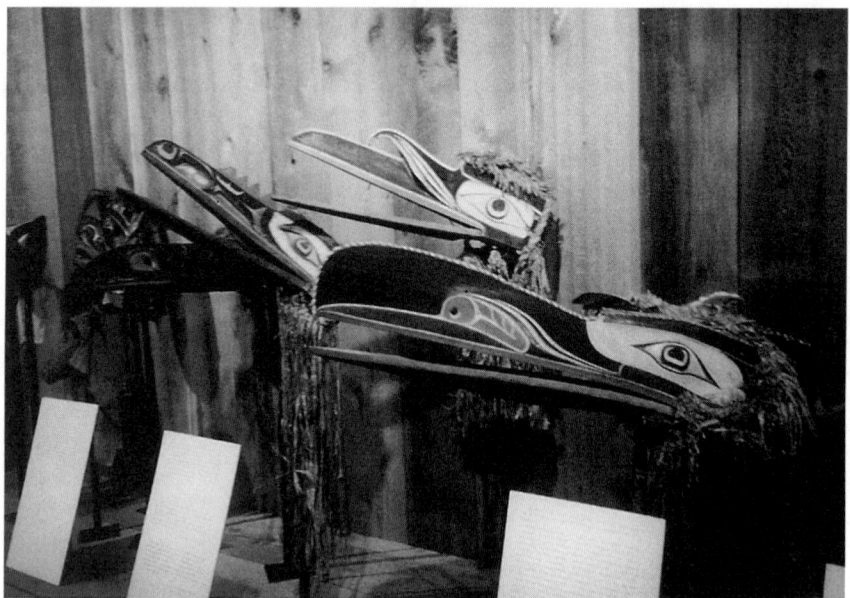

Figure 5.12. Masks from the potlatch collection, U'mista Cultural Centre, Alert Bay. Photo by James Clifford.

Tony Hunt, which contains a statement of the work's destination for use in a potlatch. In one display area, two recent acquisitions are juxtaposed: an old mask and an antique sewing machine, the latter identified as belonging to Mary Ebbets Hunt, Anisalaga, 1823–1919, originally from Alaska and wife of the Hudson's Bay agent in Fort Rupert. Her handsome machine more than holds its own among the artworks while recalling an important lineage. (Mary Ebbets Hunt was the mother of George Hunt, Franz Boas' collaborator and an ancestor of many important Kwagiulth community members.)[18]

The different cultural and political inflections of art and history in Vancouver, Victoria, Cape Mudge Village, and Alert Bay do not preclude overlap and communication. The museums have cooperated since the early 1980s, sharing curatorial expertise and exhibits. One of my aims in bringing out the strengths and limitations of majority and tribal institutions has been to argue that none can completely cover or control the important meanings and contexts generated by the objects they display. Thus, exchange and complementarity, rather than hierarchy, ideally should characterize their institutional relations. Of course, there are real obstacles to such relations: inequities in endowment, prestige, access to funding. But as tribal perspectives gain in national visibility, and as majority collections lose their claim to completeness and universality, it is to be hoped that institutional relationships will reflect the changes.[19]

The emergence of tribal museums and cultural centers makes possible an effective repatriation and circulation of objects long considered to be unambiguously "property" by metropolitan collectors and curators. The idea of majority institutions such as the Canadian Museum of Civilization and the Museum of the American Indian representing Native American cultures to the nation as a whole is increasingly questionable. So is the very existence of elaborate, enormously valuable, noncirculating collections. With better professional communication, with the manifest ability of local communities to do sophisticated, different things with artifacts from their heritage, and with the increased ability of citizens (and research scientists) to visit remote places, even the dominant scientific and political rationales for centralized collections may be questioned on their own terms. A more diverse, interesting, and fair distribution of cultural "property" should be actively encouraged by governmental agencies and private funding sources.

After visiting the U'mista Cultural Centre, I found myself reacting impatiently to accounts of protracted negotiations over the fate of the Museum of the American Indian and its cavernous Bronx warehouse bursting with Native American artifacts, most of which have never been, and may never be, displayed. Should this major, "irreplaceable" collection be attached to the American Museum of National History, subsumed by the Smithsonian Institution, or located in the Customs House in lower Manhattan? Should H. Ross Perot be allowed to move it to Texas? Does it belong to New York State? Or is it a national treasure that belongs on the Mall in Washington? (Eventually it was decided to create a new museum at the Smithsonian and use the Customs House as an adjunct.) Reading about the many millions of dollars being raised to save this unwieldy collection, I couldn't forget that the Alert Bay and Cape Mudge Village museums must constantly struggle to obtain grants for the most basic operating costs, thus diverting energy from community projects. Several large crumbs from the tables in New York and Washington could support them and dozens of emerging tribal museums. A worse irony: somewhere in the cavernous Bronx warehouse are thirty-three pieces of regalia from the Village Island potlatch. George Heye, the ever-acquisitive architect of the New York collection, bought them from W. M. Halliday in Alert Bay. (A card in the U'mista Cultural Centre display documents this purchase for an "excellent price," remitted to Ottawa. Halliday is reprimanded by his superiors for losing the pieces, seen as *Canada's* loss.) To date, the Museum of the American Indian has refused to return these last missing regalia (Webster, 1988).

Having contrasted the majority institutions in my collection with each other and with the tribal centers, I would like to suggest some differences between the two tribal museums. The U'mista Cultural Centre and the Kwagiulth Museum on Quadra Island adopt quite different strategies for displaying their shares of the returned regalia. In Alert Bay, the permanent exhibit represents the colonial history of the potlatch and particularly the story of Dan Cranmer's great ceremony of 1921 on Village Island. In Cape Mudge Village, this history is recounted but not featured; the name "Cranmer" has no prominence. In Alert Bay, a dozen or so Kwak'wala-speaking communities and origin stories are invoked, and the Cranmer potlatch story comes to stand for their common colonial history. The home to which the regalia have returned is a broad Kwakwaka'wakw unity-in-difference—a "tribal" unity forged by a common culture and history of alliance, oppression, and collective resistance.

In Cape Mudge Village, the word *Kwagiulth* in the museum's name refers to a broader unity *and* to a limited group of families. The home to which the objects have been repatriated is a community composed of named chiefs and families with continuous claims to specific objects. In his recently published memoir, Chief Harry Assu (a Lekwiltok) of Cape Mudge Village expresses the two agendas:

> Here at Cape Mudge we set up the Nuyumbalees Society to get a museum going and bring back the potlatch regalia. We chose the name Kwagiulth Museum because we wanted it to be for all our people, not just our Lekwiltok tribe. At Cape Mudge we are located where all people can easily call on their way down from our northern villages to the city—Victoria or Vancouver. It's a good place for getting together. *Nuyumbalees* means "the beginning of all legends." The legends are the history of our families. That is why our chiefs show our dances in the potlatch, so that our legends are passed on to the people. (Assu and Inglis, 1989: 106)

Harry Assu portrays the museum as primarily a site of gathering and a place for display of family histories within a diverse larger unity now denoted by the term *Kwagiulth*. Objects in the returned collection are linked to empowering family stories; they are shown in a manner analogous to the way dances are performed in the potlatch.[20] The audience for the museum is Kwagiulth, and the institution is conceived within a distinct idiom and practice of ownership, rights, and display. The museum institution, imposed as a condition of repatriation, has been reconceived in traditional Kwagiulth terms. Harry Assu continues: "It has all worked out pretty well. All our stuff that was brought back from Ottawa is in glass cases in the museum according to the family that owns them. That's what the masks and other things mean to us: family ownership. We are proud of that! It tells our family rights to the people. With our people you don't talk about what rights and dances you've got; you call the people and show them in the potlatch" (Assu and Inglis, 1989: 106).

The museum speaks *for* family rights *to* the (Kwagiulth) people. It does not foreground the different goals of speaking *for* all the Kwagiulth *to* one another and *to* a nontribal audience. The museum's primary role, in Chief Assu's account, is the expression of local family pride and rights—in objects, stories, dances, political authority. This is the prime significance of the exhibition design organized by family ownership.

Similar family claims exist in Alert Bay, but they are not featured in the U'mista display. Reflecting the fact that after sixty years there are conflicts over proper family attribution (not everyone agrees with all the Kwagiulth Museum's labels), the U'mista Cultural Centre asserts ownership at a broader level: the objects appear in the museum as treasures and historical witnesses for the Kwakwaka'wakw. In effect, the U'mista Cultural Centre aspires to a kind of majority status within the dispersed but emerging tribal unity formerly called the Southern Kwakiutl.

Perhaps we can distinguish cosmopolitan and local emphases within the shared spectrum of tribal institutions, emphases that suggest somewhat different audiences, aspirations, and politics. The U'mista Cultural Centre is both a community center (with oral-history, language, video, and education programs) and an outward-looking institution (producer of programs for wide distribution, collaborator with majority museums on traveling shows, and the like). The U'mista Society shares the aims of the Cape Mudge Nuyumbalees Society in its capacity as community catalyst and as site of storage and display for objects and histories of tribal power and significance. It also acts in the wider world of museums. For example, its tenth-anniversary exhibit on the crucial work of Mungo Martin during the worst decades of oppression will travel to Cape Mudge Village, Victoria, and UBC, as well as several other museums in Canada and possibly the United States. Gloria Cranmer Webster, as center director, has a background of collaboration with majority institutions in Victoria and with UBC.[21] And the center involves prominent local artists, notably Hunts and Cranmers, whose audiences reach well beyond Vancouver Island.

The U'mista Cultural Centre also appropriates majority anthropological tradition. Franz Boas, the white authority who put "Kwakiutl" on the social-scientific map, figures as a kind of house anthropologist. His collected Kwakiutl texts are adapted and quoted; he emerges as an ally in the potlatch exhibit. A "family" tie runs through Boas' ethnographic collaborator, George Hunt, grandfather of the important Kwagiulth artist Henry Hunt, many of whose family now live and work in Alert Bay and nearby Fort Rupert. In 1986 the U'mista Cultural Centre organized a reunion attended by thirty-four members of the Boas family, including Franz Boas' daughter, Franziska, and many Hunt descendants. Among the gifts exchanged were copies of correspondence between George Hunt and Franz Boas. Pursuing these Boas contacts, the center has tracked down early recordings of local songs, currently held in remote places such as Washington, D.C., and Indiana.[22] Salvage anthropology is repatriated.

The Quadra Island museum does not range as widely. It does not, like the U'mista Centre, portray its collection as Kwakwaka'wakw art, history, and myth, thus reclaiming in a new context the scope of Boas' "Kwakiutl" culture. Its aims are more modest, and even, in certain areas, implicitly critical of the U'mista agenda. The fact that Dan Cranmer's potlatch is highlighted in a museum directed by his daughter cannot be politically neutral. Indeed, authorities from other Kwagiulth families have taken somewhat different views of the Village Island potlatch, its animating personalities, and its continuing significance. The leading role of the Cranmers, the Hunts, and the U'mista Cultural Centre has not gone unquestioned.

At the end of the potlatch sequence in Alert Bay, we read the following testimony: "When he came home your father (Dan Cranmer) was dressed like this, bare feet in his shoes. He gave away everything. He did everything at once, to make us proud. At one time, to do all the different great things among our people. Others did one thing at a time; he was the only one who did it all at one time, because his wife was a wise woman" (Agnes Alfred, Alert Bay, 1975). The praise for Dan Cranmer is complicated by a final phrase giving credit to his wife. The phrase, enigmatic to an outsider, is elaborated in a book by Agnes Alfred's granddaughter Daisy (My-yah-nelth) Sewid Smith, *Prosecution or Persecution,* published in connection with the opening of the Kwagiulth Museum and Cultural Centre in 1979. The book, which contains accounts by potlatch participants Agnes Alfred and Herbert Martin describing their imprisonment, portrays the Village Island ceremony as collaborative work by three families, the Cranmers (Nimpkish) of Alert Bay, the Mamalillikulla nobility of Village Island, and Chief Billy Assu, a Lekwiltok of Cape Mudge Village. Daisy Sewid Smith's account gives the initiating role in the affair to Dan Cranmer's wife, Emma Cranmer, and her family. A large quantity of goods and money was gathered by Emma Cranmer's relatives and Billy Assu to facilitate Dan Cranmer's marriage repayments. Cranmer also received help from his own family (Agnes Alfred and others) to make possible the great giveaway. In Daisy Sewid Smith's version of the Village Island ceremony, Dan Cranmer appears as a central participant in a collaborative event, not as its leader. Her account brings into prominence the organizing role of Emma Cranmer and her sense of deep responsibility and guilt for those who went to prison. (She was spared, since her Nimpkish family-by-marriage surrendered their regalia.)

According to Daisy Sewid Smith, her father, Chief James Sewid, initiated the repatriation process. He insisted that Ottawa should "remember that these artifacts belonged to individual chiefs, not the tribe, and no one had the right to speak for it." A committee of elders representing the families principally involved decided that the required museum should be built at Cape Mudge Village. "Later certain members of the Nimpkish Band changed this and wanted it to be in Alert Bay. So it was decided to have two museums and that each family decide where they wanted their artifacts displayed" (Smith, 1979: 3). The division of the artifacts between two museums was not accomplished without disagreement over the proper way to commemorate the Village Island potlatch and to display its regalia. *Prosecution or Persecution* counterbalances any appearance of Nimpkish prominence.[23]

I have mentioned briefly the family histories active in the aftermath of the great potlatch and in the creation of the two museums. My intention in opening up issues I can only begin to understand is not to assert the truth of one version of events over another, or the authenticity of one museum relative to another; I want simply to make visible to outsiders the complexity that is hidden behind words such as "local," "tribal," and "community." For it is too easy to speak about "local history," the "tribe," or the "community" as if these were not differently interpreted and often contested. We need to keep in mind the constitutive disagreement featured in the Kwagiulth creation story quoted above—emblematic of a vital diversity within a shared culture and history.[24]

It would be wrong, indeed, to overstate the rivalries. The communities formerly called Southern Kwakiutl are united by a strong sense of common history, culture, kinship, and ongoing oppression. The sense of a broader Kwakwaka'wakw identity represented at the U'mista Cultural Centre is a strong reality. And wider still, the domain of Northwest Coast culture and cooperation is itself an important tribal force. (A painting by Bill Reid is displayed at the U'mista Cultural Centre; the Nimpkish Doug Cranmer worked with the Haida Bill Reid on the houses and poles behind the UBC Museum of Anthropology.) At an even more global level, the alliances of postcolonial and "Fourth World" politics impinge. The name of a women's video crew at the U'mista Cultural Centre, the Salmonistas, puns on "salmon" and "Sandinista," in reference to Alert Bay's sister relationship with a Nicaraguan fishing village. There are plans for a Kwagiulth visit to New Zealand, reciprocating the recent Maori delegation.

I returned from British Columbia with a more complex sense of distinct, but interrelated, contexts for displaying and circulating Northwest Coast artifacts. Each of the four museums is caught up in shifting power relations and competing articulations of local and global meanings. Tribal identity and power have always been fashioned through alliances, debates, and exchanges—between local communities and, since the mid-nineteenth century, with intrusive whites. These processes continue in contemporary cultural life. And as institutions such as the two Kwagiulth centers gain in visibility, escaping a merely local or minor status, they challenge the global visions embodied in the major collections. Simultaneously they function as cultural centers, sites for community education, mobilization, and the continuity of tradition. Majority museums, cosmopolitan institutions for telling inclusive stories about art and culture, begin to appear as more limited national institutions, rooted in specific metropolitan centers. These "centers" are themselves the products of powerful cultures and histories, now contested and decentered by other cultures and histories. The effects of this decentering are beginning to be felt in the major museums of Victoria and Vancouver. How much they respond and how quickly remains to be seen.

On the Northwest Coast, as elsewhere, the economies and institutions of the modern nation-state have systematically exploited, repressed, and marginalized the traditional cultures of native peoples. An unequal struggle over economic, cultural, and political power goes on, continuous in many respects from the days of Dan Cranmer's potlatch of 1921. But at least one thing has changed. It has become widely apparent in the dominant culture that many Native American populations whose cultures were officially declared moribund, who were "converted" to Christianity, whose cultural traditions were "salvaged" in textual collections such as that of Boas and Hunt, whose "authentic" artifacts were massively collected a century ago, have not disappeared. In some parts of their life dramatically changed, in others profoundly connected to tradition and place, these tribal groups continue to resist, reckon with, adapt to, and ignore the claims of the dominant culture. Exploitation—substandard schools, inferior health care, poor job prospects—continues in many places. So does political resistance and the crucial resource of a strong, supple tradition.

On Vancouver Island, the potlatch is back; so are most of the regalia confiscated in 1922. But at a price: objects illegally taken were not directly returned to the families that owned them. Rather, a museum, and in the end two museums, were imposed. It is hard to imagine a more Western, metropolitan, elite institution. Yet we have seen that it, too, can be taken over and displaced. Notice, for example, what happens to the word "museum" in a passage by Chief Harry Assu. He is evoking the Kwagiulth Museum's opening ceremony of 1979 (an event similar in spirit to the event inaugurating the U'mista Cultural Centre in 1980—recorded in the center's film *Box of Treasures*): "The Spirit of Dancing, referred to as *Klassila*, had been imprisoned in Ottawa for many years and was now being released to the Kwagiulth people. The Power of the Spirit was symbolically thrown from ship to shore, where it was 'caught' and set the catcher dancing. He in turn hurled the spirit across the beach and through the museum doors. The spirit had entered the ceremonial house (museum)."

Figure 6.1. James Bosu at the height of the Sekaka Pig Festival, 1979. From O'Hanlon (1993), Plate 7.

6

Paradise

You are walking up a ramp—wheelchair access—into a place called "Paradise." There is a subtitle: "Continuity and Change in the New Guinea Highlands." This is the Museum of Mankind, Mayfair, London. A six-foot color photo awaits you at the top of the ramp. A genial-looking man stands casually in front of a corrugated iron wall and frame window; he wears a striped apron of some commercial material, exotic accoutrements, and a gigantic headdress of red and black feathers. His face is painted black and red; a bright white substance is smeared across his chest. He looks straight at you, with a kind of smile. Arrows, on either side of the image, point left.

You follow the arrows into a light, open gallery with curving walls and raised display platforms, several spaces flowing into one another. A feeling of calm: gentle music (flutes, voices, Jew's harp), colored objects in front of soft painted landscapes, uncluttered . . . a high valley. Paradise.

A small space near the entry contains background information on the Wahgi Valley. Photographs show a street scene, a contemporary house, a netted bag whose design is based on the flag of Papua New Guinea. There is information on social structure, contact with Australian explorers in the 1920s, and the traditional livelihood. Change is there from the start: "Sweet potato, the staple food today of both the Wahgi and the herds of pigs they raise, probably only arrived in the area a few hundred years ago, with as profound effects as the recent adoption of the cash crop of coffee."

But you skip the preliminaries because the next, larger, space draws you in. It contains striking things: a reconstructed highland trade store, rows of oddly decorated shields, wicked-looking old spears, and bamboo poles covered with leaves which, on closer inspection, turn out to be paper money.

The store, beside a hand-operated coffee mill and a coffee tree, is made of corrugated iron and wood. Through a window and doorway, you observe: "PARADISE Kokonas"; "Bik Pela / SPEAR/ coarse cut / tobacco sticks"; Coke bottles; shirts on hangers (the most visible one bearing a "Los Angeles County Sheriff" patch); printed cloth—"PNG," "Jesus . . .," tropical scenes; "Cheese flavoured / TWISTIES / Baim nau"; mats, pots, spices; "HIGH MOUNTAIN Instant Coffee"; mirrors, hats, acrylic yarn, sardines, tea, rice, sugar, batteries, cassettes, hair dye . . . Paradise.

Beside the trade store stands a phalanx of five-foot-high metal and wood shields decorated with impressive designs based on South Pacific Export Lager labels and slogans such as "Six to Six." Panels explain the history and recent revival of interclan warfare in the highlands. Homemade guns hang on the wall. "Six to Six," a common expression for a party that lasts from 6 P.M. to 6 A.M., here proclaims a clan's ability to fight from 6 A.M. to 6 P.M. The phrase is combined with skulls, a border from San Miguel beer packaging (reminiscent of traditional designs), and Pacific Lager birds of paradise.

Across the room, before a painted landscape, is a cluster of spears with jagged, sculptural points (the nearest thing yet to "primitive art"). A small photographic display records the first contact of Wahgi Valley residents with whites, on a gold-prospecting expedition in 1933. One photo records a crowd of Wahgi observing the explorers' airstrip from behind a rope barrier. Another shows a smiling girl in traditional garb: she has replaced her round bailer-shell forehead ornament with a tin-can lid. Nearby, a small museum case contains forehead, neck, and nose ornaments made of shell, all showing signs of use and local repair. According to the label, one of the more perfect bailer shells is plastic.

Flanking the passage to the next exhibit are dramatic banners used in the payment of bride-wealth. You read about the process of interclan alliance and peacemaking. On the right hangs a large color photo of a banner from the 1950s: a plaque held high on a pole, ringed with dramatic black-and-red bird-of-paradise feathers and loaded with shells. A contrasting older banner, less elaborate, leans nearby. The impressive newer version reflects the inflation that has resulted from white prospectors' importation of these traditional items of wealth, as payment for goods and services. The new economy makes possible a masterpiece of traditional material culture.

Juxtaposed across the passageway, bride-wealth banners from the 1980s resemble light-green leafy panels and branches. The massed PNG banknotes, a text specifies, were "simulated by museum staff." You may be tempted to read these constructions as a kind of conceptual art. But a color photo shows a crowd dramatically presenting feathered banknote banners in the same way they previously offered shells.

You move into the next display area, which is dominated by a reconstructed *bolyim* house, a three-foot thatched structure on stilts, hung with pig jaws. A short, decorated *mond* post stands beside the house. Neither item is likely to be very striking to a Western museumgoer, yet the surrounding texts and photographs portray them as the most important objects associated with the multi-year pig festival, celebrated every generation to manifest clan fertility and power. A color photo shows the *bolyim* house and *mond* post of a 1980 festival. They are smeared with pork fat and surrounded by slaughtered pigs, a few dozen of the several hundred killed and distributed. Paradise.

You read that Wahgi men, while not objecting to display of the house and post, declined to construct them specifically for the exhibit, feeling it too dangerous. Taboos surround the activity. Moreover, it is impossible to collect authentic (that is, used) specimens, since the wood of the *bolyim* house and *mond* post must be buried, preserved for the next generation's pig festival. The artifacts in London were created by the Museum of Mankind's technical staff.

A white cross stands near the center of the ensemble. Catholics, you read, do not oppose the renewal ceremony (Lutherans and evangelicals do). A circle of beer bottles decoratively surrounds the *bolyim* house. You wonder who is appropriating whom in the mixing of these objects—traditional, commercial, and Christian.

And just for an instant, walking around the *bolyim* house, you imagine yourself stumbling over pig carcasses.

The rest of this second large display area is devoted to ornamentation used at the spectacular pig-festival dances and ceremonies. Here, as throughout, the emphasis is on "Changing Materials and Occasions": new colors and different feathers made available by expanded commerce and

Figure 6.2. Coffee mill and trade store at the "Paradise exhibition." Photo courtesy of the British Museum.

surplus coffee earnings. In a display case you discover a lovely little headband sewn from Big Boy Bubblegum wrappers, their flame color reminiscent of a feather long used in headbands. The bright white color smeared on the man's chest in the image at the exhibition entrance turns out to be baby powder. Photographs document the move away from red Raggiana bird-of-paradise feathers toward Sicklebill and, especially, long black Stephanie plumes—the latter imported from outside the Wahgi region. A wall plaque makes the essential point about cultural transformation: "Wahgi have generally seen this process as one of changing fashion rather than as a loss of 'tradition.'"

The final parts of the exhibition document missionary influences and women's changing roles and productions, particularly the making of netbags. These bags, along with the large painted war shields, are the most extensively displayed objects, suggesting a complementarity of male and female activities. Gender differences, and struggles, emerge rather clearly in the second half of the exhibit, reminding you that the earlier parts, concerned with first contact, coffee culture, new commodities, and changing ways of making war and peace, have been unmarked by gender, or are explicitly male-centered.

Now you read that the *bolyim* house and painted *geru* boards, constructed in secret by men, are part of the pig festival's assertion of male autonomy. The ceremony suppresses relationships that must be recognized elsewhere: the role of women in pig raising and the contribution of other clans as providers of women. In the pig ceremony, the male clan stands alone. However, women's agency is glimpsed in the section on missionary changes. A text presents the mixtures of tradition and innovation involved in conversion to Catholicism or to diverse Protestantisms, adding that women who don't like their husbands spending coffee money on beer may join a congregation that condemns drinking.

The netbags, traditionally associated with women and largely made by them, become an idiom for changing, and contested, gender roles. A vernacular text at the top of a label is translated: "Respectable women wear their netbags suspended from their foreheads (not over the shoulder)." Women's strength and labor, traditional values, are symbolized by larger netbags at the forehead, in opposition to smaller styles slung over the shoulder. The latter, which do not spoil hairstyles, suggest (to conservatives) a rebellious, independent, even loose woman.

The complex evolution of new netbag styles illustrates once again

Figure 6.3. Contemporary women's netbags from the "Paradise" exhibition. Photo courtesy of the British Museum.

processes of selective appropriation and change: new materials (bright yarns bought with coffee money, interwoven with marsupial fur) and fresh designs incorporating Christian and commercial elements. Some of the designs are imported, reaching the Wahgi along routes comparable to those of the older traffic in shell money. Some express a new regional identity, for consumption in an emerging national context. The show's final large wall, covered with netbags of all sorts, ends with a specimen made for sale to tourists, its woven message: "PNG BEAUTIFUL COUNTRY."

Immediately to the right of this bag, as you leave the installation, you encounter four small panels containing black-and-white photos and text: "The Making of an Exhibition." The first and largest picture shows women who provided many of the netbags, smiling, at ease. On the next panel you see an elderly man, plaiting an armband for the museum collection. Then a man, identified as Kaipel Ka, stands beside one of the shields displayed in the show. He is dressed in jeans, a Coca-Cola shirt, and light parka. An older woman, Waiang, demonstrates the abandoned accoutrements of a widow, assembled for the exhibit. A professional painter, Kaipel Ka labeled the crates that transported the collection. The crated collection is seen on the back of a truck, driven by Yimbal Aipe, soon to be elected member of parliament from North Wahgi.

On the third and fourth panels you find scenes from the Museum of Mankind: curators and conservation staff unpacking artifacts, repairing a shield, fashioning pig jaws from polystyrene for the *bolyim* house, building the exhibit (without the fabric ceiling in place), painting backdrop mountains . . .

A final color panel advertises the catalogue, *Paradise: Portraying the New Guinea Highlands,* by anthropologist and curator Michael O'Hanlon. In one of the small black-and-white photos, he can be seen unpacking crates (Figure 6.7).

My own appreciation of the "Paradise" exhibit was no doubt enhanced by the fact that I had come directly, with my six-year-old son, from the *Guinness Book of World Records* exhibit in the Trocadero, Picadilly Circus. After enduring an expensive, manipulative exercise in the exoticizing and hyperinflation of virtually everything, I found it a relief to climb the stairs at the Museum of Mankind into this airy, intelligent space. Here, too, was hyperbole—the biggest pig festival, the most shells or banknotes—but all somehow at human scale. What could be more exotic than the getup of the man pictured at the entrance? (Guinness: "World's largest feather hat!") But his smile and direct look, the mundane corrugated iron—all made his performance seem engaging, comprehensible. Contemplating jumbled commodities in the trade store, I recovered the strangeness of everyday things: cartons of Paradise . . . cookies.

From Old Persian (*pairi,* meaning "about," "around," plus *daeza,* meaning "wall"), via Greek, Latin, Old French: a garden or park, a walled enclosure. The New Guinea Highlands were one of the planet's last enclosed spaces: "lost" valleys, "uncontacted" "stone-age" peoples. The lateness of Wahgi contact with the outside world is signaled by the fact that it was accomplished by airplane, in 1933. The Leahy-Taylor patrol that quickly followed plunged the Wahgi into what the exhibition calls a "crash course in modernity." There are reasons for skepticism about "first-contact" stories, for they often establish an outsider's act of discovery by suppressing histories of prior contact and by forgetting the travel experience and knowledge of indigenous peoples. But however permeable the Wahgi Valley's "garden" walls, it is clear that many highland societies were ignorant of white people and went through unprecedented, rapid changes in the last half of the twentieth century. "Paradise" (the exhibit) tracks these processes with lucid subtlety.

Change in the New Guinea Highlands is not portrayed on a before/after axis, with a "traditional" baseline preceding the arrival of "outside" influences. Rather, we are thrown into the midst of transformations. Modernity's effects are immediately and dramatically registered in the diverse commodities of the trade store. An influx of new wealth permits the Wahgi to compensate battle deaths, to make bride-wealth payments, and to stage pig festivals in a more elaborately "traditional" way than ever before. External influence does not necessarily bring loss of tradition. By placing the trade store and beer-label-influenced shields in the space preceding the *bolyim* house and pig-festival paraphernalia, the exhibition sequence confounds a commonsense narrative that would cluster ritual with tradition and commodities with modernity. Instead, everything in the exhibit presupposes the trade store, the entanglement of Wahgi hybrid productions in regional, national, and international forces.

The use of shell wealth in "precontact" rituals would be evidence enough that Highland groups such as the Wahgi were long connected to extensive trading networks. During the 1930s the miners' airplanes re-

Figure 6.4. Trade store at the "Paradise" exhibition. Photo courtesy of the British Museum.

routed these sources, increasing the supply of shells available for ritual use. The influx of new wealth also facilitated the import of exotic bird-of-paradise feathers from other parts of New Guinea. Later, coffee income sustained the accumulation of such valuables. By the 1970s, spectacular Stephanie plumes in the headdresses of the pig-festival dancers (all of which look thoroughly "traditional" in the exhibit photos) testified to changes that also brought beer bottles into the *bolyim* house ensemble. If we wished, still, to associate Stephanie plumes with tradition and beer bottles with modernity, we would have to do so with many caveats.

It is hard to sort Wahgi material culture along a linear progression of change, a before/after model of contact. Big Boy Bubblegum wrappers might seem to belong in the trade store, but folded and woven together into a headband they clearly go with the pig-festival costumes. While formally different from feathers, they function in the same way. And, indeed, if color is the salient feature, there may be no crucial issue of translation, or even of functional equivalence. By contrast, Stephanie plumes are strikingly different, both in form and color, from the red Raggiana feathers they replaced. They, too, come from outside the Wahgi area; bought and sold, they are "commodities." On what grounds might a museum curator of indigenous Wahgi objects collect Stephanie-plume headdresses and not gum wrapper versions? What would justify selecting shell wealth but not PNG banknotes—especially when the latter hang on impressive bride-wealth banners? And what about money stuffed in arm-bands? The "Paradise" exhibition makes these questions inescapable. When, after viewing the pig-ceremony and netbag sections, one circulates back to the trade store (the articulated spaces of the small show encourage this), one looks afresh at the collected products. Definitions of traditional and modern, ritual object and commodity, have been usefully confused.

"Paradise" is gently reflexive. It makes one wonder how it was put together, juxtaposing things in ways that challenge assumptions about what is and is not worth collecting. Indeed, given the trade store—a collection within the collection—"Wahgi material culture" could simply mean *any* object used by the Wahgi. In practice, the display is more narrowly focused, showing the interaction of traditional Wahgi artifacts with new materials and commodities. So, for example, beer-label imagery and the slogan "Six to Six" are prominently displayed on metal shields, but not as they also appear on the custom-painted mini-buses that link various regions of Papua New Guinea. (One of the color plates in the exhibition catalogue features a painted bus.) The shields show the continuity and hybridization of a "traditional" activity, interclan warfare; the bus is less obviously a mediation of old and new material culture. But one could imagine an exhibit on the history of regional trade that would include it.

Be that as it may, after the initial jolt of the trade store, the exhibit sticks with objects and activities that are part of the usual repertoire of "tribal" life—showing effectively how they have been adapted to new constraints and possibilities. "Paradise" dwells on war and alliance-making, shields and weapons, bride-wealth payments, shell wealth, the pig festival's spectacular activities and adornments, religious change, and women's crafts. The fundamental strategy is to work within accepted categories of the tribal—translating, complicating, and historicizing them. Two linked stereotypes are questioned: remote tribal peoples presumed to be *either* primitive and untouched *or* contaminated by progress. Though such all-or-nothing assumptions no longer hold much sway in professional anthropology, they are certainly alive and well among the general public. Witness the continued appetite for true primitives, from the "stone-age" Tasaday (whose specific historical predicament has emerged with difficulty) to the !Kung San of the popular film *The Gods Must be Crazy* (awakened to history by a Coke bottle dropped from an airplane). The Wahgi at the Museum of Mankind are both tribal and modern, local and worldly. They cannot be seen as inhabitants of an enclosed space, either past or present, a paradise lost or preserved.

I recall the exhibit's opening image, also featured on the poster: a smiling man with painted face and chest, wearing fabulous feathers and standing in front of a corrugated iron wall. A wall text specifies: "Kauwiye Aipe decorated in black bird-of-paradise plumes to celebrate the opening of a new store which he and his brothers have established (1979)." A modern occasion and a mood of casual exoticism: Kauwiye Aipe is framed by feathers and metal, both imported. The texture and ribbing of the galvanized wall, its fresh, bluish color, locate this "tribal" performance in a contemporary moment. As I visited the exhibition, I found myself drawn to color photographs such as this. They seemed unusually prominent and, on reflection, crucial to the overall historicizing strategy.

In an ethnographic exhibit, photographs tend to signify cultural "context," and they are coded historically according to style and color. Sepia tones suggest the nineteenth century; sharp black and white registers a

Figure 6.5. *Bolyim* house and bride-wealth banners at the "Paradise" exhibition. Photo courtesy of the British Museum.

nearer, documentary past; "true" color with candid or casual poses connotes contemporary history. Faded color, for my generation at least, has a "fifties" resonance: and at least one of the exhibition's important photos, the 1950s bride-wealth banner, has this historical "tone." But most of the images are in bright, living color. Enlarged and numerous, they work against the established tendency for museum objects, even new ones, to appear as collected treasures from another time. Used in this way, color supports the critical project of bringing collector and collected into contemporaneous times (which does not mean the same time).

The only consistently noncontemporaneous times signaled by the "Paradise" photographs are explorer Mick Leahy's black-and-white records of the 1933 "first contact" and the final "Making of an Exhibition" panels. The former are appropriate and inevitable, given available technology and the historical color code. The latter seem more problematic. Why should a Wahgi man crafting objects for the exhibition be in small black and white, while other Wahgi performing at the pig festival ten years earlier are in full color? Why should the work of the museum staff appear to be taking place in some different time from the complex, contemporary, real, historical times presented elsewhere in the show? Given the limited size of the exhibit and its somewhat minimalist touch, the "Making of an Exhibition" panels register the appropriate people and activities. But given the lack of color and size in the photos, they risk appearing as an afterthought. Even at its current scale, the section might have included a large color image of the women who made many of the adjacent netbags, instead of a modest black and white. And I, at least, would have found a way to show Michael O'Hanlon in the Highlands—an image missing from both exhibition *and* catalogue. How are modesty and authority complicit in this absence?

As a consistent historicizing strategy, the use of large color photographs in "Paradise" breaks with established conventions for the *aesthetic* and *cultural* contextualization of non-Western objects in Western places. An aesthetic presentation tends to exclude, or minimize, the use of contextualizing photographs. Where they appear, they are kept small, or at a distance from objects displayed for their formal properties. Cultural treatments tend to include photographs of objects in use. But in both cases, photographs cannot become too prominent without blurring the focus on material objects. Given the overriding focus in Western museums on objects—collected, preserved, and displayed, whether for their beauty, rarity, or typicality—a distinction between object and context, figure and ground, is crucial. "Paradise," an exhibit about historical change seen through material culture, walks a fine line, both maintaining and blurring this distinction.

In places, photos challenge the object/context distinction. The bride-wealth banners made of banknotes really make sense only when one sees the nearby color photograph of men holding them aloft in a procession. The "Ah ha!" response comes when looking at the picture, not at the object. The banners are strange and beautiful in their way, but are clearly simulacra and incomplete (they lack the plumes visible in the photo). They become secondary, not the "real thing" seen so clearly in the image. Nearby, we find two bride-wealth banners from earlier periods: one a material object, the other a large color photograph. The former contains relatively few shells and no feathers; the latter, loaded with shells and stunningly feathered, is enlarged to near life-size. Here it is no longer a question of a photo providing "context" for an object. We confront an object that cannot be present physically, a 1950s bride-wealth banner— long disassembled, as is its proper fate. This banner has been "collected" in the photograph. Given its prominence, the color image seems somehow more real, in a sense more "authentic," than both the less impressive older banner propped beside it and the banknote simulacrum opposite.

The force of photographs, not as supplements but as beautiful/mean-ingful objects among beautiful/meaningful objects, is further manifested in the pig-festival section, where spectacular bird-of-paradise headdresses are shown. Feathers cannot be exported from Papua New Guinea; thus, they are legally collected with a camera. Here vivid wall-size images of dancers and crowds equal, and sometimes overpower, the mere objects displayed nearby. In museum practices that privilege the material object, this might be seen as an imbalance. But why should objects always be protected from competing messages? A great deal depends on the exhibit's goal. If one is showing historical change through hybrid objects, isn't it important to keep things contaminated by specific contexts, never allow-ing them the static autonomy of works of art or cultural icons?

The historicity of objects poses slippery problems for standard museum practices of conservation and authentification. O'Hanlon points this out in the exhibition catalogue:

I was struck, for example, by the questions which the museum's conservation staff asked as they worked on the Wahgi artefacts. One of the shields had been stored in a smoky house roof, only partially protected by a plastic wrapping: should the accumulated grime be removed from the shield's outer surface? The question raised the issue of what it is that an artefact is valued as embodying. Is it the shield as a perfect example of its type, a kind of snapshot in time, taken grime-free at the outset of its career? Or do we seek, rather, to preserve the evidence of the shield's biography through time, even when (as with the grime) the evidence also begins to obscure something of the object's original purpose?[1]

The example is far-reaching, for there is no unproblematic solution to O'Hanlon's dilemma. The same artifact cannot be both new and old. Change adds and subtracts, reveals and obscures. A before-and-after presentation could present the pre- and post-cleaning object, with the help of a photograph or other simulacrum. But in current collecting and valuing practices, the representation would never have the same value as the "original." Notions of authenticity reify and value a specific moment in the ongoing history of an object, thus evading the aporia O'Hanlon notes. But exhibits and collections seriously devoted to historical change cannot escape this fundamental tension between process and objectification. Like "Paradise," they will have to supplement, and decenter, collected objects, using photographs, texts, and reconstructions.

The historicizing of "Paradise" is aimed primarily at a visitor who believes the New Guinea Highlands to be one of the last wild, untouched places. As assistant keeper at the Museum of Mankind, routinely fielding inquiries about New Guinea, O'Hanlon knows something about his likely audience. In the catalogue he records harrowing primitivist stereotypes, laced with jokes about cannibals, directed by a television announcer at a group of Mount Hagen dancers recently performing in London (*Paradise*, 57). And for many who pass through the gallery, the notion that traditional culture must diminish in direct proportion to the increase of Coke and Christianity is axiomatic. Against this, the exhibit shows the people of highland New Guinea producing their own fusion of tradition and modernity. The Wahgi make their own history, though not in conditions of their choosing. They are part of a complex Melanesian modernity which is not, or not necessarily, following preordained Western paths. To the extent that visitors to "Paradise" come to understand something like this, the exhibit will perform an important service. Absolutist, all-or-nothing scenarios for change will be undermined, affirming the historical reality and agency of a diverse humanity.[2]

In his detailed, provocative catalogue Michael O'Hanlon reinforces this message, but with more complications and reservations. The book is not a simple reflection of the exhibit. When I spoke with O'Hanlon, he stressed this point: while the exhibition needed to maintain a clear focus, the catalogue could attempt more. *Paradise* (the book) is divided into three long chapters which discuss Highland contact history, the interactive dynamics of collecting in the Wahgi Valley, and the collaborative work of mounting an exhibit in London. O'Hanlon rightly observes (78) that most of the current critical discussion of representation and politics in museum display has not grappled with the specifics of particular exhibitions, their local histories both in the community of origin and in particular institutions.[3] *Paradise* sets a new standard for detail and reflexive analysis, especially in an exhibition catalogue intended for a nonspecialist readership. While occasionally chiding current critics of Western collecting and display for their exclusively "theoretical" focus, O'Hanlon actively takes up and illustrates many of their crucial points. He shows concretely the dialogical, contingent, and inescapably tactical nature of what he and his various collaborators produced.

The first and longest chapter provides unusually specific historical background to twentieth-century life in the Wahgi Valley. It focuses on the Komblo tribe, with whom O'Hanlon did anthropological fieldwork prior to joining the Museum of Mankind staff. After a survey of the Wahgi's sense of place and of their political and kinship structures, the account passes to the Taylor-Leahy patrol of 1933. From among Mick Leahy's extraordinary "first-contact" photos, O'Hanlon chooses images in which the Wahgi are looking concertedly at the outsiders or straight at the camera. Observation is a two-way street. Wahgi disorientation soon gives way to opportunistic appropriation.

A detailed history follows, tracking the Komblo before, and then in relation to, the patrol and its aftermaths. Unlike many tribal-contact histories, O'Hanlon's does not tell of a settled people whose life is disrupted by the advent of prospectors, police, money, commodities, world markets. In certain respects, at least, the standard narrative of disruption

Figure 6.6. Wood and metal shields from the "Paradise" exhibition. Photo courtesy of the British Museum.

is reversed. Prior to the patrol's arrival, the Komblo had been driven from their homelands in tribal fighting that got out of hand. Dispersed among communities of maternal kin, they made use of one of their number, an interpreter for the patrol, to persuade the new powers to reinstate them. With the help of the new government and local missionaries, a traditional ceremony was arranged to seal a lasting peace. For the Komblo, colonial contacts meant an end to disruption, rerooting, and a renewal of old connections. O'Hanlon's account is not, however, a simple reversal of the disruption narrative. For in crucial ways the new situation brought about by mining, missions, new markets, and Australian administration did alter the parameters within which local practices could be negotiated. The effects were uneven: some things disappeared, some were transformed, some reappeared.

Drawing on stories told to him during his fieldwork, O'Hanlon provides a complex account of Komblo mobility—both migration and diaspora— prior to the arrival of Taylor and Leahy. The Highlands appear as a historically concrete, changing, and often unsettled place. Attention to roots is here joined with an awareness of routes. Highland New Guinea societies, famous for their extreme localism, are seen to enact complex histories of dwelling and traveling. The "crash courses" of colonization and modernity do not so much introduce change as alter the terms of change, the power relations through which practices of mobility and stasis, auton- omy and interconnection, are negotiated. The second half of the chapter surveys the most salient areas of negotiation, keeping a focus on "material culture" in the Wahgi Valley. The account (more radically than the exhibit) gives "as much weight to contemporary artifacts such as vehicles, money and beer as to stone axes, spears and shells" (54). Coffee, money, transport technologies, arms, alcohol, and Christianity are treated in a contact perspective that sees the consumption of new influences and commodities as localized and inventive.

This ethnographic history is followed by chapters entitled "Collecting in Context" and "Exhibiting in Practice." The former describes the inter- active process of assembling a collection in the Highlands. O'Hanlon is forced to question his own assumptions about what could be considered "Wahgi material culture." Despite an aim to collect the "full repertoire of portable Wahgi goods," he "found [himself] unthinkingly privileging those items which were produced in the area, rather than merely used there." In search of an obsolete wooden pandanus-processing bowl, he was of- fered a specimen he knew was made in the Sepik region, for tourists.

My curatorial protests that this was not a *Wahgi* pandanus processing bowl were met with an equally firm assertion that it was. Belatedly, I realized that we were arguing at cross-purposes. For me, the bowl was ineligible on the grounds that it had been produced by a Sepik carver for sale to tourists; the seller's point was that this was a Wahgi pandanus processing bowl because (whatever its origins) it had been used by Wahgi to process pandanus, as indeed the oily stains testified. I regret now that I did not buy this, or a surprisingly wide range of other items flushed out of Wahgi houses by the opportunity to sell them but which nonetheless fell outside my somewhat puritan definition of "Wahgi material culture." (*Paradise*, 58)

The collector's criteria were soon communicated to the Wahgi, who increasingly gave him what he wanted (61). An "interpenetration" of O'Hanlon's collecting and Wahgi frames of reference took place (76). "My collecting was constrained by local processes and rules, with the upshot that the collection I made partly mirrored in its own structure local social organization. And while many comments on collecting have focused upon the 'rupture' involved in removing artefacts from their local context to install them in the rather different one of a museum or gallery, this was not necessarily the way in which the Wahgi themselves chose to view the matter" (55). The Wahgi, for example, saw themselves as already in relations with London, albeit indirectly, through the prior visit there of their neighbors, the Mount Hagan dancers. They expected O'Hanlon to organize their own trip. Failing this, his proposal that aspects of their culture be displayed at the Museum of Mankind was understood as another way of establishing relations and imposing reciprocal obligations. I will return to these issues in the next section.

The catalogue's third chapter, "Exhibiting in Practice," includes the usually forgotten record of an organizer's plans *before* they bend to the practice of putting objects and messages into specific, often limited spaces. O'Hanlon makes a virtue of necessity here, for the book's publication deadlines precluded any description of the actual installation. Writing his last chapter, he does not even know how many galleries will be available. Grant proposals are still pending. The design staff is processing his ideas. O'Hanlon records his plans for a rather large exhibit, with the hope that, if changes are made, this glimpse of the gap between vision and realization will be instructive.

The grants do not materialize. "Paradise" is reduced to a single gallery, already modified (curved walls, raised platforms, lowered ceiling) for a better-funded prior exhibit on Palestinian costume. With minor changes, however, the space works for highland Melanesia. (And indeed, the predicament of making do in an environment not entirely one's own seems all too appropriate for the exhibit's vision of modernity.) O'Hanlon is informative on the constraints of working in an established institution. He warns, however, that his is not a true ethnography of museum practices, a study which would delve into the political pressures, institutional hierarchies, and sometimes fraught personal conflicts that affect the shape of any exhibition. Such accounts of specific museum cultures and practices still need to be written, most likely by an outsider (80). O'Hanlon's tactful reflexivity is that of an insider, albeit a newcomer whose professional identification remains predominantly anthropological.

From this location, O'Hanlon analyzes his own museum practices, opening a space for critical speculation by others on curatorial roads not taken. In at least one instance, the reduced display may have improved on the original scheme. The plan recorded in the catalogue juxtaposes two large galleries, one devoted to mythic time (centered on the pig ceremony) and the other to historical time (the trade store, coffee, war and peace). This would have risked reifying a Western dichotomy which the current, more compressed and therefore mixed, exhibit questions. Another instance concerns the presentation of the Taylor-Leahy patrol of 1933. As we have seen, the present exhibit does not fall into an epochal before/after narrative, with "first contact" (the moment of "opening," "corruption," "entry" into modernity) as pivot. The plan for a larger exhibit gave considerably more space to the patrol—presented in a reflexive way. An explorers' tent would have been included, along with artifacts, such as a Leica camera of the new sort that made possible Leahy's often unposed shots. Exhibit visitors, like the Wahgi of 1933, would have been kept behind a fishing line, looking in at the alien culture of the explorers. Quotations by Wahgi on their reactions to the patrol were to be placed on the walls. And life-size blowups of Highlanders would have surrounded the tent—an image of whites under observation.

Although there is much appealing here, it would have been a risky undertaking. It is one thing to place museum visitors behind a fishing line and quite another to induce them to see an explorer's tent, camera, clothes, and gun as alien objects. (Among other things, "Banana Republic" exploration nostalgia might intervene.) And to the extent the maneuver did persuade visitors they were observing white culture with Wahgi eyes, would this not simply reinforce a sense of privileged, in this case relativized, perspective?[4] Moreover, might not increased prominence given to the "first-contact" episode inevitably encourage a historical narrative that turned on a transforming moment, thus supporting the various edenic narratives the exhibit now problematizes? On reflection, the compressed show, with one corner devoted to "first contact," seems about right—though I wish room could have been found for the Leica, in a glass case perhaps.

O'Hanlon's original plan called for the prominent use of Wahgi quotations in the "first-contact" section. Arguing for this strategy, he noted that an earlier exhibit at the Museum of Mankind, "Living Arctic," made extensive use of quotations from Native Americans, and that these had been much appreciated by visitors (87). In the current exhibit, Wahgi are very little "heard." Very brief quotations, often with allegorical resonances, are placed at the head of each long interpretive plaque, but these have no independent presence. Nor do we read, in the catalogue, any extended Wahgi interpretations of exhibit topics or process. Wahgi agency, stressed throughout, has no translated voice. As the "Living Arctic" experiment showed, this could be a powerful means of communication, albeit under curatorial orchestration. Why was the tactic dropped? So as not to over-complicate the message? So as not to privilege certain Wahgi? In order to avoid the awkwardness, even bad faith, that comes with "giving voice" to others on terms not their own?

The staging of translated, edited "voices" to produce a "polyphonic" ethnographic authority has never been an unproblematic exercise. But represented voices can be powerful indices of a living people—more so even than photographs, which, however realistic and contemporary, always evoke a certain irreducible past tense (Barthes, 1981). And to the extent that quotations are attributed to discrete individuals, they can communicate a sense of indigenous *diversity.* One of the exhibit's scattered Wahgi statements chastises young women for their new, unrespectable netbag styles. We immediately "hear" a man of a certain generation. What if longer, more numerous, and sometimes conflicting personal statements had been included? My point is not to second-guess O'Hanlon and his collaborators at the museum. There were trade-offs, and one cannot do everything in a small, or even in a large, exhibit. I wish, simply, to underline significant choices constituting both object and authority in "Paradise," choices revealed but not analyzed in the catalogue.

With two galleries available, the exhibit would have had ample space for a more extensive section than the current panels on the "making of an exhibition." O'Hanlon acknowledges that an exhibition is itself a "large artefact" worth as much attention as the objects it includes (*Paradise,* 92); but he resists including much material on its "manufacture" in the exhibition (while giving this considerable prominence in the catalogue). "Where the subject of an exhibition is anyway relatively recondite, such mixing of exhibition content, and commentary on that content, risks undermining an exhibition's capacity to convey any message at all" (92). O'Hanlon may well be right in the present instance, but I wonder whether the trade-off is quite as clear as he suggests. The assumption that reflection on the making of a message tends to weaken the message is of course familiar. Lately we have heard a chorus of warnings against too much reflexivity in ethnography—often portrayed as leading inevitably to "post-modern" hyperrelativism or narcissistic self-absorption. But the issue is seldom confronted practically in such all-or-nothing ways. There are many forms of reflexivity, and a little irony, personal voice, or reflection on process can go a long way. I, for one, am not persuaded that contemporary viewers of exhibitions (many reared on TV montage) cannot handle multiple levels of information without losing faith or attention. And what justifies the assumption that strongly focused narratives do, in fact, hold people's attention?

The concrete question, in ethnographic as well as museum practice, is always one of degree and of how specific rhetorical strategies affect different audiences. O'Hanlon's solution was to reduce reflexive materials in the exhibit while giving them prominence in the catalogue. I'm not sure what practical assumptions this division reflected. A distinction between relatively unsophisticated visitors and sophisticated readers? A feeling that stories of cultural change in highland New Guinea were appropriate to a wide London audience, whereas the details of collecting and producing a display in Mayfair were not? A greater comfort with necessarily personal material in a single-authored book, as opposed to an exhibition made by many hands? I do not know what hesitations, trade-offs, and institutional constraints influenced the negotiation of distinct zones of neutral authority (in the exhibit) and reflexive authority (in the catalogue). And I am not arguing here for a particular solution, whatever my abstract preferences might be. I am suggesting only that *some* negotiation will necessarily take place around issues of authority, reflexivity, voice, and audience, and that there is no automatic outcome. The *Paradise* ensemble (exhibit plus book) brings these issues strikingly to the fore.

O'Hanlon pushes gently, at times, against the institutional limits of his practice: "In the museum's repository, the process of unpacking the crates in which the collection had travelled was complete. The crates' contents, now safely swaddled in tissue paper, awaited fumigation, conservation, registration and careful storage as Wahgi artefacts. Meanwhile, other Wahgi artefacts—the crates themselves, no less carefully made by Michael Du, painted by Zacharias and labelled by Kaipel the sign writer—awaited disposal" (92). This poignant scene ends the catalogue. Museum basements are revealing places, and here collecting is seen to be an act of both retrieval and disposal. The scene illustrates, for O'Hanlon, "an unavoidable contingency attached to collecting and preserving some artefacts but not others." But the phrase "unavoidable contingency" may not quite do justice to the specific institutional constraints and (not inevitable) choices

Figure 6.7. Unpacking the collection. From O'Hanlon (1993), p. 79.

at work. The custom-made crates could have made striking additions to a show differently conceived. Space considerations, conventions of proper collection and display, a concern not to overcomplicate the message—all these no doubt conspired to make their disposal seem inevitable. But O'Hanlon clearly remains attached to the Wahgi crates, as he is to the individuals who so carefully made and marked them. Perhaps by giving them the last word, he expresses a wish for the leeway—in spite of museum, public, and profession—to collect and exhibit "Wahgi material culture" differently.

Paradise is directed at a certain London museum public and at a sophisticated (in places specialist) catalogue readership. That it is not addressed to the Wahgi is obvious and, given who is likely to see and read the productions, appropriate. This fact does not, however, close the personal and institutional question of responsibility to the Wahgi. It may be worth pushing the issue a bit farther than O'Hanlon does, for it is of general importance for contemporary practices of cross-cultural collecting and display. What are the relational politics, poetics, and pragmatics of representation here? In what senses do "Paradise" the exhibition and *Paradise* the book reflect Wahgi perspectives and desires? Should they?

O'Hanlon's purchase of artifacts was enmeshed in a "cultural negotiation" (*Paradise,* 60), which meant entering into specific, ongoing alliances. For Melanesians, accustomed to buying and selling objects, songs, rites, and knowledge, the purpose of payment was not to be quit but to be in relation. O'Hanlon's sponsor was a local leader, Kekanem Kinden (whose portrait appears on page 52 of the catalogue). Kinden orchestrated the necessary social transactions, including the touchy issue of who should have first access to the collector. O'Hanlon offers a sensitive account of all this, portraying himself yielding to, and working within, local protocols. He tends, overall, to present a potentially fraught process as a steady convergence of interests—a fable, if not of rapport, at least of complicity. He also gives glimpses of the relationship's more problematic aspects. As the collection is about to depart for London, it is ritually treated like a bride departing to live with her husband's people (marriage being the primary model of leave-taking for the Wahgi).

> Anamb, the local ritual expert, and a long-time friend but also someone who, on occasion, felt himself challenged by Kinden's sponsorship of me,

proposed that the collection should undergo the ceremony of beautification which is performed for a bride the evening before her departure. This was a suggestion with considerable political spin on it, a point I also noted when the same idiom of kinship was invoked in negotiating what was to be paid for artefacts. For if the collection was like a bride, then what I had paid for it was like bridewealth; and the point about bridewealth is that it is only the *first* of the payments which are owed to the bride's kin. A bride's brothers also expect payments for the children which subsequently flow from her, for they are the children's "source people." Anamb's comparison was his way of highlighting my continuing relationship of indebtedness to those who had helped me, as well as a specific attempt to constitute himself as the "source person" of any benefit which might flow to me from the collection. (*Paradise,* 77).

O'Hanlon closes his second chapter with Anamb's power play, an incident that reveals how dialogical relations of collecting both include and exclude people. Moreover, Anamb raises, Melanesian style, a far-reaching political question. What do O'Hanlon, the Museum of Mankind, and indeed the visitors and readers who "consume" these artifacts owe the Wahgi who have sent them? Payment does not end the connection with "source people." Quite the opposite: in relations of collecting, money, objects, knowledge, and cultural value are exchanged and appropriated in continuing local/global circuits. How should the benefits of these relationships be shared? If collecting is conceived as exchanging, what ongoing constraints are imposed on exhibition practices? The catalogue chapter entitled "Exhibiting in Practice" does not pursue these political issues. The prime constraints it discusses are those pragmatically imposed by funding and by the sponsoring institution and its publics. Indeed, in reading this valuable discussion of museum work and its trade-offs, one is struck by the absence of Wahgi input, direct or indirect.

According to O'Hanlon, those who helped him in the Highlands made few specific requests about the nature of the exhibit. They did, however, want the personal and political relationships involved to proceed properly. Anamb's attempt to ensure a "continuing relationship of endebtedness" (77) doubtless had more to do with keeping the exchange going and sharing the wealth than with faithfully representing his viewpoint or giving him voice. Independent of exhibit content, the issue of reciprocity remains. Does the museum officially recognize any ongoing exchange connection with Wahgi tribes or individuals? Or does it see itself as quit, having dealt as fairly as possible in the field? What is the nature of the

Figure 6.8. Kaipel Ka with his shield. From O'Hanlon (1993), Plate 14.

responsibility incurred in the making of this exhibit? Do the Wahgi understand it primarily as a personal, kinlike relation with O'Hanlon? Or is there an institutional, even geopolitical dimension? These questions, opened up by the catalogue, encourage more concreteness in our discussions of the politics of collecting and representation. A Melanesian sense that the wealthy owe something to the less wealthy who support them may or may not—or may only partially—coincide with the notions of First World / Third World, colonizer/colonized, that have tended to orient current discussions.

The most specific Wahgi request concerning the exhibition was, in fact, passed over. In the Highlands, special or restricted places are marked off by small clusters of "taboo stones" and painted posts. O'Hanlon's sponsor Kinden marked his Highland collecting camp in this way, to keep the acquisitions safe. He and others asked that the exhibit be identified as a Wahgi area by placing similar stones and posts at the entry (86). Indeed, two posts were specially painted for the purpose and given to O'Hanlon. But no stones or posts appear at the entrance to "Paradise." Apparently the museum design staff thought they might obstruct the flow of visitors (large school groups, for example) at a place where it was important that people move along.[5] In this instance, practical concerns that were surely soluble (the stones are only a foot or two high) were able to override a clearly expressed Wahgi desire for the exhibition.

London is distant from the New Guinea Highlands. There is no Wahgi community nearby that could constrain the exhibit organizers' freedom. It is worth noting this obvious fact because in many places, today, it is no longer obvious. An exhibition of First Nations artifacts in Canada will be under fairly direct scrutiny, often coupled with demands for consultation or curatorial participation. Many tribal societies now place restrictions on what can be displayed, and they participate in planning, curating, and ritually sanctioning exhibitions far from their homelands.[6] Exhibits of African materials in North America or parts of Europe may feel pressure from diasporic black communities, pressure to show certain kinds of respect—if not always to follow indigenous wishes. Compared with these examples, the Wahgi's power to coerce, to embarrass, the organizers of "Paradise" was virtually nil. O'Hanlon's rather scrupulous reciprocity in collecting did not have to be reproduced in exhibiting. A general intent to do something that would not offend the (distant) Wahgi was enough. Thus, if the taboo stones were "impractical" they could be dispensed with.

How far must an exhibition go in reflecting indigenous viewpoints? Some Wahgi urged O'Hanlon not to emphasize warfare in the exhibition.[7] The exhibit does feature war (dramatic shields and spears) but compensates by following with peacemaking. Would this satisfy the Wahgi who asked that fighting be played down? And would we want to satisfy them on this score? Indeed, who speaks for the "Wahgi"—itself a rather loose regional unit, including contentious clans? The wishes expressed might be only those of specific clan leaders, of the collection's sponsors (individuals or factions), of men, of a certain generation, of "insiders," of cultural brokers or "translators." But assuming requests come from individuals of wide local authority, should they be followed without question? Is the decision by a more powerful institution to override or supplement indigenous views always "imperialist"? Yes *and* no. In a structural sense, large metropolitan museums stand in a relation of historical privilege and financial power with respect to the small populations whose works they acquire and recontextualize. This geopolitical position is determining, at certain levels. At the same time it is cross-cut by a variety of conjunctural, negotiated, often less absolute relations; and within a general power imbalance, processes of mutual exploitation may occur. Who appropriates whom cannot be "read off" from global political economic relations. Political operations are not homologous in all contexts of interaction. People may care a lot about being compensated fairly, but not be much concerned with the details of their portrayal in a distant place. (This seems to have been the case with the Wahgi.) In other situations the priorities may be reversed. Some institutions build on a historical legacy of direct dominance over the peoples represented. Others do not. Much depends on local deals and individual contacts.

Discussions of the politics of collecting and display, especially in colonial and/or neocolonial situations, have tended to begin and end with structural dominance, overriding more local, and equally "political," contingencies. The *Paradise* catalogue explicitly sets out to provide a corrective to such sweeping, "theoretical" accounts (12, 78). While recognizing their importance, O'Hanlon focuses instead on specific practices and negotiations, providing much illuminating detail. The effect, however, of dwelling on pragmatics may be to make conjunctural negotiations seem inevitable and thus nonpolitical. Rather than contrasting abstract theory with practical interactions, I would prefer to think of connected but nonhomologous contexts of political relationship. O'Hanlon's pointed corrective, in its focus on collecting and exhibiting in practice, risks overreacting, omitting more structural or geopolitical levels of differential power. Thus, his lack of attention to the disappearance of Wahgi agency when discussing the work in London.

It is, of course, very difficult to keep all levels in view simultaneously. And it is especially hard to give the more structural determinations their due when one is immersed in the specific negotiations and relationships of a particular interaction. There is always a risk that humanist accounts of reciprocity may function as "anticonquest" narratives (Pratt, 1992) in which larger power inequalities become irrelevant because everyone treats everyone decently. But "reciprocity" is itself a translation term linking quite different regimes of power and relationality. A capitalist ideology of exchange posits individual transactions between partners who are free to engage or disengage; a Melanesian model may see ongoing relationships in which the wealthier partner is under a continuing obligation to share. It is important to keep these different practices of reciprocity in view.[8]

There will always be discrepancies, sometimes extreme, between the wishes of the people represented, the interests of academic or avant-garde consumers, and the broad public for any exhibition—in this case middle-class British primitivists. Curators and ethnographers, those at least who think it important to portray the salient conditions of their work, struggle within these pressures to produce more complex, politically accountable, broadly intelligible representations. *Paradise* is an important contribution to that struggle, both for what it does and for what it helps us see it does not do.

Since O'Hanlon cites my writings, both as charter and foil for his undertaking, I may perhaps be permitted some final responses of a more personal nature. I was engaged by *Paradise:* it confirmed my view of the world, and brought me up short. It threw me back on *my* Melanesia, a shadowed paradise. My first book (Clifford, 1982) grappled with how New Caledonian Kanaks survived a peculiarly violent (and ongoing) colonial regime, finding in hybrid Christianity new ways to be different. It led me to ask, thinking of new, complex nations in Vanuatu and Papua New Guinea: "What would it require . . . consistently to associate the inventive, resilient, enormously varied societies of Melanesia with the cultural *future* of the planet? How might ethnographies be differently conceived if this standpoint could be seriously adopted?" (Clifford, 1986: 115). *Paradise* keeps these questions open—and the questioner off center.

I keep looking at the catalogue's cover. A man, close up, wears a dramatic feathered headdress and bright orange "wig." He looks straight, unsmiling, at the camera. His nose and chin are marked with red and yellow paint. No banknotes, corrugated iron, or gum wrapper headbands here. Only on close inspection do I notice the Hawaiian cloth at his neck and "modern" materials in the wig. Coupled with the word "paradise," the picture has a decidedly primitivist effect. I recall hearing that its selection for the cover was a compromise, designed to attract a wider audience.[9] A cop-out? Maybe. But apparently this image of traditional authenticity, taken in the early 1980s of a man named Kulka Kokn, is approved by many Wahgi. It shows them as they would like to be seen: dramatically decorated, visage and skin radiant with power (O'Hanlon, 1989).

Another apparent coincidence of Wahgi and Western visions of authenticity can be seen in the catalogue's discussion of the Onga Cultural Centre (74–76). Recently established just to the west of the Wahgi by a Romonga man, Yap Kupal, the center is a museum of local culture, rather narrowly conceived. Scrupulously reconstructed precontact men's and women's houses hold a large collection of "traditional" material culture: there are no obviously hybrid objects of the sort featured in *Paradise*. Yap Kupal's aim is both to preserve the older culture for future generations and to appeal to tourists. His inspiration comes from Western-style museums in Port Moresby. Would one have wanted *Paradise* to reflect this indigenous model for the display of culture? I, for one, would hate to see the gum wrapper headbands and new netbags excluded. By foregrounding tradition as hybrid process, the London exhibit appealed to the likes of me, while offering a history lesson to primitivists (prospective Highland tourists?). It was not aimed at people like Yap Kupal. And generally speaking, hybrid exhibits like "Paradise" might not appeal to many cultural activists for whom the recovery of an indigenous past, a tradition relatively clear of the West, is a crucial political stake. They, too, might prefer the apparently untroubled traditionalism of the catalogue's cover.

This should give pause to those, like me, who have worked toward a recognition of hybrid, relational cultural processes. In normalizing inventive impurity, we have questioned purist regimes of "authenticity." But have we always been attentive enough to the ways in which articulations of authenticity are embedded in specific historical or political situations?

Figure 6.9. Kulka Kokn in ceremonial wig. From O'Hanlon (1993), cover photo.

Would we want to equate, for example, the essentialist traditionalism of the Onga Cultural Centre with an ahistorical primitivism still widespread in the West? The two might underwrite quite similar, even identical, collections of "traditional" Highland culture. But would the meaning of the collections be the same? A Western primitivist selection might confirm a historical order in which the tradition (lovingly) collected belonged irrevocably to the past. The Highland project might be concerned (like that of Yap Kupal, perhaps) with gathering past resources to ground and empower a path into the future. This "purism" would be backward-looking *and* forward-looking. And it would not necessarily be prescriptive; it could traffic in the Highland contact zone. Indeed, Yap Kupal appears in the *Paradise* catalogue wearing Western dress and holding two apparently traditional stone axes—made for sale to tourists (Figure 6.10). Assertions of local purity cannot be written off as naive or restrictive without close attention to their articulation in practice. "Authenticity" is seldom an all-or-nothing issue.

In many Western metropolitan contexts, historical visions such as that of *Paradise* seem sophisticated while those of "traditionalists" such as Yap Kupal (along with cultural activists fighting for "roots" and "sovereignty") appear simplistic. Does inauthenticity now function, in certain circles at least, as a new kind of authenticity? And having knocked certain purist assumptions off center, isn't it time to sidestep the reverse binary position of a prescriptive anti-essentialism? Struggles for integrity and power within and against globalizing systems need to deploy *both* tradition and modernity, authenticity and hybridity—in complex counterpoints.

A taste for hybridity, a taste already commodified in "sophisticated" clothing and travel advertisements, can be as unreflective as attachments to purity or absolutist tradition. Viewing, reading, enjoying *Paradise,* I gravitate toward the incongruous detail (a glimpse of Hawaiian cloth around Kulka Kokn's neck) at the expense of all the rest. A photo (Plate 6) shows pig-festival dancers at a peak moment: massed men and women dressed to the nines in traditional paraphernalia. But I focus on one woman's wary glance at the camera—for me, the image's "reality effect." James Bosu sports a mind-boggling feather headdress (see Figure 6.1), and I'm charmed by its contrast with the stub of a filter cigarette in his lips. Elsewhere Kala Wala is shown in closeup, decorated for the presentation of her bride-wealth (Figure 6.11). Shells and marsupial fur hang from her neck, and her face is brightly painted beneath abundant plumes.

Figure 6.10. Yap Kupal at the Onga Cultural Centre; Kekanem Kinden is at the left. From O'Hanlon (1993), p. 75.

On her lap she holds a cigarette pack, her armbands stuffed with leaves and banknotes. Only on reading the caption do I notice that her earrings are made from beer-can rip-tops. Once seen, they become, perversely, essential. They "complete" her.

This taste for the hybrid and the incongruous is now associated—often a bit reductively—with "postmodernism." A recent example is Charles Stewart and Rosalind Shaw's discussion of syncretizing, creolizing discourses in contemporary anthropology. I had just read their valuable collection *Syncretism/Anti-Syncretism* (1994) when I visited the "Paradise" exhibit. They end their introduction with the following query:

> We have recently acquired an englobing appetite for the irony of apparently incongruous cultural syntheses, which have in many ways become icons of postmodernism—"Trobriand Cricket"; the Igbo "White Man" masquerade on the cover of *The Predicament of Culture* (Clifford, 1988). One reason we find these so attractive, we suppose, is because we can

perceive them as already broken into parts, as deconstructed in advance. "Invention of culture" writings have demonstrated the strong political significance of syncretism and hybridization in their emphasis on the challenge that such reconstruction poses to essentialized colonial representations and to Western modernist forms of consciousness in general. But they also suit our current taste for the ironic and, far from posing a challenge to us, confirm our totalizing postmodern paradigms. And just as colonial power entailed the categorizing of people into essentialized "tribal" entities with fixed boundaries ("you are the Igbo"), anthropological hegemony now entails taking apart practices and identities which are phenomenological realities for those who use them ("your tradition is invented"). In our enthusiasm for deconstructing syncretic traditions we may have invented another kind of intellectual imperialism. (Shaw and Stewart, 1994: 22–23)

Timely and provocative observations, they trouble my encounter with *Paradise*. Is my concern (and taste) for cultural/historical juxtapositions part of an "englobing appetite," a "hegemonic," "postmodern" irony? Has my work really helped establish a new "intellectual imperialism"?

My first reaction is defensive, quibbling with terms: "hegemonic," "imperialism," "postmodern." To mention only my own work: it has been so regularly criticized in prominent publications (from *Current Anthropology* to *Signs* and *Cultural Studies*), that I have some difficulty seeing it as hegemonic. (Though of course one might respond that the terms of the *debates* establish certain horizons.) Moreover, the interest I evince in cultural collage and incongruity derives quite explicitly from *modernist* art and poetry: the Cubists, Dada and international Surrealism, Segalen, Conrad, Leiris, Williams, and Césaire (Clifford, 1988). Postmodern *avant la lettre* perhaps. But when does "postmodern" become a tag for traditions and responses that cannot be neatly periodized and from which one is having difficulty separating oneself? Shaw and Stewart's "we" clearly suggests an entanglement in the sensibility at issue.

However one names these modern/postmodern formations, there is certainly something to be concerned about. And the political question remains of how particular theories, visions, and styles assert themselves, how they manage to hold their own across different local-global contexts. Shaw and Stewart's final evocation of "imperialism" suggests that these formations impose themselves by force. The authors even go so far as to equate the situation of an essentializing colonial power which says "You

Figure 6.11. Kala Wala, decorated for the presentation of her bride-wealth. From O'Hanlon (1993), Plate 16.

are the Igbo" with that of a current "anthropological hegemony" which says "Your tradition is invented"—thus "taking apart" identities and practices people experience as "phenomenological realities." In doing so, however, they conflate rather different power situations. ("Anthropological hegemony," for me, calls up disputatious, disempowered intellectuals— privileged, no doubt, but hardly in a position to enforce their definitions.) Moreover, Shaw and Stewart seem to make an ontological distinction (which has itself become quite "political" in recent academic debates) between the *real* and the *really invented*. Why, one wonders, shouldn't people such as the Wahgi experience invention and hybrid process as part of their "phenomenological reality"? Is the "taking apart" of identities all on the side of anthropological interpretation? Elsewhere in their introduction, Shaw and Stewart argue that it is not: syncretism can be a locally recognized form of agency. Perhaps the salient difference of "phenomenological" perspective is between seeing hybridity as a process of joining together (traditions, practices, artifacts, commodities) and seeing it as one of taking them apart. Shaw and Stewart identify the latter perspective with anthropological postmodernism. But are such contemporary recognitions of invented culture necessarily "deconstructive"? One can be attracted to images of cultural hybridity not because they are *deconstructed* in advance (Shaw and Stewart) but rather because they are *historicized* in advance (the juxtaposed pieces seen as traces of power struggles and contact relations). Here a lineage of Brechtian or Benjaminian modernism would be most relevant.

Shaw and Stewart are surely right that a certain irony and allied taste for incongruous cultural syntheses can become unreflective badges of sophistication. Slipping into normativity, such attitudes lose sight of their own location (their limited, important critical task) in places that have long enjoyed the privilege of defining what counts as whole or authentic. How can we cut such critical irony down to size, without simply dismissing it as a mystification, an effect of privilege? Assuming anti-essentialism gets at something real, what is its value as a partial, *translated* truth? Cross-cultural translation is never entirely neutral; it is enmeshed in relations of power (Asad, 1986). One enters the translation process from a specific location, from which one only partly escapes. In successful translation, the access to something alien—another language, culture, or code—is substantial. Something different is brought over, made available for understanding, appreciation, consumption. At the same time, as I've argued elsewhere (Clifford, 1989, and Chapter 1, above), the moment of failure is inevitable. An awareness of what escapes the "finished" version will always trouble the moment of success. I use the dramatic word "failure" because the consciousness of being cut down to size, refuted by a constitutive "outside," is painful. It cannot be cured by revisions or by adding another perspective. If confronted consciously, failure provokes critical awareness of one's position in specific relations of power and thus, potentially, reopens the hermeneutic process. Such an awareness of location emerges less from introspection than from confrontation ("You are white"; "You are a postmodernist") and from practical alliance ("On this, at least, we can work together").[10]

The contemporary sensibilities evoked by Shaw and Stewart need to grapple with the failure that accompanies their success—as translations not descriptions. "Postmodern" theories, descriptions, ironies, and tastes have entered their moment of public contestation and crisis. Their critiques of authenticity get us somewhere *and* fall apart. They both travel and are lost in transit. We (a pronoun and location I share with Shaw and Stewart) begin to see both what hybridity theories illuminate and where the shadowed edges are. Such theories have been good for displacing purisms of all sorts, for bringing contact zones and borders into view, and for appreciating the ruses of cultural agency. But they tend to homogenize hybridities—those produced in different historical situations and relations of power, hybridities imposed from "above" and invented from "below."[11] And when every cultural agent (especially global capitalism) is mixing and matching forms, we need to be able to recognize strategic claims for localism or authenticity as possible sites of resistance and empowerment rather than of simple nativism.

I'm still looking at the painted face of Kulka Kokn on the catalogue's cover. His photographed eyes meet mine with a slightly baleful stare. His big mustache, his set (slightly smiling?) mouth . . . He looks tough. Luminous feathers, almost day-glo, orange and red, surround him. He looks out. I wonder how he would appear in a Hawaiian shirt. I take away the face paint, the headdress. He becomes many people: a taxi driver in Los Angeles, a politician in Fiji, a British novelist. And though I know he is a New Guinea Highlander, I can't help seeing him now as dressed up for the pig festival, acting the part: a "postmodern native."

Paradise suggests a different translation. It tells me that this is the way modern Wahgi (men) would like to be seen: strong and radiant. This is

Figure 6.12. Contemporary netbags. From O'Hanlon (1993), p. 48.

also the way the exhibition and book represent New Guinea Highlanders: "traditional," and appropriating new materials. A paradise of local resilience, of *hybrid authenticity*. Turning the book over, I see a confident-looking young woman displaying her "PNG Beautiful Country" netbag. Women gain in independence; the local appropriates the national. I turn to the frontispiece: a group of young men are concentrating on something: one studies an open notebook (Figure 6.13). They all wear plain polo shirts. Nothing whatsoever in the picture suggests New Guinea. An image of complete Westernization? The caption reads: "Zacharias (left) and Wik (right) calculate the distribution of pork at the author's leaving party." Still Melanesian: modern men in polo shirts working the (anthropological) contact zone.

Three photographs of the "Wahgi." Together they signify hybrid authenticity: the message, and hope, of *Paradise*. A cultural history and a possible future. A translation. A brightly illuminated clearing. I notice some of the dark edges, questions.

Coffee. The cash crop brings money into the valley, making possible elaborate traditional ceremonies in the postwar decades. In line with new, culturally sensitive studies of "consumption" (Thomas, 1991; Miller, 1987, 1994), the exhibit and catalogue stress how Wahgi men and women have appropriated and customized the new currency and products. The Wahgi are seen to be holding their own. But coffee plantations have also edged out traditional agriculture and pig raising, increasing dependence on trade store goods. The *Paradise* catalogue and exhibit register the negative consequences of increasing reliance on a single cash crop: new inequalities of wealth in the region, dependence on world market prices, which have fluctuated wildly in recent decades (43–44). Indeed the very image of "paradise" here—the full trade store, the exuberant and abundant plumes, the elaborate pig festival—depends on a distant contingency. Brazil, 1975–1976: a destructive frost raises the world price of coffee beans, and fuels the Wahgi "good years." Prices quadruple in the 1970s; after 1990, they plummet. The Wahgi are increasingly at the mercy of forces beyond their control. The exhibition panel on coffee begins with a statement by Kekanem Paiye, speaking in 1980: "Coffee bears us aloft." Are people in 1994 saying, "Coffee drags us under"? To what extent does *Paradise* reflect a transient historical moment?

Netbags. The panel quotation: "'Respectable women wear their netbags suspended from their foreheads (not over the shoulder).' Kekanem Kinden

(1990)." These words from Michael O'Hanlon's sponsor in the Highlands—an authority, peacemaker, builder of the future—express norms that would restrict women's mobility. Powerful men think women should remain in traditional roles, with big netbags of sweet potatoes suspended from their foreheads, rather than flirting in the roadside markets. But what else are women doing with their new mobility? What are their different stakes in tradition and modernity, continuity and change? How do they manage hybrid cultural processes, and how are they managed by them? What is the ongoing power of men in *Paradise?*

War. Some Wahgi were willing to sell O'Hanlon their shields because they expected that fighting would become more individualized, and would henceforth use guns. The recent revival of warfare in the Highlands ("pacification" was never, in fact, complete) and the emergence of larger-

Figure 6.13. Zacharias (left) and Wik (right) calculate the distribution of pork at the author's leaving party. From O'Hanlon (1993), frontispiece.

scale "tribal" rivalries, new economic inequalities, and marauding bands of robbers (called *raskol*) all cast shadows on the story of peacemaking and alliance featured in the exhibition and catalogue. O'Hanlon points to an ambiguous prospect: new stresses leading to violence, but also successful peacemaking initiatives and voluntary local limitations on the use of guns (51–54). So far, coalitions of local and national authorities have contained fresh unrest, and people are not starving in the Highlands. But if things take a turn for the worse economically, *Paradise* could look like a history of the halcyon days.

Still looking at the picture of Kulka Kokn . . . It's ten years old. What is he up to now? Is he driving a truck? Amassing wealth? Is he a Christian leader? A *raskol?* What happens when, again, I remove his feathered headdress but see him now singing a hymn, or behind the wheel, or holding a semi-automatic rifle . . . ? Other futures for the Highlands? Or connected, but discrepant, possibilities? How should we translate multiple local futures in places such as this—sites linked with national politics, with world markets, with ongoing, always already spliced histories of gender, local power, land, and custom?

In *The Predicament of Culture* I argued that metanarratives of destruction and invention needed to be held in a kind of unresolved ethnographic tension (Clifford, 1988: 17). Not complementarity ("The bad news . . ., the good news . . .") but a simultaneous awareness of different possibilities. The formula, albeit crude and binary, was intended to hold a place for historical uncertainty. It was not a prescription for specific ethnographic accounts, which can legitimately emphasize one or another pole or local resolution. But it was a claim that the tension would not, should not, disappear. In this spirit, I find myself wanting a more ambivalent *Paradise;* I look for the shadows already there to lengthen, to trouble the hopeful story of hybrid authenticity. Trouble, not erase.

7

Museums as Contact Zones

In early 1989 I found myself sitting around a table in the basement of the Portland Museum of Art, Portland, Oregon. About twenty people had gathered to discuss the museum's Northwest Coast Indian collection. The group included museum staff, several well-known anthropologists and experts on Northwest Coast art, and a group of Tlingit elders, accompanied by a couple of younger Tlingit translators. I was present as a "consultant," part of a grant supporting the proceedings.

The museum's Rasmussen Collection was amassed in the 1920s in southern Alaska and along the coast of Canada. Long displayed in a drab, somewhat "ethnographic" manner, it was overdue for reinstallation. The director of the Portland Art Institute, Dan Monroe, who had worked with native tribes in Alaska, took the unusual step of inviting a representative group of Tlingit authorities, prominent elders from important clans, to participate in planning discussions.

In the museum basement, objects from the collection were brought out, one by one, and presented to the elders for comment: a raven mask, an abalone-inlaid headdress, a carved rattle . . . What transpired was a series of complicated, moving performances, by turns serious and lighthearted.

The curatorial staff seems to have expected the discussions to focus on the objects of the collection. I, at any rate, anticipated that the elders would comment on them in a detailed way, telling us, for example: this is how the mask was used; it was made by so-and-so; this is its power in terms of the clan, our traditions, and so forth. In fact, the objects were not the subject of much direct commentary by the elders, who had their own agenda for the meeting. They referred to the regalia with appreciation and respect, but they seemed only to use them as *aides-mémoires,* occasions for the telling of stories and the singing of songs.

The songs were sung and stories told in accordance with clear protocols governing the authority of particular individuals and clans, rules establishing performance rights. An elder representing one clan would perform his or her songs and stories; then an elder from another clan would offer thanks and reciprocate. The whole event had a ceremonial dimension, punctuated by intense emotion, silences, and laughter. The objects in the Rasmussen Collection, focus for the consultation, were left—or so it seemed to me—at the margin. For long periods no one paid any attention to them. Stories and songs took center stage.

Amy Marvin says of the prayers she sings that they "balance" her, "as in a boat," so that she can tell stories. She begins haltingly, seeming to search for points in a familiar landscape, places "over there . . ." She tells the "Glacier Bay story" about a village covered with ice: a sense of great loss. She sings a memorial song. "Where is my land?" "I'm not going to see my village again . . ." She refers to the previous day, when a killer-whale drum was brought out—a drum the clan did not know had been preserved. A very heavy moment, she says. Jimmy George, an elder nearly ninety years old, had offered the killer-whale story, which belongs to his clan . . . a story he once told at San Diego Sea World. She thanks him.

The Glacier Bay recitation concerns her present homeland around Hoonah, Alaska. This becomes explicit when Amy Marvin connects the loss of tribal lands in the story with current Forest Service policies regulating their use.

A headdress representing an octopus is brought out. So she tells an octopus story about an enormous monster that blocks the whole bay with its tentacles and keeps the salmon from coming in. (All the stories are told in Tlingit with translation and explanation by the younger participants—elaborate performances, sometimes interrupted by dialogue.) The Tlingit hero has to fight and kill the octopus to let the salmon come into the bay, salmon which are the livelihood of the group. The hero opens the bay so the group can live. And by the end of the story the octopus has metamorphosed into state and federal agencies currently restricting the rights of Tlingit to take salmon according to tradition.

As performed in the museum basement, "traditional" stories and myths suggested by the old clan objects end up as specific histories with pointed meanings in current political struggles.

One of the younger Tlingit says: There will be a day when we're back fishing there. And an older man, Austin Hammond, speaking for the Raven House in Haines, Alaska, supports Amy Marvin, saying he could feel her emotions as she spoke. He is weeping. The Glacier Bay story reminds him, he says, of how he used to fish and trap there. Now the same monster is coming underneath our canoe again. The land's being taken from us, and that's why I'm telling this. We're sharpening our knives, so to speak. Words are that strong, he says.

She thanks him for his words: words need to be caught, she says. Then Austin Hammond tells about the octopus blanket made for his father (not in the museum collection), about its power. We're telling you these things, he says to the white people assembled. We hope you'll back us up.

Lydia George, a city councilwoman, fills in details about current land claims. She stresses that different clans and places come together in these struggles. She avoids generalizations about the "Tlingit."

Austin Hammond tells a long Raven story, his father's blanket spread in front of him. He goes into great detail about different kinds of fish, the specific times of their entry into the bay and rivers. He tells how the Raven determined these things—all the species of salmon, the rules of their behavior, and of our fishing. Why am I telling this? he asks. Four people from Washington, D.C. came to our convention. They told us we were taking up all our salmon. I told them the story—how the Raven worked on the salmon for everyone here on our land.

A beaded jacket is laid on the table. Austin Hammond tells a "Bible story"—a Raven tale reminiscent of Jonah and the Whale. We have no writing, he says, so we make copies in our jackets, blankets. He thanks another elder for permission to tell the story. In it, the Raven flies down the whale's blowhole, sets up a little stove, and cooks the salmon the whale swallows. But he can't get out. The humorous tale turns tragic. To our white brothers here, Hammond says, our prayers are like the Raven's. Who will cut open the whale, so we can come out? We're in need of all our ancestors, our land is being taken. Our children . . . Who will look after them? Maybe you can help us, help cut open the whale. That's how I feel.

Sadly, he tells of being alone in his clan house. He invokes his grandfathers and ancestors, then sings a song composed by his uncle, Joe

Wright, weaving a portion of it into his urgent speech. We're losing our grounds, he says, so I hold onto this song.

More speeches, stories, and explications follow—formal responses to the speakers. After lunch, the mood is lighter: love songs are sung, spiced with off-color humor and innuendo. Anyone can sing along with these. A younger Tlingit explains that at memorials and parties there is a heavy part—dealing with loss, the ancestors, name giving—and a lighter side: humor and expressions of love for one another.

As the process continues over three days, objects from the Rasmussen Collection lie on the museum tables or in storage boxes.

Reciprocities

The experience of "consultation" left the Portland Art Museum staff with difficult dilemmas. It was clear that from the elders' viewpoint the collected objects were not primarily "art." They were referred to as "records," "history," and "law," inseparable from myths and stories expressing ongoing moral lessons with current political force. The museum was clearly informed that the elders' voices should be presented to the public when the objects were displayed. This demand presupposed a real degree of trust, since many of the stories and songs were proprietary. Specific permissions were needed. Indeed, a prior agreement stipulated that any information revealed at the consultation would be jointly controlled by the museum and the elders. On more than one occasion during the proceedings, the museum was directly admonished: We're taking the risk of confiding important things to you. It's important that these be recorded for posterity. What will you do with what we give you? We'll be paying attention.[1]

Staff at the Portland Museum were genuinely concerned that their stewardship of the Rasmussen Collection include reciprocal communication with the communities whose art, culture, and history were at stake. But could they reconcile the kinds of meanings evoked by the Tlingit elders with those imposed in the context of a museum of "art"? How much could they decenter the physical objects in favor of narrative, history, and politics? Are there strategies that can display a mask as simultaneously a formal composition, an object with specific traditional functions in clan/tribal life, and as something that evokes an ongoing history of struggle? Which meanings should be highlighted? And which community has the power to determine what emphasis the museum will choose? Should the museum now search out individuals with clan authority connected to other tribal objects in the collection—Kwagiulth, Haida, Tsimshian? Could it establish relations of trust with all the relevant groups and individuals? To what extent was the whole process dependent on specific personal contacts? How could the relationship deal with conflicts within contemporary tribal communities? (The Tlingit elders who came to Portland did not represent all the clans connected to the objects.) How much discussion and negotiation is enough? And how many grants could a single museum expect to receive in support of such activities? I cannot go into the personal, institutional, and funding contingencies that have delayed reinstallation of the Rasmussen Collection. Suffice it to say that the choices posed by the elders remain unresolved, their gift (and challenge) unanswered.[2]

As the meeting progressed, the basement of the Portland Art Museum became something more than a place of consultation or research; it became a *contact zone.* I borrow the term from Mary Louise Pratt. In her book *Imperial Eyes: Travel and Transculturation* (6–7), she defines "contact zone" as "the space of colonial encounters, the space in which peoples geographically and historically separated come into contact with each other and establish ongoing relations, usually involving conditions of coercion, radical inequality, and intractable conflict." Unlike the term "frontier," which is "grounded within a European expansionist perspective (the frontier is a frontier only with respect to Europe)," the expression "contact zone"

> is an attempt to invoke the spatial and temporal copresence of subjects previously separated by geographic and historical disjunctures, and whose trajectories now intersect. By using the term "contact" I aim to foreground the interactive, improvisational dimensions of colonial encounters so easily ignored or suppressed by diffusionist accounts of conquest and domination. A "contact" perspective emphasizes how subjects are constituted in and by their relations to each other. [It stresses] copresence, interaction, interlocking understandings and practices, often within radically asymmetrical relations of power.

When museums are seen as contact zones, their organizing structure as a *collection* becomes an ongoing historical, political, moral *relationship*—a power-charged set of exchanges, of push and pull. The organizing structure of the museum-as-collection functions like Pratt's frontier. A center and a periphery are assumed: the center a point of gathering, the periphery an area of discovery. The museum, usually located in a metropolitan city, is the historical destination for the cultural productions it lovingly and authoritatively salvages, cares for, and interprets.[3]

What transpired in the Portland Museum's basement was not reducible to a process of *collecting* advice or information. And something in excess of consultation was going on. A message was delivered, performed, within an ongoing contact history. As evoked in the museum's basement, Tlingit history did not primarily illuminate or contextualize the objects of the Rasmussen Collection. Rather, the objects provoked (called forth, brought to voice) ongoing stories of struggle. From the position of the collecting museum and the consulting curator, this was a disruptive history which could not be confined to providing past tribal *context* for the objects. The museum was called to a sense of its responsibility, its stewardship of the clan objects. (Repatriation was not, at this time, an explicit issue.) The museum was asked to be accountable in a way that went beyond mere preservation. It was urged to act on behalf of Tlingit communities, not simply to represent the history of tribal objects completely or accurately. A kind of reciprocity was claimed, but not a give-and-take that could lead to a final meeting of minds, a coming together that would erase the discrepancies, the ongoing power imbalances of contact relations.

Before we explore this uneven reciprocity, it is important to realize the limits of the contact perspective I am developing here. For example, some of what went on in Portland was certainly not primarily contact zone work. Some of the songs, speeches, stories, and conversations were performances among Tlingit, not directed to the museum and its cameras but interclan work—what had to be done if the objects were to be addressed at all. (This dimension was largely obscure to me in my marginal location.) Moreover, although one cannot separate a history of loss, displacement, and reconnection from the meanings these masks, drums, and garments hold for clan elders, it would be wrong to reduce the objects' traditional meanings, the deep feelings they still evoke, to "contact" responses. If a mask recalls a grandfather or an old story, this must include feelings of loss and struggle; but it must also include access to powerful continuity and connection. To say that (given a destructive colonial experience) all indigenous memories must be affected by contact histories is not to say that such histories determine or exhaust them. The "tribal" present is a fabric some of whose strands extend before (and after) the encounter with white societies—an encounter that may appear endless but is actually discontinuous and, in some respects, terminable.[4] The old objects certainly invoked these other histories (memories, hopes, oral traditions, attachments to land). But in the contact zone of the Portland Museum's basement, the meanings addressed to white interlocutors were primarily relational: "This is what the objects inspire us to say in response to our shared history, the goals of ongoing responsibility and reciprocity we differently embrace."

While *reciprocity* is a crucial stake, it will not be understood in the same way by people from different cultures in asymmetrical power relationships. Reciprocity in the Tlingit's demands for help was not, as in a commercial transaction, the goal of being paid up, quit. Rather, the intent was to challenge and rework a relationship. The objects of the Rasmussen Collection, however fairly or freely bought and sold, could never be entirely possessed by the museum. They were sites of a historical negotiation, occasions for an ongoing contact.

In Chapter 6, I discussed another museum space and practice in a contact perspective. There, the Museum of Mankind in London was shown to be enmeshed in potentially complex, asymmetrical relations with groups and individuals in Highland New Guinea. The museum, though not necessarily its ethnographer/curator, Michael O'Hanlon, wanted to be quit in its obligations to the Wahgi, whose culture and history were on display in its galleries. But glimpses of the Waghi side of the transaction, or at least the aspirations of certain individuals, suggest a more ongoing, differently politicized understanding of the relationship. "Reciprocity," a standard for fair dealings, is a translation term, whose meanings will depend on specific contact situations. Thus, the term's different contexts and meanings, the locations of power from which it is asserted, must always be kept in view. These differences of location and meaning were at issue in the Portland Museum's basement.

In contact zones, Pratt tells us, geographically and historically separated groups establish ongoing relations. These are not relations of equality, even though processes of *mutual* exploitation and appropriation may be at work.[5] As we have seen, fundamental assumptions about relationship itself—notions of exchange, justice, reciprocity—may be topics of struggle and negotiation. Moreover, contact zones are constituted through reciprocal movements of people, not just of objects, messages, commodities, and money. Highland New Guinea is distant from London, yet the Wahgi who cooperated with O'Hanlon to amass a collection of "material culture" for the Museum of Mankind felt connected, indeed entitled to visit. Their expectation was that a London tour would be arranged, similar to one several years before by a group of their neighbors, a Mount Hagen dance troupe. Certain Wahgi, at least, were ready to "work" this London-Highlands contact zone for their own purposes. O'Hanlon had to explain that his mandate from the museum did not include funds for their travel. Differences of power, control, and design of budgets determined who would be the collectors and who the collected.

Stanford University in California is also far from Highland New Guinea. It has recently been the site of a rather different set of contact relations. A dozen or so sculptors from the Highlands recently traveled to Palo Alto to carve and install a sculpture garden on the university's campus. The project was organized on a shoestring by Jim Mason, a student in anthropology, with small grants and contributions. Once at Stanford, the sculptors occupied a wooded corner of the central campus and set to work. Throughout the summer of 1994 they transformed tree trunks brought from New Guinea and soft stone from Nevada into human figures entwined with animals, fantastic designs. Their workplace was open to everyone passing by, and on Friday evenings it turned into a party, with barbecues, face painting, drumming, and dancing. The New Guinea artists taught their designs to interested Palo Altoans. Growing numbers turned up every week to hang out, make art, and celebrate.

When I visited in the autumn of 1994, the artists had returned to the Highlands and the "New Guinea Sculpture Garden" consisted of several dozen carved trunks and stones scattered among the trees. The former were secured by cables (one had recently been stolen) and protected from the rain by sheets of transparent plastic. People wandered in and pulled back the plastic shrouding crocodiles and long-beaked birds. A leaflet informed visitors that the project still needed to raise $40,000 for site installation and landscaping. Suggested contributions ranged from $10,000 for travel from New Guinea, to $250 for a fern, to $100 for a spotlight, to $25 for artists' spending money. As of this writing, a year later, the garden is taking shape. Volunteers have set the poles in cement and installed the stone carvings. Mounds of earth and plants follow New

Guinea landscaping styles. The tallest poles form a "spirit house," and other brightly painted, or elaborately carved, twisting wooden poles and slit gongs are scattered throughout the grove.

At the New Guinea Sculpture Garden, interactive process was as important as the production and collection of "art" or "culture." Although there is a long tradition of bringing exotic people to Western museums, zoos, and world fairs, the sculptors at Stanford were not offered as specimens on display. They were presented as practicing "artists," not as "natives." People could, of course, view them as exotica, but this went against the spirit of the project, which invited people to participate, financially and personally, in the making of the garden. The traveling artists pursued their own adventures, collecting prestige, information, and fun, while staying in touch with the Highlands by phone. They made friends from the various communities around Stanford. They were taken to Disneyland and the Esalen Institute, entertained by local firefighters and the WO'SE African Community Church in Oakland. Hundreds of people were at the airport to see them off. Return visits, in both directions, have been planned. A regular visitor to the campus grove: "It is like a miracle dropping here from outer space, in a very lily-white, upper-class community." A carver: "All the people who come are good. People are happy to see us, and they bring us food" (Koh, 1994: 2B).

We can defer, for now, the important issue of how the garden will ultimately be owned and used, and consider how the interactive process of its making opens up a different range of relations from those normally practiced in contexts of collecting and display. Richard Kurin (1991) describes similar phenomena during two exhibitions/performances held on the Mall in Washington, D.C., as part of the 1985 Festival of India. The events were titled "Aditi: A Celebration of Life" and "Mela! An Indian Fair." The former brought rural Indian craftspeople and performers into the national Museum of Natural History; the latter was a "composite fair presenting rituals, crafts, performances, foodways, and commercial traditions from a variety of Indian regions" (319). Kurin details many ways the artisans and street performers shaped and stretched their "exhibition" settings. He also explores the event's different political interests—for the Smithsonian Institution, the Indian government, and the street performers from India. The last-named used the recognition afforded by the trip to Washington to raise their impoverished status at home, to induce politicians to reconsider harsh beggary laws applied to folk artists, and in some cases to acquire title to land. Kurin's complex account of the happenings on the Mall suggests a utopian space of interaction and performative improvisation, hedged around by caste and class politics in India and by the commodification of "folk" traditions and "culture" in the geopolitical marketplace of national "festivals." Recent Indian immigrants to the United States who translated and assisted at the popular events found themselves identifying with "vulgar" street performances they would have shunned in India. Class and caste hierarchies were leveled, at least for a time, as performers were invited home for meals. Respect for the diversity of Indian subcultures was stimulated. And the sponsoring museum was obliged to modify its objectifying modes of display to accommodate visitors who thought of the occasion as just another fair, this time on the Mall in Washington, D.C. As organizer of the event, Kurin was caught between the needs of the performance and those of institutional order. His daily exhortations to the monkey-men of Mela to get out of the trees, with threats of possible arrest by park police, "were taken neither as official warnings nor as stage directions but as straight lines to be incorporated into the performance routine for the enjoyment of the audience" (324).[6]

Exploitations

It is important to keep the possibilities for subversion and reciprocity (or relatively benign mutual exploitation) in tension with the long history of "exotic" displays in the West. This history provides a context of enduring power imbalance within and against which the contact work of travel, exhibition, and interpretation occurs. An ongoing ideological matrix governs the understanding of "primitive" people in "civilized" places. As Coco Fusco and Guillermo Gómez-Peña discovered when they performed a broad satire in which "undiscovered" Amerindians were confined in a golden cage, more than a few visitors took them literally. Fusco (1994) discerns an "other history" of intercultural performance, which runs from Columbus' kidnapped Arawacs and Montaigne's "cannibals," to populated "villages" and "streets" at world exhibitions, to Ishi at the University of California Anthropological Museum. She extrapolates the history to include all more or less coerced performances of identity: the spectacularization of "natives" in documentary films or the collection of "authentic" Third World art (and artists) for exhibitions such as "Les Magiciens de la Terre" in Paris. A growing body of writing has begun to provide details of this quite extensive and continuous history of exhibitionary contacts (Rydell, 1984; Bradford and Blume, 1992; Corbey, 1993; Fusco, 1995). It reveals the racism, or at best the paternalist condescension, of spectacles which offered up mute, exoticized specimens for curious and titillated crowds. The degradation was physical as well as moral, not infrequently resulting in the travelers' untimely deaths. Exhibitions were contact zones where germs made their own connections.[7]

A wholly appropriate emphasis on coercion, exploitation, and miscomprehension does not, however, exhaust the complexities of travel and encounter.[8] Montaigne, for example, derived something more than an ethnocentric *frisson* from his meeting with Tupinamba in Rouen. Even encounters that are ethnocentric—which they all are to a degree—can produce reflection and cultural critique. The critical reflections and agency of the exotic "travelers" are most difficult to discover, given limited records and a tendency, in what records exist, to accord such travelers *behavior* rather than independent *expression*. Since they were generally treated as passive specimens (or victims), their views seldom entered the historical record. Their "captivity narratives" remain to be discovered or pieced together, inferred, from historical shreds.[9] Some of those displayed in European courts, museums, fairs, and zoos were kidnapped, their travel anything but voluntary. In many cases, a mix of force and choice was at work. People lent themselves to the projects of explorers and entrepreneurs for a range of reasons, including fear, economic need, curiosity, a desire for adventure, a quest for power.

"One of my colleagues," writes Raymond Corbey, "who grew up in postwar Berlin told me of his astonishment when, as a boy, he came across an African man whom he had seen only hours before in native attire in Castan's Panoptikum, now in European clothes on a tramcar, smoking a cigarette" (Corbey, 1993: 344). Astonishment, mixed perhaps with a sense of betrayal, was an appropriate response for someone accustomed to a carefully staged primitivity. But what was the African's attitude to the movement between racial/ethnic spectacle and common streetcar? Was acting the "African" an ordeal? A satire? A source of pride? Just a job? All of these? And more? An adequate answer depends on knowing about individual histories and specific power relations. In most cases the details are unavailable. But documentation does exist for a revealing experience in which native culture was made into a spectacle—an experience which, though far from typical, can help clarify the social relationships and different investments at stake.

In 1914 Edward Curtis, the elegiac photographer of North American Indians, made a feature-length movie called *In the Land of the Headhunters*. Working on northern Vancouver Island, Curtis hired a large contingent of Kwakiutl Indians to act in a tale of precontact Northwest Coast life, complete with boy-meets-girl romance, evil sorcerers, masks, war canoes, and severed heads. With the help of local authorities—notably George Hunt, Franz Boas' principal assistant—a serious attempt was made to re-create authentic traditional settings, artifacts, dances, and ceremonies. T. C. McLuhan, in her film *The Shadow Catcher* (1975), records the reminiscences of three elderly people who participated in Curtis' re-creation. They recall that it was a lot of fun, dressing up and doing things the old way. Everybody had a good time. Bill Holm's conversations with other surviving participants at screenings of the restored film in 1967 confirm their point (Holm and Quimby, 1980).

In an important sense, the Kwakiutl were exploited by Curtis, made to act out a stereotype of themselves for white consumption. The sensational title featuring "headhunters" is indicative of what Fusco argues is the inescapable violence of such projects. And one wonders: Had the film been a commercial success, how much of the profit would have found its way back to northern Vancouver Island? In other important senses, however, relations were not exploitative. The participants in *Headhunters* earned good money and enjoyed themselves. They willingly donned wigs, shaved their mustaches, and endured the tickle of abalone nose-rings. They knew that Curtis' portrayal of their traditions, while sensational, was respectful. Spectacle was, after all, very much a part of Kwakiutl culture, and Curtis tapped a rich tradition of acting. Moreover, George Hunt played a crucial role in the process, interpreting tradition, recruiting actors, and gathering costumes and props. Surviving snapshots of the filming show Curtis behind the camera, with Hunt beside him, holding a megaphone and directing the action (Holm and Quimby, 1980: 57–61). By local standards, in the context of prior trade and ethnographic contacts, Curtis dealt fairly with the communities he mobilized. His interest in a "vanishing" culture seems to have overlapped productively with their own interest in a way of life which some knew through their parents and grandparents and with which they felt a strong continuity through changing times.[10]

The staging of cultural spectacles can thus be a complex contact process with different scripts negotiated by impresarios, intermediaries, and actors. Of course Curtis' film, made on native grounds with the assistance of local authorities, was quite different from the traveling shows and exhibitions, which tended to be more domineering and exploitative. The most famous of all the purveyors of stereotypes, Buffalo Bill's Wild West Show, was generally sustained by respectful personal relations with its Native American participants. But the conditions of travel were hard, and few stayed for more than a season or two. Some joined the show for the wages it offered (low, but there was no way to make money on the new reservations); others wanted to escape the inaction imposed by "pacification"; occasionally "troublemakers" were sent by the government as an alternative to imprisonment; others wanted to travel and to observe the world of whites (Blackstone, 1986: 85–88). Black Elk, an Oglala Sioux, joined Buffalo Bill for the last-mentioned reason, and his memories of Chicago, New York, London, and Paris provide a precious glimpse of travel and cultural criticism from a native viewpoint (Black Elk, 1979; DeMallie, 1984; see also Standing Bear, 1928). It is critical to recognize that the cultural performances in such spectacles were scripted and their actors frequently exploited. But it is also important to recognize a range of experiences and not to close off dimensions of agency (and irony) in their participation. The crucial issue of power often appears differently at different levels of interaction, and it cannot simply be read off from ascribed geopolitical locations. Power and reciprocity are articulated together in specific ways. Who calls which shots? When? Do structural and interpersonal power relations reinforce or complicate each other? How are differing agendas accommodated in the same project?

On the contemporary scene, the performance of culture and tradition—what Robert Cantwell (1993) calls "ethnomimesis"—may include empowerment and participation in a wider public sphere *as well as* commodification in an increasingly hegemonic game of identity. Why would tribal people be eager to dance in New York or London? Why come to Stanford? Why play the game of self-representation?[11] Such visitors, their hosts, and impresarios are not free of colonial legacies of exoticism and neocolonial processes of commodification. Nor are they entirely confined by these repressive structures. It is important to recognize this complexity. For what exceeds the apparatus of coercion and stereotype in contact relations may perhaps be reclaimed for current practice in movements to expand and democratize what can happen in museums and related sites of ethnomimesis. The historical possibilities of contact relations—negative and positive—need to be confronted.

In cases where coercion is not direct, when non-Western artists, culture makers, and curators enter Western museums on their own (negotiated) terms, the collection sites of art and anthropology can no longer be understood primarily in terms of Promethean discovery and discerning selection. They become places of crossing, explicit and unacknowledged, occasions for different discoveries and selections. Some illuminating current examples are found in *Fusion: West African Artists at the Venice Biennale,* interviews conducted by Thomas McEvilley (1993). Tamessir Dia—a Senegalese, born in Mali, raised in Ivory Coast, and educated in France— expresses an African "contact perspective." After noting his admiration for Delacroix, Cézanne, and especially Picasso, Dia adds:

> To my perception, what's happening in Europe and America belongs to me. One day someone asked me what I thought about Picasso and other European painters and I said, "In France, I took what belongs to me. Picasso came and took things from my home. I went to France and took things that are mine." For me the European tradition was a way of reunderstanding my own civilization's value, because Europe after the First World War was having a crisis of imagination, a crisis of development in an artistic sense, a cultural sense. And they turned to Africa. I also understand that they used my heritage to develop their own, so why can't I take theirs, whatever is technically useful to me, to express myself?

McEvilley responds: "When you say that you went to France and took what belongs to you, you don't mean that you were taking back purloined elements of African culture but that you were taking elements of European culture which belonged to you in exchange for them." Dia clarifies: "I am not limited to African culture—that would be absurd; it would be ridiculous for any African today to speak of Africanity or Negritude. What you are is in everything, it's in your spirit. As an African you can never live exactly like a European—at least the people in my generation" (McEvilley, 1993: 61).

Africa and Europe have been thrown together by destructive and creative histories of empire, commerce, and travel; each uses the other's traditions to remake its own. Pratt (1992: 6), following Fernando Ortiz and Angel Rama, calls such processes "transculturations." Until recently in the West, transculturation has been understood hierarchically, in ways that naturalize a power imbalance and the claim of one group to define history and authenticity. For example, Africans using Europe's heritage were seen to be imitating, losing their traditions in a zero-sum game of acculturation; Europeans using African cultural resources appeared to be creative, progressive, inclusive modernists. Views such as those of Tamessir Dia suggest a more complex history of translations and appropriations.

Contact history is evoked in two titles—"Africa Explores" and "Digesting the West"—from Susan Vogel's innovative exhibition and catalogue on twentieth-century African art (Vogel, 1991). In this instance a contemporary museum, the Center for African Art in New York, collects work that has, for more than a century, itself been collecting the West through transcultural processes ranging from infatuation and forced feeding to satire, syncretic conversion, and critical selection. The New York museum operates in long-established circuits of travel and transculturation. On the one hand, it replays, in new forms, established practices of discovering, gathering, and valuing art and culture—a restless curatorial exploration and construction of Africa. In this practice it brings peripheral work to an established center, for appreciation and commodification. On the other hand, the Center for African Art increasingly operates in an awareness of Africa as not simply "out there" (or "back then") but as part of a network, a series of relays forming a diaspora that includes New York City. This diaspora has well established, branching routes and roots in slavery, in migration from Caribbean, South American, and rural North American places, and in current circuits of commerce and immigration from the African continent. In this context, the museum's contact work takes on local, regional, hemispheric, and global dimensions. In the center's recent exhibition of African and African American altars, "Face of the Gods," it grappled explicitly with the challenge of exhibiting (in) diaspora. This project brought artist/practitioners of African-based religions into the museum work, both in New York and in the altars' successive gatherings, and changes, on the road.

Africa 95 offers a more extensive example of a contact approach. This extraordinary ensemble of art exhibits, music and dance performances, films, conferences, workshops, residencies, TV and radio shows, and children's events was provoked by a planned exhibition at London's Royal Academy of Arts, "Africa: The Art of a Continent." The Royal Academy project, a major "comprehensive" selection, was conceived according to a classic model: a single European curator gathered what he considered the finest and most representative work, while limiting the exhibition to "art" produced before 1900. The organizers of *Africa 95* in effect folded this project into a more heterogeneous and future-oriented vision. Without rejecting its historical/aesthetic agenda, they surrounded and decentered it. Instead of bringing art from Africa, *Africa 95* brought artists. It recognized that African artists had long been in contact with Europe and were currently working both within and beyond the African continent, moving in and out of the "West."

The first *Africa 95* event, "Teng/Articulations," was an artist-led workshop in Senegal. It was followed by an "international sculpture workshop" at the Yorkshire Sculpture Park, where for three months artists from a dozen African countries joined with artists from the United States and the United Kingdom to create on-site works. More than twenty exhibitions of contemporary African art and photography took place throughout the autumn of 1995 in London and other British cities. These were coordinated with colloquia and extensive film, music, dance, and literature programs. There was a consistent policy of involving Africans as authorities and curators. At the Whitechapel Art Gallery, a counterpoint to the Royal Academy show was titled "Seven Stories about Modern Art in Africa." Five of the seven curators were leading African artists and art historians, and their personal visions of modern African art effectively complicated assumptions of a unified continental aesthetic.

Clémentine Deliss, artistic director of *Africa 95,* stressed that the project was conceived not merely as a site of exhibitions, but also of meetings among artists, an occasion for developing ongoing contacts (Deliss, 1995: 5). That the contact zones of *Africa 95* were not political or economic free-spaces is signaled by prominent advertisements for transnational corporate sponsors, notably banks, in the program brochure and by recurring complaints that the event was being held in Britain rather than in Africa (Riding, 1995). Europe still enjoyed the power to collect and exhibit Africa on its own terms and terrain. However, for many of the artists and musicians Europe and America were already sites of work, and the event was an opportunity to expand their audiences and sources of inspiration.

Africa 95, working in and out of museums and galleries, had something in common with the current spate of national festivals (Festival of India, of Indonesia, and so on) in which Third World regions display their arts in First World places with the aim of increasing global legitimacy and attracting investors. But there were major differences. Although corporate sponsors such as CitiBank used the event to portray themselves as good transnational "African" citizens, *Africa 95* did not directly represent any major commercial interest or national polity, and its diverse occasions and participants, its stress on cross-national exchanges, were not easily channeled. It did, of course, help produce a modern, hybrid "Africa" as a marketable commodity for international art markets. But this product was, significantly, the contact work of Africans who may profit from it. *Africa 95* used, and was used by, transnational circuits tied to colonial and neocolonial relations—making spaces for contacts that exceed those relations.

Contestations

The notion of a contact zone, articulated by Pratt in contexts of European expansion and transculturation, can be extended to include cultural relations within the same state, region, or city—in the centers rather than the frontiers of nations and empires. The distances at issue here are more social than geographic. For most inhabitants of a poor neighborhood, located perhaps just blocks or a short bus ride from a fine-arts museum, the museum might as well be on another continent. Contact perspectives recognize that "natural" social distances and segregations are historical/political products: apartheid was a relationship. In many cities, moreover, contact zones result from a different kind of "travel": the arrival of new immigrant populations. As in the colonial examples evoked by Pratt, negotiations of borders and centers are historically structured in dominance. To the extent that museums understand themselves to be interacting with specific communities across such borders, rather than simply educating or edifying a public, they begin to operate—consciously and at times self-critically—in contact histories.

We have seen some of the ways that museum practices of collecting and display look different in a contact perspective. Centers become borders crossed by objects and makers. Such crossings are never "free" and indeed are routinely blocked by budgets and curatorial control, by restrictive definitions of art and culture, by community hostility and miscomprehension. The examples I have chosen so far suggest ways these borders can be more democratically negotiated, a choice reflecting the reformist tenor of my analysis. I could have begun, however, not with border crossings, but with border *wars*. Two recent disputes have sent shock waves through the museum world in Canada and to a lesser degree the United States: the Lubicon Cree boycott of the "Spirit Sings" exhibition in Calgary, and the widely publicized conflict over "Into the Heart of Africa" at the Royal Ontario Museum, Toronto, during 1989 and 1990. In both cases, communities whose cultures and histories were at stake in prominent exhibits mobilized to seriously trouble the museum.

"The Spirit Sings: Artistic Traditions of Canada's First Peoples" was organized by the Glenbow Museum in Calgary to coincide with the 1988 Winter Olympics. It brought together a large number of artifacts from collections in Canada and abroad, with the goal of presenting a detailed and diverse picture of Native Canadian cultures at the time of early contact with Europeans. The exhibition further explored the distinctive world view shared by these cultures and their resilience in the face of outside influence and domination (Harrison, 1988). For many, including some Native Canadian groups, the exhibit was successful, though it was criticized for its relative lack of attention to contemporary manifestations of its guiding themes. But the content of "The Spirit Sings" was not, primarily, what provoked a widely supported boycott. The Lubicon Lake Cree of Northern Alberta, to dramatize their pending land-claim, called a boycott of the Winter Olympics, a highly visible political stage. The action focused on the Glenbow Museum because the exhibition's chief sponsor, Shell Oil (which provided $1.1 million of the exhibition's total budget of $2.6 million), was drilling on land claimed by the Lubicon. To a growing number of Lubicon supporters, native and nonnative, it was hypocritical for "The Spirit Sings" to celebrate the beauty and continuity of cultures whose current survival was threatened by the exhibit's own corporate sponsor. Supporters of the exhibit pointed out that no museum of any size can survive without corporate or government sponsors, whose hands are never perfectly clean. The museum was being unfairly targeted, dragged without warning into the Lubicons' struggle.

Whatever the different perceptions of fairness and exploitation, the affair raised questions of broad importance. Should museums be able to assemble exhibits of Indian artifacts (including loans from other institutions) without permission from relevant tribal communities? What is involved in control over "cultural property"? What kind of consultation and involvement in planning is proper? (Glenbow had consulted with nearby tribes but not with the Lubicon, who did not respond to a blanket invitation. Curatorial control of the show was, in any event, undiluted.) Must some attention to current issues and struggles be part of any exhibition on native art, culture, or history? Can museums claim political neutrality? How accountable are they for the activities of their public or private sponsors?[12] In response to these questions, the Canadian Museums Association and the Assembly of First Nations commissioned a Task Force on Museums and First Nations, whose report gained wide acceptance and which established guidelines for collaboration between native representatives and museum staff (Hill and Nicks, 1994). Serious collaboration is now the norm in Canadian exhibitions of First Nations art and culture.

"Into the Heart of Africa," at the Royal Ontario Museum, was inspired in part by recent critical writings on the history of collecting and museum display. "Studying the museum as an artifact, reading collections as cultural texts, and discovering life histories of objects," it sought to "understand something of the complexities of cross-cultural encounters" (Cannizzo, 1989: 92). The exhibition's approach was reflexive, relying strongly on juxtaposition and irony. Statements by missionaries and imperial authorities were presented without comment beside African artifacts. The exhibit clearly did not condone the sometimes racist images and words it displayed, nor did it maintain a consistently critical perspective. Objects and images were often left to "speak for themselves." But the attempt to complicate curatorial didacticism backfired. Colonialist perspectives were all too clear in the nineteenth-century quotations and images; African responses remained implicit. People absorbed quite different messages from the presentation. While some visitors found the exhibit provocative, if somewhat confusing in its presentation, others were offended by what they took to be a suspension of criticism that bordered on indifference. Many—though not all—African Canadians who visited the museum were shocked by glorified colonialist images and condescending statements about Africans prominently and apparently uncritically displayed. They were not seduced by an ironic treatment of the violent destruction and appropriation of African cultures. The museum and its guest curator, anthropologist Jeanne Cannizzo, had misjudged the exhibit's discrepant audiences.

A bitter controversy ensued in the media. There were clashes between picketers at the Royal Ontario Museum and the police; all of the museums that were scheduled to host the exhibit during its traveling phase canceled. This is not the place (nor am I well placed) to survey the controversy and adjudicate the extremes of mutual suspicion and miscomprehension that emerged. (See, among others, Ottenberg, 1991; Cannizzo, 1991; Hutcheon, 1994; and Mackey, 1995.) "Into the Heart of Africa" was denounced as racist colonization by other means, part of an ongoing suppression of African achievements and African Canadian experiences. The exhibit's critics were dismissed as narrow ideologues and censors, unable to grasp irony or a complex historical account. The controversy has since rippled through museum contexts, and as Enid Schildkraut, in a sensitive critique, confesses: "It made many of us working in the field of ethnographic exhibitions, particularly African exhibitions, tremble with a sense of 'There but for the grace of God go I.' How could an exhibition have gone so wrong? How could it have offended so many people from different sides of the political spectrum?" (Schildkraut 1991: 16).

The museum became an inescapable contact (conflict) zone. Distinct audiences brought differently attuned historical experiences to "Into the Heart of Africa." M. Nourbese Philip makes this point trenchantly, chastising the museum for missing an opportunity in the controversy to confront its publicly stated goals: to understand the "museum as an artifact" and the "complexities of cross-cultural encounters." The exhibition was clearly not sensitive to African Canadians' stake in the history of white Canadians and the African colonial enterprise. Its story was understood to be continuous with ongoing racist structures in officially "multicultural" Canadian life. African history could not be distanced in time and space. The museum learned, the hard way, about the risks (and Philip insists: the opportunities) of working in relation to an African diaspora within a fissured Canadian public sphere. The exhibit was a "cultural text" that could not be read from a stable location. "The same text resulted in contradictory readings determined by the different life histories and experiences. One reading saw these artifacts as being frozen in time and telling a story *about* white Canadian exploration of Africa; the other inserted the reader—the African Canadian reader—actively into the text, who then read those artifacts as the painful detritus of savage exploration and attempted genocide of their own people" (Philip, 1992: 105).

Would fuller "consultation" with the relevant "communities" (including the white Canadians whose family histories were at issue) have prevented polarization? Would more explicit narration of an African "side" to the story in the exhibit have helped, as Schildkraut argues? Surely. But Philip sees—as do some museum professionals thinking in the wake of "The Spirit Sings" and "Into the Heart of Africa"—that structures of power are fundamentally at stake (Ames, 1991: 12–14). Until museums do more than consult (often after the curatorial vision is firmly in place), until they bring a wider range of historical experiences and political agendas into the actual planning of exhibits and the control of museum collections, they will be perceived as merely paternalistic by people whose contact history with museums has been one of exclusion and condescension. It may, indeed, be utopian to imagine museums as public spaces of collaboration, shared control, complex translation, and honest disagreement. Indeed, the current proliferation of museums may reflect the fact that, as historically evolved, such institutions tend to reflect unified community visions rather than overlapping, discrepant histories. But few communities, even the most "local," are homogeneous. In practice, different groups may come together around a specific issue or antagonism (as many African Canadians did in response to the Royal Ontario Museum), yet divide on others. The tribal response to "The Spirit Sings" was not uniform. And on certain issues, black Canadians whose families have been in Canada for two centuries may differ from people with close connections to places in the Caribbean or from Africans who have recently arrived. On the general issue of Africa and colonial history, they may share a common outrage. But when practical problems of interpretation and emphasis, issues of repatriation and compensation, are raised, the unanimity can dissolve.

Who, after all, is best qualified by "experience" (what kinds?), by depth and breadth of knowledge (what knowledges?), to control and interpret an African collection? African Canadians who have never been to Africa and who may hold an idealized vision of its cultures? White anthropologists and curators who have spent considerable time on the continent and have studied its history in depth, but have never viscerally known racism or colonization? Contemporary Africans? (From which ethnicity, nation, or region? Living in Africa? In Canada?) Sometimes, as in the case of the Tlingit at the Portland Museum of Art, the connection of current community members to old objects is very direct. In other cases, what is at issue is "cultural property" or a more distant "historical" relationship. Since communities and collections are seldom unified, museums may have to address sharply discrepant publics.

Clearly, there is no easy solution to these problems, no formula based on unassailable principle. Neither community "experience" nor curatorial "authority" has an automatic right to the contextualization of collections or to the narration of contact histories. The solution is inevitably contingent and political: a matter of mobilized power, of negotiation, of representation constrained by specific audiences. To evade this reality—resisting "outside" pressures in the name of aesthetic quality or scientific neutrality, raising the specter of "censorship"—is self-serving as well as historically uninformed. Community pressures have always been part of institutional, public life. Museums routinely adapt to the tastes of an assumed audience—in major metropolitan institutions, largely an educated, bourgeois, white audience. National sensibilities are respected, the exploits and connoisseurship of dominant groups celebrated. Donors and trustees exercise very real "oversight" (a more polite word than "censorship") on what kinds of exhibits a museum can mount. One has no difficulty imagining the drying up of grants, donations, and bequests that would follow, should a major museum adopt a consistently critical stance toward the art market or a view of American or Canadian history that gave a prominent, permanent place to the perspectives of economically, racially, or colonially oppressed people.[13]

Museums do not like to offend their publics, especially the sources of their material support. In normal, "nonpoliticized" times, this accountability to particular interests and tastes is simply business as usual. It is only when curatorial perspective and social location are challenged by a differently interested public (as in debates about the 1987 "Hispanic Art" exhibit at the Houston Museum of Fine Arts, for example), or when an exhibit's message offends powerful constituencies (the Smithsonian's recent critical view of the American frontier; the Hiroshima / Enola Gay display), or when communities are publicly divided over a proposal (whether or not to include a slave market at colonial Williamsburg) that things are perceived as "political." But such debates and negotiations are inherent in the contact work of museums. More than ever before, curators reckon with the fact that the objects and interpretations they display "belong" to others as well as to the museum.

Ownership and control of collections have never been absolute; individual donors routinely attach conditions to their gifts. But now communities that are socially distant from the museum world can effectively constrain the display and interpretation of objects representing their cultures. In contemporary Canada and the United States, at least, there are strong, overtly political limits on how Native American, Latino, or African American art can be displayed and interpreted. Emerging notions of "cultural property" impinge on abstract assumptions about freedom of ownership. Of course, major museums have never owned their artworks in quite the same way that an individual does. Their collections are held in trust for a wider community—defined as a city, class, caste or elite, nation, or projected global community of high culture. The objects in a museum are often treated as a patrimony, someone's cultural property. But whose? Which communities (defined by class, nationality, race) have a stake in them? Carol Duncan's research on the history of the Louvre, an institution that has served as a model for major museums throughout the world, shows how its transition from palace to museum was linked to the creation of a "public" in postrevolutionary France, the development of a secular, national community (Duncan, 1991, 1995). The homogeneity of such a public is currently at issue in struggles over multiculturalism and equality of representation. Borders traverse the dominant national or cultural spaces, and museums that once articulated the cultural core or high ground now appear as sites of passage and contestation.

In counterpoint with the decentering of established institutions, alternate "museums" make new demands on the contact work of managing and interpreting patrimonies, cultural traditions, and histories. Tribal museums and minority cultural centers collect and exhibit community productions in ways that both overlap with and diverge from the practices of more conventional museums (see Canadian Museums Association, 1990; Karp, Kreamer, and Lavine, 1992; and Chapter 5, above). Community museums / cultural centers (the distinction may be blurred or irrelevant) are differently centered, expressing partial histories and locally inflected aesthetic, cultural contexts. The fact that an altar or a tribal mask can mean quite different things in different locations makes inescapable the recognition and display of multiple contexts for works of art or culture. Innovative museum professionals have long been interested in ways to put objects in a fresh light, to make them new. Explicit contact relations now place this kind of search in a different conjuncture, imposing new collaborations and alliances. Thus, the multiplication of contexts becomes less about discovery and more about negotiation, less a matter of creative curators having good ideas, doing research, consulting indigenous experts, and more a matter of responding to actual pressures and calls for representation in a culturally complex civil society.

Contact work in a museum thus goes beyond consultation and sensitivity, though these are very important. It becomes active collaboration and a sharing of authority. This development is clearly traced in Fath Davis Ruffins' excellent survey of forms of cultural memory, the black museum movement, and the (partial) entry of African American professionals into historically white museums in the United States (1992). From the standpoint of museum professionals, it is one thing to call on one's "native informant" and quite another to work with a co-curator.[14] In matters of minority or tribal art, collaboration entails complex processes that Charlotte Townsend-Gault has described in terms of culturally and politically limited translation work and the tactical negotiation of boundaries (Townsend-Gault, 1995; see also Irving and Harper, 1988; Ames, 1991; González and Tonelli, 1992).

One of the most difficult areas of negotiation around tribal objects and colonial histories concerns repatriation. In a contact perspective, the movement of objects out of tribal places into metropolitan museums would be an expected outcome of colonial dominance. Such movements would not be confused with progress or with preservation (a kind of immobility/immortality) in a cultural "center." In contact zones, cultural appropriations are always political and contestable, cross-cut by other appropriations, actual or potential. Museums and the market manage the travel of art objects between different places. Objects of value cross from a tribal world to a museum world as a result of political, economic, and intercultural relations that are not permanent. For example, a powerful tradition of collecting in the salvage mode has long been justified by the idea that authentic tribal productions are doomed: their future can only be either local destruction or preservation in the hands of knowing collectors, conservators, and scientists. But it is harder now to see the destiny of collections as a linear teleology of this sort (Clifford, 1987). By positing the disappearance of tribal worlds, salvage collecting presumed (and to an extent created) the rarity of "authentic" tribal art. Some tribal communities did indeed disappear, often violently. Others hung on, against terrible pressures. Sometimes this meant putting on camouflage, coming out of hiding when the situation was less repressive. Others changed, finding new ways to be different. In light of these diverse histories, the notion that indigenous artworks somehow *belong* in majority (scientific or fine-art) museums is no longer self-evident. Objects in museums can still go elsewhere.

Repatriation of tribal works is not the only proper response to contact histories, relations which cannot always be reduced to colonial oppression and appropriation. But it is a possible, appropriate route. And although the return of objects may be a fortunate homecoming, it is not always obvious where home is for collected objects. The situation can be complicated and ambiguous.[15] Indeed, some native groups do not want physical possession of traditional objects; they simply want ongoing connection and control. In practice, the notion of cultural property can mean that a metropolitan or state museum holds collections in trust for specific communities. Indeed, some museums may come to resemble a depository and lending library, circulating art and culture beyond their walls—with varying constraints—to local museums or community centers and even for use in current ritual life (Blundell and Grant, 1989). This is relatively easy to imagine between national and tribal or ethnic museums. But can a museum allow art and artifact to travel in and out of the "world of museums" (an emerging network considerably larger than what is usually called the "museum world")? Movement of collections in and out of the world of museums is still quite difficult for curators and boards of directors to accept, given the traditional economy and mission of the Western museum. It would require breaking with strong traditions of conservationism. For example, shudders were surely felt by many museum professionals over the recent repatriations of Zuni war-god figures, *Ahauutas*, which are now rotting on secret mesa tops, completing their interrupted traditional life journey.

This history of rotting sculptures—a story of destruction for one culture and of renewal for another—is one possible travel story for repatriated objects. There are others. As we saw in Chapter 5, an important potlatch collection recently returned to Kwagiulth clans on Vancouver Island ended up in two tribal *museums*. As a condition for relinquishing the objects, the conservation-minded museum world successfully extended itself into the tribal world. But at the same time, the tribal world appropriated and transculturated the museum, along with the very notion of the "collection" and the kinds of cultural/aesthetic/political meanings it could embody. In this new, hybrid context the museum becomes a cultural center and a site of storytelling, of indigenous history, and of ongoing tribal politics. It is also caught up with Fourth World tribal circuits, with "cultural tourism" by natives and whites, and with commercial tourism at regional, national, and international levels.

"Museums" increasingly work the borderlands between different worlds, histories, and cosmologies. Is the Kwagiulth U'mista Cultural Centre a museum? Yes and no. An art museum? Yes and no. Is the San Francisco Galeria de la Raza a museum? Yes and no.[16] Contact zones—places of hybrid possibility and political negotiation, sites of exclusion and struggle—are clear enough when we consider tribal or minority institutions, but what would it take (and why would it matter?) to treat the Metropolitan Museum of Art in Manhattan as a contact zone rather than a center? Or the Louvre? To give marginal, "between" places a tactical centrality is ultimately to undermine the very notion of a center. All sites of collection begin to seem like places of encounter and passage. Seen this way, objects currently in the great museums are travelers, crossers—some strongly "diasporic" with powerful, still very meaningful, ties elsewhere. Moreover, the "major" museums increasingly organize themselves according to the dictates of tourism, national and international. This rethinking of collections and displays as unfinished historical processes of travel, of crossing and recrossing, changes one's conception of patrimony and public. What would be different if major regional or national museums loosened their sense of centrality and saw themselves as specific places of transit, intercultural borders, contexts of struggle and communication between discrepant communities? What does it mean to work within these entanglements rather than striving to transcend them?

Such questions evoke some of the conflicting demands currently felt by museums in multicultural and multiracial societies. By thinking of their mission as contact work—decentered and traversed by cultural and political negotiations that are out of any imagined community's control—museums may begin to grapple with the real difficulties of dialogue, alliance, inequality, and translation.

In the World of Museums

My account of museums as contact zones is both descriptive and prescriptive. I have argued that it is inadequate to portray museums as collections of universal culture, repositories of uncontested value, sites of progress, discovery, and the accumulation of human, scientific, or national patrimonies. A contact perspective views all culture-collecting strategies as responses to particular histories of dominance, hierarchy, resistance, and mobilization. And it helps us see how claims to both universalism and to specificity are related to concrete social locations. As Raymond Williams showed in *Culture and Society* (1966), nineteenth-century bourgeois articulations of a high/universal "culture" were responses to industrial change and social threat. Conversely, "minority" and "tribal" articulations of a discrete culture and history respond to histories of exclusion and silencing. They claim a locally controlled place in the broader public culture, while speaking both within particular communities and to a wider array of audiences. Museums/cultural centers can provide sites for such articulations.

My account argues for a democratic politics that would challenge the hierarchical valuing of different places of crossing. It argues for a decentralization and circulation of collections in a multiplex public sphere, an expansion of the range of things that can happen in museums and museum-like settings. It sees the inclusion of more diverse arts, cultures, and traditions in large, established institutions as necessary but not as the only or primary point of intervention. Indeed, any pluralist vision of full inclusivity at privileged sites (such as the Mall in Washington, D.C.—a national museum of museums) is questioned.[17] A contact perspective argues for the local/global specificity of struggles and choices concerning inclusion, integrity, dialogue, translation, quality, and control. And it argues for a distribution of resources (media attention, public and private funding) that recognizes diverse audiences and multiply centered histories of encounter. Given the history of museums in the Euro-American bourgeois state and indeed in national contexts everywhere, this view may seem utopian. It is utopia in a minor key, a vision of uneven emergence and local encounter rather than of global transformation. It makes a place for strong, if precarious, initiatives that pull against established hierarchical legacies.

These legacies have recently been subjected to searching critical and historical analysis. The growth of public museums in nineteenth-century Europe and America was part of a general attempt to purvey and organize "culture" from the top down. Museums accumulated the "symbolic capital" of traditional and emergent elites (Bourdieu, 1984). They institutionalized a hardening distinction between "highbrow" and "lowbrow" activities (Levine, 1988). The "publics" whom they addressed and whose "patrimonies" they collected were constituted by bourgeois nationalist projects (Duncan, 1991). In the nineteenth century, a series of important "legislative and administrative reforms . . . transformed museums from semi-private institutions restricted largely to the ruling and professional classes into major organs of the state dedicated to the instruction and edification of the general public" (Bennett, 1988: 63). In the twentieth century, museums have been central to the production and consumption of "heritage" in a dizzying range of local, national, and transnational contexts (Walsh, 1992), integral elements in expansive tourist industries (MacCannell, 1976; Horne, 1984; Urry 1990). As an institution that emerged with the national, bourgeois state and with industrial and commercial capitalism, the museum's destiny is linked to their global diffusion and local adaptations.

The link with capitalist marketing and commodification has been traced by Neil Harris (1990) in his provocative comparison of museums and department stores in nineteenth- and twentieth-century North America. By the 1940s, he argues, museums had been widely eclipsed by commercial emporia as sites for the display of art and objects and for the edification of popular taste. But recently many major museums have become more consumer-oriented, with a concomitant change of image.

> If attractiveness and public appeal become the museum's objectives, how in effect does it differ from any commercial institution which exists chiefly for the purpose of selling? . . . Has the museum, a new entertainment palace, become merely another asylum, an asylum not for objects and art but for special kinds of memory baths and gallery-going rituals, a quantified, certified, collective encounter that may shape purchase patterns but hardly improve them? At one time, museums were charged with paying too little attention to the wants and needs of millions of laymen. Now, in another era, they are taxed with pandering to delight in relevance, drama, and popularity. (Harris, 1990: 81)

However these developments are evaluated, and whatever possibilities of cultural/political advocacy are opened up by the increasingly frank abandonment of older ideals of aesthetic and scientific neutrality (95), Harris concludes that "the changing fortunes of the museum as a public influence suggest capacities that are great, growing, and endowed with almost infinite variation" (81).[18]

The "museum" Harris refers to is a Western, largely metropolitan institution. But his vision of a dynamic, consumer-oriented machine for gathering and displaying objects of artistic, cultural, and commercial value has evident global ramifications. The "flexible accumulation" (Harvey, 1989) of traditions, identities, arts, and styles associated with contemporary capitalist expansion supports the proliferation of museums in what might cynically be called a global department store of cultures. Kevin Walsh (1992) develops this general perspective in a trenchant critique of "museums and heritage in a postmodern world." Walsh extends David

Harvey's view of globalizing capitalist culture: a relentless erosion of "place," of local and continuous senses of collective time, and the substitution of shallow, spectacular, and merely nostalgic conceptions of the past. Heritage replaces history, contributing to a hegemonic articulation of national and class interests. Building on Robert Hewison's *The Heritage Industry* (1987), Walsh grounds the recent rapid growth of museums in Britain in a period of industrial/imperial decline and Thatcherite retrenchment. He finds similar neoliberal hegemonies at work wherever changing societies, engaged with expansive capitalism, represent and consume their past as heritage. The commodification of local pasts is part of a global process of cultural "de-differentiation."

Walsh and Harvey's analysis of the "postmodern" marketing of heritage is a necessary, but not a sufficient, account of the many activities happening in and through museums. A contact perspective, as Pratt argues, complicates diffusionist models, whether they be celebratory (the march of civilization and Western exploration) or critical (the relentless spread of capitalist commodity systems). Walsh recognizes, at times, that his approach oversimplifies, and he cites Mike Featherstone's caution: "The binary logic which seeks to comprehend culture via the mutually exclusive terms of homogeneity/heterogeneity, integration/disintegration, unity/diversity, must be discarded. At best, these conceptual pairs work on one face only of the complex prism which is culture" (Featherstone, 1990: 2). The burden of Walsh's account falls, however, on the first terms of the series.[19]

With different political valences, museums express the interests of nation-states, of local and tribal communities, of transnational capital. Wherever local custom, tradition, art (elite or popular), history, science, and technology are collected and displayed—for purposes of prestige, political mobilization, commemoration, tourism, or education—museums and museum-like institutions can be expected to emerge. The spaces of collection, recollection, and display marked by the term "museum" are multiplex and transculturated. Different histories lead into these contact spaces, different engagements with modernity/postmodernity, different "nostalgias" (Stewart, 1988; Ivy, 1995). Tribal "museums," for example, reflect indigenous as well as Western forms of accumulation, memory, and display. They project a vision of history as struggle, survival, renewal, and ongoing difference. Barnaby and Hall (1990) provide an informative account of the Dene Cultural Institute, initiated in 1986 by delegates of the

Dene Nation representing the Gwich'in, Slavery, Dogrib, Chipewyan, and Cree peoples of Canada's Northwest Territories. The institute reflects a conscious tribal decision to preserve and restore Dene culture as part of a movement for aboriginal rights and control of resource development. The institute has been concerned with oral history, language revitalization, traditional medicine, land use, public education, and collection of archives and artifacts. An exhibition space for Dene materials is planned. Here, clearly, the museum function is integral to the larger work of a cultural center. It is crucial to be attentive to the interrelation, relative weight, and political impetus of these functions in different institutional articulations of heritage.[20]

Compare Schildkraut's account (1996) of the opening of the Asante Manhyia Palace Museum in Ghana, a very different assertion of traditional, here royal, authority. Alternate visions of tradition and modernity may be expressed in museums to the extent that they reflect local initiatives and embody real alliances and conversations between community members and outside professionals—the ideal of Georges-Henri Rivière's "eco-museum" (Rivière, 1985). And within dominant national contexts, important distinctions can be made in the production and consumption of "heritage." As Tony Bennett has noted, the politics of British conservation has generally been conservative—an assumption that Raphael Samuel (1995) complicates. Australia, however, offers a different "official" context. A museum such as the Sydney Hyde Park Barracks reflects the inclusive politics of Labor's "new nationalism." By taking up residence in buildings originally built to house transported criminals, the museum announced its intention to represent Australian histories that were excluded from more celebratory, consensualist visions (Bennett, 1988: 80).

Why have museum practices proved so mobile, so productive in different locations? Several interlocking factors are at work. The ability to articulate identity, power, and tradition is critical, linking the institution's aristocratic origins with its modern nationalist and "culturalist" disseminations. Museums also resonate with a broad range of vernacular activities of collecting, display, and entertainment. Accumulating and displaying valued things is, arguably, a very widespread human activity not limited to any class or cultural group. Within broad limits, a museum can accommodate different systems of accumulation and circulation, secrecy and communication, aesthetic, spiritual, and economic value. How its "public" or "community" is defined, what individual, group, vision, or ideology it celebrates, how it interprets the phenomena it presents, how long it remains in place, how rapidly it changes—all these are negotiable. Gathering an individual's or a group's treasures and history in a museum overlaps with practices such as collecting memorabilia, making a photo album, or maintaining an altar. In some cases, museums are sustained with relatively few resources: the energy of a local collector/enthusiast and some volunteers. Communities or individuals who might have traditionally expressed their sense of identity and power by holding a festival or building a shrine or church may now (also) support a museum.

In a global context where collective identity is increasingly represented by having a culture (a distinctive way of life, tradition, form of art, or craft), museums make sense. They presume an external audience (national and international connoisseurs, tourists, scholars, curators, "sophisticated" travelers, journalists, and the like). These may not be the sole or even the primary audience for cultural displays and performances, but they are never entirely absent. When a community displays itself through spectacular collections and ceremonies, it constitutes an "inside" and an "outside." The message of identity is directed differently to members and to outsiders—the former invited to share in the symbolic wealth, the latter maintained as onlookers, or partially integrated, whether connoisseurs or tourists. From their emergence as public institutions in nineteenth-century Europe, museums have been useful for polities gathering and valuing an "us." This articulation—whether its scope is national, regional, ethnic, or tribal—collects, celebrates, memorializes, values, and sells (directly and indirectly) a way of life. In the process of maintaining an imagined community, it also confronts "others" and excludes the "inauthentic." This is the stuff of contemporary cultural politics, creative and virulent, enacted in the overlapping historical contexts of colonization/decolonization, nation formation / minority assertions, capitalist market expansion / consumer strategies.

The "world of museums" is diverse and dynamic. To varying degrees, the different contact zones I have been tracking partake of a postmodern marketing of heritage, the display of identity as culture or art. And there is no doubt that the museum-structure of culture—objectified tradition, construed as moral/aesthetic value and marketable commodity—is increasingly widespread. Aspirations of both dominant and subaltern populations can be articulated through this structure, along with the material interests of national and transnational tourism. To "have" a culture, Richard Handler has argued (1985, 1993), is to be a collector, caught up in the game of possessing and selectively valuing ways of life. But how completely caught? What *else* goes on in tribal and other local articulations of culture? How unified is the constellation of cultural/economic formations we call the postmodern? . . . The world system? . . . Late capitalism? Let us not foreclose too soon. Museums, those symbols of elitism and staid immobility, are proliferating at a remarkable rate: from new national capitals to Melanesian villages, from abandoned coal pits in Britain, to ethnic neighborhoods in global cities. Local/global contact zones, sites of identity-making and transculturation, of containment and excess, these institutions epitomize the ambiguous future of "cultural" difference.

8

Palenque Log

Consider the new world that faces the three-month-old Magnolia Warbler after finding its way to the tropics. Raised in a young stand of conifers, this small bird faces one of the most complex and diverse habitats in the world—the canopy of a lowland tropical rain forest. How migratory birds explore and learn about their new environments remains a fascinating mystery for behavioral scientists.

—Russell Greenberg, *El Sur de Mexico: Cruce de caminos para los pajaros migratorios*

7:15 A.M.: Outside my hotel, I flag a bus for Las Ruinas, joining some other early-bird tourists and people who work at the site. Cornfields are visible through the mist on steep slopes behind the ruin. The temples remain hidden by dense foliage.

7:30–8:00: The parking lot is mostly empty. A group of men, women, and children are playing no-net volleyball at the far end. Behind them, above some small trees, is the Temple of the Inscriptions. My camera, which I dropped on the bathroom floor this morning, jams. After some futile attempts at repair, I give up on it.

A couple of guys in cowboy hats begin sweeping the lot. It rained hard last night, and many leaves are mixed in with the litter. Some long-haired Lacandon Indians in loose white smocks and loafers lug cartons filled with bows and arrows from a VW "combi" van to their selling place near the entrance. Their kids, similarly dressed but barefoot, eat a breakfast of bananas and tortillas in the cool of a nearby shelter.

It's already warm. The ruin opens at 8:00. Lots of bird songs, slap of hands on the rubber ball, low talk, an occasional laugh. "Independent travelers," mostly young Europeans, arrive in VW combis from the town of Palenque, eight kilometers away. A few cars. The volleyball stops.

8:00–8:25: Ticket sales start. Mexican sellers of handicrafts and souvenirs, non-Indian *ladinos,* begin to set up in their stalls along one side of the parking area. One family eats an elaborate breakfast, standing around their car's trunk. The first big bus arrives at 8:15.

I buy a ticket and go to the entry at the far end of the lot. This gate is an innovation since my visit to Palenque two years ago, when we entered directly from the parking area. Now, a detour has been arranged, a transition from lot to site, looping through trees and up stone steps. The gate has been moved a hundred yards to the side and farther from the cars. Here, as we sign a large register, guides offer their services in several languages: a complete tour costs seventy pesos ($23) and includes a "jungle walk."

Inside the gate: a loud buzzing, singing sound from the forest hillside. People are already perched atop the Temple of the Inscriptions and the

Figure 8.1. The Temple of the Inscriptions. Photo by James Clifford.

Palace tower. Their little bodies, colored caps and shorts, scatter across the open park.

Snapshot: walking from left to right, against the flow of visitors and along the base of the Temple of the Inscriptions: a man followed by a boy. Both carry heavy loads. The man is bent, a tumpline across his forehead, aiming straight for the gate and the parking lot. He and the boy look neither at the giant pyramid on their left nor at the tourists squinting into cameras. .

I move into the shade halfway up the Palace steps. From here I can see where a trail climbs into the hills behind the Temple of the Inscriptions. The man and boy must have come down this way. Two years ago, I walked a little way up the trail in search of a "pre-excavation" feeling: the tangled foliage and intense sounds which would have greeted early explorers like Del Río, Dupaix and Castañeda, Waldeck, Walker and Caddy, Stephens and Catherwood. A few hundred yards in, I found the partly cleared Casa del Léon, trees still gripping its roof, the "romantic" ruin made famous in a drawing by Count Waldeck in 1833. This was something like what Catherwood actually saw—not the cleaned-up renditions Stephens published, and nothing like the manicured, rebuilt monuments of the current *parque nacional*.

As I pushed further on, the trail seemed to merge with roots and tangled vines. I wondered whether a heap of partly covered stones might belong to some hidden structure. Nothing but forest sounds, deep shadows, and shafts of light. I was alone . . . with the mosquitoes. But suddenly six men rushed past, lugging a complete set of instruments for a mariachi band. Surreal moment: ordinary explanation. Three hours' walk up the trail is a Chol Mayan village. Their route to town emerges from the trees behind the Temple of the Inscriptions, crosses its base, and passes through the *zona arqueológica* to the road.

8:30–8:45: Arrival of the first leaf-sweeper in the main plaza. An older woman, a Mexican tourist, stops to chat with him. He's ignored by the others, who aim their cameras where he's not. So far, the big space of the site contains, disperses, all the small bodies.

Guides speaking in raised tones, the first groups make their appearance. I notice attendants standing atop the large structures. They wear blue INAH baseball hats (Instituto Nacional de Antropología e Historia). I walk to the site's lower end, past the newly cleared ball court, beside the stream that flows through the ruin, to the Campamento INAH.

Things have changed there, too, in the past couple of years. What was once a little museum is now a restoration lab. Through an open door I hear taped music and see young people in white coats—mostly women, one man—piecing together large clay tubes, elaborately molded with human and animal features. More than seventy of these *cilindros,* whose function remains uncertain, have recently been found among bones buried at the base of the Temple of the Sun.

Campamento: the word harkens back to a time when Palenque was hard to get to, when archaeologists actually camped here. Now the INAH installation includes permanent workrooms, storage areas, a dining room, and a kitchen. When digging is in full swing, as many as three hundred may be employed here. Now only a few dozen are working, mostly on restoration and site maintenance.

8:45–9:00: Several trucks marked "INAH" roll in on a dirt road that cuts across the park. There's a strong forest buzz—cut by the intermittent sound of a machine somewhere in the trees. I slap my neck a few times at the fringe of the mosquito-free tourist zone. Now the tape from the lab emits a reggae bass line: "Get up, stand up. Stand up for your rights . . ."

Men are walking slowly to work in the park. One carries a machete and an electronic device of some sort; another a hammer and, over his shoulder, several long strips of wood.

Beyond the restoration lab the path slopes down past a shed, where several wheelbarrows are propped together. Then it fords the stream at a spot some tour guides call the "queen's bathtub." A faded sign: "Prohibido Bañarse En Este Lugar." Across the stream: some dilapidated houses, a few hammocks slung under tin roofing, a man splashing himself with water from a tub. Temporary quarters for some of the local Chols and other laborers who do the heavy work of excavation. The dark camp in the forest is what Erving Goffman called the "back area" of a performative space—located behind, and making possible, the bright spectacle of the ruin proper.

9:00–9:15: Walking out into the clearing, I find the temples of El Grupo Norte roped off. Excavations at their base have revealed important sculptures, sheltered now by corrugated iron. Why did these buildings seem so finished, two years ago? Was it the grass, neatly mowed right up to them? The permanent interpretive plaques?

Several men are now on top, moving slowly in the hot sun, picking up stones, washing something in liquid from a big plastic jug. All over the site, seventh-century roofs are being chemically treated against seepage. (Freud: the destruction of Pompeii began when it was dug up.)

The men take a break from the heat, shaded by a temple door. They sip from a shopping bag. In the distance, little multicolored lines of people coil around the summit of the Temple of the Inscriptions. Faint voices, a shout from the top . . .

9:15–9:45: I walk behind the Palace, toward the Temples of the Sun, the Cross, the Foliated Cross. This whole area, site of very recent discoveries—including a major tomb—is closed to visitors. All I can see of the ongoing work is the rebuilt base of the Temple of the Sun. What two years ago was a little building on a grassy mound is now the summit of a pyramid. The space enclosed by the three temples will feel different, surely, when we are allowed in again. What will become of their special lightness and grace?

A giant heap of rubble, produced by the excavations, spills down the slope above me. A woman sits on top, presumably to keep out the unauthorized. A Mexican man, academic looking, with a beard and wire-rimmed glasses, enters the roped-off area and climbs the trail behind her.

Disappointed, I turn away, mount the freshly excavated west steps of the Palace, and enter the famous large patio. The subtle asymmetry of the portico is more apparent now that this side has been cleared and rebuilt. Inside, the brilliant proportions conceived by ancient architects have a calming effect.

Sounds collect in the big patio (I'm glad, now, that I can't take pictures): voices of the tour guides blending with bird calls and forest hum. At one moment I hear French, Spanish, and English, from three sides of the patio . . . later German. Forest of Interpretations.

Everywhere I glance, it seems, someone is pointing a camera. Brief hallucination: the hundreds of photos per hour (per minute?) generated by these stones . . . like masses of birds taking off, scattering. Where do they go?

9:45–10:00: It's very hot now, and I decide to postpone my climb to the top of the Temple of the Inscriptions (with obligatory descent into Pacal's sweaty tomb). Back in the parking lot a man collects the last of yesterday's plastic bottles and dead leaves, sweeping alongside five coaches, all transporting Mexicans. These are the only big buses in the lot, and I'm struck by what I only half-noticed in the site: the large number of Mexican tourists.

Why are they here? I have a clear, no doubt stereotypical sense of why Europeans and North Americans visit Palenque. The international circuit is well established—from the 1840s, when Stephens and Catherwood's bestseller put Palenque on the travel map, to the present generation, with their zoom lenses, backpacks, running shoes, and New Age crystals. But the Mexicans in these big buses seem different. For one thing, they are working-class and petit bourgeois in appearance. Chatting easily in the shady spots, yelling from the tops of monuments, many of them seem to enjoy the ruin without the reverential museum attitude of the international pilgrims. They are more at home, somehow. Theirs seems a more social outing.

I don't know. Tourists (especially the ones in big buses) are a mystery, everyone's "Other," never given any social or individual complexity. And tourism still tends to be seen as a uniquely First World activity. How do ancient Mayans figure in the Mexican national imagination? In Mexican schools? How are they commodified in the second-class resort circuit? Are the builders of Palenque equal to the Aztecs, premier "First Mexicans"? How have Mayan symbols been used to articulate mestizo regional identities? And what is the special allure of Palenque, site of that most spectacular of archaeological finds—the discovery in 1952 of Pacal's hidden tomb by a Mexican, Alberto Ruz L'Huillier?

A guide at the site tells me that whenever there's a *telenovela* featuring an archaeologist, they can expect an influx of Mexican tour groups: one called "Más Allá de la Muerte" has just ended. There may be something to what he says, but the snobbism leaves me suspicious. Tourist as dope again.

I go to the restaurant for a Coke and watch the *artesanía*/souvenir trade picking up across the lot. Back near the gate, Lacandons are doing a brisk business in bows and arrows. I already have some from last time. Somewhere (in the forest? in town?) a lot of people are making these things. A truck carrying bottles of "COYAME: Agua Mineral y Sabores" rolls up.

I had expected that the Chamulan women would be in the parking lot by the time I left the ruin. They are highland Mayans, unmistakable in their *traje*—dark wool skirts, blue or white blouses, wide red belts. Two years ago they circulated freely among the cars and as close as possible to the ticket window and entry gate. In their heavy skirts made for the chilly mountains, arms and shoulders laden with woven goods, sometimes lugging a baby in a *rebozo,* managing a flock of kids who sell the wares, an eye out for the authorities, the *Chamulitas* seemed ubiquitous. Where are they now?

10:00–11:00: In a combi bound for town I join several other weary tourists, a few *campesinos,* and a Lacandon mother with her toddler. A fifteen minute drive takes us to the Cristóbal Colón first-class bus depot and the "Cabeza Maya," on the edge of town. The latter is a monumental white head gazing toward the sky: exaggerated Maya profile, lips ecstatically parted. I need to cash a travelers' check and change hotels.

"RRRRadio Palenque!" . . . Then something about a thousand watts of power and the greatness of "la cultura Maya."

Palenque is a fast-growing regional center of some seventy thousand inhabitants. (In 1950 the population was only 6,206.) Virtually every building appears to have been built recently. Although tourism and the famous *ruinas* have a lot to do with its rapid growth, Palenque is also a market/agricultural center. As I walk along the main street, Calle Juarez, I pass gift shops, camera stores, travel agencies (offering trips to the cascades of Agua Azul, or the remote Mayan sites of Yaxchilan and Bonampak), restaurants, food stores, video parlors, pharmacies, "Sombrerería Juarez" (a bright little room stuffed with cowboy hats), and "Agropecuaria Palenque" (saddles, plastic rope, shelves of chemicals, fertilizer bags, trays lined with squirming chicks).

Among the multicolored signs and painted walls cracked by sun and streaked by torrential rains, I make out some bright blue blouses and red belts. The Chamulans are on the streets, selling their woven belts, bracelets, and dolls. These wares, along with imported Guatemalan bags, shawls, shirts, pants, and sandals, are heaped along the sidewalks. A few older women sit in the shade, but the sellers are mostly young women, with some preteenage boys. They're working in *tierra caliente,* I find out, on two-week rotations, largely from the poor barrios around San Cristóbal de las Casas: La Hormiga, Paraiso, Nueva Palestina.

The Chamulans have recently been excluded from the *zona arqueológica.* No more ambulatory sellers. The only Mayan Indians now working the site are the Lacandons, offering an image of (archaic) authenticity, still privileged in their station near the gate. Apparently they have political clout somewhere, for assertions of their special connection with the builders of Palenque are dubious. If any living Mayans are the "Last Lords of Palenque" (title of a recent book about the Lacandons), it is probably the local Chols. Their language, at least, can be directly linked to the glyphs. But the Chols, aloof, have not yet chosen or been forced to enter the tourist economy in a major way. Chamulan women—men do not sell handicrafts publicly—are now a fixture of Palenque street life, renting strips of sidewalk outside stores and enjoying an apparent monopoly in their sphere. Expelled from Las Ruinas, they're angry but helpless.

Snapshot: a Chamulan boy draped with souvenir belts and woven goods, playing a Bart Simpson video game.

Snapshot: two girls in blue chat intensely, one tipped back in a tiny chair, the other on the curb. They ignore two boys wrestling inside a cardboard carton.

Stopping at a camera store, I acquire a "Memory Maker" (by Minolta). And on the way to my new hotel (La Cañada: I've heard it's where the archaeologists hang out) I pay three streetsellers for a portrait. The money's good, but the girls are nervous about the snapshot and want to get it over with. They divvy up the coins fast, looking over their shoulders. We talk awkwardly for a minute, about the heat, San Cristóbal.

11:00–1:30: Checking in at La Cañada. Jungle atmosphere in the hotel restaurant: moldings of reliefs from the ruin propped among the vines. Only a dozen rooms: not one of the new tourist hotels. This suits my "independent traveler" image. Exhausted from walking around in the sun, I switch on the air conditioning and collapse on my bed—staring blankly at a map of Palenque. A rectangular street grid.

Reminds me of New York City, my native land . . . And my mind wanders to John L. Stephens, another New Yorker, arriving here in 1840 after descending from the Chiapas highlands, as I did, over what he describes as the worst mountain and jungle trail he ever encountered. Finally reaching the goal of his expedition—his "furthest point of navigation," Conrad might say—Stevens finds people who seem in closer touch with New York than with their administrative center, Ciudad Real (San Cristóbal). Ship captains and merchants in the logwood trade linking Campeche with Manhattan have been visiting the area for some time. Several have inscribed their names on the walls of the ruin, and at least

Figure 8.2. Chamulan street sellers in Palenque. Photo by James Clifford.

one lives in the area. So much for lost cities and the ends of the earth.

I saw a local kid today with a T-shirt: "New York I ♥ U." (Also: "Chicago Bulls," "Aztec Calendar," and "Hard Rock Café: Palenque, Chiapas.") Stevens took five days to descend from Ocosingo through the mountains and jungle. I took four hours in a minivan. "Independent travelers" often like to associate themselves with John L. Stephens.

I doze off.

1:30–2:00: In the afternoon I plan to visit the new museum and visitor center, a kilometer or so downhill from the site. After an early lunch in the hotel restaurant, I walk out to the Cabeza Maya and catch a ride back to the ruin. Even as the hours of *comida* and *siesta* begin, there are plenty of buses and combis running.

Paying my fifty-cent fare, I get the feeling Las Ruinas are a kind of suburb. Stephens and Catherwood took half a day to get from town to the site, and as late as the early 1950s the only transport was by horse. When Alberto Ruz entered Pacal's tomb in 1952, putting Mexican archaeology in the limelight, Mexico's president paid a visit and immediately ordered construction of a road. As we crawl across the speed bump at the gate to the *zona,* I read a large sign, dated 1981, officially proclaiming Palenque a national park and announcing plans to pave the highway.

Just two years ago, when I drove down from San Cristóbal, people spoke excitedly about the new band of continuous asphalt linking the Pan American Highway in the highlands with Palenque, Villahermosa, and Merida in *tierra caliente.* "Mundo Maya," the international tourist circuit that is fueling the latest burst of site development at Palenque, depends on the existence of such roads, suitable for rental cars and first-class buses.

The network is being extended to include a *frontera* road through the jungle, following the border with Guatemala and connecting Palenque with Yaxchilan, Bonampak, several newly discovered ruins, ecological tourist settings in the Lacandon forest, and the scenic Lagos de Montebella in southern Chiapas. In addition to tourism, the projected road has obvious military and development potential (logging, coffee production).

"Parque Nacional," 1981. As we roll along the *zona's* relatively smooth asphalt toward the forested hills, I recall that 1981 was the last year of Mexico's oil boom. The next decade brought debt crisis, shrinking opportunities, unemployment. It was *la crisis* that forced most women from Chamula into handicraft production for tourists, and a growing number into selling on the streets of San Cristóbal. Now they are traveling further afield, to Palenque, Merida, Villahermosa, and Cancun, following routes laid down by Chamulan men who have long supplemented an inadequate subsistence economy at home with labor in lowland plantations, cornfields, public works, and construction. After 1982 most of the jobs for men vanished; and what remained, degrading work in the coffee fields, was taken over by desperate Guatemalans fleeing their own crisis, political as well as economic.

During the 1980s Chamulan women and children took to the streets, scratching out a living in one of Mexico's few expanding sectors, tourism— a sector driven by forces and desires far from debt-ridden Latin America. The alternatives were cruel: permanent migration to a hostile city or to distant homesteads in the Lacandon forest. Staying home, a woman and her children could perhaps sell firewood and earn enough to get by. But the market price for a load—which took four to six hours of hard work to cut, split, and transport—was only twenty U.S. cents.

2:00–3:00: The new administrative and visitor center is luxurious. Three handsome modern buildings, all with structural motifs recalling pyramids: the site museum, an auditorium with office and laboratory complex, a restaurant / gift shop.

The museum was officially opened by President Carlos Salinas de Gortari just three months ago. A large sign on the road gathers logos from the powers at work:

Consejo Nacional para la Cultura y las Artes
Gobierno del Estado
INAH
FONCA: Fondo Nacional para la Cultura y las Artes
BANCO BCH

Figure 8.3. The New Site Museum. Photo by James Clifford.

DOMECQ
NESTLE
VITRO: Envases Norteamerica
GUTSA: Construcciones
FEMSA–COCA COLA
BANCOMER
VISA

The museum surrounds an interior garden, with large glass windows outside. Objects are displayed in modern, formal/aesthetic style, individuated in pools of light. Uncluttered and spacious, the museum's interpretive tone is one of scientific overview, restrained, even minimalist. Short texts on the walls refer to ancient Mayan religion, culture, ecology, architecture, calendars, writing, and so on. The elaborately sculpted clay *cilindros* recently discovered at the Temple of the Sun are scattered throughout the museum. Big glyph panels fill several walls. The class system of the ancient Maya is summarized, with sections on priests, artisans, bureaucrats, traders, unskilled workers, and peasants. (Slaves are not included, though their possibility is mentioned.)

I've got the museum pretty much to myself. Because the new complex is a kilometer by road from the ruin, with no free shuttle, tired pyramid-climbers tend to pass it up. This will change, I hear, in the future. Long-range plans call for the museum complex to become the main entrance and parking area. A climb through the forest, on foot or in electric cars, will dramatically transport visitors from the modern to the ancient world. It is felt that currently the magic space of the ruin is too close to the parking lot, with its buses, food, and commerce. Even the new gate, with its detour through the trees, doesn't eliminate the feeling of proximity. As a sometime postmodern, I like this contamination, and regret the improvements.

Nostalgia and the sophisticated traveler: "When I was first here [before touristification], everything was better." Nostalgia can work over quite short intervals. Witness my feelings about the old and new museums. Two years ago, the *museo* was a few crowded rooms in the farthest corner of the ruin. Outside, Palenque's only stele stood in rain and sun, the open door of a bathroom visible just behind. Now this white, artistically eroded figure dominates the new museum's covered entry, elegant against a blue wall. The former *museo* had scant space for aesthetic isolation; everything was crowded, something of a jumble. Coming on this collection, one had a feeling of discovery, of stumbling on a small treasure. I recall the fascination exerted on me by some witty and intricate stucco glyphs, eight inches from my sweaty nose.

In the new, air-conditioned space, I look from distances controlled by attendants, cords, and glass. I long for the old *museo,* its casual intimacy, *my* piece of an old Palenque, at the same time admitting that the new one isn't so bad, after all. There's a lot here, very clearly presented. And where would they have put all these marvelous new *cilindros,* anyway?

A small bird, having flown into the glass, lies dead outside.

When was the "good time" to be at Palenque? The issue arose on my way here when I stopped at Toniná, a Mayan ruin in the highlands near Ocosingo. (Stephens and Catherwood were there, but for a day only, so great was their impatience to reach Palenque.) A large site, Toniná has only recently emerged as an important Late Classical center. Off the beaten track, it was a discovery for me.

I felt I had arrived at the perfect moment. The ruin, about a quarter excavated, gave a sense of the whole while leaving much to the imagination. Just enough knowledge, not too much. Carvings lying around, not locked up. A bumpy dirt road, few visitors, horses grazing on the site. An "independent traveler," contemplating the beautiful Ocosingo Valley from atop Toniná's observatory, could think a bit smugly of all those *other* tourists rushing past to Palenque.

But was this really the good time to visit Toniná? What about discoveries to come? Had I arrived a few years earlier, I would have missed the stupendous stucco mural that was the highlight of my visit. What was I missing now, still buried beneath the romantic trees and vines?

Compared to Toniná—and many other partly cleared sites now accessible to travelers willing to walk, bump around in a van, or take a small plane—Palenque seems a "completed" ruin. Everything is ordered, cleaned, rebuilt to just the degree permissible. Reconstruction beyond a certain shadowy line could turn an authentic ruin into a theme park.

For the traveler seeking discovery and an experience of communion, would the best time to visit Palenque be at the moment of discovery, whenever that was? Whose discovery? Before the first foreigners—Dupaix, Waldeck, Stephens, and Co.? But in the eighteenth and nineteenth centuries at least, until the extensive clearing supervised by Alfred Maudslay in 1891, one would not have seen very much. Stephens writes that he could walk right past a large pyramid and not know it was there.

Perhaps, for the "independent" visitor, the best time would have been just after the series of mappings and excavations conducted from the 1920s to the 1940s, but before construction of the access road. In 1949 one would have had a fairly visible "whole" site, the fully reconstructed Palace tower, and a chance to hear the birds, gaze at the stars, and commune with the stones without interruption. But then one would have missed Pacal's tomb, opened several years later. And if one had come in the late fifties, when the site still averaged only six or seven visitors a day, one would not yet have had the benefit of the dramatically revised knowledge of ancient Mayan society, soon to emerge from the glyph decipherments of the seventies, work which focused on Palenque.

When I was here just two years ago, the main entrance to the Palace was a dirt slope. And I haven't seen what they're finding in the Temple of the Sun . . .

Trajectory of a ruin: (1) discovery: uncovering secrets, reading fragments; (2) excavation: analysis, mapping, reconstruction; (3) museumification: collecting, displaying, making art-science; (4) touristification: providing access, developing the "attraction," mass pedagogy. One can't be present at every moment. "Independent travelers," like me, tend to vacillate ideologically between step 1 and step 3, while being materially located at step 4.

Desire to be alone in (with) the ruin. I'm talking with a Frenchwoman who guides "adventure" tours. "Palenque isn't as wonderful as last year," she says. "It's jammed with tourists." Last time, her group was caught in the rain atop the palace. It was marvelous. Clouds and mist, all the birds, no one around: "Il n'y avait *personne!*"

Alone with the stones, with nature. This much is required if ancient sites are to transmit wisdom and sublimity to romantic individualists. "Alone" meaning with special people like oneself. Not with tourists, attendants, workers, INAH trucks, *campesinos* lugging stuff through . . .

Virtually everyone I spoke with who "knows" Palenque—archaeologists, veteran visitors—tells of some personal moment of discovery: sunrise at the Temple of the Sun, stars from the observatory tower, a foggy morning, silence (with birds). The glossy picture books also remove the people.

Notebook entry: from John L. Stevens (1969: 119), *Incidents of Travel in Central America, Chiapas and Yucatan* (at Copan, 1839).

The ground was entirely new; there were no guide-books or guides; the whole was a virgin soil. We could not see yards before us, and never knew what we would stumble on next. At one time we stopped to cut away branches and vines which concealed the face of a monument, and then to dig around and bring to light a fragment, a sculpted corner of which protruded from the earth. I leaned over with breathless anxiety while the Indians worked, and an eye, an ear, a foot, or a hand was disentombed; and when a machete rang against the chiselled stone, I pushed the Indians away, and cleared out the loose earth with my hands.

3:00–4:00: Leaving the site museum, I encounter in an exit passageway four large, uncaptioned photos of contemporary Mayans: (1) a Lacandon man with an inscrutable look and an enormous homemade cigar; (2) a woman (Chol?) tending a smoky fire; (3) a man in a traditional hat, holding some corn; and (4) a group of women and kids, at ease, several laughing toward the camera. The message is uncertain: what connection do these people have or not have with the artifacts and history on display?

The photos are a kind of bridge to the restaurant and gift shop in the next building. There, I sip a soda surrounded by the craftwork of living Mayans. One large section of the long, open restaurant area is given over to traditional *artesanía*. At the far end I see a Chamulan woman in her distinctive bright-blue blouse and dark skirt. "So they've let them in, down here . . ." Then I do a double-take and realize she's a mannequin.

The restaurant display features highland Indian costumes. There are photos of the three big crosses / trees-of-life outside San Juan Chamula. Ribboned hats from Zinacantan hang on the walls. Near the Chamulan woman: a featureless Lacandon man. What is his relation to the other men wearing these clothes, selling arrows up at the gate?

I'm in another museum here: folklore and authentic culture displayed, aestheticized and valued, for purchase. The clothes and artifacts around the dummies are not for sale. But the "museum effect" extends into the gift shop across the restaurant area, where similar goods are available. An interpretive plaque details the place of woven goods in traditional Indian life. There are similar labels for the basketry and pottery sections. This is an upscale boutique, conceived for people who will pay with American Express cards. It includes a few books, mostly in English, including one of Robert Laughlin's scholarly collections of Tzotzil texts. Arrows, but no T-shirts.

Notebook entry: from Maruch Komes Peres and Diane L. Rus (1991: 12), *Ta Jlok'ta Chobtik Ta K'u'il (Récit d'une tisserande de Chamula)*.

Figure 8.4. *Artesanía* display, restaurant area. Photo by James Clifford.

A *rebozo* or shawl should take fifteen days. If you want it to be pretty, you have to embroider it by hand, which takes four days—full days. The colored pompoms, two more days. Weaving of each part of the wool blouse we call *tchilil tzotz* takes three or four days. This *huipil* has three parts: one for each sleeve and the other for the torso, so it takes nine days to finish. Like all wool garments, after weaving you have to treat it so it won't shrink when washed. That's two days per piece, a week for the three. Only then can you sew the sleeves. Embroidering the neck, that can be a week. Then you sew its cotton ball and the three pompoms on each side: six days.

In the new, improved *Zona Arqueológica,* Mayans are admissible as authenticated folklore. Streetsellers, however "traditional" their clothes, are matter out of place, generally scorned by the local *ladinos.* I hear it said that they are "prostituted" by the tourist trade. They belong in their villages. I'm not surprised to learn, too, that a plan was proposed to reroute the forest trail emerging at the Palace of the Inscriptions so that descending Chol villagers would pass behind the pyramid, out of sight and outside the ruin proper. So far, objections have blocked the plan. And it's unlikely the Chols would go along, especially now that the word is out (thanks to the New Epigraphy) that "Pacal spoke Chol."

4:00–4:15: Back to town in a combi. I pay the driver extra to stop for a few photos: cornfields above the ruin, the entry to the national park, a statue of "La Madre Maya" (with baby, in the same style as the Cabeza).

4:15–5:30: A pause at the Cristóbal Colón bus station to reserve a seat back to the highlands. Then, walking downtown, as the sky darkens for the late-afternoon downpour, I watch streetsellers unfurl big sheets of plastic and stuff their wares into garbage bags. Sitting out the rain in a café, I write postcards and decline woven belts and bracelets.

Later that evening: My souvenir: a bas-relief carved in soft stone by some boys who work in the "Taller des Artesanías" outside the hotel. It's a reduced copy of Pacal, from the sarcophagus in the Temple of the Inscriptions, shown at the moment of his last breath.

I ask the oldest boy, about sixteen years old, about his life in Palenque, the ruin, and so on. "For us," he says, "the ruin is no big deal. We respect it, sure, but it's nothing special. Palenque . . . people say its exciting, but for us . . . We do this *artesanía* for the money, that's all." It's said without apparent bitterness. A fact.

The little king reclines on glyphs for death and life, as he falls into the underworld . . . looking skyward in an attitude of bliss.

I answer with the cliché that our homes always become too familiar. Travel makes things fresh. I don't really appreciate the beauty of my home in California, and so forth.

The figure in my hand is part of an elaborate carving still in the crypt and a bit hard to see. This is the first time I've looked closely at the ecstatically dying king.

The boy doesn't respond. My words seem to fall flat. The difference in our situations, the privilege assumed by my cliché, is too apparent. I *can* travel. He can't . . . at least not for novelty and pleasure.

Pacal's hands and feet are marvelously expressive, sensuous. I feel I've gotten something special.

Note: This log, written from notes made at Palenque in July 1993, draws on information readily available around the site and in well-known published works. For Chamulan streetsellers I have relied on Diana L. Rus, *La crisis economica y la muher indigena: El caso de Chamula, Chiapas* (1990), and on Kathleen Sullivan's work-in-progress on ambulatory sellers in San Cristóbal—research which she kindly discussed with me. Special thanks to Moises Morales for several illuminating conversations about the ruin and its history. Of course, he bears no responsibility for my general optique.

Several months after the initial publication of these notes, travel to the ruin was disrupted by the Zapatista rebellion—temporarily.

Everything is written from the location of a meta-"independent traveler" within the tourist circuit.

FUTURES

Weather satellite photograph: North Pacific region. (*Image courtesy of Julian Bleecker.*)

9

Year of the Ram:
Honolulu, February 2, 1991

"'What you see is horns in the front and then the backbone and then the legs on both sides and the tail going out beyond the legs,' she said."

The new Chinatown atrium. Available cuisines: Japanese, Thai, Korean, Hawaiian, Chinese, Italian, Mexican, Filipino, Singapore, Lulu International, U.S. . . .

Night in the crowded streets: smoke from food stands, running young men and women from a martial-arts club, a dragon, University of Hawaii jazz ensemble, all-Asian saxophone section.

The beautiful Hawaiian capes made of feathers were worn in battle. Nearby, a high school band finishes its recital with the Looney Tunes theme, immediately followed by "The Star-Spangled Banner."

In a desert the tank is hit and sends up a plume of black smoke.

Heavy flowers around our necks.

"Each day at sunrise the light was radiant in my hut. The gold of Tehamana's face illuminates everything around it, and the two of us go to refresh ourselves in a nearby stream, naturally, simply, as in Paradise."

The Hilton Hawaiian Village (2,200 rooms): black football players (Pro Bowl weekend) loom in elevators over white art-museum directors (A.A.M.D. annual meeting). Leisure attire, exposed skin, beaches . . .

In a desert the tank is hit, explodes inside, sears the men's faces, and sends up a plume of black smoke.

"The goat is more earthy, the ram more scholarly."

Football players signing autographs. Museum directors debating multicultural-ism. While in the art collector's beautiful home, one wall is covered with flickering video screens.

"A woman soldier is reported missing in action." Maps. "This will not be another Vietnam." Talking general (apparently African American). Bombsight footage.

Man (apparently Anglo) in California: "We should go all the way this time, do it right, just get rid of those people."

In slow motion a building implodes.

The museum's dark garden overlooks a million city lights, as if seen from an incoming plane or missile. The performance artist in his mariachi suit and Indian war bonnet says, "It is very strange being here, in the beginning of the third world war."

"Ram or ewe? 'That's anybody's guess,' she said."

In a desert the tank is hit, explodes inside, sears the men's faces, tears sharp pieces of metal into their bodies, and sends up a plume of black smoke.

This garden, this city: "Montezuma entertaining Cortez." Smell of flowers and blood. Writhing dragon. Meat cooking. The different bodies mingle.

"This will not be another Vietnam."

A Hawaiian man plays with three children on the beach. He seems to be their father. In bathing suits, each one appears distinct, as if from a separate painting. The man is young and muscular. The four build something in the sand. When the smallest begins to cry, the man quickly takes him on his lap.

"First we will cut it off, then we will kill it."

And just beneath a white, floating platform, the battleship *Arizona* holds onto her 1,100 drowned men.

"There is no confirmation that women and children were killed in the raid."

Art museum directors discuss the problem of aesthetic universals. The football crowd whoops it up in the bar.

Heavy flowers around our necks.

"The *China Daily,* the only English-language newspaper published in Beijing, is calling it the Year of the Sheep. But the China Institute of America in Manhat-tan, which bills itself as this country's oldest bicultural institution concentrating on China, decided that this was the Year of the Ram by taking a vote among its staff."

Tonight, as the year 4688 gets underway, I rub ointment on my sleeping son's chapped lips.

In a desert, the tank is hit, explodes inside, sears the men's faces, tears pieces of sharp metal into their bodies, suffocates them, ignites their uniforms, and sends up a plume of black smoke.

This will not be Vietnam.
This will not be America.

Where do we come from?

In a desert,

What are we?

The tank is hit,

Where are we going?

Explodes inside . . .

Quotations: New York Times, article on the Chinese Year of the Ram (or Sheep); Paul Gauguin, *Noa Noa;* Gulf War Media Coverage; Guillermo Gómez-Peña; President George Bush; General Colin Powell; Gauguin, *D'où venons-nous? Que sommes-nous? Où allons-nous?* (Museum of Fine Arts, Boston).

10

Diasporas

This essay asks what is at stake, politically and intellectually, in contemporary invocations of diaspora. It discusses problems of defining a traveling term, in changing global conditions. How do diaspora discourses represent experiences of displacement, of constructing homes away from home? What experiences do they reject, replace, or marginalize? How do these discourses attain comparative scope while remaining rooted/routed in specific, discrepant histories? The essay also explores the political ambivalence, the utopic/dystopic tension, of diaspora visions that are always entangled in powerful global histories. It argues that contemporary diasporic practices cannot be reduced to epiphenomena of the nation-state or of global capitalism. While defined and constrained by these structures, they also exceed and criticize them: old and new diasporas offer resources for emergent "postcolonialisms." The essay focuses on recent articulations of diasporism from contemporary black Britain and from anti-Zionist Judaism: quests for nonexclusive practices of community, politics, and cultural difference.

A few caveats are in order. This essay has the strengths and weaknesses of a survey: one sees the tips of many icebergs. Moreover, it attempts to map the terrain and define the stakes of diaspora studies in polemical and sometimes utopian ways. There is sometimes a slippage in the text between invocations of diaspora theories, diasporic discourses, and distinct historical experiences of diaspora. These are not, of course, equivalent.

But in practice it has not always been possible to keep them clearly separate, especially when one is discussing (as I am here) a kind of "theorizing" that is always embedded in particular maps and histories. Although this essay strives for comparative scope, it retains a certain North American bias. For example, it sometimes assumes a pluralist state based on ideologies (and uneven accomplishments) of assimilation. While nation-states must always, to a degree, integrate diversity, they need not do so on these terms. Words such as "minority," "immigrant," and "ethnic" will thus have a distinctly local flavor for some readers. Local, but translatable. I have begun to account for gender bias and class diversity in my topic. More needs to be done here, as well as in other domains of diasporic complexity where currently I lack competence or sensitivity.

Tracking Diaspora

An unruly crowd of descriptive/interpretive terms now jostle and converse in an effort to characterize the contact zones of nations, cultures, and regions: terms such as "border," "travel," "creolization," "transculturation," "hybridity," and "diaspora" (as well as the looser "diasporic"). Important new journals, such as *Public Culture* and *Diaspora* (or the revived *Transition*), are devoted to the history and current production of transnational cultures. In his editorial preface to the first issue of *Diaspora*, Khachig Tölölian writes, "Diasporas are the exemplary communities of the transnational moment." But he adds that diaspora will not be privileged in the new journal devoted to "transnational studies" and that "the term that once described Jewish, Greek, and Armenian dispersion now shares meanings with a larger semantic domain that includes words like immigrant, expatriate, refugee, guest-worker, exile community, overseas community, ethnic community" (Tölölian 1991: 4–5). This is the domain of shared and discrepant meanings, adjacent maps and histories, that we need to sort out and specify as we work our way into a comparative practice of intercultural studies.

It is now widely understood that the old localizing strategies—by bounded *community,* by organic *culture,* by *region,* by *center and periphery*— may obscure as much as they reveal. Roger Rouse makes this point forcefully in his contribution to *Diaspora*'s inaugural issue. Drawing on research in the linked Mexican communities of Aguililla (Michoacán) and Redwood City (California), he argues as follows:

It has become inadequate to see Aguilillan migration as a movement
between distinct communities, understood as the loci of distinct sets of
social relationships. Today, Aguilillans find that their most important kin
and friends are as likely to be living hundreds or thousands of miles away
as immediately around them. More significantly, they are often able to
maintain these spatially extended relationships as actively and effectively
as the ties that link them to their neighbors. In this regard, growing
access to the telephone has been particularly significant, allowing people
not just to keep in touch periodically but to contribute to decision-mak-
ing and participate in familial events from a considerable distance
(Rouse, 1991: 13).

Separate places become effectively a single community "through the continuous circulation of people, money, goods, and information" (14). "Transnational migrant circuits," as Rouse calls them, exemplify the kinds of
complex cultural formations that current anthropology and intercultural
studies describe and theorize.[1]

Aguilillans moving between California and Michoacán are not in diaspora; there may be, however, diasporic dimensions to their practices and
cultures of displacement, particularly for those who stay long periods, or
permanently, in Redwood City. Overall, bilocale Aguilillans inhabit a border, a site of regulated and subversive crossing. Rouse appeals to this
transnational paradigm throughout, giving it explicit allegorical force by
featuring a photo of the famous wedding of Guillermo Gómez-Peña and
Emily Hicks, staged by the Border Arts Workshop of San Diego–Tijuana
at the point where the U.S.-Mexico *frontera* crumbles into the Pacific.
Border theorists have recently argued for the critical centrality of formerly
marginal histories and cultures of crossing (Anzaldúa, 1987; Calderon and
Saldívar, 1991; Flores and Yudice, 1990; Hicks, 1991; Rosaldo, 1989).
These approaches share a good deal with diaspora paradigms. But borderlands are distinct in that they presuppose a territory defined by a geopolitical line: two sides arbitrarily separated and policed, but also joined by
legal and illegal practices of crossing and communication. Diasporas usually presuppose longer distances and a separation more like exile: a constitutive taboo on return, or its postponement to a remote future. Diasporas also connect multiple communities of a dispersed population.
Systematic border crossings may be part of this interconnection, but
multilocale diaspora cultures are not necessarily defined by a specific
geopolitical boundary. It is worth holding onto the historical and geographic specificity of the two paradigms, while recognizing that the con-

crete predicaments denoted by the terms "border" and "diaspora" bleed into each other. As we will see below, diasporic forms of longing, memory, and (dis)identification are shared by a broad spectrum of minority and migrant populations. And dispersed peoples, once separated from homelands by vast oceans and political barriers, increasingly find themselves in border relations with the old country thanks to a to-and-fro made possible by modern technologies of transport, communication, and labor migration. Airplanes, telephones, tape cassettes, camcorders, and mobile job markets reduce distances and facilitate two-way traffic, legal and illegal, between the world's places.

This overlap of border and diaspora experiences in late twentieth-century everyday life suggests the difficulty of maintaining exclusivist paradigms in our attempts to account for transnational identity formations. When I speak of the need to sort out paradigms and maintain historical specificity, I do not mean the imposition of strict meanings and authenticity tests. (The quintessential borderland is El Paso–Juárez. Or is it Tijuana–San Diego? Can *la ligna* be displaced to Redwood City, or to Mexican American neighborhoods of Chicago?) William Safran's essay in the first issue of *Diaspora*, "Diasporas in Modern Societies: Myths of Homeland and Return" (1991), seems, at times, to be engaged in such an operation. His undertaking and the problems he encounters may help us see what is involved in identifying the range of phenomena we are prepared to call "diasporic."

Safran discusses a variety of collective experiences in terms of their similarity to and difference from a defining model. He defines diasporas as follows: "expatriate minority communities" (1) that are dispersed from an original "center" to at least two "peripheral" places; (2) that maintain a "memory, vision, or myth about their original homeland"; (3) that "believe they are not—and perhaps cannot be—fully accepted by their host country"; (4) that see the ancestral home as a place of eventual return, when the time is right; (5) that are committed to the maintenance or restoration of this homeland; and (6) whose consciousness and solidarity as a group are "importantly defined" by this continuing relationship with the homeland (Safran 1991: 83–84). These, then, are the main features of diaspora: a history of dispersal, myths/memories of the homeland, alienation in the host (bad host?) country, desire for eventual return, ongoing support of the homeland, and a collective identity importantly defined by this relationship.

"In terms of that definition," Safran writes, "we may legitimately speak of the Armenian, Maghrebi, Turkish, Palestinian, Cuban, Greek, and perhaps Chinese diasporas at present and of the Polish diaspora of the past, although none of them fully conforms to the 'ideal type' of the Jewish diaspora" (84). Perhaps a hesitation is expressed by the quotes surrounding "ideal type," a sense of the danger in constructing, here at the outset of an important comparative project, a definition that identifies the diasporic phenomenon too closely with one group. Indeed, large segments of Jewish historical experience do not meet the test of Safran's last three criteria: a strong attachment to and desire for literal return to a well-preserved homeland. Safran himself later notes that the notion of "return" for Jews is often an eschatological or utopian projection in response to a present dystopia. And there is little room in his definition for the principled *ambivalence* about physical return and attachment to land which has characterized much Jewish diasporic consciousness, from biblical times on. Jewish anti-Zionist critiques of teleologies of return are also excluded. (These strong "diasporist" arguments will be discussed below.)

It is certainly debatable whether the cosmopolitan Jewish societies of the Mediterranean (and Indian Ocean) from the eleventh to the thirteenth centuries, the "geniza world" documented by the great historian of transnational cultures, S. D. Goitein, was oriented as a community, or collection of communities, primarily through attachments to a lost homeland (Goitein, 1967–1993). This sprawling social world was linked through cultural forms, kinship relations, business circuits, and travel trajectories, as well as through loyalty to the religious centers of the diaspora (in Babylon, Palestine, and Egypt). The attachment to specific cities (sometimes superseding ties of religion and ethnicity) characteristic of Goitein's medieval world casts doubt on any definition that would "center" the Jewish diaspora in a single land. Among Sephardim after 1492, the longing for "home" could be focused on a city in Spain at the same time as on the Holy Land. Indeed, as Jonathan Boyarin has pointed out, Jewish experience often entails "multiple experiences of rediasporization, which do not necessarily *succeed* each other in historical memory but echo back and forth" (personal communication, October 3, 1993).

As a multiply centered diaspora network, the medieval Jewish Mediterranean may be juxtaposed with the modern "black Atlantic" described by Paul Gilroy, whose work will be discussed below. Although the economic and political bases of the two networks may differ—the former commercially self-sustaining, the latter caught up in colonial/neocolonial forces—

the cultural forms sustaining and connecting the two scattered "peoples" are comparable within the range of diasporic phenomena. In Safran's prefiguration of a comparative field—especially in his "centered" diaspora model, oriented by continuous cultural connections to a source and by a teleology of "return"—African American / Caribbean / British cultures do not qualify. These histories of displacement fall into a category of quasi-diasporas, showing only some diasporic features or moments. Similarly, the South Asian diaspora—which, as Amitav Ghosh has argued (1989), is oriented not so much to roots in a specific place and a desire for return as around an ability to recreate a culture in diverse locations—falls outside the strict definition.

Safran is right to focus attention on defining "diaspora." What is the range of experiences covered by the term? Where does it begin to lose definition? His comparative approach is certainly the best way to specify a complex discursive and historical field. Moreover, his juxtapositions are often very enlightening, and he does not, in practice, strictly enforce his definitional checklist. But we should be wary of constructing our working definition of a term like "diaspora" by recourse to an "ideal type," with the consequence that groups become identified as more or less diasporic, having only two, or three, or four of the basic six features. Even the "pure" forms, as I've suggested, are ambivalent, even embattled, over basic features. Furthermore, at different times in their history, societies may wax and wane in diasporism, depending on changing possibilities—obstacles, openings, antagonisms, and connections—in their host countries and transnationally.

We should be able to recognize the strong entailment of Jewish history on the language of diaspora without making that history a definitive model. Jewish (and Greek and Armenian) diasporas can be taken as nonnormative starting points for a discourse that is traveling or hybridiz-ing in new global conditions. For better or worse, diaspora discourse is being widely appropriated. It is loose in the world, for reasons having to do with decolonization, increased immigration, global communications, and transport—a whole range of phenomena that encourage multilocale attachments, dwelling, and traveling within and across nations. A more polythetic definition (Needham, 1975) than Safran's might retain his six features, along with others. I have already stressed, for example, that the transnational connections linking diasporas need not be articulated pri-marily through a real or symbolic homeland—at least not to the degree that Safran implies. Decentered, lateral connections may be as important as those formed around a teleology of origin/return. And a shared, ongoing history of displacement, suffering, adaptation, or resistance may be as important as the projection of a specific origin.

Whatever the working list of diasporic features, no society can be expected to qualify on all counts, throughout its history. And the discourse of diaspora will necessarily be modified as it is translated and adopted. For example, the Chinese diaspora is now being explicitly discussed.[2] How will this history, this articulation of travels, homes, memories, and transnational connections, appropriate and shift diaspora discourse? Different diasporic maps of displacement and connection can be compared on the basis of family resemblance, of shared elements, no subset of which is defined as essential to the discourse. A polythetic field would seem most conducive to tracking (rather than policing) the contemporary range of diasporic forms.

Diaspora's Borders

A different approach would be to specify the discursive field diacritically. Rather than locating essential features, we might focus on diaspora's borders, on what it defines itself against. And, we might ask, what articulations of identity are currently being replaced by diaspora claims? It is important to stress that the relational positioning at issue here is a process not of absolute othering but rather of entangled tension. Diasporas are caught up with and defined against (1) the norms of nation-states and (2) indigenous, and especially autochthonous, claims by "tribal" peoples.

The nation-state, as common territory and time, is traversed and, to varying degrees, subverted by diasporic attachments. Diasporic populations do not come from elsewhere in the same way that "immigrants" do. In assimilationist national ideologies such as those of the United States, immigrants may experience loss and nostalgia, but only en route to a whole new home in a new place. Such ideologies are designed to integrate immigrants, not people in diasporas. Whether the national narrative is one of common origins or of gathered populations, it cannot assimilate groups that maintain important allegiances and practical connections to a homeland or a dispersed community located elsewhere. Peoples whose sense of identity is centrally defined by collective histories of displacement and violent loss cannot be "cured" by merging into a new national community.

This is especially true when they are the victims of ongoing, structural prejudice. Positive articulations of diaspora identity reach outside the normative territory and temporality (myth/history) of the nation-state.[3]

But are diaspora cultures consistently antinationalist? What about their own national aspirations? Resistance to assimilation can take the form of reclaiming another nation that has been lost, elsewhere in space and time, but that is powerful as a political formation here and now. There are, of course, antinationalist nationalisms, and I do not want to suggest that diasporic cultural politics are somehow innocent of nationalist aims or chauvinist agendas. Indeed, some of the most violent articulations of purity and racial exclusivism come from diaspora populations. But such discourses are usually weapons of the (relatively) weak. It is important to distinguish nationalist critical longing, and nostalgic or eschatological visions, from actual nation building—with the help of armies, schools, police, and mass media. "Nation" and "nation-state" are not identical.[4] A certain prescriptive antinationalism, now intensely focused by the Bosnian horror, need not blind us to differences between dominant and subaltern claims. Diasporas have rarely founded nation-states: Israel is the prime example. And such "homecomings" are, by definition, the negation of diaspora.

Whatever their ideologies of purity, diasporic cultural forms can never, in practice, be exclusively nationalist. They are deployed in transnational networks built from multiple attachments, and they encode practices of accommodation with, as well as resistance to, host countries and their norms. Diaspora is different from travel (though it works through travel practices) in that it is not temporary. It involves dwelling, maintaining communities, having collective homes away from home (and in this it is different from exile, with its frequently individualist focus). Diaspora discourse articulates, or bends together, both roots *and* routes to construct what Gilroy (1987) describes as alternate public spheres, forms of community consciousness and solidarity that maintain identifications outside the national time/space in order to live inside, with a difference. Diaspora cultures are not separatist, though they may have separatist or irredentist moments. The history of Jewish diaspora communities shows selective accommodation with the political, cultural, commercial, and everyday life forms of "host" societies. And the black diaspora culture currently being articulated in postcolonial Britain is concerned to struggle for different ways to be "British"—ways to stay and be different, to be British *and something else* complexly related to Africa and the Americas, to shared histories of enslavement, racist subordination, cultural survival, hybridization, resistance, and political rebellion. Thus, the term "diaspora" is a signifier not simply of transnationality and movement but of political struggles to define the local, as distinctive community, in historical contexts of displacement. The simultaneous strategies of community maintenance and interaction combine the discourses and skills of what Vijay Mishra has termed "diasporas of exclusivism" and "diasporas of the border" (1994).

The specific cosmopolitanisms articulated by diaspora discourses are in constitutive tension with nation-state / assimilationist ideologies. They are also in tension with indigenous, and especially autochthonous, claims. These challenge the hegemony of modern nation-states in a different way. Tribal or Fourth World assertions of sovereignty and "first-nationhood" do not feature histories of travel and settlement, though these may be part of the indigenous historical experience. They stress continuity of habitation, aboriginality, and often a "natural" connection to the land. Diaspora cultures, constituted by displacement, may resist such appeals on political principle—as in anti-Zionist Jewish writing, or in black injunctions to "stand" and "chant down Babylon." And they may be structured around a *tension* between return and deferral: "religion of the land" / "religion of the book" in Jewish tradition; or "roots" / "cut 'n' mix" aesthetics in black vernacular cultures.

Diaspora exists in practical, and at times principled, tension with nativist identity formations. The essay by Daniel and Jonathan Boyarin that I will discuss below makes a diasporist critique of autochthonous ("natural") but not indigenous ("historical") formulations. When claims to "natural" or "original" identity with the land are joined to an irredentist project and the coercive power of an exclusivist state, the results can be profoundly ambivalent and violent, as in the Jewish state of Israel. Indeed, claims of a primary link with the "homeland" usually must override conflicting rights and the history of others in the land. Even ancient homelands have seldom been pure or discrete. Moreover, what are the historical and/or indigenous rights of *relative* newcomers—fourth-generation Indians in Fiji, or even Mexicans in the southwestern United States since the sixteenth century? How long does it take to become "indigenous"? Lines too strictly drawn between "original" inhabitants (who often themselves replaced prior populations) and subsequent immigrants risk ahistoricism. With all these qualifications, however, it is clear that the claims to political legitimacy made by peoples who have inhabited a territory since before recorded history and those who arrived by steamboat or airplane will be founded on very different principles.

Diasporist and autochthonist histories, the aspirations of migrants and natives, do come into direct political antagonism; the clearest current example is Fiji. But when, as is often the case, both function as "minority" claims against a hegemonic/assimilationist state, the antagonism may be muted. Indeed, there are significant areas of overlap. "Tribal" predicaments, in certain historical circumstances, are diasporic. For example, inasmuch as diasporas are dispersed networks of peoples who share common historical experiences of dispossession, displacement, adaptation, and so forth, the kinds of transnational alliances currently being forged by Fourth World peoples contain diasporic elements. United by similar claims to "firstness" on the land and by common histories of decimation and marginality, these alliances often deploy diasporist visions of return to an original place—a land commonly articulated in visions of nature, divinity, mother earth, and the ancestors.

Dispersed tribal peoples, those who have been dispossessed of their lands or who must leave reduced reserves to find work, may claim "diasporic" identities. Inasmuch as their distinctive sense of themselves is oriented toward a lost or alienated home defined as aboriginal (and thus "outside" the surrounding nation-state), we can speak of a diasporic dimension of contemporary tribal life. Indeed, recognition of this dimension has been important in disputes about tribal membership. The category "tribe," which was developed in U.S. law to distinguish settled Indians from roving, dangerous "bands," places a premium on localism and rootedness. Tribes with too many members living away from the homeland may have difficulty asserting their political/cultural status. This was the case for the Mashpee, who in 1978 failed to establish continuous "tribal" identity in court (Clifford, 1988: 277–346).

Thus, when it becomes important to assert the existence of a dispersed people, the language of diaspora comes into play, as a moment or dimension of tribal life.[5] All communities, even the most locally rooted, maintain structured travel circuits, linking members "at home" and "away." Under changing conditions of mass communication, globalization, postcolonialism, and neocolonialism, these circuits are selectively restructured and rerouted according to *internal and eternal* dynamics. Within the diverse array of contemporary diasporic cultural forms, tribal displacements and networks are distinctive. For in claiming both autochthony and a specific, transregional worldliness, new tribal forms bypass an opposition between rootedness and displacement—an opposition underlying many visions of modernization seen as the inevitable destruction of autochthonous attachments by global forces. Tribal groups have, of course, never been simply "local": they have always been rooted and routed in particular landscapes, regional and interregional networks.[6] What may be distinctively *modern,* however, is the relentless assault on indigenous sovereignty by colonial powers, transnational capital, and emerging nation-states. If tribal groups survive, it is now frequently in artificially reduced and displaced conditions, with segments of their populations living in cities away from the land, temporarily or even permanently. In these conditions, the older forms of tribal cosmopolitanism (practices of travel, spiritual quest, trade, exploration, warfare, labor migrancy, visiting, and political alliance) are supplemented by more properly diasporic forms (practices of long-term dwelling away from home). The permanence of this dwelling, the frequency of returns or visits to homelands, and the degree of estrangement between urban and landed populations vary considerably. But the specificity of tribal diasporas, increasingly crucial *dimensions* of collective life, lies in the relative proximity and frequency of connection with land-based communities claiming autochthonous status.

I have been using the term "tribal" loosely to designate peoples who claim natural or "first-nation" sovereignty. They occupy the autochthonous end of a spectrum of indigenous attachments: peoples who deeply "belong" in a place by dint of continuous occupancy over an extended period. (Precisely how long it takes to *become* indigenous is always a political question.) Tribal cultures are not diasporas; their sense of rootedness in the land is precisely what diasporic peoples have lost. Yet, as we have seen, the tribal-diasporic opposition is not absolute. Like diaspora's other defining border with hegemonic nationalism, the opposition is a zone of relational contrast, including similarity and entangled difference. In the late twentieth century, all or most communities have diasporic dimensions (moments, tactics, practices, articulations). Some are more diasporic than others. I have suggested that it is not possible to define "diaspora" sharply, either by recourse to essential features or to privative oppositions. But it is possible to perceive a loosely coherent, adaptive constellation of responses to dwelling-in-displacement. The currency of these responses is inescapable.

The Currency of Diaspora Discourses

The language of diaspora is increasingly invoked by displaced peoples who feel (maintain, revive, invent) a connection with a prior home. This sense of connection must be strong enough to resist erasure through the normalizing processes of forgetting, assimilating, and distancing. Many minority groups that have not previously identified in this way are now reclaiming diasporic origins and affiliations. What is the currency, the value and the contemporaneity, of diaspora discourse?

Association with another nation, region, continent, or world-historical force (such as Islam) gives added weight to claims against an oppressive national hegemony. Like tribal assertions of sovereignty, diasporic iden-tifications reach beyond mere ethnic status within the composite, liberal state. The phrase "diasporic community" conveys a stronger sense of difference than, for example, "ethnic neighborhood" used in the language of pluralist nationalism. This stronger difference, this sense of being a "people" with historical roots and destinies outside the time/space of the host nation, is not separatist. (Rather, separatist desires are just one of its moments.) Whatever their eschatological longings, diaspora communities are "not-here to stay." Diaspora cultures thus mediate, in a lived tension, the experiences of separation and entanglement, of living here and remem-bering/desiring another place. If we think of displaced populations in almost any large city, the transnational urban swirl recently analyzed by Ulf Hannerz (1992), the role for mediating cultures of this kind will be apparent.

Diasporic language appears to be replacing, or at least supplementing, minority discourse.[7] Transnational connections break the binary relation of "minority" communities with "majority" societies—a dependency that structures projects of both assimilation and resistance. And it gives a strengthened spatial/historical content to older mediating concepts such as W. E. B. Du Bois's notion of "double consciousness." Moreover, diaspo-ras are not exactly immigrant communities. The latter could be seen as temporary, a site where the canonical three generations struggled through a hard transition to ethnic American status. But the "immigrant" process never worked very well for Africans, enslaved or free, in the New World. And the so-called new immigrations of non-European peoples of color similarly disrupt linear assimilation narratives (see especially Schiller et al., 1992).[8] Although there is a range of acceptance and alienation associ-ated with ethnic and class variations, the masses of these new arrivals are kept in subordinate positions by established structures of racial exclusion. Moreover, their immigration often has a less all-or-nothing quality, given transport and communications technologies that facilitate multilocale communities. (On the role of television, see Naficy, 1991.) Large sections of New York City, it is sometimes said, are "parts of the Caribbean," and vice versa (Sutton and Chaney, 1987). Diasporist discourses reflect the sense of being part of an ongoing transnational network that includes the homeland not as something simply left behind but as a place of attachment in a contrapuntal modernity.[9]

Diaspora consciousness is thus constituted both negatively and positively. It is constituted negatively by experiences of discrimination and exclusion. The barriers facing racialized sojourners are often reinforced by socioeconomic constraints, particularly—in North America—the development of a post-Fordist, nonunion, low-wage sector offering very limited opportunities for advancement. This regime of "flexible accumulation" requires massive transnational flows of capital and labor—depending on, and producing, diasporic populations. Casualization of labor and the revival of outwork production have increased the proportion of women in the workforce, many of them recent immigrants to industrial centers (Cohen, 1987; Harvey, 1989; Mitter, 1986; Potts, 1990; Sassen-Koob, 1982). These developments have produced an increasingly familiar mobility "hourglass"—masses of exploited labor at the bottom and a very narrow passage to a large, relatively affluent middle and upper class (Rouse, 1991: 13). New immigrants confronting this situation, like the Aguilillans in Redwood City, may establish transregional identities, maintained through travel and telephone circuits, that do not stake everything on an increasingly risky future in a single nation. It is worth adding that a negative experience of racial and economic marginalization can also lead to new coalitions: one thinks of Maghrebi diasporic consciousness uniting Algerians, Moroccans, and Tunisians living in France, where a common history of colonial and neocolonial exploitation contributes to new solidarities. And the moment in 1970s Britain when the exclusionist term "black" was appropriated to form antiracial alliances between immigrant South Asians, Afro-Caribbeans, and Africans provides another example of a negative articulation of diaspora networks.

Diaspora consciousness is produced positively through identification with world-historical cultural/political forces, such as "Africa" or "China." The process may not be as much about being African or Chinese as about being American or British or wherever one has settled, differently. It is also about feeling global. Islam, like Judaism in a predominantly Christian culture, can offer a sense of attachment elsewhere, to a different temporality and vision, a discrepant modernity. I'll have more to say below about positive, indeed utopian, diasporism in the current transnational moment. Suffice it to say that diasporic consciousness "makes the best of a bad situation." Experiences of loss, marginality, and exile (differentially cushioned by class) are often reinforced by systematic exploitation and blocked advancement. This constitutive suffering coexists with the skills of survival: strength in adaptive distinction, discrepant cosmopolitanism, and stubborn visions of renewal. Diaspora consciousness lives loss and hope as a defining tension.

The currency of diaspora discourses extends to a wide range of populations and historical predicaments. People caught up in transnational movements of capital improvise what Aihwa Ong has termed "flexible citizenship," with striking differences of power and privilege. The range extends from binational citizens in Aguililla / Redwood City or Haiti/Brooklyn to the Chinese investor "based" in San Francisco who claims, "I can live anywhere in the world, but it must be near an airport" (Ong, 1993: 41). This pseudo-universal cosmopolitan bravado stretches the limit of the term "diaspora." But to the extent that the investor, in fact, identifies and is identified as "Chinese," maintaining significant connections elsewhere, the term is appropriate. Ong says of this category of Chinese immigrants: "Their subjectivity is at once deterritorialized in relation to a particular country, though highly localized in relation to family" (Ong, 1993: 771–772). Since family is rarely in one place, where exactly do they "live"?

What is the political significance of this particular crossing-up of national identities by a traveler in the circuits of Pacific Rim capitalism? In light of bloody nationalist struggles throughout the world, the investor's transnational diasporism may appear progressive. Seen in connection with exploitative, "flexible" labor regimes in the new Asian and Pacific economies, his mobility may evoke a less positive response. The political and critical valence of diasporic subversions is never guaranteed. Much more could be said about class differences among diasporic populations. In distinguishing, for example, affluent Asian business families living in North America from creative writers, academic theorists, and destitute "boat people" or Khmers fleeing genocide, one sees clearly that degrees of diasporic alienation, the mix of coercion and freedom in cultural (dis)identifications, and the pain of loss and displacement are highly relative.

Diaspora experiences and discourses are entangled, never clear of commodification. (Nor is commodification their only outcome.) Diasporism can be taken up by a range of multicultural pluralisms, some with quasi-official status. For example, the Los Angeles Festival of 1991, orchestrated on a grand scale by Peter Sellars, celebrated the lumpy U.S. melting pot by giving the bewildering diversity of Los Angeles a global reach. The festival connected Thai neighborhoods with imported dancers from Thailand. The same was done for Pacific islanders and various Pacific Rim peoples.[10] Transnational ethnicities were collected and displayed in avant-garde juxtaposition, ostensibly to consecrate a non-Eurocentric art/culture environment. Los Angeles, successful host to the Olympics, could be a true "world city." The festival was well funded by Japanese and American corporate sponsors, and for the most part it delivered a nonthreatening, aestheticized transnationalism. The low-wage sweatshops where many members of the celebrated populations work were not featured as sites for either "art" or "culture" in this festival of diasporas.[11]

Reacting to trends in the U.S. academy, bell hooks has pointed out that international or postcolonial issues are often more comfortably dealt with than antagonisms closer to home, differences structured by race and class (hooks, 1989, 1990; see also Spivak, 1989). Adapting her concern to the present context, we see that theories and discourses that diasporize or internationalize "minorities" can deflect attention from long-standing, structured inequalities of class and race. It is as if the problem were multinationalism—issues of translation, education, and tolerance—rather than of economic exploitation and racism. While clearly necessary, making *cultural* room for Salvadorans, Samoans, Sikhs, Haitians, or Khmers does not, of itself, produce a living wage, decent housing, or health care. Moreover, at the level of everyday social practice, cultural differences are persistently racialized, classed, and gendered. Diaspora theories need to account for these concrete, cross-cutting structures.

Diasporic experiences are always gendered. But there is a tendency for theoretical accounts of diasporas and diaspora cultures to hide this fact, to talk of travel and displacement in unmarked ways, thus normalizing male experiences. Janet Wolff's analysis of gender in theories of travel is relevant here (Wolff, 1993). When diasporic experience is viewed in terms of displacement rather than placement, traveling rather than dwelling, and disarticulation rather than rearticulation, then the experiences of men will tend to predominate. Specific diaspora histories, co-territories, community practices, dominations, and contact relations may then be generalized into gendered postmodern globalisms, abstract nomadologies.

Retaining focus on specific histories of displacement and dwelling keeps the ambivalent politics of diaspora in view. Women's experiences are particularly revealing. Do diaspora experiences reinforce or loosen gender subordination? On the one hand, maintaining connections with homelands, with kinship networks, and with religious and cultural traditions may renew patriarchal structures. On the other, new roles and demands, new political spaces, are opened by diaspora interactions. Increasingly, for example, women migrate north from Mexico and from parts of the Caribbean, independently or quasi-independently of men. While they often do so in desperation, under strong economic or social compulsion, they may find their new diaspora predicaments leading to renegotiated gender relations. With men cut off from traditional roles and supports, with women earning an independent, if often exploitative, income, new areas of relative independence and control can emerge. Life for women in diasporic situations can be doubly painful—struggling with the material and spiritual insecurities of exile, with the demands of family and work, and with the claims of old and new patriarchies. But despite these hardships, they may refuse the option of return when it presents itself, especially when the terms are dictated by men.

At the same time, women in diaspora remain attached to, and empowered by, a "home" culture and a tradition—selectively. Fundamental values of propriety and religion, speech and social patterns, and food, body, and dress protocols are preserved and adapted in a network of ongoing connections outside the host country. But like Maxine Hong Kingston (1976), who redeems the woman warrior myth from all the stories transmitted to her from China, women sustaining and reconnecting diaspora ties do so critically, as strategies for survival in a new context. And like the Barbadian women portrayed in Paule Marshall's *Brown Girl, Brownstones* (1981)—who work hard to make a home in New York while keeping a basic "aloofness" from "this man's country"—diaspora women are caught between patriarchies, ambiguous pasts, and futures. They connect and disconnect, forget and remember, in complex, strategic ways.[12] The lived experiences of diasporic women thus involve painful difficulty in mediating discrepant worlds. "Community" can be a site both of support and oppression. A couple of quotations from Rahila Gupta offer a glimpse of a South Asian ("black British") woman's predicament:

> Young women are . . . beginning to question aspects of Asian culture, but there is not a sufficiently developed network of Black women's support groups (although much valuable work has been done in this area) to enable them to operate without the support of community and family. This is a contradiction in which many women are caught: between the supportive and the oppressive aspects of the Asian community . . .
>
> Patriarchal oppression was a reality of our lives before we came to Britain, and the fact that the family and community acted as sites of resistance to racist oppression has delayed and distorted our coming together as women to fight this patriarchal oppression. (Gupta, 1988: 27, 29).

The book from which these quotations are taken, *Charting the Journey: Writings by Black and Third World Women* (Grewal, 1988), maps a complex overlapping field of articulations and disarticulations in contemporary Britain—what Avtar Brah has called a "diasporic space."[13] Grewal's anthology presents common experiences of postcolonial displacement, racialization, and political struggle, as well as sharp differences of generation, of region, of sexuality, of culture, and of religion. A possible coalition of diverse "black British" and "Third World" women requires constant negotiation and attention to discrepant histories.

Do diasporic affiliations inhibit or enhance coalitions? There is no clear answer. Many Caribbeans in New York, for example, have maintained a sense of connection with their home islands, a distinct sense of cultural, and sometimes class, identity that sets them apart from African Americans, people with whom they share material conditions of racial and class subordination. Scarce resources and the mechanisms of a hierarchical social system reinforce this response. It is not inevitable. On the one hand, feelings of diasporic identity can encourage antagonism, a sense of superiority to other minorities and migrant populations.[14] On the other, shared histories of colonization, displacement, and racialization can form the basis for coalitions, as in the anti-Thatcherite alliances of "black" Britain which mobilized Africans, Afro-Caribbeans, and South Asians in the 1970s. But such alliances fall apart and recombine when other diasporic allegiances come into focus—a loyalty to Islam in the Salman Rushdie dispute, for example. There is no guarantee of "postcolonial" solidarity. Interdiaspora politics proceeds by tactics of collective articulation *and* disarticulation. As Avtar Brah has written concerning the debates of the late 1980s surrounding terms for diasporic community in Britain, "The usage of 'black,' 'Indian' or 'Asian' is determined not so much by the nature of its referent as by its semiotic function within different discourses. These various meanings signal differing political strategies and outcomes. They mobilize different sets of cultural and political identities, and set limits to where the boundaries of a 'community' are established" (Brah, 1992: 130–131).

The Black Atlantic

Diaspora communities, constituted by displacement, are sustained in hybrid historical conjunctures. With varying degrees of urgency, they negotiate and resist the social realities of poverty, violence, policing, racism, and political and economic inequality. They articulate alternate public spheres, interpretive communities where critical alternatives (both traditional and emergent) can be expressed. The work of Paul Gilroy sketches a complex map/history of one of the principal components of diasporic Britain: the Afro-Caribbean / British / American "Black Atlantic."

In *There Ain't No Black in the Union Jack* (1987), Gilroy shows how the diaspora culture of black settler communities in Britain articulates a specific set of local and global attachments. On one level, diaspora culture's expressive forms (particularly music) function in the defense of particular neighborhoods against policing and various forms of racist violence. On another level, they offer a wider "critique of capitalism" and a network of transnational connections. In Gilroy's account, the black diaspora is a cosmopolitan, Atlantic phenomenon, embroiled in and transcending national antagonisms such as Thatcherite England's "cultural politics of race and nation." It reinvents earlier strands of Pan-Africanism, but with a postcolonial twist and a 1990s British-European tilt. St. Clair Drake has distinguished "traditional" from "continental" Pan-Africanist movements (1982: 353–359). The former had its origins in the Americas, and it emerged strongly in the late nineteenth century through the work of black churches, colleges, and the political movements associated with Marcus Garvey and W. E. B. Du Bois. It was a transatlantic phenomenon. With the postwar emergence of African states, African nationalist leaders moved to the forefront, and Pan-Africanism's center of gravity moved to continental Africa. The allied political visions of Kwame Nkrumah and George Padmore would lead the way. Writing in the 1980s and 1990s in the wake of this vision's retreat, Gilroy returns the "black" cultural tradition to a historically decentered, or multiply centered, Atlantic space. In the process, he breaks the primary connection of black America with Africa, introducing a third paradigmatic experience: the migrations and resettlings of black British populations in the period of European colonial decline.

Gilroy's brilliantly argued and provocative new book, *The Black Atlantic: Modernity and Double Consciousness* (1993a), projects in historical depth a diverse black diaspora culture that cannot be reduced to any national or ethnically based tradition. This map/narrative foregrounds histories of crossing, migration, exploration, interconnection, and travel—forced and voluntary. A collection of linked essays on black intellectual history, *The Black Atlantic* rereads canonical figures in a transoceanic perspective, questioning their inscription in an ethnically or racially defined tradition: Du Bois in Germany; Frederick Douglass as ship caulker and participant in a maritime political culture; Richard Wright in Paris, connecting with the anticolonial Présence Africaine movement. Transnational culture-making by musicians is also given prominence, from the nineteenth-century Fisk University Jubilee Singers to contemporary reggae, hip-hop, and rap. Gilroy is preoccupied with ships, phonograph records, sound systems, and all technologies that cross, and bring across, cultural forms. The diaspora cultures he charts are thoroughly modern—with a difference.

Gilroy tracks moving vinyl, locally scratched and dubbed. But he roots—or routes—music in a wider transcultural and subaltern history of the Atlantic. Drawing on recent historical research by Peter Linebaugh and Marcus Rediker that uncovers a multiracial radical political culture spanning the eighteenth-century Atlantic (1990), Gilroy's account questions "national, nationalistic, and ethnically absolutist paradigms" (Gilroy, 1992a: 193), on both the Right and the Left. He counters reactionary discourses such as those of Enoch Powell (and a growing chorus) that invoke a "pure" national space recently invaded by threatening aliens, that assume the entanglement of Britain in black history to be a postwar, post–British Empire phenomenon (see also Shyllon, 1982). He also supplements E. P. Thompson's "making of the *English* working class" with the making of the *Atlantic* working class (a multiracial group), and challenges recent arguments from within the British labor movement for a popular "Left nationalism" to counter Thatcherism. Finally, Gilroy's black Atlantic decenters African *American* narratives, bringing the Caribbean, Britain, and Europe into the picture.

"The history of the black Atlantic," he writes, ". . . continually criss-crossed by the movement of black people—not only as commodities—but engaged in various struggles toward emancipation, autonomy, and citizenship, is a means to reexamine the problems of nationality, location, identity, and historical memory" (Gilroy, 1992a: 193). Gilroy brings into view "countercultures of modernity," bringing "black" not only into the Union Jack but also into debates over the tradition of Enlightenment rationality. This "black" element is both negative (the long history of slavery, the legacy of scientific racism, the complicity of rationality and terror in distinctively modern forms of domination) and positive (a long struggle for political and social emancipation, critical visions of equality or difference that have been generated in the black diaspora).

If there is a utopian agenda in Gilroy's transnational counterhistory, it is counterbalanced by the antagonistic violence, displacement, and loss that are *constitutive* of the cultures he celebrates: the Middle Passage, plantation slavery, old and new racist systems of dominance, and economic constraints on travel and labor migration. In *There Ain't No Black in the Union Jack*, the long fifth chapter on music and expressive culture ("Diaspora, Utopia, and the Critique of Capitalism") follows and depends for its effect upon four chapters that establish the discursive, political power of racist structures in postwar Britain. Some version of this utopic/dystopic tension is present in all diaspora cultures.[15] They begin with uprooting and loss. They are familiar with exile, with the "outsider's" exposed terror—of police, lynch mob, and pogrom. At the same time, diaspora cultures work to maintain community, selectively preserving and recovering traditions, "customizing" and "versioning" them in novel, hybrid, and often antagonistic situations.

Experiences of unsettlement, loss, and recurring terror produce discrepant temporalities—broken histories that trouble the linear, progressivist narratives of nation-states and global modernization. Homi Bhabha has argued that the homogeneous time of the nation's imagined community can never efface discontinuities and equivocations springing from minority and diasporic temporalities (1990). He points to antiprogressive processes of repetition (memories of slavery, immigration, and colonization, renewed in current contexts of policing and normative education), of supplementarity (the experience of being "belated," extra, out of synch), and of ex-centricity (a leaking of the national time/space into constitutive outsides: "The trouble with the English," Rushdie writes in *The Satanic Verses*, "is that their history happened overseas, so they don't know what it means"). Diasporic "postcolonials," in Bhabha's vision, live and narrate these historical realities as discrepant, critical modernities. He invokes the "scattered" populations gathering in the global cities, the *diaspora* where new imaginings and politics of community emerge.[16]

Gilroy probes the specific "diaspora temporality and historicity, memory and narrativity that are the articulating principles of the black political countercultures that grew inside modernity in a distinctive relationship of antagonistic indebtedness" (1993a: 266). Arguing against both modernist linear progressivism and current projections of a continuous connection with Africanity, *The Black Atlantic* uncovers a "syncopated temporality—a different rhythm of living and being." Gilroy cites Ralph Ellison: "Invisibility, let me explain, gives one a slightly different sense of time, you're never quite on the beat. Sometimes you're ahead and sometimes behind. Instead of the swift and imperceptible flowing of time, you are aware of its nodes, those points where time stands still or from which it leaps ahead. And you slip into the breaks and look around" (Gilroy, 1993a: 281). Ellison (via Gilroy) offers a black version of Walter Benjamin's practice of countermemory, a politics of interrupting historical continuities to grasp the "monads" (Ellison's "nodes"?) or "fissures" in which time stops and prophetically restarts (Benjamin, 1968). In syncopated time, effaced stories are recovered, different futures imagined.

In diaspora experience, the co-presence of "here" and "there" is articulated with an antiteleological (sometimes messianic) temporality. Linear history is broken, the present constantly shadowed by a past that is also a desired, but obstructed, future: a renewed, painful yearning. For black Atlantic diaspora consciousness, the recurring break where time stops and restarts is the Middle Passage. Enslavement and its aftermaths—displaced, repeated structures of racialization and exploitation—constitute a pattern of black experiences inextricably woven in the fabric of hegemonic modernity. These experiences form counterhistories, off-the-beat cultural critiques that Gilroy works to redeem. Afrocentric attempts to recover a direct connection with Africa, often bypassing this constitutive predicament, are both escapist and ahistorical. The "space of death" reopened by memories of slavery and in continuing experiences of racial terror casts a critical shadow on all modernist progressivisms. Gilroy supplements the analyses of Zygmunt Bauman (1989) and Michael Taussig (1986) on the complicity of rationality with racial terror. At crucial moments, the choice of death or the risk of death is the only possibility for people with no future in an oppressive system. Gilroy's reading of Frederick Douglass' struggle with the slave-breaker probes such a moment, paired with the story of Margaret Garner, whose killing of her children to spare them from slavery is retold in Toni Morrison's *Beloved*. The resulting sense of rupture, of living a radically different temporality, is expressed in an interview with Morrison quoted extensively in *The Black Atlantic*:

> Modern life begins with slavery . . . From a woman's point of view, in terms of confronting the problems of where the world is now, black women had to deal with post-modern problems in the nineteenth century and earlier. These things had to be addressed by black people a long time ago: certain kinds of dissolution, the loss of and need to reconstruct certain kinds of stability. Certain kinds of madness deliberately going mad in order, as one of the characters says in the book, "in order not to lose your mind." These strategies for survival made the truly modern person. (Gilroy, 1993a: 308).

Morrison's "modern person" is the result of struggle with a "pathology." "Slavery broke the world in half," she goes on to say. And not only for Africans: "It broke Europe." It made Europeans slave masters.

Diaspora cultures are, to varying degrees, produced by regimes of political domination and economic inequality. But these violent processes of displacement do not strip people of their ability to sustain distinctive political communities and cultures of resistance. Obviously the mix of destruction, adaptation, preservation, and creation varies with each historical case and moment. As counterdiscourses of modernity, diaspora cultures cannot claim an oppositional or primary purity. Fundamentally ambivalent, they grapple with the entanglement of subversion and the law, of invention and constraint—the complicity of dystopia and utopia. Kobena Mercer works with this constitutive entanglement in a penetrating essay, "Diaspora Culture and the Dialogic Imagination."

> There is no escape from the fact that as a diaspora people, blasted out of one history into another by the "commercial deportation" of slavery (George Lamming) and its enforced displacement, our blackness is thor-

oughly imbricated in Western modes and codes to which we arrived as
the disseminated masses of migrant dispersal. What is in question [in
recent black British film] is not the expression of some lost origin or
some uncontaminated essence in black film-language, but the adoption
of a critical "voice" that promotes consciousness of the collision of
cultures and histories that constitute our very conditions of existence.
(Mercer, 1988: 56)

There are important differences between Mercer's and Gilroy's conceptions of diaspora. Mercer's version is rigorously antiessentialist, a site of
multiple displacements and rearticulations of identity, without privilege to
race, cultural tradition, class, gender, or sexuality. Diaspora consciousness
is entirely a product of cultures and histories in collision and dialogue.
For Mercer, Gilroy's genealogy of British "blackness" continues to privilege
an "African" origin and "vernacular" forms—despite his stress on historical
rupture and hybridity and his assault on romantic Afrocentrisms (Mercer,
1990).[17] For Gilroy, Mercer represents a "premature pluralism," a postmodern evasion of the need to give historical specificity and complexity
to the term "black," seen as linked racial formations, counterhistories, and
cultures of resistance (Gilroy, 1993a: 32, 100).

I do not want to oversimplify either position in an important, evolving
dialogue that is probably symptomatic of a moment in cultural politics
and not finally resolvable. In this context it may be worth noting that,
because the signifier "diasporic" denotes a predicament of multiple locations, it slips easily into theoretical discourses informed by poststructural-
ism and notions of the multiply positioned subject. Indeed, many of these
discourses have been produced by theorists whose histories are, in varying
degrees, diasporic. The approach I have been following (in tandem with
Gilroy) insists on the routing of diaspora discourses in specific maps/
histories. Diasporic subjects are distinct versions of modern, transnational,
intercultural experience. Thus historicized, diaspora cannot become a
master trope or "figure" for modern, complex, or positional identities,
cross-cut and displaced by race, sex, gender, class, and culture.

Gilroy's specific map/history is certainly open to amendment and critique—for skewing "black Britain" in the direction of an Atlantic world
with the Afro-Caribbean at its center, for focusing on practices of travel
and cultural production that have, with important exceptions, not been
open to women, for not giving sufficient attention to cross-cutting sexualities in constituting diasporic consciousness. Moreover, his diasporic

intervention into black history reflects a specific predicament: what he has called "the peculiarities of the Black English" (Gilroy, 1993b: 49–62). *The Black Atlantic* decenters, to a degree, a sometimes normative African *American* history. To a degree. The specific experiences of plantation slavery, emancipation, South-North mobility, urbanization, and race/ethnic relations have a regional, and indeed a "national," focus that cannot be subsumed by an Atlanticist map/history of crossings. Although the roots and routes of African *American* cultures clearly pass through the Caribbean, they have been historically shaped into distinct patterns of struggle and marks of authenticity. They are not transnational or diasporic in the same way or to the same degree. Important comparative questions emerge around different histories of traveling and dwelling—specified by region (for example, the "South" as a focus of diasporic longing), by (neo)colonial history, by national entanglement, by class, and by gender. It is important to specify, too, that black South America and the hybrid Hispanic/black cultures of the Caribbean and Latin America are not, for the moment, included in Gilroy's projection. He writes from a North Atlantic / European location.[18]

Gilroy is increasingly explicit about the limitations of his "strictly provisional" undertaking (1993a: xi), presenting it as a reading of "masculinist" diasporism and as a first step open to correction and elaboration. There is no reason his privileging of the black Atlantic, for the purposes of writing a counterhistory in some depth, should necessarily silence other diasporic perspectives. With respect to contemporary Britain, one can imagine intersecting histories based, for example, on the effects of the British Empire in South Asia, or on the contributions of Islamic cultures to the making and critique of modernity. Gilroy's work tactically defines a map/history in ways that may best be seen as "anti-antiessentialist," the double negative not reducible to a positive. If diaspora is to be something about which one could write a history—and this is Gilroy's politically pointed goal—it must be something more than the name for a site of multiple displacements and reconstitutions of identity. Like "black England," the black Atlantic is a historically produced social formation. It denotes a genealogy not based on any direct connection with Africa or foundational appeal to kinship or racial identity.

In the current theoretical climate of prescriptive antiessentialism, diaspora discourses such as Gilroy's refuse to let go of a "changing same," something endlessly hybridized and in process but persistently there—

memories and practices of collective identity maintained over long stretches of time. Gilroy attempts to conceive the continuity of a "people" without recourse to land, race, or kinship as primary "grounds" of continuity.[19] What, then, is the persistent object of his history? How to circumscribe this "changing same"? The black Atlantic as a counterhistory of modernity is crucially defined by the still-open wound of slavery and racial subordination. It is also a "tradition" of cultural survival and invention out of which Gilroy writes. But before he can invoke the much-abused term "tradition"—site of a thousand essentialisms—he must redefine it, "wrench it open":

> [Tradition] can be seen to be a process rather than an end, and is used here neither to identify a lost past nor to name a culture of compensation that would restore access to it. Here, too, it does not stand in opposition to modernity nor should it conjure up wholesome, pastoral images of Africa that can be contrasted with the corrosive, aphasic power of the post-slave history of the Americas and the extended Caribbean. Tradition can now become a way of conceptualizing the *fragile communicative relationships across time and space* that are the basis *not of diaspora identities but of diaspora identifications*. Reformulated thus, [tradition] points not to a common content for diaspora cultures but to evasive qualities that make inter-cultural, trans-national diaspora *conversations between them* possible. (Gilroy, 1993a: 276, emphasis added)

Identifications not identities, acts of relationship rather than pregiven forms: this *tradition* is a network of partially connected histories, a persistently displaced and reinvented time/space of crossings.[20]

Jewish Connections

Gilroy rejects "Africa" as privileged source (a kind of Holy Land) while retaining its changing contribution to a counterculture of modernity. His history of black Atlantic diversity and conversation echoes the language of contemporary Jewish diasporism, anti-Zionist visions drawn from both Ashkenazic and Sephardic historical experiences. As we shall see, their critique of teleologies of return to a literal Jewish nation in Palestine parallels Gilroy's rejection of Afro-centered diaspora projections. The ongoing entanglement of black and Jewish diaspora visions, often rooted in biblical imagery, is salient here, as are the shared roots of Pan-Africanism and Zionism in nineteenth-century European nationalist ideologies—the influence of Heinrich von Treitschke on Du Bois, or Edward Wilmot Blyden's interest in Herder, Mazzini, and Hertzl. Nor should we forget a common history of victimization by scientific and popular racisms / anti-Semitisms, a history that tends to be lost in current black-Jewish antagonisms. (For a corrective, see Philip, 1993; and West, 1993.) Gilroy confronts these connections in the last chapter of *The Black Atlantic*. Here I merely suggest a homology between defining aspects of the two diasporas. A full discussion of the differences, tensions, and attractions of the traditions is beyond my present compass.

When understood as a practice of dwelling (differently), as an ambivalent refusal or indefinite deferral of return, and as a positive transnationalism, diaspora finds validation in the historical experiences of both displaced Africans and Jews. In discussing Safran's constitution of a comparative field, I worried about the extent to which diaspora, defined as dispersal, presupposed a center. If this center becomes associated with an actual "national" territory—rather than with a reinvented "tradition," a "book," a portable eschatology—it may devalue what I called the lateral axes of diaspora. These decentered, partially overlapping networks of communication, travel, trade, and kinship connect the several communities of a transnational "people." The centering of diasporas around an axis of origin and return overrides the specific local interactions (identifications and ruptures, both constructive and defensive) necessary for the maintenance of diasporic social forms. The empowering paradox of diaspora is that dwelling *here* assumes a solidarity and connection *there*. But *there* is not necessarily a single place or an exclusivist nation.

How is the connection (elsewhere) that makes a difference (here) remembered and rearticulated? In a forcefully argued essay, "Diaspora: Generation and the Ground of Jewish Identity," Daniel and Jonathan Boyarin defend an interactive conception of genealogy—kinship not reducible to "race" in its modern definitions—as the matrix for dispersed Jewish populations (1993). They offer sustained polemics against two potent alternatives to diasporism: Pauline universalist humanism (we are all one in the spiritual body of Christ) and autochthonous nationalism (we are all one in the place that belongs, from the beginning, to us alone). The former attains a love for humanity at the price of imperialist inclusion/conversion. The latter gains a feeling of rootedness at the expense of excluding others with old and new claims in the land. Diaspora ideology, for the Boyarins, involves a principled renunciation of both universalism and sovereignty—an embrace of the arts of exile and coexistence, aptitudes for maintaining distinction as a people in relations of daily converse with others.

Permanent conditions of relative powerlessness and minority status justify and render relatively harmless ethnocentric survival tactics—for example, imposing marks of distinction on the body (special clothing, hairstyles, circumcision), or restricting charity and community self-help to "our people." In conditions of permanent historical exile—or what amounts to the same thing, in an exile that can end *only* with the Messiah—ethnocentrism is just one tactic, never an absolute end in itself. Rabbinical diasporist ideologies, developed over twenty centuries of dispersion and drawing on biblical traditions critical of Davidic monarchy and of all claims to authenticity in the "land," in effect continue the "nomadic" strand of early Judaism. For the Boyarins, this is the mainstream of Jewish historical experience. And they assert unequivocally that the Zionist solution to the "problem" of diaspora, seen only negatively as *galut* ("exile"), is "the subversion of Jewish culture and not its culmination . . . capturing Judaism in a state" (Boyarin and Boyarin, 1993: 722, 724). Drawing on the scholarship of W. D. Davies (1992) and others, they stress the ambivalence in Jewish tradition, from biblical times to the present, regarding claims for a territorial basis of identity. "Return," defined as exclusive possession of the "land," is not the authentic outcome of Jewish history. Against the national/ethnic absolutism of contemporary Zionism, Jonathan Boyarin writes, "we Jews should recognize the strength that comes from a diversity of communal arrangements and concentrations both among Jews and with our several others. We should recognize that the copresence of those others is not a threat, but rather the condition of our lives" (1992: 129).

The Boyarins' account of diaspora aspires to be both a model *of* (historical Jewish experience) and a model *for* (contemporary hybrid identities). This aim is apparent in the following passage:

> Diasporic cultural identity teaches us that cultures are not preserved by being protected from "mixing" but probably can only continue to exist as a product of such mixing. Cultures, as well as identities, are constantly being remade. While this is true of all cultures, diasporic Jewish culture lays it bare because of the impossibility of a natural association between this people and a particular land—thus the impossibility of seeing Jewish culture as a self-enclosed, bounded phenomenon. The critical force of

this dissociation among people, language, culture, and land has been an enormous threat to cultural nativisms and integrisms, a threat that is one of the sources of anti-Semitism and perhaps one of the reasons that Europe has been much more prey to this evil than the Middle East. In other words, diasporic identity is a disaggregated identity. Jewishness disrupts the very categories of identity because it is not national, not genealogical, not religious, but all of these in dialectical tension with one another. When liberal Arabs and some Jews claim that the Jews of the Middle East are Arab Jews, we concur and think that Zionist ideology occludes something very significant when it seeks to obscure this point. The production of an ideology of a pure Jewish cultural essence that has been debased by Diaspora seems neither historically nor ethically correct. "Diasporized," that is disaggregated, identity allows the early medieval scholar Rabbi Sa'adya to be an Egyptian Arab who happens to be Jewish and also a Jew who happens to be an Egyptian Arab. Both of these contradictory propositions must be held together. (Boyarin and Boyarin, 1993: 721)

The passage expresses a powerful and moving vision, especially for a world riven by absolute oppositions of Arab and Jew. It need not detract unduly from its force to ask whether Rabbi Sa'adya's disaggregated identity would have been restricted, or differently routed, if he had been a woman. How did women "mix" cultures? And how have they transmitted, "genealogically," the marks and messages of tradition? How have women embodied diasporic Judaism, and how has Judaism marked, empowered, or constrained their bodies?

The Boyarins, in this essay at least, are silent on such questions. They do briefly invoke feminist issues in the sentences that immediately follow the passage quoted above.

Similarly, we suggest that a diasporized gender identity is possible and positive. Being a woman is some kind of special being, and there are aspects of life and practice that insist on and celebrate that speciality. But this is not simply a fixing or a freezing of all practice and performance of gender identity into one set of parameters. Human beings are divided into men and women for certain purposes, but that does not tell the whole story of their bodily identity. Rather than the dualism of gendered bodies and universal souls—the dualism that the Western tradition offers—we can substitute partially Jewish, partially Greek bodies, bodies that are sometimes gendered and sometimes not. It is this idea that we are calling diasporized identity. (Boyarin and Boyarin, 1993: 721)

Arguments from antiessentialist feminism are implicitly deployed here, and the figure of "woman" is joined to that of the Jew to evoke a model of identity as a performed cluster/tension of positionalities.[21] Would it make the same sense to say that a body was sometimes black, sometimes not, sometimes lesbian, sometimes not, sometimes poor, and so forth? Yes and no. For we approach a level of generality at which the specificities and tensions of diasporist, racialist, class, sex, and gender determinations are erased. Moreover, in this assertion of a common predicament we glimpse the hegemonizing possibilities of diasporist discourse. Skimmed over in the identification of "diasporized" gender identity are a series of historical specifications. "Human beings are divided into men and women for certain purposes." Whose purposes? What are the unequal dividing structures? How do these functional "purposes" appear from different sides of the gender divide? I have already argued that it is important to resist the tendency of diasporic identities to slide into equivalence with disaggregated, positional, performed identities in general. As they necessarily draw from antifoundationalist feminism, postcolonial critique, and various postmodernisms, contemporary diaspora discourses retain a connection with specific bodies, historical experiences of displacement that need to be held in comparative tension and partial translatability.

I have dwelt on one instance of too-quick diasporic equivalence in the Boyarins' essay to identify a persistent risk in "theoretical" comparisons, a risk that haunts my own project. Overall, the Boyarins maintain the specificity of their point of engagement, their "discrepant cosmopolitanism" (see Chapter 1, above). As observing Ashkenazic Jews, they contest for a tradition, from within. But their theory and practice preclude this "inside" as an ultimate, or even principal, location. Perhaps, as they recognize, in allegorizing diasporism they run the risk of making Jewish experience again the normative model. But in the passage just cited, diaspora is portrayed in terms of an almost postcolonial vision of hybridity. Whose experience, exactly, is being theorized? In dialogue with whom? It is clear that the Boyarins have been reading and reacting to minority and Third World authors. And Paul Gilroy is a close student of Walter Benjamin. Moreover, Asian American diaspora theorists are reading black British cultural studies. Diasporas, and diaspora theorists, cross paths in a mobile space of translations, not equivalences.

The Boyarins do not, in fact, say very much about the specific mechanisms of "genealogy" (or "generation," as they also call it). Their chief effort is devoted to critical ground-clearing, making space for multifaceted, nonreductive transmissions of the marks and messages of peoplehood. Against Pauline spirituality, they insist on carnal, socially differentiated bodies. The bodies are gendered male, which is to say they are unmarked by gender—at least in this essay.[22] (Daniel Boyarin's *Carnal Israel* [1993b], as well as his work on Saint Paul [1993a], centrally engages feminist issues.) The Boyarins argue persuasively that the multiple social transmissions of genealogy need not be reduced to a "racial" matrix of identity. But in deploying the language of "generation" and "lineage," they risk naturalizing an androcentric kinship system. As in Gilroy's history, which leans toward the diasporic practices of men, there is considerable room for specification of gendered diaspora experiences.[23]

Diasporic Pasts and Futures

The Boyarins ground their defense of diaspora in two thousand years of rabbinical ideology, as well as in concrete historical experiences of dispersed community. They state: "We propose Diaspora as a theoretical and historical model to replace national self-determination. To be sure, this would be an idealized Diaspora generalized from those situations in Jewish history when the Jews were relatively free from persecution and yet constituted by strong identity—those situations, moreover, within which promethean Jewish creativity was not antithetical, indeed was synergistic with a general cultural activity" (Boyarin and Boyarin, 1993: 711). Jewish life in Muslim Spain before the expulsions—a rich, multireligious, multicultural florescence—is one of the historical moments redeemed by this vision. "The same figure, a Nagid, an Ibn Gabirol, or a Maimonides, can be simultaneously the vehicle for the preservation of traditions and of the mixing of cultures" (721). We enter, here, the whole "geniza world" of S. D. Goitein, the Mediterranean of the eleventh to the thirteenth centuries (and beyond) where Jews, Muslims, and Christians lived, traded, borrowed, and conversed in the process of maintaining distinct communities.[24]

There are no innocent periods of history, and the geniza world had its share of intolerance. Without reducing these centuries to a romanticized multiculturalism, one can recognize an extraordinary cosmopolitan network. As Goitein and his followers have shown, lines of identity were drawn differently, often less absolutely than in the modern era. For long periods and in many places, people of distinct religions, races, cultures, and languages coexisted. Difference was articulated through connection, not separation. In his book *After Jews and Arabs,* which draws generously on Goitein's research and vision, Ammiel Alcalay portrays a Levantine world characterized by cultural mixing, relative freedom of travel, an absence of ghettos, and multilingualism—the antithesis of current national, racial, and religious separations. A sweeping work of counterhistory and cultural critique, Alcalay's study begins to make room for women's histories, specified by class, in its world of intersecting cosmopolitan cultures. In this he builds on Goitein's awareness of "the chasm between the popular local subculture of women and the worldwide Hebrew book culture of the men" (quoted in Alcalay, 1993: 138). This "chasm" need not be taken to mean that men were cosmopolitan, and women not: affluent women, at least, traveled (sometimes alone), were involved in business, held property, crossed cultural borders—but in particular ways that Jewish diaspora studies have only begun to recognize and detail.

Alcalay's history gives "regional" concreteness to a diasporist Jewish history which, in the Boyarins' version, is not connected to a specific map/history. "Jewish history" is, of course, diverse and contested. In the present Israeli state, a division between Ashkenazic and Sephardic/Mizrahi populations reflects distinct diaspora experiences. As reclaimed in Alcalay's book, the Sephardic strand offers a specific counterhistory of Arab/Jewish coexistence and crossover. Sephardic/Mizrahi histories may also generate "diasporist" critiques by Arab-Jewish exiles within the Israeli "homeland" (Lavie, 1992; Shohat, 1988, 1989). Sephardic regional roots and emerging alliances with "Third World" or "Arab" movements can articulate networks that decenter both the diasporist figure of the "wandering Jew" and the overwhelming importance of the Holocaust as defining moment in modern "Jewish history." In Israel, a minority of European Jews have taken a leading role in defining an exclusivist Jewish state—predicated on religious, ethnic, linguistic, and racial subordinations. Sephardic/Mizrahi counterhistories question this state's hegemonic self-definition. Important as these struggles may be, however, one should not overgeneralize from current hierarchical oppositions in Israel. Both Sephardic and Ashkenazic traditions are complex, containing nationalist and antinationalist strands. There are strong resources for a *diasporist* anti-Zionism in pre-Holocaust Ashkenazi history. (Indeed, the recent signing of a fragile peace accord between Israel and the Palestine Liberation Organization makes this vision, these historical resources, seem less anachronistic. If a viable political arrangement for sharing the land of Palestine finally emerges, Jews and Arabs will need to recover diasporist skills for maintaining difference in contact and accommodation.)

Max Weinreich's historical research has shown that the maintenance of Ashkenazic Jewishness (*yidishkeyt*) was not primarily the result of forced, or voluntary, separation in distinct neighborhoods or ghettos. This relatively recent "ghetto myth" supports an ethnic absolutism (as Gilroy might put it) that denies the interactive and adaptive process of historical Jewish identity.

> Ashkenazic reality is to be sought between the two poles of absolute identity with and absolute remoteness from the coterritorial non-Jewish communities. To compress it into a formula, what the Jews aimed at was not isolation from Christians but insulation from Christianity. Although, throughout the ages, many Jews must be supposed to have left the fold, the community as a whole did succeed in surviving and developing. On the other hand, the close and continuous ties of the Jews with their neighbors, which used to be severed only for a while during actual outbreaks of persecutions, manifested themselves in customs and folk beliefs; in legends and songs; in literary production, etc. The culture patterns prevalent among Ashkenazic Jews must be classified as Jewish, but very many of them are specifically Ashkenazic. They are mid-course formations as those found wherever cultures meet along frontiers, in border zones or in territories with mixed populations. (Weinreich, 1967: 2204)

Weinreich's prime specimen of Ashkenazic border culture is Yiddish, the "fusion language" of which he is the preeminent historian. He also lays great stress on the open-ended process of Talmudic interpretation through which laws (*dinim*) and customs (*minhogim*) are continuously adapted and clarified anew in the light of the Torah (which, the Yiddish saying goes, "contains everything"). The defining loyalty here is to an open text, a set of interpretable norms, not to a "homeland" or a even to an "ancient" tradition. I have been quoting from a summary essay of 1967 in which Weinreich characterizes Ashkenazic diasporic history without any mention of return, Holy Land, or Israel. The distinction of Jew and non-Jew is critical, but processual and nonessentialist: "It turns out that the very existence of a division is much more important than the actual location of the division line . . . More often than not, it appears, the distance between Jewish and non-Jewish patterns is created not by a difference in the ingredients proper but rather by the way they are interpreted as elements of the given system" (Weinreich, 1967: 2205). Difference, for Weinreich, is a process of continual renegotiation in new circumstances of dangerous and creative coexistence.[25]

What is at stake in reclaiming these different Ashkenazic and Sephardic diasporist visions, beyond their evident contribution to a critique of Zionism and other exclusivist nationalisms? An answer is suggested by my own belated route to the geniza world and the company of Goitein admirers: a remarkable hybrid work of ethnography/history/travel, *In an Antique Land,* by Amitav Ghosh (1992). An Indian novelist-cum-anthropologist, Ghosh writes of his fieldwork in the Nile Delta, and in the process uncovers a deep history of transnational connections between the Mediterranean, Middle East, and South Asia—a history onto which he grafts his own late-twentieth-century travel from one Third World place to another. In the dispersed Cairo geniza archive, he tracks the almost forgotten story of an Indian traveler to Aden, the slave and business agent of a Jewish merchant residing in Mangalore. (The history of this archive is itself an engrossing subplot.) Ghosh's search for his twelfth-century precursor opens a window on the medieval Indian Ocean, a world of extraordinary travel, trade, and coexistence among Arabs, Jews, and South Asians. Like Janet Abu-Lughod's important overview, *Before European Hegemony* (1989), and like the earlier world-historical visions of Marshall Hodgson (1993), Ghosh's account helps us remember/imagine "world systems," economic and cultural, that preceded the rise of an expansionist Europe. In the late twentieth century it is difficult to form concrete pictures of transregional networks not produced by and/or resisting the hegemony of Western techno-industrial society. These histories of alternate cosmopolitanisms and diasporic networks are redeemable (in a Benjaminian sense) as crucial political visions: worlds "after" Jews and Arabs, "after" the West and the "Rest," and "after" natives and immigrants.

Such visions and counterhistories can support strategies for nontotalizing "globalization from below." The phrase, paired with "globalization from above," is proposed by Brecher et al. (1993) to name transregional social movements that both resist and use hegemonizing technologies and communications. This constitutive entanglement is, I have argued, characteristic of modern diaspora networks. Entanglement is not necessarily cooptation. Recalling older histories of discrepant cosmopolitan contacts can empower new ways to be "traditional" on a more than local scale. Epeli Hau'ofa's recent recovery of a long history of Pacific travels in the projection of a new "Oceanian" regionalism ("our sea of islands") is a case in point (Hau'ofa et al., 1993).

The works I have been discussing maintain a clear, at times crushing, awareness of the obstacles to such futures, the constant pressure of transnational capital and national hegemonies. Yet they express, too, a stubborn hope. They do not merely lament a world that has been lost. Rather, as in diaspora discourses generally, both loss and survival are prefigurative. Of what? We lack a description and are reduced to the merely reactive, stopgap language of "posts." The term "postcolonial" (like Arjun Appadurai's "postnational") makes sense only in an emergent, or utopian, context.[26] There are no postcolonial cultures or places: only moments, tactics, discourses. "Post-" is always shadowed by "neo-." Yet "postcolonial" does describe real, if incomplete, ruptures with past structures of domination, sites of current struggle and imagined futures. Perhaps what is at stake in the historical projection of a geniza world or a black Atlantic is the "prehistory of postcolonialism." Viewed in this perspective, the diaspora discourse and history currently in the air would be about recovering non-Western, or not-only-Western, models for cosmopolitan life, nonaligned transnationalities struggling within and against nation-states, global technologies, and markets—resources for a fraught coexistence.

COWGIRL / Kou'gurl.
Custom-made cardboard box (13.2" × 10" × 2.5"), labeled; photocopied photograph of
the outlaw Jennie Metcalf; two china creamers in the form of cows.

Collated 1992

11

Immigrant

"The goal of all life is death."—Sigmund Freud

Walking down from Hampstead Station along a well-to-do residential street. It's April, and the gardens are starting to bloom in earnest. English Gardens—squeezed into boxes behind Council houses, strips along railroads. I recall reading about British soldiers carving plots in the blasted battlefields of the Somme, the Marne. Daydreaming along tranquil sidewalks, brushing against flowered shrubs, I almost miss one of the nicer homes, a small sign out front. The Freud Museum: 20 Marsfield Gardens, London NW3.

A poster: nineteenth-century photograph of a woman in Victorian dress and broad-brimmed hat. She looks coolly at the camera, fingering a big six-shooter. "Susan Hiller at the Freud Museum."

Museum and shrine, the house has a lived-in quality. Freud's study is preserved, filled with favorite images and objects, his desk half-covered with statuettes from ancient Egypt, Greece, Rome, Asia. The famous analytic couch is there.

Freud's collection of antiquities traveled with him to London when he fled the Nazis in 1938. At 20 Marsfield Gardens, terminally ill, he would spend the last year of his life, finishing *Moses and Monotheism*. He gathered

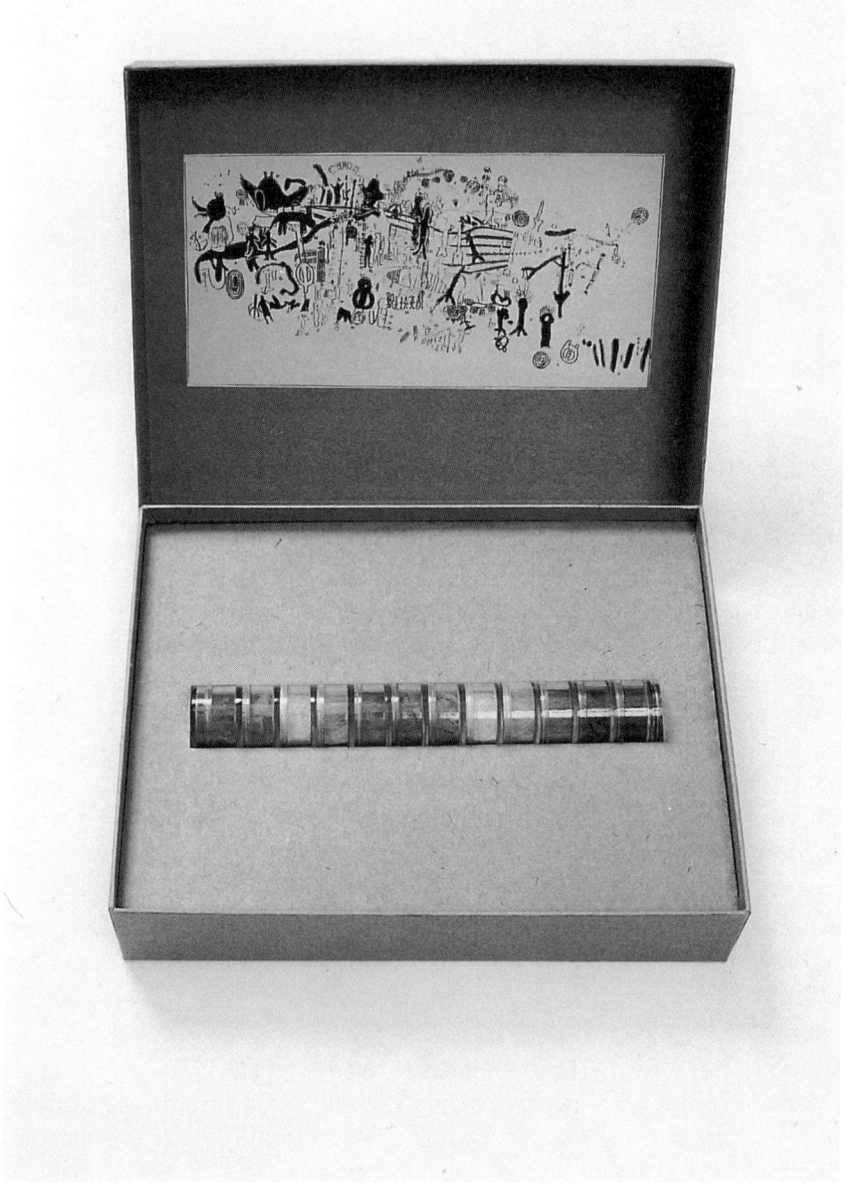

NAMA-MA / Mother.
Custom-made cardboard box (10" × 13.25" × 2.5"), labeled; photocopy of diagram showing Uluru cave paintings; Australian native earths collected at Papunya, in cosmetic
containers.

Curated 1991

himself in this house: a kind of vessel, box, a boat of the dead—carrying a body across with its beloved things.

Sources

"The term 'origin' does not mean the process by which the existent came into being, but rather what emerges from the process of becoming and disappearing. Origin is an eddy in the stream of becoming."

—Walter Benjamin

Susan Hiller brings twenty-two cardboard boxes into the Freud Museum. Opened, they are a series of small collections, displayed in a vitrine along one side of a first-floor room. They comment on Freud's archaeology, reworking his themes: memory and forgetting, antiquity, illness, comedy, cure, death, male, female, primitive, civilization, light, dark, Greek and Jewish histories, progress, repetition . . . His world. Hers.

"That's me, displaying a beautiful dress . . ."

Archaeological collecting boxes: their lids propped open, with images and writing on the inside. The bottoms contain objects, often in hollowed-out compartments. Each ensemble has been labeled with a card, printed in museum style, recording exact size, origin, a description, and the date of processing: collected 1992, collated 1992, sampled 1993, edited 1994, . . . surveyed, located, compiled, assembled, classified, bound.

One of the boxes, *"NAMA-MA/mother,"* holds a reproduction of aboriginal rock paintings from Uluru cave (Ayers Rock, Australia), along with twelve transparent cosmetic cases. Each contains soil of a slightly different color. "Native earths" are used for painting rocks and (as the cosmetic cases suggest) faces. The earths suggest an ongoing process: marking of origin, nature, bodies, kinship . . . "Archaic" and "modern," contemporary.

Movable dream labs.

PANACEA/Cure
Custom-made cardboard box (13.25" × 10" × 2.5"), labeled; photocopied newspaper advertisement; book entitled *The Life of Joanna Southcott,*

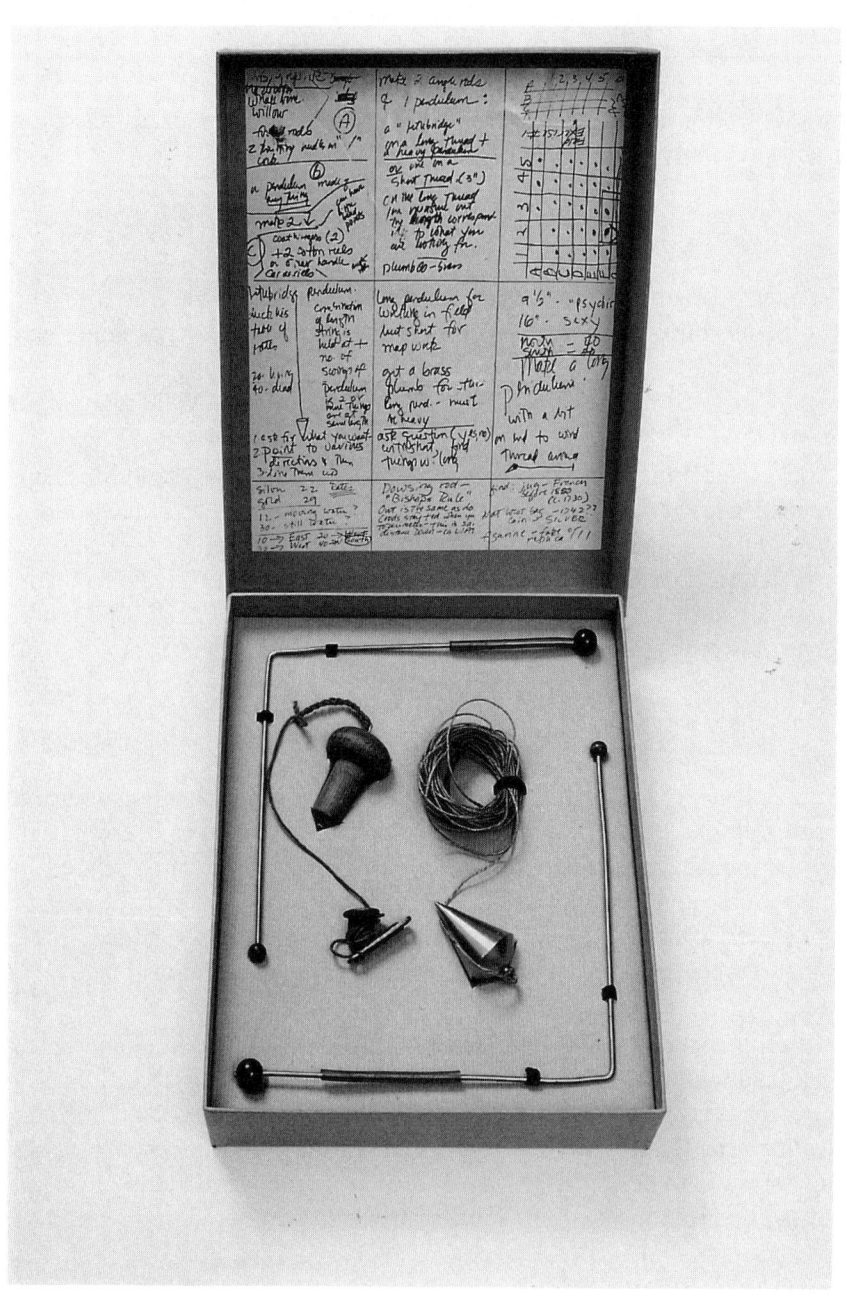

VIRGULA DIVINA / Water-Witching.
Custom-made cardboard box (13.2" × 10" × 2.5"), labeled; photocopy of artist's notes on dowsing methods; artist's handmade divining rods; two pendulae, one hand-made.

Displayed 1991

annotated and extended by the artist with photograph, flower and news-paper cutting; cover added by the artist.

Filed, 1991

Inside the lid: an advertisement (*London Evening News,* 1977) from the Panacea Society, proclaiming that "CRIME & BANDITRY, DISTRESS OF NATIONS & PERPLEXITY will continue until the Bishops open JOANNA SOUTHCOTT'S BOX of sealed writings."

"Another summer, near Vienna . . ."

Joanna Southcott, the eighteenth-century prophet, was to have given birth to the Messiah. Instead, she left a sealed box of writings which could be opened only by a convocation of the twenty-four bishops of England and Wales. (What annotations have been added to the book displayed here?)

Source of rebirth and transformation. "What does woman want?" Her closed box, book, word. Her cure for . . .

"These are just pictures of the waiting room . . ."

"*VIRGULA DIVINA/Water-Witching.*" The artist's divining rods, string, and pendulae. In the lid, her notes on dowsing.

In other boxes, I find the Greek rivers Lethe, Mnemosyne, and Acheron: corked bottles with old-fashioned tags. "*INITIATION/Beginning.*" Sources. How do we know when water's below? Where should we dig?

His room: figurines like stalagmites on every table. Egypt, Greece, Rome, Assyria, Asia . . . (And just visible in photos of his Vienna desk, two Kiddush cups, one marked with the Tablets of the Law.) An Egyptian funerary boat rests on a shelf.

Her collections: Native American potsherds (in plastic bags); massed ar-rowheads and (xeroxed) Mayan glyphs; an African weapon bundle (made for tourists); earth from the six North Ireland counties.

Where are the sources? He excavates something long buried; and she . . .

Room

Born and educated in the United States, Susan Hiller does fieldwork on Mayan archaeology and ethnology in Mexico, Belize, Guatemala. In the late sixties she moves to London to pursue an art career.

COWGIRL/Kou'gurl
Custom-made cardboard box (13.25" × 10" × 2.5"), labeled; photocopied photograph of the outlaw Jennie Metcalf; two china creamers in the form of cows.

Collated, 1992

Immigrant, she encounters a new slur on women: "cows." At home, cows meant only milk, pitchers, domesticity. In London the American outlaw cradles her gun / her creamer.

KOMOIδIA/Comedy
Custom-made cardboard box (10" × 13.25" × 2.5"), labeled; photocopy of Victorian illustration with poem; modern English toy; two slide viewers with one replica magic-lantern slide each.

Organized, 1932

In the lid: a Victorian image of Punch and Judy. Printed below: "Look here—a quarrel has begun. See how they wield their sticks . . . Cruel Punch kills Judy . . . What naughty . . ." In the bottom she has placed modern puppets: Judy without a stick.

"I don't think I'd be a good subject for biography—not enough 'action'! You would say all there is to say in a few sentences—she spent her life with children!"

—Anna Freud

The room preserves her workplaces: a light writing table and a large loom. Notebooks, wool and scissors, analytic couch. Along one wall, memorabilia are gathered in a series of glass cases: books, photos, a brooch . . .

The museum pamphlet: "Anna Freud: Her Life and Work."

"In 1923 Sigmund Freud began suffering from cancer and became increasingly dependent on Anna's care and nursing. Later on, when he needed treatment in Berlin, she was the one who accompanied him there. His illness was also the reason why a 'Secret Committee' was formed to protect psychoanalysis against attacks. Anna was a member, and like the others was given a ring as a token of trust. After her father's death she was to convert one of his rings into a brooch. The Roman intaglio bears the figure of Jupiter enthroned, crowned by Victory with Minerva in attendance."

From her first-floor window I peek out at the garden, bathed in sun. It's not open to the public. Inside: subdued light, carpeted floors, stairs . . . Voices down the hall, where three videos play in series: Eli Wallach (a documentary based on photos of the Freuds' Vienna apartment, Berggasse 19); Sigmund Freud (defining his achievement for the BBC); Anna Freud (narrating home movies of the family).

The dining room: ". . . painted peasant furniture which came from Anna Freud's and Dorothy Burlingham's country cottage at Hochrotherd in Austria. Also in the room is a souvenir painting of the alpine region where Freud usually spent his holidays, walking in the countryside he loved."

"Later she was to say of this period: 'Back then in Vienna we were all so excited—full of energy: it was as if a whole new continent was being explored, and we were the explorers.'"

Euch/Prayer
Custom-made cardboard box (10" × 13.25" × 2.5"), labeled; photocopied map; tesserae and modern marble slab found at the entrance to the Underworld near Vathia.

Presented, 1991

Home Movie

Her voice from the next room.

In front of translucent curtains, a video screen, moving images. The veiled garden. "This is Paula, our housekeeper, still with us . . ."

Sunday visits to his mother. "As you see, she had lovely white hair . . ." Martha Freud and her sister, Minna Bernays. Sigmund Freud and his "very beloved" Chow dog, "Jofi."

"My father didn't like to be photographed, and usually made a face."

Candid shot in a garden, happily talking archaeology with a friend from Rome. "Another summer, near Vienna." Visitors offering gifts—the Freuds' fiftieth anniversary. "Now you will see . . ."

His sister, who died in the concentration camps (her hand on his knee).

ADHS/Hades
Custom-made cardboard box (13.25" × 10" × 2.5"), labeled; photocopied photograph taken near the Necromanteion of Ephyra, ancient oracle of the dead and sanctuary of Persephone and Hades; water collected from the river Acheron, in chemical flask, sealed and tagged.
Surveyed, 1993

A movie camera wanders through gardens filled with flickering shades. Stills: "My father as a boy . . . My grandmother as a younger woman . . . My father and mother, again, in one of their summer rental houses . . ."

Princess Marie Bonaparte, who made most of these films, sits in Freud's waiting room.

Berggasse 19. Swastikas. Vienna crowds. "That's some stranger . . ."

En route for London, her father wrapped in blankets, ailing. On the terrace at Marie Bonaparte's in Paris. Meeting of Freud's new Chow, "Lün," and the princesses' Chow, "Tatoun." Curly tails waving . . . His stiff face.

London: "Jumbo," the little Pekinese. "We were hoping my father would take to him as a temporary replacement." (She speaks as of a child . . .) But he is loyal to Lün, in quarantine. Glimpse of Ernest Jones.

"(Simchas)/Joy." Microscope and magic-lantern transparencies, found at the

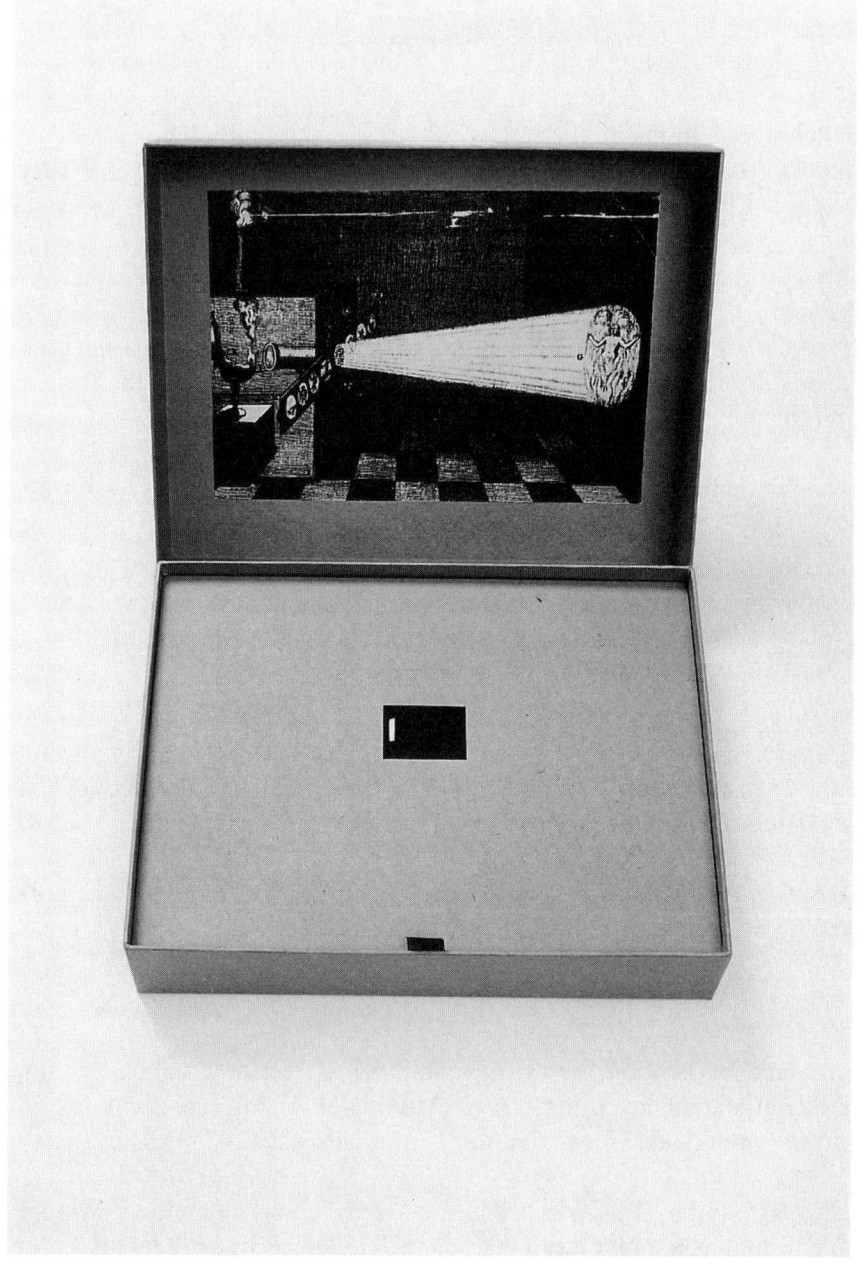

SEANCE / Seminar.
Custom-made cardboard box (10" × 13.25" × 2.5"), labeled; photocopied engraving from
Athanasius Kircher, *Ars Magna Lucis et Umbrae,* 1671; miniature television monitor (l.c.d.,
type) showing a program by the artist entitled *Bright Shadow.*

Edited 1994

Freud Museum: blow fly, dandelion head, bird beak, the royal family, Swiss Family Robinson, heroes (coast guards), Snow White and the Seven Dwarfs, Mickey Mouse in Africa . . .

Twenty Marsfield Gardens: more visitors, "the last birthday" . . . Swaddled outdoors, on a couch of some kind. People approach, he nods . . .

The flickering.

Women of 20 Marsfield Gardens: Martha Freud, Minna Bernays, Anna Freud, Paula Fichtl, and Dorothy Burlingham (Anna's "American companion").

> *HEIMLICH/Homely*
> Custom-made cardboard box (13.25" × 10" × 2.5"), labeled; photocopy of Breton angel of death; 45 rpm record of Johnny Ray singing "Look Homeward Angel."
>
> Referenced, 1994

Freude. Animated, he's standing in the garden to receive a delegation from the Royal Society, writing his name in a big book. Happy (she says) to see his signature near Charles Darwin's.

Crossing

A tiny TV monitor nestled in one of her boxes plays a program called "Bright Shadow."

Lucid: Freud refused morphine, until he asked for a lethal dose.

". . . everything went downhill rapidly. A distressing symptom was an unpleasant odor from the wound, so that when his favorite Chow was brought to visit him she shrank into a far corner of the room, a heart-rending experience which revealed to the sick man the pass he had reached. He was getting very weak and spent his time in a sick bay in his study from which he could gaze at his beloved flowers in the garden."

"Lucid" [Latin *lucidus,* light, clear] . . . In astronomy, visible to the naked eye: said of a star.

MOROR / Bitter.
Custom-made cardboard box (10" × 13.25" × 2.5"), labeled; photocopied illustration from a book; two books modified by the artist: *Essai d'Ethnographie Traditionelle des Mellahs* . . . , Elie Malka (Morocco, n.d.), and *Juifs et Arabes*, Salamon D. Gottein (Paris, 1957).

Labeled 1993

". . . it was as if a whole new continent . . ."

"*LA PESTE / Plague.*" Photograph (in a rearview mirror). Glimpse of the artist and a *memento mori* of the Great Plague: stone skulls at a London churchyard. Inside the lid: world map, charts, data on "the current global situation of the HIV/AIDS pandemic."

Crumbling borders . . .

Wandering

"*PLIGHT/Plite.*" A modern sandpainting. The Teepee: ". . . made of sands collected from the deserts and mountains of the southwestern United States. This painting is durable and can be dusted with a soft dry cloth."

"Plight": v.t. to weave, to braid, to plait. (Obs.) "A *plighted* garment of diverse colors."—Milton

"The skin is transparent and allows light from the sun to shine through, thereby giving light and heat within."

Through his clenched lids, a bright garden . . .

"I Wander thro' each charter'd street . . ."

From Old Street Station I take City Road to Bunhill Fields Burying Ground. Across the street is Wesley's Chapel and House (museum). In the cemetery, a collection of Old London, I find the graves of William and Catherine Blake, Bunyan, Defoe. There are others of note: antislavery crusaders, writers of hymns, an inventor of insurance. Some of the stones were moved here, replanted.

Eddying waters of Mnemosyne and Lethe.

Next, the modern wasteland of the Barbican, where "Defoe" and "Shakespeare" are towers of flats, looming over pedestrian walkways. Arrows point to the Museum of London, at the far side of the vast complex. I

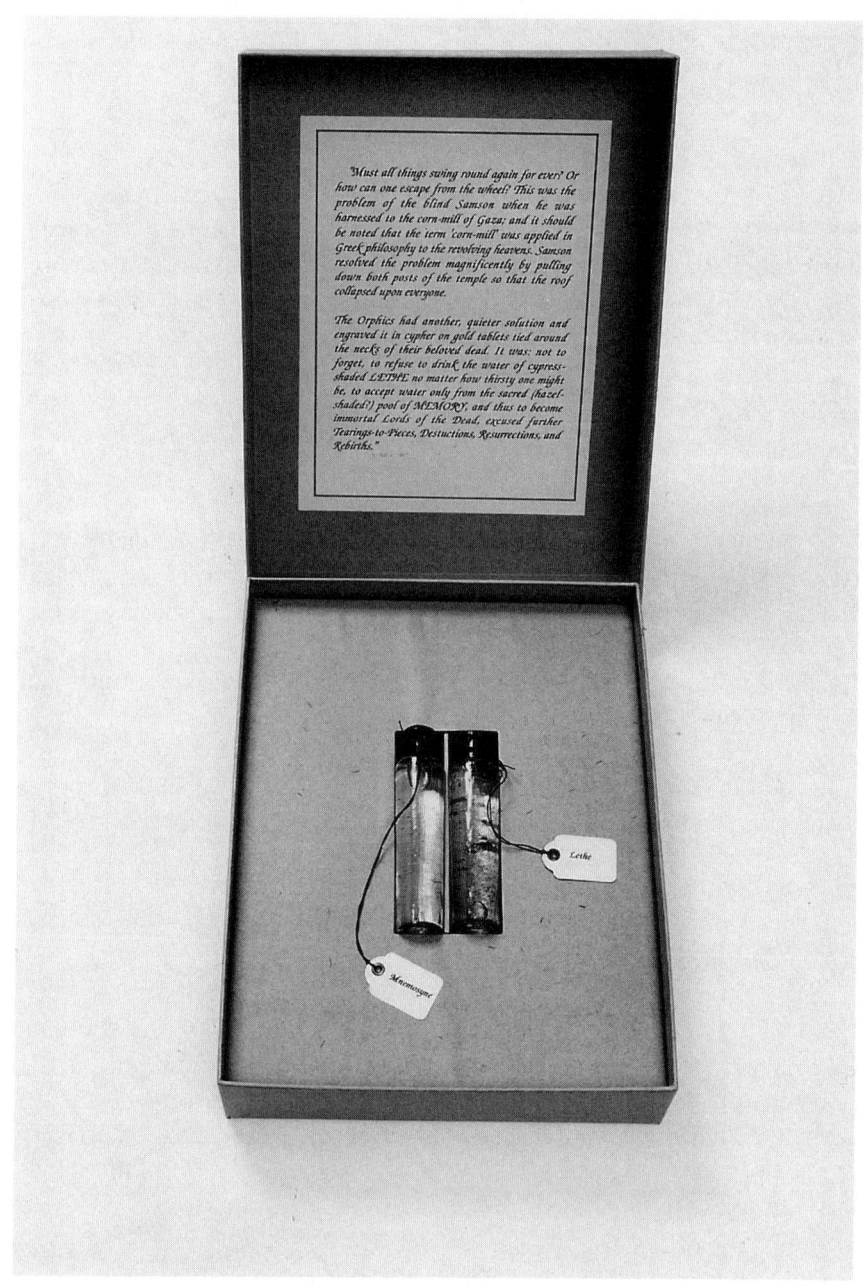

EAUX-DE-VIE / Spirits.
Custom-made cardboard box (13.2" × 10" × 2.5"), labeled; photocopy of text by Robert Graves; water collected from the Lethe and the Mnemosyne, in antique bottles, corked sealed and tagged.

Annotated 1993

meet only half a dozen people on my way—including an elderly woman, who grips a wheeled walker, inching along, head down.

Wandering vine . . .

"Blake had left Poland Street in 1790, soon after the death of his mother . . . [He] and Catherine now moved to 13 Hercules Buildings, Lambeth, on the south bank of the Thames."

> CHAMIN-HA' / *House of Knives*
> Custom-made cardboard box (10" × 13.25" × 2.5"), labeled; photocopy of Mayan calendar glyphs, numerals, and day names; obsidian blades.
> Collected, 1992

"Gilchrist describes the house as a humble, one-storeyed building; but Frederick Tatham, a friend of Blake's later years, remembers it as 'a pretty, clean house of eight or ten rooms,' a typical London terrace house of the eighteenth century, with the usual strip of garden behind. In this garden grew a 'wandering vine,' unpruned, to form the arbor, where, according to one of those legends which no official denial can kill, Mr and Mrs Blake were once surprised by a friend in the dress of Eden, with the addition only of helmets (a detail which comes through the painter George Richmond), occupied in the reading aloud of *Paradise Lost*."

Dwelling/traveling . . .

"The Peopling of London" exhibition: a city of outsiders, from its Roman, Saxon, Viking, Norman beginnings through waves of Europeans, Asians, Jews, Huguenots, Irish, Arabs, Cypriots, Latin Americans . . . , ending with the recent influx from former colonies.

I pick up a telephone in the Museum of London and hear the voice of a woman recalling her arrival from Jamaica in 1955: her astonishment, looking out a window on her first day, to see white men digging up the street.

Postcards: an eighteenth-century black merchant seaman and street singer who wears a model ship on his hat; suffragettes picketing, one of them an Indian princess. And in the museum's foyer: a traveling exhibit on London's Sephardim: Greece, Morocco, Spain, Iraq, India, Guatemala . . .

Outside the Barbican and heading for Saint Paul's, I again pass the woman, bent over her walker. She doesn't look up from the pavement. Where, *where in the world,* is she going?

Gathering

Anna Freud traveled frequently to America.

Susan Hiller goes back and forth to Ireland, Greece, Australia, the Native Americas . . . She collects things without apparent value. Tourist art, scraps of pottery, toys, forgotten books, stones, dirt, water. Archaeologist and pilgrim: scavenger of futures . . . In Delphi she collects from the Castillian Spring; in Ireland her bottle fills from the Well of Saint Brigit; she returns from Australia with "native earths."

Where (in the world) are her sources . . .

"MOROR/Bitter." "Famille israélite." There's an Arabic inscription. An old photograph shows Arab Jews posing serenely: two bearded men in turbans; two demure children; a woman, impassive, in draped scarf and richly flowered dress.

In another box . . . White patriots hurl stones at dark Jews: illustration photocopied from a 1927 pamphlet, *The Jewish Minority in Roumania* . . . , "showing ethnic cleansing."

Bloodlines and the "New Europe." A dying man wrapped in blankets. English Channel.

"If Moses was an Egyptian . . ."

From Vienna, Freud traveled as a pilgrim, she says . . . especially to Rome, where he discovered "inner" meanings and archaeological images for the psyche. She says her own travels are pilgrimages, too.

Pilgrimage: an activity long open to women; close to tourism (her souvenirs recall); discovery as repetition.

". . . my father and mother, again."

Freud collected the world, its origins and history. On his desk, a beloved figure of ancient Egypt . . . "Everything is decontextualized," she says, "and put in a situation of being possessed by a European of a certain generation. Of course, I'm aware that even my collection could come to look like that eventually."

". . . an eddy in the stream of becoming."

She gathers souvenirs, scraps, and secrets, bringing them into his house, among his things. Her open suitcases.

Anna Freud traveled frequently to . . .

Worlds

Outside 20 Marsfield Gardens, afternoon light edges new leaves in the English gardens.

Europe seems far from California, where I live on a bay facing west, toward the East.

In boxes of memory and forgetting, our belongings.

Growing up in New York, London was my source. But now . . .

Limahuli Gardens: native plants on the island of Kaua'i.
A house, trees, a spring in the south of France.
Egyptian night-jar's song.

And the palms, araucaria pines. Valley of Hienghène, New Caledonia.

I'm telling my Melanesian guide that, to me, the dwellings seem strangely

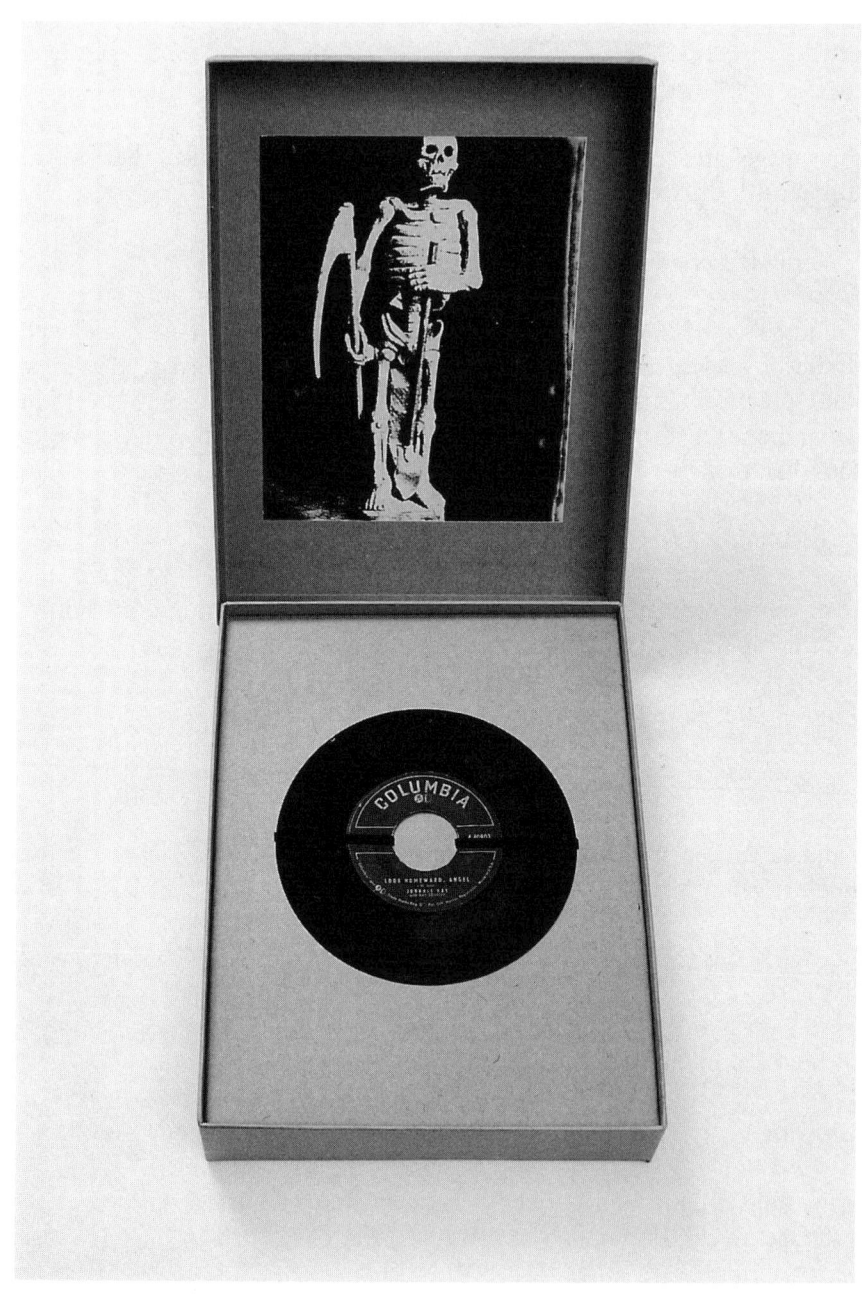

HEIMLICH / Homely.
Custom-made cardboard box (13.2" × 10" × 2.5"), labeled; photocopy of Breton angel of death; 45-rpm record of Johnny Ray singing *Look Homeward Angel*.

Referenced 1994

bare . . . while the habitat is so full, so carefully tended. He pauses a moment. "Mais, c'est *ça* la maison."

A sweep of the arm collects trees, river, breeze, stones, mountains— the dead.

Sources

Boxes: Susan Hiller, installation at the Freud Museum, 1994. Photos courtesy of Book Works. From Susan Hiller, *After the Freud Museum* (London: Bookworks, 1995).

Sigmund Freud, quoted in Norman O. Brown, *Apocalypse and/or Metamorphosis,* 182.

Walter Benjamin, *The Origin of German Classic Drama,* 45.

Anna Freud, quoted in Robert Coles, *Anna Freud: The Dream of Psychoanalysis,* 3.

From "Anna Freud: Her Life and Work" and "Freud Museum." Orientation pamphlets, Freud Museum, London.

Anna Freud: video commentary on family movies at the Freud Museum.

William Blake, "London," from *Songs of Experience.*

Kathleen Raine, *William Blake,* 63.

Ernest Jones, *The Life and Work of Sigmund Freud,* vol. 3, 245.

Susan Hiller, *Thinking about Art: Conversations with Susan Hiller,* ed. Barbara Einzig (forthcoming).

Sigmund Freud, *Moses and Monotheism,* 17.

Jean-Marie Tjibaou, Valley of Hienghène, New Caledonia.

All other quotations are from Susan Hiller's boxes at the Freud Museum.

Postcards: Egyptian funerary boat in Freud's collection; desk in his study at the Freud Museum. Reproduced by permission.

Thanks to Judith Aissen and Ty Miller for help with this experiment.

Aleut seahunter's hat, Unalaska. Given to the Peabody Museum, Salem, Massachusetts, in 1829 by Captain William Osgood. Made of bent wood with walrus whiskers, this hat is painted red, green, yellow, black and turquoise blue. It is adorned with ivory birds, trade beads, and incised, inlaid metal ears (or eyes). The hat's form suggests it may have functioned like a mask, identifying its wearer with mobile predatory seabirds as well as with cosmological cycles (Black, 1991). (*Courtesy Peabody Essex Museum, Salem, Mass. Photo by Mark Sexton.*)

12

Fort Ross Meditation

The Orchard

The orchard is on a hillside facing west. The fort spreads out below. And beyond: sparkling, swaying, the big ocean.

Paintings and sketches of the Russian settlement, made before 1850, take this viewpoint. Perhaps the artists sat somewhere just below the orchard; perhaps they worked under one of these large, unkempt pear trees. But the trees, newly planted then, would not have given much shade. Maybe the artists ate pears.

Their pictures show a walled enclosure, with blockhouses at two corners and a chapel at a third. Several large wooden buildings with reddish sloping roofs are scattered near the walls. Outside the fort, one sees clusters of smaller buildings, fenced fields, and a windmill. The structures spread along a bluff, below which a path descends to a cove and a small beach.

In 1995, seen from the old orchard, the fort's main structures don't look much different. They have been accurately reconstructed. The surrounding houses are gone, and some large new trees—eucalyptus and cypress—have taken hold. Behind the trees, you can see a parking lot. A paved road—California Route 1—curves in front.

A pamphlet informs me that the orchard was begun in 1814, with peaches brought from Peru on the schooner *Chirikov*. In the next few years, more peaches, as well as grapes, arrived on the *Kutuzov* from Peru and from the Spanish mission in Carmel, 150 miles to the south. Olive trees also can be traced to the mission. Over the next three decades of Russian settlement in Alta California, more seeds and cuttings arrived: pears, apples, plums, evergreen bitter cherries, and figs. Their provenance is not entirely clear, but the routes were certainly various: from Europe and Russia, by ship around Cape Horn to Alaska, and thence to the Ross colony; up the coast from Chile, Peru, and Spanish California; from the eastern United States by boat, and later overland by wagon.

By 1842, when the Russian-American Company abandoned its Ross outpost, the orchard extended to five acres, tended by local Indian workers and partly enclosed by an eight-foot board fence. The site of a house is still faintly discernible, probably a dacha for the fort's last commandant, Alexander Rotchev. Through the mid- and late nineteenth century, the orchard was maintained and expanded by German and Anglo Californian ranchers who acquired Fort Ross, first from the Russians and then from the Mexicans, who considered the Sonoma coastline north of San Francisco as part of their domain. In 1906 the property passed to the State of California. And in the same year, the site, located directly over the San Andreas Fault, was badly damaged by the great earthquake. Sliding earth uprooted or buried many of the trees. Thereafter things fell into neglect, and it was not until the late 1970s that a preservation project was begun, largely by local volunteers.

Currently, the "Russian Orchard" is mowed and enclosed by an electrified deer-fence. Some of the old apples and pears are surrounded by new "daughter trees," made from cuttings. Seven numbered posts refer the visitor to descriptions in the pamphlet, available at the Fort Ross State Historic Park Visitor Center. The orchard doesn't seem to be much visited (there's a combination lock to negotiate), and the general feeling is one of unkempt repose.

There has been some debate, and no doubt wishful thinking, about which, if any, of the trees growing here were actually planted by the Russians. Some of them look the part. There are several thirty-five-foot pear trees, which the pamphlet says were "possibly" planted before 1841. A clump of large evergreen bitter cherries, preserved from rot by their hard wood, are linked to the Russians by the story that their fruit was used to flavor the fort's vodka. The old olives "probably" go back to the Carmel Franciscans. All the apples are of later origin, though possibly connected to the original arrivals by seeds or cuttings. A single Gravenstein, the only one to survive the 1906 quake, twists near the fence.

The aged trees are unpruned, sometimes toppled and overgrown, lightly hung with moss. One of the pears still produces a small round fruit of gritty texture. The tall pears and cherries are planted in groups, as described in Russian accounts. Indentations in the earth, a sag pond and long fault trough, register the effect of the Pacific Plate's sliding beneath the North American. In the trough bank an enormous old pear tree—more horizontal than vertical—has miraculously survived 1906. A few dark leaves can be seen at the tips of its bare branches, and a couple of fruit—shrunken moons—against the sky.

I try a green-and-brown apple that has fallen from a "daughter tree." Its rough skin is covered with blemishes, and it tastes good—tart and sweet. The flavor reminds me of apples I ate sitting on a branch in an old orchard in Vermont, where I spent summer vacations as a boy. Did these apples come across the continent, or around Cape Horn from the eastern states— migrants, like me, to this coast? And how must such apples have tasted to Russian, Yankee, Aleut, Native Alaskan, or Hawaiian voyagers who put in at Fort Ross after months at sea? A taste of land, home, childhood? A strange taste? Did the California Indians who worked here like the alien fruit?

An empty ocean. In the old Russian paintings of Fort Ross, the horizon's line is broken by a ship. Under full sail, it seems to hover on the water, too large to be quite real. Always desired. Always arriving.

History

I'm looking for history at Fort Ross. I want to understand my location among others in time and space. Where have we been and where are we going? But instead of a clear direction or process, I find different, overlapping temporalities, all in differing ways "historical." The long rhythm of the San Andreas fault, which began moving 50 million years ago, makes little distinction between 1906 and 1996. Geological time is inhuman in scale, yet its effects on human life have been direct, catastrophic. The cyclical temporalities of weather—fog, water, wind, erosion. Looking down the coast from the old Russian orchard in the autumn of 1995, I see dust from the earth-moving trucks of CALTRANS in their endless struggle to keep Route 1 from slipping into the sea. Plants keep their own times: distinct life-spans, forms of propagation and travel. Seeds and spores get around with help from animals, including people—hair, digestive tracts, hands, clothes, wagons, boats, airplanes. Germs and viruses have their histories, deadly when long-separated populations come into contact. The histories of animals are entwined with those of humans: most notoriously, on this coast, the lives of gray whales and sea otters, both hunted till nearly extinct but now returning. Finally, the mix of human times we commonly call history: the long span of indigenous traditions and folk histories; the waxing and waning of tribes and nations, of empires; the struggles and ruses of conquest, adaptation, survival; the movements of natives, explorers, and immigrants, with their distinct relations to land, place, and memory; the changing rhythms of markets, commodities, communications, capital—organizing and disorganizing everything.

At Fort Ross, I hope to glimpse my own history in relation to the movements of others in a regional contact zone. Call it, for convenience, but too simply, the North Pacific. I want to ask some large and ultimately unanswerable questions in a personal way. To think historically, I need to be both globally aware and locally situated. For the forces—economic, political, environmental—that have brought us all together here are materialized as historical reality only through particular local projects and stories. These are neither uniform nor finally determined. Historical reality, what happens in nonrepeating time, is a changing set of determinations, not a cumulative process or a teleology. This, at least, is my assumption— and hope. Fort Ross is a place to start in again with history. Located on the rim of the Pacific, my home of eighteen years, the fort's nineteenth-century stories, seen from an uncertain fin-de-siècle, may provide just enough "depth" to help make sense of a future, some possible futures.

"Where do we come from? What are we? Where are we going?" Gauguin affixed those questions to his largest canvas, painted in a real Pacific place of his imagination. They are the questions we endlessly ask of history. With a critical and growing uncertainty: Who is asking? I, my parents, my grandparents did not come to this coast from China, Japan, the Philippines, Mexico, Guatemala, Samoa, Cambodia, Vietnam . . . We do not remember a time on the coast before strangers arrived.

Standing at the reconstructed Russian fort, one finds it odd to recognize that when its builders gazed at the Pacific horizon, they were looking back, not out. Odd, that is, for someone conditioned to think that the direction of historical development in the "New World" was from east to west. The national space of the United States has long been conceived as an expansion west, and (less canonically) south. This westward-looking dream topography had its origin along the Asiatic and African edges of Europe, over centuries of violent and creative contacts. The dream—productive, expansive, violent—had a destination: the Pacific. Here the "West" culminated. Beyond the final ocean lay the East.

At Fort Ross, even "Western" history arrives from the wrong direction. And it comes contaminated, an extension of Russia's great Asian encounter: the Siberian frontier. In fact, few of the builders of Russian America were, in any pure sense, European. Most of the pioneers at Fort Ross were, after all, Siberians (mixed Russian, creole, and native), Aleuts, and Alaskans. It is strange to stand on the California coast and imagine yourself at the farthest extension of an eastward-expanding empire centered in St. Petersburg. And it is disorienting to realize that what brought so diverse a crew to this isolated coast in 1830 was a trading network centered on Chinese luxury goods. The China Trade, fueled by the Anglo-American love of spices, porcelain, and especially tea, transformed much of the Pacific. The search for commodities to sell in Canton unleashed destructive scrambles for sandalwood, sea cucumber, and, in Alaska and California, sea-otter pelts. Fort Ross is as much part of Asian as of Western history.

It is also part of hemispheric history. The presence of Russia in America accelerated Spanish (and, after 1821, Mexican) colonization of Alta California. The relations of Fort Ross with the religious and military centers at Carmel, San Francisco, San Rafael, and Sonoma were both tense and cooperative. Here a frontier moving west-to-east encountered one moving south-to-north. Moreover, the links with South America were palpable, via Pacific sea routes. The very-American George Washington Call, whose ranch occupied the fort in the late nineteenth century, came to the Sonoma coast from Valparaiso with his Chilean wife, Mercedes.

Today these transpacific and hemispheric involvements make renewed sense. They prefigure something . . . As contemporary California fills with Pacific and Asian immigrants, many linked across the ocean in familial and financial diasporas, and as the state's southern border becomes ever more porous, the mix of forces and peoples on the 1830 Sonoma Coast seems less distant. The fact of Fort Ross helps dislodge a dominant "American" history, making room for other stories, other discoveries and origins, for a United States with roots and routes in the Asian Pacific, in the Américas. And around the fort I begin to feel the ongoing presence of native histories, stories differently situated, linking other origins and futures—histories that tell the experiences of those who saw sails appear on an empty horizon with emotions very different from joy.

Russian America

Russian America was an extension of Siberia. The famous Cossack *promyshlenniki,* self-governing freelance hunters and frontiersmen who in sixty years burst across the Ural Mountains and raced to the Eastern Sea of Okhotsk, did not hesitate when faced with a mere ocean.* Their conquest of Siberia had been driven by what the Russians called "soft gold"—the skins of beaver, silver fox, and especially sable, which brought high prices in Europe and China. Where the fur-bearing animals were killed off—and it did not take long—the hunters moved on. When the land stopped, they continued by other means. Rumors told of places beyond the water. Vitus Bering's expeditions of 1728 and 1741 glimpsed Alaska and touched on the Aleutian Islands. Survivors from his luckless second voyage returned to the Kamchatka Peninsula, after a winter of shipwreck, with little more than their lives (Bering lost his). But they did collect 900 sea-otter skins, which fetched an amazing 90,000 roubles on the China market. After Bering's crews reported that the Aleutian coasts teemed with otters, the race was on. Within twenty-five years, *promyshlenniki* in crude boats had tracked the Aleutian chain as far as the Alaskan Peninsula and Kodiak Island, 2,700 miles from Okhotsk. By 1799 the Russian-American Company, a private, quasi-governmental body, had obtained a monopoly from the czar to hunt furs in North America. Under the energetic leadership of Alexander Baranov, it moved its headquarters from Kodiak further east to Sitka (New Archangel). Fort Ross, far south on a temperate coast Sir Francis Drake had named New Albion, would be the company's farthest outpost.

Russian America was a coastal-extractive, not a settler, colony. At its peak, no more than several hundred ethnic Russians lived there. The major work of hunting and exploration was accomplished by indigenous and creole employees. The *promyshlenniki* had routinely intermarried, or

---

*The principal sources for the facts and interpretations in this "meditation" are cited in a postscript. References for direct quotations appear in the text.

at least cohabited, with the indigenous peoples of Siberia, and the practice was continued by Russians of all classes in America. A large creole population developed, which occupied intermediate places in a graded, not a binary, racial hierarchy. These mixed-race employees worked with indigenous conscripts under the direction of a small minority of ethnic Russian leaders and experts.

The colony was heavily dependent on native labor organized in large hunting parties. Some of the work called for very special skills. Fur seals could be easily clubbed as they bred by the thousands on the Pribilov Islands; beavers could be trapped much as they had been in Siberia; but sea otters, the linchpin of the American operation, were another matter. Mobile, living in treacherous coastal waters, they usually were speared from moving boats. Only Aleuts and Koniags from Kodiak Island (the Russians called them all "Aleuts") were good at this. The Aleuts in particular, trained from childhood to hunt on the water in superbly designed *baidarkas* (kayaks), were virtuosos of the otter hunt.

The freelance Russians who worked their way along the Aleutians were quick to exploit native hunters. This was accomplished by the familiar early-colonial combination of carrot and stick: mutually beneficial trade, alternating with naked terror. Some of the explorers were fair in their dealings; and some stayed on, marrying local women. Others were brutal. They organized work parties, sending the conscripts to remote coastlines, sometimes for extended periods. Aleut men were cajoled or coerced onto these expeditions, often after their families had been taken hostage. With organization of the extractive system, work for the invaders became a required tribute. Payment tended to be minimal, sometimes in the form of goods produced by Aleut and Koniag women, themselves forced to work at Russian settlements. The disruption of island subsistence patterns was serious, at times devastating. A wave of epidemics, brought by the invaders, decimated the Aleutian and coastal Alaskan populations, continuing their devastations well into the nineteenth century.

By the early 1760s, the generally peaceful Aleuts had had enough. Several eastern groups carried out a well-prepared attack on five Russian ships, destroying four and killing most of their crews. The response was exemplary: scores of villages on Unalaska and neighboring islands were destroyed, their inhabitants tortured and killed. Concerted resistance ended. Processes of assimilation, forced and voluntary, followed: local chiefs, supported by the Russians, controlled the regular supply of hunting parties; individual islanders were taken to Siberia, educated, converted, and returned to serve as translators and local leaders. With the help of liberal priests such as Ioann Veniaminov (an important early ethnographer/historian and colonial reformer), by the end of the eighteenth century virtually all Aleuts were nominally Russian Orthodox—a faith to which they gave an indigenous stamp. Though conversion to Christianity was not coerced, as it often was in Spanish America, it occurred against a backdrop of superior power and sporadic terror. The same was true of somewhat more liberal labor regimes instituted at the end of the century by the Russian-American Company. St. Petersburg regularly exhorted the pioneers to treat American natives well, but with limited effect. The realities of the distant colony, undermanned and needing to hunt in ever more distant regions, left it wholly dependent on indigenous labor. Resupply expenses were high, profit margins narrow.

The quest for new hunting grounds continued south along the American coast, sometimes with the help of New England trading vessels, to whom Baranov supplied parties of Aleuts and Koniags with their kayaks. The hostile Tlingit impeded work in the inlets and islands south of Sitka. Here British and Yankee traders, willing to pay better prices and trade on native terms, did better. But farther south in California, there was less resistance and the otters were still plentiful. Aleuts aboard Yankee ships worked all the way to the Sea of Cortez in Baja California. The first Russians with their hunting teams arrived at Bodega Bay, just north of San Francisco, in 1809. Then, in 1812, concerned about Spanish opposition, the company moved its base up the coast to a more defensible site that would become Fort Ross ("Ross," short for *Rossiia;* thus "Fort Russia"). From this base the Koniags and Aleuts prowled coastal waters as far south as Monterey. They carried their light *baidarkas* across the Marin Peninsula, to poach in the great bay that was ineffectively guarded by a small presidio at San Francisco.

The fort was conceived as a permanent settlement. Although its primary reason for existence was sea otters, and to a lesser degree fur seals, the supply of "soft gold" would not last. Further expansion down the coast was blocked by the Spaniards. By the 1820s, the outpost's secondary function, agricultural production in support of the Alaska colony, was becoming its prime rationale. And with the turn to large-scale farming, the Russians required increased local labor. Having brought along their own teams of hunters, they had not initially depended on the coastal

Pomos and Miwoks. Indeed, relations, though not without tension and mutual fear, were relatively friendly. Ivan Kuskov, the fort's first manager, chose a site long occupied by a Pomo settlement, Métini (Mad-Zhi-Ni). He negotiated a formal treaty with local chiefs of the band that would later come to be called Kashaya Pomo, acknowledging their permission to use the land. This formal recognition of indigenous rights may have had as much to do with producing a "legal" right to occupation, against prior Spanish claims, as it did with respecting Native American ownership. In any event the Kashaya had little choice, confronting invaders armed with rifles and cannons. Although they fought sporadically among themselves and with their neighbors—raids and revenge killings—the Kashaya were not a warlike group.

According to oral tradition, the Russian sailing ships were at first thought to be giant bird-spirits. the Kashaya learned better when the strange winged vessels anchored in the cove at Métini and began unloading cannons, supplies, and fleets of kayaks. Perhaps referring to the appearance and disappearance of ships on the horizon, the Kashaya called the newcomers, both Europeans and Alaskans, "undersea people." They entered into relations of trade and cohabitation with the newcomers, maintaining the indigenous settlement at Métini near the fort during thirty years of Russian occupation. The Kashaya, a small Pomo group probably less than a thousand in number, moved among summer coastal villages and winter settlements inland atop steep ridges. There was a good deal of coming and going along the thirty miles of their coastal territory, bordered by Central Pomo on the north at the Gualala River and by Coast Miwok on the south, just beyond the mouth of the Russian River. A significant number of California Indians lived near the Russian fort. At first, Russian protection, trade goods, and cohabitation with Alaskans and creoles kept Kashaya, largely women and their offspring, at the fort. Later, extensive agriculture and husbandry would require a large labor force, especially at harvest times. When they found themselves shorthanded, the Russians resorted to force, sweeping into more distant Kashaya villages, rounding up work parties at gunpoint, and taking hostages to ensure discipline.

But this was not their preferred method; nor could they practically keep large numbers of people at the fort by raw coercion, as the Spanish and Mexicans did in their mission and ranch colonial system. On the whole, the Indians who worked at Fort Ross did so under a more flexible system of constraints and rewards. Among colonizers, the Russians in California were far from the worst. They left native culture alone, so long as the colony's economic goals could be met. Theirs was not a civilizing or a proselytizing mission. Intermarriage and the growth of creole populations were encouraged. The Kashaya, who had been quickly apprised of the harsh prospects offered by the presence of whites north of San Francisco Bay, recognized the relative advantage of alliance with the Russians. There was significant communication among the region's Indian groups. The Pomo were divided into seven mutually unintelligible language groups, but multilingualism was common, and the Kashaya had (and still have) strong trading and kin ties to the Coast Miwok. The Miwok knew the Spanish (and later Mexican) colonial system at first hand. Many of their men had been subjected to forced labor, some of their women raped. The inhabitants of native villages were moved to the missions, where Spanish language and religion were imposed. Even when they were kindly treated, there was always pressure to give up Indian ways. News of these harsh realities, and of the invader's superior military power and deadly diseases, spread quickly. California Indians had good reason to fear the arrival of whites.

At Fort Ross, a significant number of Miwok women figure in the censuses. Many had fled north to join their allies, the "Fort Ross Pomo," for protection from the Spanish invaders. The stories they told would have been chilling. The Russians at least provided a relatively safe zone, a barrier against the more destructive settler colonization of the Spanish and Mexicans. Indeed, one of the things that impressed the Kashaya at Fort Ross, if the stories collected by linguist Robert Oswalt in the 1950s are any indication, was the Russians' willingness to discipline "undersea men" (probably creoles or Alaskans) who mistreated Kashaya women. At Métini, if one worked and followed certain rules, one could live as an Indian, with enough food and a real degree of protection in a world newly darkened by uncertainty and terror. Other Indians living nearby, or passing through the Fort Ross complex, no doubt had a different mix of motives. The undersea people had goods to trade. They were, culturally, a very mixed lot. You could deal with them.

Fort Ross was a cluster of settlements, with the vast majority of people living outside the walls. Inside, the governor, his family, and a handful of other privileged Russians dwelt in a half-dozen large houses which also held provisions, trade goods, furs, arms, and gunpowder. There were workshops, offices, kitchens, a lockup. A Russian Orthodox chapel stood at one corner of the stockade. Outside, just above the cove, a Koniag village sheltered the sea-mammal hunters who made up half of the population in the 1820s. Indian settlements were scattered inland. And various creole and lower-class Russian/Siberian workers and artisans lived in another cluster of dwellings surrounded by barns, a wind-driven flour mill, workshops, and other outbuildings. A ship-building operation and a forge were located near the cove, along with a crucial building, especially for sailors and oceangoing hunters: the steam bath.

Who, exactly, lived at Fort Ross? A census made in 1820 by the first governor, Ivan Kuskov, gives a reliable snapshot. Of 260 inhabitants, 14.6 percent were Russians, 6.5 percent creoles, 51.2 percent Eskimos (126 Koniags, 7 Chugach), and 21.5 percent California Indians. In addition to these principal groups, the census records three Aleuts, five Siberian Yakuts, four "Sandwichians" (Hawaiians), two Tlingits, one Tanaina Indian, and one unidentified. The proportions varied over the years, and there was a good deal of coming and going. Kirill Khlebnikov's travel journals of 1822 record several discontented *promyshlenniki* (lower-class Russians) deserting to the Spaniards south of San Francisco. Some later returned, under duress. And there were transients, deposited by the various ships that made port at Fort Ross or at Bodega Bay. On May 29, 1822, "a Negro and an Irishman" disembarked from the *Lady Blackwood,* a British East India Company ship en route from Calcutta. The "Negro" proved to be a good carpenter and farmer, skills desperately needed at the fort. Before moving on, he repaired farm implements and constructed two devices for threshing grain.

Of the local Indians counted, 84 percent were women. (Later, as the scale of agriculture increased, more men would reside at the fort, at least seasonally.) Of the forty-eight women counted in 1920, twenty-six were "from the vicinity of Ross" (Kashaya); twenty-one had come from the south (Miwok from Bodega Bay, Pomo and Miwok from the Russian River area); one hailed from Point Arena in the north. Most of the Indian women were living with Koniags and Chugach. A few lived with Russians and creoles. Some Russian and creole men cohabited with creole, Koniag, or Aleut women, of which forty-seven were counted. In 1920, almost all of the Indian men living at Fort Ross were "convicts," serving sentences for acts such as attacking Koniags hunting in their coastal waters or killing Russian horses. There was a punitive aspect to the colony's peaceful coexistence with the coastal tribes.

It was a remarkable social mix, governed by complex, cross-cutting ethnic and racial hierarchies. Russians were at the top, followed in descending order by Russian/Siberian creoles, Russian/Alaskan creoles, the various Alaskans (including Aleuts), Alaskan/Californian creoles, and, at the bottom, the California natives. This, at least, was the hierarchy as seen from above. How affiliations were negotiated across the various levels is unclear, and there must have been a range of alliances. The largest number of "marriages," or cohabitations, were between Koniags and Californians. What sorts of exchanges occurred in these relationships? Current archaeological work outside the walls of the fort is turning up some clues. Russian "loan words" in contemporary Kashaya speech, some with detectable features of Koniag pronunciation, are tantalizing reminders of a heteroglot history. The alliances were, for the most part, temporary. When the Alaskans departed for extended hunting expeditions, their partners might go to a home village to await their return. Relations with family outside Métini were sustained. When the Russians left Alta California in 1842, six Kashaya women accompanied their partners to Sitka. In Russian accounts, their departure is voluntary; in Kashaya oral tradition, it is coerced.

In the 1820s a Dena'ina (Tanaina) Athabaskan named Qadanalchen worked for a spell at Fort Ross. On his return to Cook Inlet, Alaska, he was rebaptized Nikolai Kalifornsky, and he founded a village near his home which for many years bore his name: "From California." In March 1979 his great-great-grandson Peter Kalifornsky visited Fort Ross Historic Park, spending the night as an honored guest of the Kashaya Pomo at their Stewarts Point reservation. It is likely that he sang a song for his hosts, a song for homesickness, composed by his ancestor during his time at Fort Ross. Qadanalchen sang it while rubbing the bottoms of his feet with dirt he had brought in a small bag from his home village (Kalifornsky, 1991: 253).

> Ki q'u ke sha nuntalghatl'.
> Quint' a hk'u, qildu ki.
> Shesh t'qelani.
> Shi k'u ki.

> Another dark night has come over me.
> We may never be able to return home.
> But do your best in life.
> That is what I do.

Histories

We have very unequal access to the experiences of those in the Fort Ross / Métini contact zone. The records of Russian and other European visitors are abundant. They, along with company documents, make possible the history I have just sketched. The visitors tell of hospitality at the isolated stockade, and provide more or less reliable details on the California Indians and local flora and fauna. Such accounts predominantly represent views from a base inside the stockade, or on shipboard. But most of the life of the fort took place outside and around the stockade. Here the traces—textual, archaeological, and oral—of the different histories are more scattered. The experiences of the visiting Koniag, Chugash, Aleut, and Athabaskan voyagers are the most obscure. Russian observers, perhaps overly familiar with the populations from Alaska, record little of their social life at the fort.

Kashaya oral traditions contain first-hand accounts of the Ross experience, stories that reflect Indian perspectives and critical sensibilities. Some of these are recorded in *Kashaya Texts* (1964), transcribed in Kashaya and translated into English by the linguist Robert Oswalt. Two elders, Herman James and Essie Parrish, provided most of the myths, stories of unusual or supernatural events, and folk histories, supplemented by songs, recipes, prophecies, and conversations. Oswalt collected the texts in 1958 as records of a dying language and as sources for folklorists and historians. Today they are available to Kashaya and others as foundations for local tradition, as sources for an emergent Kashaya "literature," and as autoethnographic representations for a wider audience, products of a particular contact relationship with white anthropologists and linguists.

Stories that conform to Western historical ontologies—events in nonrecurring time, without supernatural interventions—are grouped by Oswalt in a section titled "Folk Histories." (He notes that the Kashaya do not distinguish these stories from tales he groups under the "supernatural," a category including unusual occurrences that are not myths.) Folk histories in principle, sometimes in practice, can be mapped onto Western chronologies. Glenn Farris (1989a) has argued that these oral histories should not be considered inferior to written records. And he demonstrates the point by comparing the accounts of an event provided by Herman James and Essie Parrish with archival sources on the same occurrence. In 1833 a large trapping expedition organized by the Hudson's Bay Company passed Fort Ross / Métini on its way up the coast. The effect was spectacular: 163 men, women, and children, with 450 horses and mules, appeared on a hilltop, the rising sun behind them, and paraded past the Kashaya village in a seemingly endless train. "They went on and on . . ." The stories of Parrish and James record astonishment, fear, curiosity; and they include many details of the strangers' speech, dress, and behavior, as well as the observations of a Kashaya man fishing nearby who was captured and spent a day with the train. Herman James also records that "the undersea people were afraid, too, and gave them food even though they didn't ask for it" (Oswalt, 1964: 253). Presumably this memory refers to Alaskans or creoles at the fort, for the Russians knew of the Hudson's Bay party and had, grudgingly, given permission for it to pass. Farris concludes: "The fact that the 'undersea people' reacted similarly [to the Kashaya] indicates how removed from the council of the tiny ruling minority of white European Russians was the populace of Fort Ross" (Farris, 1989a: 479).

Kashaya oral histories offer more concrete and detailed accounts of the event than do the journals of the expedition leaders, which have little to say about the Fort Ross settlement. The Kashaya texts are thus "good history," providing factual information and glimpses of Indian reactions to the events of early contact. "Folk histories" are conventionally defined as stories whose historical "reality" can be verified and dated by reference to independent sources, usually written accounts. Essie Parrish's story of the first sighting of a Russian boat, seen in the distance as a big bird-person, evidently refers to a real "historical" event. And Herman James's descriptions of how the Russians grew and milled grain are quite particular. They reflect a willingness to observe new processes closely and to learn, in this case to learn to eat flour. But the new would not, should not, cancel the old. Herman James ends thus: "Later on, when [the Russians] had lived there a while, [the Indians] ate flour, too. And they also ate pinole in their own way" (Oswalt, 1964: 269). Learning was reciprocal. One story about two "undersea youths" who freeze to death in the rain ends with Kashaya teaching the newcomers how to protect their bodies from the coastal moisture.

The tales, while recording historical events, also have a didactic purpose. Stories about the Russians' harsh beatings of men who abused their wives convey a clear warning, as does an account from the years following the Russians' departure, a story Oswalt titles "A Lynching." Two Indian youths kill a white man. Each one, thinking the other has been captured, gives himself up to the whites and is summarily hanged. The story ends with Indian threats of revenge petering out in the face of ever-more-numerous settlers. ("White men" here refers to American settlers who arrive after the Ross colony; Russians, creoles, and native Alaskans are always called "undersea people.") In these cautionary tales, colonial "justice" appears spectacular and fearsome. The new rule of the game, for Indians: don't be violent; and especially, don't hurt whites.

One of the most intriguing texts in Oswalt's "folk history" section, while offering an account of events now somewhat vague, gives a good sense of how Kashaya viewed the Russian operation. The story has been titled by the editor: "Hunting Sea Otter and Farming." I will quote it in full and explore some of its implications as Kashaya history. Like most of the accounts directly concerning Fort Ross, it derives from Herman James's maternal grandmother, Lukaria.

> Lukaria lived almost her entire life in the vicinity of Métini and was about eight years old when Fort Ross was founded there. She lived through the Russian occupation, the subsequent filling of the land with American settlers, and the consequent dying of much of the old Indian way of life. Herman James was brought up mainly by Lukaria and acquired his knowledge of myths, tales of the supernatural, and folk history directly from her. He was a grown man in his twenties when she died in 1908. By this fortunate circumstance of an intimate overlapping of two long life spans, we are able to transcribe, at only second-hand, accounts of personal experiences as much as 150 years old. (Oswalt, 1964: 9)

Although the history retold here is clearly intended to represent a general, moral viewpoint, it is never separated from personal experience. As Herman James insists at the end of each retelling, these stories are true because they were told to him by his grandmother, she who had first-hand knowledge.

Most of James's tales reflect a woman's perspective. (This is true of virtually all the materials in *Kashaya Texts*.) One story centers on a mother's defense of her children against white marauders. And the accounts of punishment for wife beaters at the fort focus on strong women: one protests her treatment in a dramatic suicide; the other declines to return to her abusive husband, despite his public reformation. The tales pointedly refuse "happy endings" through male redemption. In the story "Sea Otter Hunting and Farming," quoted below, one feels a moral sensibility which may have a gendered aspect, while the story also reflects a general Kashaya judgment of the activities of the "undersea people." Parts of the account reflect Lukaria's direct observations at Métini; other parts must derive from Kashaya conversations with Alaskan hunters at the fort.

"Hunting Sea Otter and Farming"
(Told by Herman James, September, 1958)

1. *I am going to tell about what the undersea people did. When they first came up, they lived at Métini. They lived there a long time.*

2. *After a while, it turned out that they had sailed out and found a land up north. After sailing a while, they arrived during what we call leafing-out time [early spring]; the land was already starting to warm up. When they had been traveling for six months, they sailed south from there. Sailing along, they were long overdue. They must have found what we call otter—otter skin is valuable; they sell one skin for a lot. When they arrived back, they told about it—their own people, the undersea people—the Indians didn't know about that yet.*

3. *After a while they filled a slightly larger boat with everything—food, guns, ammunition. Having gotten everything ready, they sailed off at pinole time [summer]. They sailed for a while—it was perhaps one month that they were sailing towards that place. At that time the ships moved around by sail only. There were no motors at that time operating to propel boats.*

4. *Then they sailed up to that place. That land in the north was a cold place. We Indians called it Ice Country [Alaska]. After staying a while, they sailed southward. They were transporting south many skins—many otter skins. They say it was six months before they showed up.*

5. *Once in a while they ran out of food; they saw hard times. Many times that happened to them, but they didn't listen [profit from their mistakes]. They sailed off for long periods and sold those skins. Loading up the boats, they sent them off to some other place. When they sold [the skins], they made quite a lot of money. Other things they didn't do much. They only did that work. They went collecting in the north.*

6. *One time, many young men sailed out in two boats. Still others had already sailed on ahead. One [of the two boats] sailed off after them. That one didn't find the others, but the second one did sail up to the north to the Ice Country. Nowadays that has become a big town [Sitka]. But at that time it was wild country; there was no one there—only a lot of wild animals.*

7. The other was absent for a long time; it turned out to be lost; it had sailed a little off course. They set out to search for it and unexpectedly found it way off somewhere else. [The lost ship] accompanied the others now; when they sailed off, they followed. They landed over there. They were starving, having run out of food. For a while, for a week perhaps, they had been starving. Some had become very weak; only a few of the stronger ones could walk around.

8. When the two [crews] had landed there, rested a while, become a little stronger, then they went out hunting. They found a lot [of sea otter]: they are said to have killed quite a few in one day—about twenty or thirty. Some of the men skinned them, dried them, put them in sacks, and loaded them in the boats. There were many, about two or three hundred skins, when they returned. That is what they did.

9. They did that for a long time. With that money they lived there—the undersea people. They didn't grow anything; they didn't even keep cattle. They only did that one thing. With that they made money for food to eat and clothes to wear and food to feed their wives and children. They did that for a long time.

10. After a while it got so that they couldn't sail up there because of the ice. They say that in that country the ice was like houses floating around, it was so cold. It was like mountains rising from the sea. Once in a while when a boat was bumped by one, it was smashed to pieces. When that happened the people drowned and froze stiff from the cold. One time when that must have happened to a boat, the undersea people—there were perhaps twenty in the boat—were all drowned. They were never found, never heard from again; they were never to return again.

11. They still didn't listen but still sailed off to gather and shoot the many [otter], and having loaded up the boats with them, sail off to their home—which was Métini. One time, after a while, as I said before, the route where they were accustomed to sailing up turned out to be closed off by ice rearing up like mountains. It was blocked where they usually went, it having really begun to turn cold. It got so that they couldn't return; there was no way to sail forward. When that happened, they said, "Let's go back; it's too hard for us to break a way through," and, having turned around, they started back. When they were sailing along the way, they, too, ran out of food—the food ran short. Starving, they sailed along.

12. When they didn't show up from there, the other undersea people from Métini set out to search; they already knew what had happened to them when they didn't show up for so long. Now they set sail. They found [the lost ship]

when it had sailed about halfway back. Some of the men had already died— starved—only the few stronger ones were sailing the ship. The ship that had sailed out from Métini was carrying a lot of food, for they had known the others would be starving. They gave them a lot of food. After a while the others [rescuers] took over the operation of the ship, letting them relax and just live on the boat while being fed. They became stronger. They sailed along. They sailed in without anything. They had just turned back on the way without otter skins. They didn't catch even one.

13. They say that it was on the last trip that that happened to them. "Let's quit. We can't sail up there any more," they said to the commander. At first the commander didn't agree. "It's true," they said. "These sick people are sick from starvation," said one [captain of the expedition]. While speaking, he announced that he wasn't going to sail off any more. The commander then said, "We'll find something else [to do]."

14. Then they sold the skins and got a lot of money for them. With that they bought what they could grow for food [seeds], because they couldn't sail off northwards any more. With that they bought wheat to plant where the fields stretch out at Métini. The whole land was covered; that was their business now. By growing they learned how to grow the food, all the things they ate. They lived there a long time. That was the only way they prospered.

15. Other people didn't do that work that they had discovered—of valuable otter skins. When they sold those, everywhere they prepared clothes—made expensive coats. Poor people, however, couldn't buy them; they were so expensive then. But they made their own coats, everything for their women and for the children. They sewed them for wearing in winter. That's what they say they did, realizing they couldn't get them any more, couldn't find otter skins any more.

16. This, too, is true; this, too, my grandmother saw and told about. She had remembered well everything they did. Then she told it to me. I have remembered it for a long time. It was sixty-five years ago that my grandmother told me that; I still remember it and have told it true. She also said that it was true about how they first landed, and made money for food to eat, and did those things. This is all. (Oswalt, 1964: 261–265)

Lukaria's account, retold by Herman James, describes several dangerous hunting expeditions and rescues. It also explains the basic economics of the sea-otter trade and the transition at Fort Ross from exclusive reliance on commercial hunting to agricultural production. In these domains, it is true to historical "fact."

But there are additional dimensions in which this historical account is true. Its narration of the facts is faithful to a Kashaya way of seeing the undersea people at "Métini"—not, significantly, at "Fort Ross," a name that does not appear. The old Kashaya settlement becomes the undersea people's home base. Their forays north to Alaska begin and end at Métini. How are we to understand this historical recentering? The story's fourth sentence says that, after living a long time at Métini, the undersea people "had sailed out and found a land up north." Robert Oswalt supplies a clarifying footnote: "Herman James was under the impression that the undersea people came to Fort Ross first and then discovered Alaska from there rather than the reverse, true sequence." Here the story diverges from the "facts." But Oswalt's footnote opens up new questions.

Herman James was scrupulously retelling what he heard from his grandmother. Whatever changes may have occurred in the process of oral transmission and recollection, it is unlikely that the centering of the tale in Métini would have been added. In this respect, Herman James was certainly retelling the story as it had come down to him. Thus, if Oswalt asked him whether he believed it was true that the undersea people came first to Métini and then sailed to Alaska, and if James answered yes, what would this mean? Would it mean that it was true in the story, or true independently of the story? And if Oswalt asked James whether he knew that the Russians and Alaskans had come to Métini after Alaska and the answer was no, would it follow that the story told to him by Lukaria was not true on this important point? On the occasion of this retelling, was James primarily concerned with being true to the story, or to an independent historical reality referred to by the story? If the former, on this occasion, does it preclude recognition of the latter at another time, in a different relational context?

Whatever Herman James believed about the independent historical facts of discovery, the truth of the story he told cannot be separated from *a way of narrating, and judging, history.* This truth depends on a specific location at Métini, an important Kashaya center and the place Lukaria spent most of her life. It must have seemed mysterious to the Kashaya, at first, that the undersea people could feed and clothe themselves without producing the necessities of life. How could they live, when all they did was hunt for sea-otter skins? There was no place—no land, plants, animals—from which they drew their sustenance. Soon, however, the workings of a distant market became clear, and the story explains them. Moreover, the

Kashaya's most substantial contacts with the newcomers were with native Alaskans. Where did they come from? What did they do on their hunting trips? Why did they travel so far? Lukaria passes on stories that Kashaya women surely heard from their domestic partners. Indeed, the stories probably refer to actual experiences; but given imperfect knowledge of each other's languages, and lacking the detail that comes with eyewitness accounting, the stories have a vague, somewhat dreamlike quality.

The Ice Country, with its intense cold, dangerous floating mountains, and constant threat of starvation, is anything but inviting. Why would anyone go there? The stories take a dim view of the only conceivable reason: hunting otters for sale at a great profit. The hunters, driven by this aim, always end up starving or lost at sea. "They didn't listen [profit from their mistakes]," the narrator says repeatedly, using phrases common in the teaching of children. The story clearly approves the fact that the undersea people eventually turn away from sea-otter hunting to agriculture, away from selling skins for coats poor people can't afford and toward making their own coats. Self-sufficiency is valued over reliance on a faraway market. The sea-otter trade, dangerous like the shifting northern ice, brings famine when things go wrong. A cautionary tale. Don't cut yourself off from producing your own food and clothing. Don't be seduced by the lure of the market.

A critique of mercantile capitalism? Or merely a warning to stay home, stay connected to the land, avoid floating mountains? There's a risk of overinterpretation here. But it's hard not to see this Kashaya history in relation to ongoing struggles to *stay*, actively, to resist being subsumed by a mobile world, a world of abstract commodities and exchange values. How does this story continue to make sense of contact history in light of twentieth-century Kashaya histories of separatism and wary engagement with white society? Herman James, a recent Mormon convert when he recited the story to Oswalt, had lived most of his life under the influence of the Bole Maru Dreaming Religion, a revivalist movement. Its most powerful Kashaya prophets, Annie Jarvis and Essie Parrish, promoted traditional values and local attachments. Before the Second World War, Jarvis actively resisted federal proposals to relocate the Kashaya on lands more accessible to employment. What might the recurring themes of "Sea Otter Hunting and Farming"—the themes of rescue, nourishment, and return "home" to Métini—signify at these later moments, when many Kashaya were leaving the land for work elsewhere?

In the story, active staying meant keeping "Métini" (a Kashaya center) from becoming "Fort Ross" (outpost of a foreign empire). In this history the stretch of Sonoma coastland is a homeland, a place of return, rather than a discovered, frontier place. Seen in this light, the centering of contact history at Métini is less a historical error than a narrative strategy, with moral and political consequences. Oswalt (1956: 11) points out that the Kashaya storytellers always set the scene for their tales in a known territory. So vague a place as Alaska (let alone Russia) could be located concretely only in relation to a narrative center at Métini. Moreover, this repositioning of the factual history of discovery would have the added effect of establishing a moral center for the tale, literally grounding its critique of the sea-otter trade.

Narrative histories organize facts in meaningful series. They make sense in spatial/temporal "worlds" which situate the truth of the story, its concrete reality for specific communities. What different forms of "history" are juxtaposed at Fort Ross / Métini? Nonrepeating events in linear time are recalled here, retold from distinct perspectives. Can the "facts" be extracted from the different records, sifted and compared? Yes, but only as known from a specific place in time and at the cost of evacuating the historical *content* of the different narratives' *form*—the differently centered maps/histories they presuppose. The "facts" come to us encoded in concrete experiences and projections. Can we accept the historical reality of complex contact relations where events are construed by differently positioned subjects in overlapping but nonidentical ways? Is it possible that historical reality is not something independent of these differently centered perspectives, not their sum total, and not the result of a critical sifting of different viewpoints by independent experts "at the end of the day"? Can we conceive of historical reality as an overlay of contextual stories whose ultimate meanings are open-ended because the contact relations that produced them are discrepant, unfinished?

Lukaria's repositioning of contact history at Métini takes on fresh significance in current contexts of native resurgence. The recent anniversary of Columbus' arrival in the "New World" provoked a chorus of objections from indigenous peoples to the very idea of "discovery." For the notion, uncritically repeated for centuries, made Europe the exclusive center of historical dynamism and consciousness. Historical visions with deep sources in the Americas were inconceivable—recognized, if at all, only as legend or myth. All this has changed. Indigenous stories of contact recenter familiar stories of discovery, conflict, acculturation, and resistance. The line between myth and history can no longer be drawn along a border between Western and non-Western epistemologies. And in the wake of growing arguments over the cultural and political location of historical narratives, it becomes harder and harder to sustain a unified, inclusive historical consciousness capable of sorting and reconciling divergent experiences. Hegel's synthetic historical realism was turned on its head by Marx, but not decentered. That would be the philosophical project of Nietzsche, and the practical task, still unfinished, of decolonization.

Commodities

I'm wandering around the reconstructed fort, peering into rooms filled with trade goods—china plates and teapots, bales of tea, animal traps, coils of rope. On a desk: pens and ink, ledgers . . . In another room I observe the animal skulls, insects, plant samples, and notebooks of a naturalist. Downstairs: scores of muskets, powder horns, and casks of gunpowder. The buildings have been reconstructed according to original plans, using thick redwood timber and Russian building techniques when possible. (Modern roofing, glass, and fire extinguishers are also in evidence.) I recall reading somewhere that the carpenters who built Fort Ross used maritime joinery. And I find myself thinking of the fort as a kind of beached, reconfigured ship.

The one house still incorporating Russian materials was built by the fort's last governor, Alexander Rotchev, for his wife, a princess, and their family. According to a French visitor, it contained a "choice library, a piano, and a score of Mozart." Now the house is empty, except for a series of interpretive panels. Outside the door a docent and some visitors are sitting in the shade of an apple tree. She is filling in historical details. I approach warily, wanting to hear what she's saying but jealous of my dreamy independence, reluctant to become just another tourist. When the guide passes around some objects, I join the group for a closer look.

We take turns holding a flat black square, about the thickness of an average book and embossed with Chinese writing and designs. She tells us it is compressed tea in the form it traveled across the Pacific, around Cape Horn to New England and Europe. We sniff the dry square to see if we can pick up a faint scent of tea, or even of the ox blood with which it was mixed for travel.

Then I am holding the thing I have been wanting to touch: a sea-otter pelt. The docent passes around a Californian and an Alaskan otter skin, each one thick and soft—the latter, she tells us, preferred by nineteenth-century consumers for its especially dark luster and thickness. Sea-otter fur has more hairs per square inch than the coat of any other creature. Chinese traders in Canton paid a hundred dollars each for skins speared along the American coast. A hundred dollars, in 1820, was the profit made by a Pennsylvania farmer for a year's work! I register these facts as the "soft gold" slips between my fingers . . . And as our guide hastens to add: "These otters died of natural causes."

I cannot quite get my mind around the fact that pelts like these could have driven the whole undertaking—the far-flung enterprise of Russian America, with its violent disruption of Aleut and Koniag societies; the crucial expansion (in conjunction with whaling) of New England merchant economies; the establishment of the North Pacific as a zone of imperial competition, thus hastening Spanish colonization of Alta California. The Russian-American Company would never have attempted its costly Alaska operation without the wildly profitable sea otter. And for the early New England–China trade, these animals, bought cheap on the American coast and sold dear in Canton, were a crucial link. What else could North America or Russia offer the Chinese luxury market? What other item of exchange could fill ships with tea, spices, and porcelain, generating the profits needed to sustain risky navigation in badly charted seas? The challenge of the China trade was to find things that would sell in Canton. In the later nineteenth century, sandalwood and sea cucumber from Hawaii and the South Pacific would fill the bill. During the Fort Ross years, the fur trade which had fueled Russian imperial expansion was already in decline.

A century and a half later, here on the edge of the Pacific, a sea-otter pelt reminds me of the overwhelming influence of Chinese demand for exotic goods—its power in the eighteenth and nineteenth centuries, and again today. Much has changed, and Asia feels nearby again. Now Japanese are buying up prime properties along the Sonoma coast. Chinese exports disrupt the U.S. balance of trade. The otter pelt lies limp in my hands. What did it feel like to Manchu aristocrats in 1800? How could this thing somehow equal a year of farmwork? What does it equal now? How could these remains of dead animals create such wealth, driving people to perilous exploits, to death, and to conquest?

Marx called the commodity "a mysterious thing, simply because in it the social character of men's labor appears to them as an objective character stamped upon the product of that labor; because the relation of the producers to the sum total of their own labor is presented to them as a social relation, existing not between themselves, but between the products of their labor" (Marx, 1961: 72). Seen as commodities, sea-otter skins and bales of tea exist as relations of equivalence independent from the work of Aleut hunters or Chinese coolies. The skins are valuable because they can be exchanged in Canton. Tea is worth producing in quantity because strangers will pay for it with rare luxury items. Exchange value, as Marx recognized, determines production. An Aleut might hunt sea otters for skins or meat (also for fun and a challenge), but he would not hunt in large teams, far from home, without the material compulsion of the market and the labor discipline it required. The value of the products of his labor, in no proportion to any wage received or to the risk and social disruption imposed, would remain a mystery. As a commodity, the sea-otter skin would take on an independent, alien existence, an abstract relation between things traded in Canton, or at the Mongolian trading city of Kiakhta. We hear this abstraction, this distance, when Lukaria (through Herman James) says: "They sailed off for long periods and sold those skins. Loading up the boats, they sent them off to some other place."

Recalling Marx, as I stroke the luxurious, dead otter skin, I think of the human activities—the hunting skills of men, the tanning skills of women—that, around 1800, transformed living animals into pelts, counted, bundled, priced. These "productive" activities resulted in the virtual extermination of the sea otter. And today, as capitalist markets expand, virtually unopposed, throughout the planet, and as the gap between rich and poor grows apace, I hold on to the need Marx recognized for some ethical and political purchase on these global equations, with their transforming local consequences. At a moment of rampant neoliberalism, the question is urgent.

Corn, for example. Under the present North American Free Trade Agreement, peasant corn farmers in Chiapas, Mexico, must compete with large-sale agribusiness in Kansas, USA. The peasant corn economy, with all of its rich symbolism and long tradition, is subjected to an international market that has the power to sweep it away, swiftly and violently. And coffee. In eastern Chiapas, where barefoot *campesinos* and Mayan Indians arduously carved plantations out of the Lacandon forest, a drop in global coffee prices and a "liberal" withdrawal of government support have meant ruin. It is not surprising that the Zapatista rebellion was centered in Chiapas and that its outbreak coincided with implementation of the Free Trade Agreement.

In 1995 I hold a sea-otter pelt and think of its power in 1830. This skin, in Canton, equaled a year of farm labor . . . The fact still does not compute. And it should not—any more than a sack of corn in Chiapas should, somehow, equal a sack from Kansas. Corn weeded by hand on steep hillsides by people who eat tortillas with every meal cannot be equivalent to something dispensed from giant grain elevators.

I struggle to keep commodities mysterious, to grasp the sheer incongruity and violence of their fantastic equivalences. This mystery is not something to be reduced, as Marx wished, to a true measure of equivalence in social labor. (What a world of different circumstances is hidden in the word "social"!) But rather, the mystery inheres in commodities' openness to diverse appropriations, their capacity for being historically made and remade. What is corn for a Mayan Indian? A fax machine for Subcommandante Marcos? What is a sea-otter skin to an eco-tourist? A VCR or acrylic paint in the hands of Australian aboriginal artists? A rum bottle in a Santeria altar? A Bob Marley recording in Hawaii? A Rambo T-shirt in Lebanon? A pack of cigarettes and a beer can left at the Vietnam War Memorial? A car used by California Indians to return to their reservation for a festival?

Animals

The first detailed scientific descriptions of American sea otters were provided by the German naturalist Georg Wilhelm Stellar. In 1741–1742, Stellar accompanied Vitus Bering aboard the *St. Peter* on its disastrous final voyage. Shipwrecked for a winter off the Kamchatka coast, Stellar had ample opportunity to observe the curious creatures. Otters were the survivors' staple food for six months, and they were killed by the hundreds for their skins—in hopes of profit in the event of a safe return, and to serve as stakes in the endless card games that occupied the men all winter. Stellar disapproved of this excess.

> [The sea otter] is an extraordinarily beautiful and pleasant animal, as well as amusing and comical in its habits; at the same time it is a very cajoling

and amorous one. When one sees them running, the gloss of their hair exceeds the blackest velvet. They lie together as families; the male is with its female, the half-grown offspring called *koshloki,* and the nursing young. The male caresses its female by stroking, for which he uses the front feet like a dog, and lies on her, but she teasingly often pushes him away from her. Not even the most loving human mother engages in the same kind of playing with her children, and they love their children in such a way that they expose themselves to the obvious danger of death.

In Stellar's account, as in many other conservationist portrayals of the sea otter, anthropomorphism abounds.

They stand in the sea upright like humans and hop up with the waves, hold the front foot over the eyes and look at one as though the sun were bothering them. They lie on their backs and scratch their noses with their front feet, they throw their children in the water and catch them again. When a sea otter is attacked and cannot see an escape route anywhere, he blows and hisses like an infuriated cat. When he receives a blow, he gets ready to die in this fashion: he lies on his side, pulls his hind feet after him, and covers his eyes with his front feet: and when he is dead he lies like a dead person, since he crosses his front feet on his chest. (Stellar, 1988: 147–148)

Since Stellar's time, this most human of animals, forever playful and sad, has gained pride of place in the ecological pantheon of endangerment. Its destruction during the late eighteenth and early nineteenth centuries was swift and relentless. By the time Nicolai Resanov, the visionary architect of Russian America who visited Fort Ross in 1806, began to talk of sea-mammal conservation, the damage had been done.

Today, gray whales, also hunted to the brink of extermination, pass Fort Ross on their migrations between Baja California and the Arctic Ocean. Boatloads of tourists trail in their wake. Sea otters, their small population closely monitored, are glimpsed again in the waters near Carmel, or playing starring roles at the Monterey Bay Aquarium. From deadly to benign commodification: these creatures have, at least, survived the techno-capitalist history that visited them in the late eighteenth century. The efficient killing and processing machine of the nineteenth-century whaling ship, the relentless *baidarkas* with their organized, quick spears, are gone, replaced by a safe-zone of human love, a bubble of compassion in which to live.

In the years around 1800, piles of skins and barrels of whale oil were prized by an expanding mercantile capitalism. The "life" of the otters, seals, and whales was a natural obstacle which had to be overcome, something processed and discarded in the course of production. Today this "life" is itself commodified. It is figured on T-shirts, in stuffed animals, consumed at gift shops, toy stores, at the Monterey Bay Aquarium, and on the Santa Cruz tourist pier—where the *baidarkas* once hunted. The endangered otters and whales are once again historical actors, limiting, to a degree, what can be done in the coastal environment. Whales and otters versus offshore oil rigs. There is some power here.

Historical "actors"? Surely this is going too far. For what I have said suggests only that whales and otters have become a new kind of raw material for human appropriation and commodification. They hinder development only inasmuch as they are mobilized as potent symbols by environmentalist culture and politics. The agency, surely, is all human. Yet if environmentalism teaches anything, it is that "we," humans, are not the only actors in the nonreversible course of the planet, and it questions a worldview that keeps "history" exclusively located in human action and consciousness. Leaving aside the overlay of species- and ethnocentrism in such a worldview (Kashaya histories can include animals as conscious agents), human-centered historicisms increasingly seem dated, legacies of nineteenth-century notions of progress and development that cannot be sustained. The nature of historical agency and consciousness is newly uncertain.

A symptom, perhaps, of this uncertainty is my hankering to ask an absurd question. What does the history of changing environments, including their own near extinction, commodification, and consumption since 1700, look like to sea otters? How might this history appear to them? The arrival of a new predator? Holocaust? The predator's removal? Survival? Can we imagine a nonhuman historical consciousness? The anthropomorphism of such a question makes Stellar's projections seem tame by comparison. Why this desire to find something like historical consciousness and agency in nonhumans?

What temporalities define the consciousness of sea otters? Days and nights? Tides? Seasons and currents? The life cycles of kelp and other food? Reproduction? Birth and death? Perhaps even generations—a sense of living through offspring? None of these temporalities, the feelings, actions, and skills associated with them, come within distant translation-range of "history" in its human senses. Still, the life of California sea otters in 1995 is clearly different from that in 1800. They are drastically fewer; their environment is more polluted; the flora and fauna around them have changed. Could otters have a feeling that the environment in which they now live is not the one for which they evolved? The changes have been abrupt, the destruction nearly total. And two hundred years is very short in evolutionary time. Could the discrepancy between evolutionary and historical temporalities register somewhere in the otter's experience? A feeling of being in a world that doesn't quite work? In this sense—a consciousness of "historical" change? Is the perception of a rupture a kind of bare minimum of historical consciousness, a before and an after that break the flow of cyclical, repeatable time? Could historical consciousness be minimally defined as the awareness of a linear sequence different in quality from other sequences—for example, transitions between fall and winter, or between generations?

Why indulge in such speculations? Perhaps to glimpse, from a translated place of animal difference, the enveloping waters in which I myself swim, the environment in which my "life" unfolds, a habitat called history. Otters have been part of this history. We both, with our different consciousnesses, are affected by its changes, constraints, possibilities. And we have a future, perhaps, together—sharing a "nature" that is being ruined, transformed, and preserved largely by humans. The life of sea otters, once destroyed by human ambition, enterprise, and greed, is now sustained by human environmental vision. This vision, emergent and embattled, is composed of scientific interest, romanticism, and guilt, as well as by a positive sense that terms like "history" and "nature" are not mutually defining opposites but, rather, linked terms in a global transformative process, a process whose endpoint and even direction escape certain knowledge. Something that cannot be grasped by a single "consciousness."

Perhaps this explains the clumsiness of my questions about sea otters' "historical consciousness." For as we struggle, in the late twentieth century, to articulate a historical imagination that no longer assumes humans to be the godlike subjects of destiny, are we not still entangled in a nineteenth-century ideology where attaining fuller, more complete consciousness is the progressive goal of being-in-history? But is consciousness, a process which presupposes a central, individual subject, the ultimate crystallization of life-in-history? "Historical consciousness" may be only one form of historical imagination, a form which came to a kind of apogee, with

Hegel, in a context of nineteenth-century belief in the knowing, "Western" self. A certain Reason. And although the global reach of this form of historical consciousness has been pervasive, and although it now defines "reality" for many people in non-Western, twentieth-century contexts, it is no longer adequate to the heterogeneous experiences of environment, continuity, and change which clamor for recognition as properly "historical," as different paths into and beyond modernity. Perhaps this splitting up of "historical consciousness" enables me to ask about nonhuman temporalities which intersect with but are not reducible to human history. An impossible translation exercise, since the code to which I compare these experiences is premised precisely on their exclusion. This is my predicament within a historical ontology, a specific sense of the real becoming visible at the fraying limits of a triumphant West.

Standing at Fort Ross, remembering the San Andreas Fault, its obscure, devastating temporality and the short span of human intervention and management. Why do I want, still, to call the whole uncontrollable process "history"? What sense does it make to speak of natural history, the history of the planet, the history of the universe? As if dates and linear time could consolidate all the temporalities, aligning them with human agency. Yet I seem to need historical meanings, the way an otter needs a kelp forest. A place to live.

Empires

Having stumbled onto the Sandwich Islands (Hawaii), Captain Cook put in at Nootka Sound on Vancouver Island during the spring of 1778. Relations with the Indians were friendly, and some metal was traded for sea-otter skins. He then explored the Bering Sea, refuted theories of the Northwest Passage, mapped many islands and coasts, and returned to winter in Hawaii. After conflicts with the Hawaiians resulted in Cook's death, his ships proceeded to Kamchatka, and thence homeward. In Macao the few pelts casually acquired at Nootka fetched £2,000. With this news and the availability of the Sandwich Islands as a base and stopover, the North Pacific soon teemed with English and Yankee traders and whalers. It became a site of intense imperial competition. The arrival of British and American ships broke the Spanish and Russian monopolies. Between 1810 and 1850, the disposition of power from Hawaii to Alaska and Baja California was largely settled in its present form.

Not long after the Russians arrived in Alta California, the Transcontinental Treaty of 1819 established 42° north, the current Oregon-California border, as the extent of Spanish aspirations. The Oregon Territories, as far north as Sitka, were claimed by Americans, English, and (sporadically) Russians. Alta California, though formally Spanish (and soon Mexican), was in fact under little effective imperial control. The Spanish Empire, overextended and distracted by European wars, could not provide colonists in large numbers. Its overland supply lines were uncertain, and a maritime presence along the coast virtually nil. After the Mexican Revolution of 1821, the Californios, whose leaders were padres, royalists, and independent rancheros, became even more disconnected from the center, ejecting Mexican governors who displeased them. They traded with Yankee and British ships and with the Russians at Fort Ross (while formally insisting that the intruders depart). A trickle of settlers had arrived from the United States, including the Swiss-American Johann August Sutter, whose Sacramento fort became a welcoming point for overland arrivals. Sutter's discovery of gold in 1849 would transform Alta California's population and economy. Mexican California was quickly overrun—and the rest, as we say, is history.

History: what happened, what had to occur. In retrospect. Can we imagine Los Angeles as part of Mexico? Or perhaps California, New Mexico, and Arizona as an independent, Spanish-speaking country? It is still a shock to come across a map from 1845. The border begins at New Orleans, twists north and west until it reaches the forty-second parallel in what is now Montana, and then runs straight to the Pacific. The vast area south of this line is labeled "Mexico." This is not one of those early maps one finds amusing because they contain distortions of topography and blank spaces. Just 150 years old, the map shows a fully recognizable North America, in which the United States has a very odd form. The familiar cut-out of the continental United States—a shape we saw every day on the wall in school, from sea to shining sea, its southern edge naturally following the Rio Grande—is not there.

Could things have happened differently? If Japan had not been closed to commerce for centuries and had helped solve Russian America's resupply problem? If the czars had taken an active interest in their eastern frontier? In the 1830s Ferdinand von Wrangell, governor of Russian America, was arguing that Fort Ross should expand into the Sacramento River valley, territory which no empire yet controlled. What if the czar had not refused the price of Mexican agreement: recognition of their revolution? Straws in the wind.

Or what if British Canada had gained control over the entire Oregon Territory? What if the U.S. election of 1844 had gone the other way, putting a brake on expansionist politics? And what if Santa Ana had been a better tactician in Texas, or had, with British help, persuaded the Texans to stay independent? And if this had slowed the move to annex Alta California, would there have been a Treaty of Guadaloupe Hidalgo in 1848?

Straws in the wind. In retrospect, everything is all too clear. Mexico and Russia were overextended. England could control coasts and trade, but not fill a territory with colonists. The demographically and economically expansive United States had to prevail. But if the Civil War had taken a different turn . . .? Playing against History is always a losing proposition. The deck is stacked.

Yet the counterhistorical work of reaching into the past for alternative futures is not about claiming that it could—or should—have been different. It's a process of thinking historically in the present, breaking the spell of inevitability. I return, again, to the U.S. map, and to the crucial decades before 1850, when it was made. Isn't the "naturalness" of the U.S.-Mexico border at the Rio Grande mocked by the blatant arbitrariness of the U.S.-Canada border? In school, I wondered how this line could be so straight. Why that particular parallel? Who chose it? Individual statesmen at a contingent moment reflecting a balance of power. It could easily have been pushed up a bit. Or down.

Is the shape of Canada permanent? In 1995 Quebec just missed, by the slimmest of margins, provoking a constitutional crisis, perhaps separating from the union. Large areas of the Arctic have been returned to Inuit control. Moreover, Canada's economic and cultural ties with the United States are profound. On many levels, the border does not exist. On others, it is vehemently defended. Indeed, virtually everywhere one looks nations and empires seem both powerful and fragile, united and disunited, discrete and permeable. Complex balances of power and interest sustain and undermine them.

Britannia once ruled the waves; now America rules the airwaves. But how completely? For how long? The British Empire, which on my schoolroom maps painted large red swaths across Africa, declined in less than a half-century. Shrunk now to a few small islands, the United Kingdom includes populations who reject "English" national, cultural, and racial hegemony: Caribbeans, Africans, South Asians. Nationalist movements in Ireland, Scotland, and Wales disturb the English peace. European affiliations make the "English" Channel a very permeable border.

The Soviet Union, in many ways a continuation of the Russian Empire, is in disarray. Centuries of expansion across a vast continent suddenly appear less inevitable, less driven by historical necessity. This geopolitical fact, which colored my schoolroom maps with a different red, splits into different regional facts and histories reflected in the reappearance of names such as Azerbaijan, Georgia, Uzbekistan, Kazakhstan. The suddenness of the Soviet/Russian imperial crisis is shocking: without even a fifty-year "decline"—and nothing like the slow erosion of the Roman or Spanish empire.

Fort Ross. The West Coast of the United States, not long ago the eastern edge of Russia, is being bought up by investors from Japan and Hong Kong. Is the U.S. American empire in decline? Or perhaps in metamorphosis? It's unclear. We are not yet able to recognize these wavering contradictions as the beginning of an end that some "history" might judge definitive. Currently the changes look more like realignments, recenterings. "Transnational capitalism" is the inheritor of Euro-American imperial dynamics, "Americanization" a common shorthand for the spread of techno-capitalist, market, and media systems throughout the globe. And simultaneously, Anglo California is being displaced by the Pacific and Latin America. People, capital, commodities, driven by global political-economic forces, do not stop at national borders. Will "English Only" movements, immigration restrictions, xenophobic terror attacks, and back-to-basics initiatives be able to stem the tide? Can a rusting "American" assimilation/exclusion machine be repaired?

It would be ironic if the United States were transformed by sheer numbers of people. For in the crucial decades, 1840–1860, when Texas, California, and Oregon were annexed, when the national map took shape, it was sheer numbers of uncontrolled immigrants who took over the lands claimed by Mexico and Britain, creating facts on the ground that battles and treaties would eventually ratify. Now, new facts are being created in transnational cities and in immigrant enclaves throughout the land. The homogeneous territory and history ("Westward-ho") of the United States is complicated, challenged, by populations from the Latino South, from Asia and the Pacific. The new immigrants are racially marked in ways the prior generations from Europe were not, or were marked only temporarily. For them, like the slaves who came from Africa, the melting (whitening) pot works unevenly or not at all. Normative immigrant experiences of assimilation are interrupted by relations of border crossing, by diasporic attachments "elsewhere."

Commodities and markets release forces that tear down borders and unsettle empires; they also consolidate dominant polities. Because economic globalization works both with and against national attachments, it is premature to decree either the end or the consolidation of nation-states. And although the centers of capitalist power are still largely in the European and North American "West," this is changing. Asian economic power is an inescapable reality, whether centered in Japan, Korea, Indonesia, or—most powerfully perhaps—in diasporic and mainland China. Can we still say that global economics, because it is capitalist, is inherently "Western"? As Marx understood, capitalism is revolutionary, destructive *and* productive. And it does not usher in a unified, "bourgeois," or "Western" sociocultural order as it spreads. It has proved to be flexible, working through as well as against regional differences, partially accommodating to local cultures and political regimes, grafting its symbols and practices onto whatever non-Western forms transculturate its logic. It does business with monarchies, dictatorships, oligarchic bureaucracies, and democracies, with neo-Confucians, Hindus, Orthodox Jews, a range of Islamic societies.

Fort Ross, 1830/1995: the progress of the "West," as teleology, as the end or cutting edge of History, falters. Why these dates, this place? In his "Theses on the Philosophy of History" Walter Benjamin saw the need to break the thrall of historicist inevitability, "how it really was." Historical reality was always the story of the victors. A materialist, he said, shuns universal history and works to "blast" past times, "charged with the time of the now . . . out of the continuum of history." In a present emergency, forgotten or doomed elements from the past flash up in consciousness, projecting different, discontinuous futures. The materialist historian labors to stop time, to interrupt the flow of thoughts, "in a configuration pregnant with tensions . . . a monad" (Benjamin, 1969: 262–263).

Fort Ross, 1812–1841, is my monad. It helps disarticulate California, showing it as historically constituted from Asia as well as from Europe; relocating it in the shifting borderlands of the Américas, connected to the Island Pacific, to the Alaska/Siberia crossroads. And it opens an alternate space of contacts between whites and Indians: unequal, often violent relations, but not based on the stark alternatives of extermination or assimilation. It offers resources for thinking historically in the present emergency—linked, disparate pasts and futures.

Walls

The Great Wall of China was many walls—border fortifications built, ruined, rebuilt by different dynasties over nearly two thousand years. At times "China" was defined against the north by wall-building, at other moments by commerce and diplomacy. The wall came and went. Its last and most spectacular version, constructed by the Ming in the sixteenth and seventeenth centuries, was probably financed, in significant degree, by Peruvian silver. As much as a fifth of the production of New World mines was shipped by galleon to Manila, where Chinese merchants traded luxury goods. Borders close and open, selectively. The Great Wall is a monument to failure: Ming inability to manage relations in a changing frontier zone. A two-thousand-mile wall could not preserve them; the Manchus swept in.

In his novel *The Shadow Lines,* Amitav Ghosh writes of an Indian family whose members cross and recross two geopolitical borders. One border joins and divides Calcutta and London, the other Calcutta and Dhaka. Toward the end of the book the narrator's failing grandmother prepares for a return visit to the city she left, years before, when India was partitioned: Dhaka, East Pakistan, now Bangladesh. A short flight from Calcutta. The old woman asks whether, from the plane, she will see the border. Her son informs her that it won't look like a map, with different colors on either side of a dark line. "But surely," the old woman persists, "there's something—trenches perhaps, or soldiers, or guns pointing at each other, or even just barren strips of land. Don't they call it no-man's-land?" Her son laughs: "No you won't be able to see anything except clouds and perhaps, if you're lucky, some green fields." She remains puzzled: "But if there aren't any trenches or anything, how are people to know? I mean, where's the difference then? And if there's no difference, both sides will be the same; it'll be just like it used to be before, when we used to catch a train in Dhaka and get off in Calcutta the next day without anybody stopping us. What was it all for then—Partition and all the killing and everything—if there isn't something in between?" (Ghosh, 1989: 148).

Gloria Anzaldúa writes from a place where the 1,950-mile U.S.-Mexico border meets the Pacific. At the beginning of *Borderlands / La Frontera* she walks through a hole in the chain-link fence, feeling with her fingers the wire, "rusted by 139 years / of the salty breath of the sea." Mexican kids chase a soccer ball across. Her subversive borderland draws from everyday life along the *frontera:* multilingualism, code switching, migration back and forth, a peculiar savvy or *facultad,* undoing binary structures . . . But then the borderland shrinks to a narrow line, a wound: "This is my home / this thin edge / of barbwire" (Anzaldúa, 1987: 3).

"In Berlin, the prevailing winds are from the west. Consequently a traveler coming in by plane has plenty of time to observe the city from above. In order to land against the wind, a plane must cross the city and the wall dividing it three times: initially heading east, the plane enters West Berlin airspace, banks left in a wide arc across the eastern part of the city, and then, coming back from the east, takes the barrier a third time on the approach to Tegel landing strip. Seen from the air, the city appears perfectly homogeneous. Nothing suggests to the stranger that he is nearing a region where two political continents collide" (Schneider, 1983: 3). Writing in the early 1980s, Peter Schneider tells of casual crossings, "for the hell of it," to see a movie and return—many subversive crossings, but also internalized walls, the hardest to jump. Today Berlin's wall is rubble—swept away, among other things, by television, which never respected the partition.

Inside the stockade at Fort Ross, cannons, powder, supplies and trade goods, residences for the few relatively genteel Russians. Outside, a cluster of villages, hierarchies, social relations. Inside, a place of refuge and purity; outside, contacts, contaminations. By 1833 there were more than sixty mixed-race children at the colony. Outside the wall a "Russian village" was composed of European-style houses, gardens, and orchards. It housed lower-class ethnic Russians, ethnic Siberians, and Creoles. A Native Alaskan neighborhood was built, Koniag style, facing the water, on a bluff just over the cove. Russian-style plank houses were mixed with several Alaskan semi-underground sod houses, or *barabaras*. The houses over the cove were inhabited by single men, by native Alaskan couples, by a large number of Alaskan men coupled with local Pomo or Miwok women, and by more or less transient kin of those women. A third "village," actually several hamlets scattered on hillsides behind the fort, was inhabited by Pomos and Coast Miwoks. Métini. Contemporary accounts describe cone-shaped houses of redwood, and archaeological research has identified at least one large indented circle, with remains of a center post—probably a sweat lodge or ceremonial structure of some kind.

It is intriguing to speculate about everyday mixing in the communities outside the walls of Fort Ross. Contemporary accounts, archaeological excavation, and Kashaya oral history offer many hints. The role of Pomo and Miwok women as cross-cultural mediators and brokers is particularly significant. They made up the bulk of the "permanent" native Californian population at the fort, complemented by men increasingly recruited, or coerced, for seasonal agricultural labor. Women lived with their Alaskan partners, observing new ways, exchanging stories and skills, bearing chil-dren, preparing unfamiliar foods (for example, sea-lion meat, a staple at the fort) in Kashaya/Miwok ways, introducing venison and acorn mush to the sea-mammal hunters. They maintained regular connections with their families inland and along the coast.

Why did so many women come to the fort? The reasons would have been complex. Coercion? Possibly, but escape to remote Kashaya villages on the high ridges inland was always possible. Protection from Spanish and Mexican abuses? Certainly, in the case of Miwok refugees. And the Kashaya, though not under direct pressure from the padres and rancheros, certainly realized that the Russians could offer a useful barrier. Perhaps women lived at the fort to sustain relations with the undersea people, to observe, to understand and control them. Perhaps they were there because Fort Ross was still Métini, in Kashaya eyes—their place. Archaeological evidence from the native villages at the fort confirms a long-standing pattern of Kashaya contact history: wary and selective engagement. There seems to have been little accumulation of Western trade goods.

Russian colonization had long encouraged intermarriage with native peoples; their cultural policy was live and let live. Unlike the Spanish Empire, the regime at Fort Ross undertook little forced resettlement and religious conversion; and the priority was extractive trade and agriculture, rather than the massive expropriation of lands that came with later Yankee colonization. In the early nineteenth century, the Kashaya were able to sustain traditional lifeways along the coast and atop the high inland ridges. Métini, alongside Fort Ross, was a link in a living Kashaya chain of settlements and kin relations, a site of multiple crossings, never a closed frontier or bastion. In spite of bad working conditions and the Russians' occasionally brutal roundups of indigenous labor at harvest times, Kashaya comings and goings in the neighborhoods around the stockade reflected indigenous agency and were never strictly controlled.

Contacts. In the early nineteenth century, a wave of epidemics swept through Kashaya country. At Fort Ross in 1823, twenty-nine Creoles and native Alaskans, along with an unrecorded number of Indians, succumbed to measles. A second wave of measles struck in 1833. Between 1836 and 1839, epidemics of smallpox, whooping cough, measles, and chicken pox raced through Russian America from the Aleutians to California. Here, as elsewhere, the epidemiological assault, often preceding the establishment of forts, missions, and presidios, was devastating. Indian communities reeled under successive blows, regrouping, holding on. Physical and cultural survival meant making the best of bad situations. If the Kashaya, in contrast to the Miwok and other native Californians, were able to sustain their language and many elements of traditional culture into the 1950s, this was due, in part, to the protection offered during crucial decades by the relatively laissez-faire Russians. The interventionist paternalism and slave regimes of the Spanish and Mexicans were held off; traditional lifeways were adapted to the new contact situation. And one should not underestimate the importance of seeing the "undersea people" depart in 1841. Even as the new "white men" moved in, the possibility, the hope, of a time *after* invasion was renewed.

Fort Ross / Métini: a coming and going of empires: walls built, ruined, rebuilt. When Indian revivalist movements, related to the Ghost Dance, arrived in California during the late nineteenth century, they took hold in Kashaya country. In the twentieth century, the Bole Maru Dreaming Religion was strongly traditionalist and localist, particularly under the charismatic leadership of Annie Jarvis and Essie Parrish. The Kashaya reservation, atop a ridge inland from Stewart's Point, was not abandoned in the 1930s, despite government offers of resettlement in a more practical area of the Russian River valley. The Second World War, with its job opportunities and other disruptions, largely emptied the reservation. When people returned in 1945, their attitude was less insular. Soon Mormon proselytizing divided the community. With Essie Parrish's death in 1979, the Kashaya lost a powerful spiritual leader, yet to be replaced.

In 1996, less than a hundred Kashaya live on the reservation. Signs of poverty abound—patched together houses, dead cars with grass growing through them, planks thrown across rutted driveways. Some elders keep the old ways alive, passing on the stories. Members of the tribe who work in Santa Rosa or the Bay Area return for seasonal reunions. Some no longer attend. The Bole Maru ceremonial house is locked, waiting for a new dreamer.

Just up the road, surrounded by a moat-like lagoon, Odiyan, a large new Tibetan Buddhist study center, displays its eighty-foot-high temple and gleaming copper dome. Constructed by exiles and members of North America's growing Buddhist movement, Odiyan is a replica of Samye, Tibet's first Buddhist monastery.

Pasts

Kashaya maintain a presence in the Fort Ross Interpretive Association (FRIA), which supports interpretive and research activities at the state historical park. Violet Chappelle, daughter of Essie Parrish, serves on the board of directors. During my visit to the fort in December 1995, I joined the association. In its newsletter I found statements by new candidates for the board. Some excerpts:

John Allen (community-college instructor of Asian and American history): "My interest in history is wide-ranging: Byzantine and Russian history and culture, Siberian expansion and the development of the Pacific Rim. As a native of Alaska and long-time resident in my adopted state of California, I also take a special interest in the Russian involvement in North America."

Ludmilla Ershow (professor of Russian at San Francisco State): "I accompany my students to St. Petersburg, and my friends and relatives keep me in touch with Russians, who are very excited about Fort Ross and Russian America. My chief interest in Fort Ross is the Russian period. My serving on the Board would put to work for FRIA my contacts in the local Russian community and my access to academic and cultural circles in Russia."

Otis Parrish (former clockmaker and counselor at the Oakland Consortium of United Indian Nations, Inc. Currently doing graduate work in anthropology at Berkeley): "I am a member of the Kashaya Band of Pomo Indians, whose aboriginal territory encompassed the Fort Ross State Park lands . . . I am a teller of traditional Kashaya stories. My life-long interest has been education and the use of education to get a clearer picture of the lifeways of my Kashaya people. My interest spans the time from the future to the present to the historic, and most importantly the prehistory of the Kashaya people. For me to better understand the future, I must have a better understanding of the people who have come into contact with the Kashaya during its historic periods . . . I believe that the Kashaya part of the park's plan could be further developed, thereby enhancing other components as well."

John Sperry (engineer; teacher of physics and math at Sierra College): "At Fort Ross I've been up to here in Call House restoration work—foundation, roof, and fund raising. I plan to turn now to the building of a baidara and seeking grants to fund the project. Baidaras, thirty-foot skin boats, were important freight craft here at the fort. They were of Aleut design."

Doni Tunheim (architectural color consultant): "As co-founder and co-chairman of the Adobe Coalition, I worked for ten years with all levels of local and state governments as we successfully promoted, funded, and oversaw the restoration of Santa Cruz Mission State Historic Park . . . As co-chair of the First Annual Home Sweet Home tour to benefit the Call Ranch, I am enjoying my involvement in the community."

Jerry Wheeler: "I am a longtime resident of the Fort Ross area and have participated in Living History Day for the last two years as the blacksmith. I know that my talents and skills would enhance the programs at the fort."

The state park at Fort Ross represents three important histories—of Russians, native Californians, and California ranchers—histories that intersect in partial ways. Moreover, each constituency is internally complex. Russian American history includes Siberians, Aleuts, and especially Koniags, along with ethnic Russians and creoles. Kashaya Pomo, along with some Coast Miwok, make up the native Californian constituency. The early history of California during the Ranch period (1842–1906, at the fort) includes Anglo and other European pioneers, along with Mexican cowboys, loggers, farmworkers, and charismatic individuals such as the Chilean ranch-wife Mercedes Call. Initially, the reconstructed fort and historic park were assumed to be primarily a Russian story; and this emphasis continues to dominate the presentation at the site and visitor center. In recent years, however, the park's official interpretive policy has embraced a "flow-of-history" approach. In this vision, the significance of the site includes the natural environment and precontact Kashaya history, as well as the Russian and Ranch periods. The different emphases are connected in a single historical flow.

This policy formally resolves a question that often besets historical (or "heritage") museums and sites: Whose history, whose heritage? The flow-of-history idea answers, in effect: Everyone's history—each finding its proper place in an overlapping sequence. But the policy does not resolve pragmatic, often political, problems of relative emphasis. After the fort was abandoned by the Russians, it became a ranch, then a sawmill; it contained a dance hall, barns, elaborate equipment for loading timber on ships. The reconstructed Russian stockade, chapel, and dwellings largely erase this moment in the flow. The Ranch period is condensed in the lovely old Call Ranch House not far from the stockade. There, restoration projects are well advanced, including plans for Mercedes Call's garden overlooking the Pacific. The Kashaya settlement at Métini, the Koniag and Russian villages, are left to the imagination. Staff at the fort would like to represent them more concretely. But it is hard enough, with a shrinking state-parks budget, to find funds to maintain what already exists. Currently, one wall of the stockade is down, its reconstruction delayed by a shortage of funds.

A docent tells me that the flow-of-history idea is nice, but people don't get it. They ask, for example, what the Russians did in the ranch house. They look, she says, for a core experience, a central moment . . . It has been said that history is just an arrangement to make sure everything doesn't happen at once. Chronology, history's orderly "flow," must be among its least intuitive devices.

Archaeological research has for some time been reconstructing the life that took place outside the walls of the Russian fort. The community's interethnic mix is documented by excavations at the old Russian cemetery, directed by Lynne Goldstein, and by ongoing work on the Koniag village and the Kashaya settlements, organized by Kent Lightfoot. The cemetery and Koniag-village project required consultation and permission from native organizations on Kodiak Island. The Métini work, in its early stages, can be pursued only with active Kashaya support. If this is forthcoming, and when detailed knowledge becomes available, how will the native aspects of the Ross contact zone be publicly represented? Who will control the story to be told?

Current interpretive signs at the fort portray good interethnic relations, a happy family. Russian-Alaskan relations are seen as voluntary and fair. The plaques stress that the Russians, unlike other colonizers, paid, fed, and clothed their native workers. There is no account of forced recruitment or hostage-taking. Accounts of relations at the fort with the local Indians stress intermarriage, but do not mention epidemics. Today's Kodiak Island natives and many Pomo and Miwok take a less charitable view of the Russians and their historical legacy. Park staff agree that the interpretive plaques at the fort and the introductory displays at the visitor venter are, to put it kindly, outdated. When resources become available to replace them, who will write the new narratives? And how will the different historical constituencies be balanced? Will it be possible to celebrate California's ranch history without describing the forced expulsion of Kashaya from Métini, not long after the Russians left? Will the stories of lynchings, the tales of harassment and protection of native women by ranchers—accounts that appear in *Kashaya Texts*—appear alongside Mercedes Call's garden?

And if the Kashaya villages around the fort are described, how will any differences between oral history and scientific archaeology be reconciled? If a settlement were to be reconstructed, what historical moment would be chosen? Must it fall within the Russian period? Important community stakes direct such questions, as well as issues of relative historical truth. For example, what would be done with any large round indentations, which may be ceremonial structures? How would such structures be related to the circular, semi-subterranean dance houses that became prominent during the revivalist movements of the later nineteenth century and which, according to many scholars, were offshoots of the Ghost Dance? Indigenous memory contradicts this history, giving such dance houses an older, local origin. How should the difference be resolved? Would scientific dating of the site and its contents adequately settle the matter, as a practical, indeed a political issue?

If the excavations are completed and interpreted at the fort, or if a portion of Métini is reconstructed, the story told there will be a Kashaya story. The current politics of excavation and public interpretation demand this. But why should the Kashaya, who do not necessarily speak with a single voice, want to tell their history to outsiders, in this arena? And if they do, what will their story be like? I don't know. That will be negotiated among different tribal authorities, scholars (native and nonnative), funding sources, and park staff. But it seems evident that the Kashaya will and should have a determining role. And their story would certainly present Métini as much more than an addendum to the Russian fort. The ongoing story of Indian life here reaches back to the primordial land, to animals and plants, to the activities of Coyote and other mythic or ancestral actors. It long predates and has outlasted the Russian decades. Thus, Kashaya history does not so much complement or fill in Russian and Euro-American histories as cut across, intersect with them. In the public space of Fort Ross Historic Park, would this narrative need to be reconciled with the histories of Russian America or of California ranching? Should the primary purpose of such an addition be to present a "full" slice of historical reality, if only during the early and mid-nineteenth century? I do not think so. Its principal purpose, and achievement, would be to make a space for the telling of a Kashaya story, a differently centered history drawing on overlapping historical and archaeological traditions, but not limited by them. This presupposes the activity of Kashaya as more than simple consultants or advisors in the process of narration and reconstruction. Something more than an articulation of "heritage," this public re-membering of Métini would be historical work by a community both reckoning itself among others and articulating a tribal past-becoming-future. The project's primary task would be to tell history "our way."

Outside the visitor center, hanging beneath the wooden sign that reads "Fort Ross," is a smaller plaque: "May-Tee-Nee." Noticing it, I wonder how Kashaya history can be made present in a way that does not seem merely added on, supplementary, to the history of Russian America? Current plans for the addition of "culture trails" around the fort would not actually reconstruct portions of Koniag or Kashaya villages, but would evoke them through displays of archaeological excavations, sheltered and under glass. Such an approach, while beginning to fill in the complex lives outside the walls, would leave the imposing reconstructed fort, and the Russian history it incarnates, as the park's centerpiece. Other histories would remain ancillary (ranching located at the Call house) or literally in fragments (the Kashaya/Miwok and Alaskan settlements). Perhaps this is inevitable. But perhaps a reconstructed Métini could be combined with other strategies to offset Russian "monumentalism." These would be reinforced by a revised display at the visitor center, helping people visualize (and hear?) the complexly rooted, intersecting lives outside the walls.

However the different stories at Fort Ross / Métini are materially represented, the difficult dialogue of the three constituencies must continue. A proper "balance" of messages and sensibilities will always reflect openended, political relationships in an ongoing contact history. Final agreement may not—should not—be possible. Told from Native Alaskan and Californian perspectives, the story of Russian America can appear bleak, as invasion and plague, with the Russians portrayed as exploiters. Is such a view one-sided? How do the interested Russian communities react to so negative an assessment? How do Native Californians respond to the adventure of early California ranching, a history that includes their expulsion from ancestral lands? And within the costumed Living History days celebrated each summer at the fort, is there a place for a person dying of measles? Can the representation of heritage ever be balanced—inclusive and consensual—when the flow of history is actually an overlay of different, conflicting, and ongoing stories, histories continuously reinterpreted?

Futures

To make a story, one starts with a place and a span of time, beginnings that are never simply given. The histories at Fort Ross highlight specific pasts, prefiguring certain possibilities. The years of Russian Alta California, 1812–1841, take center stage. This historical moment brings into focus a Northern Pacific zone of trade and exploration, linking California, Moscow, New England, China, Latin America, Hawaii, London. These were years of devastating colonial contact for indigenous populations in North America, a time of rivalry among imperial powers during which the United States achieved continental dominance. But in this relatively recent past we also glimpse other Americas in which outcomes now taken for granted seem less assured. Contact relations, borders and powers, line up differently before "definitive" mid-century events such as the California Gold Rush or the Treaty of Guadaloupe Hidalgo.

In 1830 the "United States of America" was still the weakest of the three contenders for the Sonoma coast. Fort Ross was the easternmost outpost of a vast Russian empire. Today, even Russia's continental reach is in doubt. Will the United States of America be united a hundred years hence? Will California still be thought of as belonging to an empire with roots in

Europe? In the early nineteenth century, China was a potent economic force in the transformation of this coast. And in the future? In the year 2100, the North Pacific will surely look different as a site of empire, commerce, the traveling and dwelling of peoples. Will the "west" coast be an "eastern" border again?

As the twentieth century draws to a close, apparently overwhelming forces connect and differentiate the world's peoples—global capitalism, nationalism, modern communications. The recent history of these forces in the expansion and structural dominance of Euro-American industrial society is fairly clear. What is less clear is the ultimate reliance of global-izing forces on Western cultural institutions. Capitalist culture, flexible and locally adaptive, is not a single thing. Nationalism, often a destabiliz-ing power, can be articulated in contradictory situations, as domination and as resistance to domination. Advanced communications technologies are used by Western and non-Western religious fundamentalisms, by movements for social justice and tribal rights, by Coca Cola, Toyota, and CitiBank. But in recognizing the enormous power of capitalism, national-ism, and communications technology, we need not make them all-power-ful. Historically linked processes, they work together and pull against one another; they are made and unmade in local contexts. Unevenness, con-tradiction, instability, and invention are inseparable from recent global developments some call a "new world order," others an "empire of chaos" (Amin, 1994).

I derive something like hope from unexpected news—for example, accounts of the pope's visits to New Guinea and Africa. The Catholic faithful, bare-chested in traditional regalia, perform tribal dances to greet the costumed white man. What historical changes have brought John Paul II, of all people, to preach the value of indigenous culture? Where are these forces leading us, separately and together? What are we to make of the fact that Russian Orthodoxy, among Aleuts, Koniags, and Yup'ik Eski-mos, has become a mark of *native* identity? What has been lost? What has survived? What is being reinvented in the ordered disorder of contempo-rary "cultures"?

Something like hope . . . Not prophecy or a revolutionary vision. A recognition, perhaps, of contingency, of minor utopias. But is it not blind, even perverse, to speak of hope in the face of so many devastating facts: relentless environmental degradation, neocolonialism, overpopulation, a growing gap between privileged and desperate people virtually everywhere? The question is inescapable, crushing. Yet pessimism gets one nowhere, and frequently lapses into cynicism, a predictable "toughmindedness." That temptation, today, is all too familiar. It must be possible to reject pessimism along with its opposites—the celebratory, ameliorist visions of progress through development, techno-science, the internet, neoliberal consensus at the "end of history." Can we sustain a more complex and unstable sense of constraint and possibility, bleak and hopeful prospects? Gramsci named a problem, not a solution, with his formula, "Pessimism of the intellect, optimism of the will." But why is hope always on the side of the nonintellectual "will"?

At Fort Ross, something like hope . . . The North Pacific is a geopolitical space whose transformation by capital and empire is less than two centuries old. Is it possible, as one contemplates the area's "Russian period," to feel, for a crucial instant, that nothing has been settled? That the historical processes unleashed then—the power of markets over vast spaces, the making and unmaking of political borders, the decimations and movements of peoples—are incomplete? The "West Coast," the "United States of America" . . . Such things did not exist here a century and a half ago. Will they be here a century hence?

Pried out of the continuum of a triumphal (or tragic) American History, the moment of "Fort Ross" offers strands of historical contingency. In its entwined stories I glimpse the rise and fall of empires, the historical shallowness of U.S. American hegemony, the perseverance and renewal of native peoples, the unfinished relations of north and south in the continent, the ongoing Asian influence in North Pacific history. Living and thinking inside a triumphant Western history, I am brought up short by statements like the following, by Barbara Shangin, an Alutiq (Koniag) elder, descendent of the sea-otter hunters at Fort Ross:

> Our people have made it through lots of storms and disasters for thousands of years. All the troubles since the Russians are like one long stretch of bad weather. Like everything else, this storm will pass over some day. (Pullar and Knecht, 1995: 15)

A different vision. Does it translate? What inspiration can I derive from Barbara Shangin's words? Can they be taken seriously—here, in "postmodern" California—without romanticism? History is thought from different places within an unfinished global dynamic. Where are we in this process?

Is it too late to recognize "our" diverse paths into and through modernity? Or too early?

Fort Ross history draws me north to Alaska, the Bering Strait, the Aleutian Islands: places where America and Asia merge. As a schoolchild I was fascinated, troubled, by the maps which stopped precisely there: a line of tiny dots where west somehow ended, starting over as east on the opposite side of the world. In the Aleutians, "east" and "west" stopped making sense.

Another line of northern dots fascinated and terrified me. (Perhaps this was the line I first wanted to cross, to erase, at Fort Ross.) It stretched across Alaska north of the Arctic Circle: the DEW line. Distant Early Warning: the dots were radar outposts supposed to give us a few extra minutes before the End. In my school we marched out of class to sit on metal stairs, heads between our knees. My family's apartment building in New York City was marked with a yellow and black civil-defense plaque, announcing a shelter in the basement somewhere. (I could never find anything except some barrels marked "Water.") We formed vague images of Russian missiles crossing the Bering Strait and the Arctic Ocean. Then there would be sirens, perhaps some kind of a roar . . . East becoming West.

I grew up in the everyday fear of this implosion and the real possibility that I and everyone I knew might not survive. The fear, a fact of life for more than three decades, has receded. I, my family, and my friends will probably live into the next century—a time with its own dangers, known and unknown, but at least without the threat of imminent extermination. All at once, the millennium feels like a beginning.

In the middle of the Bering Strait, two tiny islands lie within sight of each other: Big Diomede and Little Diomede. For many centuries, Yup'ik-speaking and later Inupiaq-speaking Eskimos inhabited the two islands, in close and continuous contact with each other and with Eskimo populations on the Seward and Chukchi peninsulas of Alaska and Russia. The dotted U.S.-Russia Convention Line, ruler-straight on the map, passes between the two Diomedes. Just to the south in the Bering Sea, St. Lawrence Island has long been the home of Yup'ik Eskimos who share a virtually identical language with Eskimos on the Asian shore, a twenty-four-hour row away. Close ties have existed for centuries, both before and after 1867, when St. Lawrence Island, culturally and geographically an extension of Asia, was included in the Alaska Purchase and became part of America.

Cold War politics turned the ancient borderland into a sealed frontier. In 1948 Soviet authorities evacuated residents of Big Diomede to the mainland—those who had not already moved to Little Diomede. Ten years later, the Eskimo populations of coastal communities along the Bering Strait and opposite St. Lawrence Island were moved inland, out of range of any visits with their Alaskan kin. For forty years the borderland was effectively closed, except for a few secret crossings, some possibly organized by intelligence services. But as the political ice began to thaw in the late 1980s, pressure grew for an opening of the Beringia "crossroads," as it was coming to be called. In 1987 an American, Lynne Coxe, obtained permission to swim from Little to Big Diomede. Some Diomeders came along in a boat and renewed connection with Naukanski Yup'iks who had journeyed from the Soviet shore to meet them.

In the three years that followed, politicians, journalists, natives, and businessmen crisscrossed the area. Visa-free travel for Eskimos was reestablished. By 1991 more than ten thousand people a year were traveling between Anchorage and various Soviet locations on regularly scheduled Aeroflot and Alaska Airlines flights. Sister cities exchanged delegations. Eskimo groups renewed their former relations, and Aleuts of the Commander Islands agitated to contact their American kin. Cruise-ship tourism was up. In July 1991, Chukchi and Eskimos from Siberia visited Little Diomede for the first time in four decades, crossing dangerous seas again in open boats.

Sources

This essay draws on conversations with people knowledgeable about Fort Ross and its history. Lyn Kalani, Dan Murley, and Bill Walton, staff at the Historic Park, were generous with their time and advice. Archaeologists Lynne Goldstein, Kent Lightfoot, and Glenn Farris provided leads and corrected errors. Robert Oswalt carefully answered my questions on the Kashaya texts published in his collection; Otis Parrish discussed with me his vision of Kashaya cosmology and history in relation to archaeology at the fort; and Greg Sarris offered stimulating perspectives on Kashaya and Miwok histories. The Fort Ross library was particularly useful. Dan Murley generously made available to me his unpublished lectures on Alaskan sea-mammal hunters and on interethnic relations outside the stockade.

The Orchard. The paintings of Fort Ross to which I refer are by V. Ushanoff (after a sketch by Bernard Duhaut-Cilly), 1828, and by I. Voznesensky, 1841. On the orchard's history: Stainbrook (1979); and collected plans, photos, and memorabilia at the Fort Ross Library.

History. Said (1978) provides a genealogy of the "West" sustained against the "East." On "American history" seen from Asia and the Pacific, I have learned from the work-in-progress of Glen Mimura. On rewriting "America" as the "Américas," see, among others, Saldívar (1991). For a complex vision of North Pacific history, I draw on McDougall (1993).

Russian America. For the contact history of Russian America, I have relied on standard works by Chevigny (1951, 1965) and Tikmenev (1978), supplemented by Gibson (1976, 1988); Black (1977); Starr (1987); Fitzhugh and Crowell (1988); Fitzhugh and Chaussonnet (1994); Oswalt (1988); Farris (1989b); Istomin (1993); Kari (1983); and a sampling of contemporary accounts—for example, Khlebnikov (1990); Alekseev (1987); and Farris (1988).

Histories. In addition to Oswalt (1964) and Farris (1989), I have drawn on Sarris' dialogical approach to Native Californian texts (Sarris, 1993). The notion of a spatialization prior to storytelling is derived from Leenhardt (1947) and from Bakhtin's concept of "chronotope" (Bakhtin, 1937). On Pomo ethnography and the Bole Maru dreaming religion, I have consulted Dubois (1939); Kennedy (1955); McLendon and Oswalt (1978); and Sarris (1993, 1994).

Commodities. For a complex sense of local/global commodity systems, I have been influenced by the work of Daniel Miller (1987, 1994, 1995); also Taussig (1980, 1987); Sahlins (198); and Thomas (1991).

Animals. On the diversity and structure of "historical" consciousness, see, among many recent works, Rosaldo (1980) and White (1987). My general approach to nature-in-history reflects that of Cronin (1995). On history as a "European" phenomenon, globally articulated but possibly displaced or "provincialized," see Chakrabarty (1992). The final paragraphs of this section owe a great deal to comments by Chris Healy.

Empires. McDougall (1993); Sahlins (1988); Benjamin (1968). My general approach to globalizing processes reflects that of Stuart Hall (1991); also Abu-Lughod (1991) and Hannerz (1991). For a survey of recent developments in anthropology, see Kearney (1995). For a brilliant discussion of the "geo-body" of the modern nation reminiscent of my comments on the cartographic image of the United States, see Winichakul (1994).

Walls. Schneider (1983); Anzaldúa (1987). On the Great Wall, see Waldron (1990). On borders and borderlands, the literature is now quite large. For a survey of recent work centered on the U.S.-Mexican border, see Alvarez (1995). For recent archaeology around the walls at Fort Ross, I draw especially on Lightfoot, Wake, and Schiff (1981); also on Martinez (1995).

Pasts. On FRIA doings, I have sampled recent newsletters and discussed projects with staff at the fort. Sketches of the "flow-of-history" approach, as well as initial plans for "culture trails" and restoration of the Call House, are available in the Fort Ross library. My discussion of possible Kashaya projects at the fort is indebted to Otis Parrish. See Chapter 7 for further sources on dilemmas and opportunities in museums/heritage sites seen as "contact zones."

Futures. On Gramscian politics adapted to current circumstances, I have learned from Stuart Hall (1985, 1988). Richard Gordon (1994) provides a view of the world capitalist economy as composed of contradictory processes, including disparate sites of innovation and regional mobilization. Jonathan Friedman (1994) very suggestively explores a paradoxical "world system" which fosters not hegemony but rather a systematic disorder productive of cultures and identities. Samir Amin (1994) sees capitalist global regulation as unable, over the long run, to control nationalist revolts and disorders. For diasporic dis- and rearticulations of culture and nation, see Chapter 10; also Gupta (1992) on the instability of national and transnational identities. On Russian orthodoxy as a "native" religion, see Black (1977) and Fienup-Riordan (1990). Arguing for "a kind of hope," I often find myself struggling with the compelling *noir* visions of Mike Davis and Talal Asad. On histories of partition and crossing in Beringia, I rely especially on Krauss (1994); also on Fitzhugh and Crowell (1988) and Chaussonnet (1995).

Notes

1. Traveling Cultures

1. The phrase "spatial practice" is derived from Michel de Certeau (1984). My overriding emphasis here, and in the more extended discussion of fieldwork in Chapter 3, will to some degree obscure the fact that these are always spatio-*temporal* localizations. In the words of Adrienne Rich (1986), "A place on the map is also a place in history." The temporal dimensions elided in this paper have been fully explored in Fabian (1983); see also Clifford (1986).

2. For a glimpse of the tent flap as threshold for certain practices of writing, see Clifford (1990: 67).

3. Of course, the relevant populations did not always come clustered in stable villages. See Clifford (1988: 230–233), for Margaret Mead's difficulties "locating" the Mountain Arapesh in highland New Guinea.

4. Of course, fieldworkers also pass through. Their departure is a crucial moment, articulating separate "places" of empirical research and theoretical elaboration, fieldnotes and writing up; see Clifford (1990: 63–66). Classically, ethnographies have given some prominence to arrivals, little to departures. But seeing fieldwork as a form of travel, a multi-locale spatial practice, brings the end (and loose ends) of "dwelling" into the picture.

5. Homi Bhabha (1990) has reminded us about the discrepant temporalities and histories that do not add up to a homogeneous language/time/culture or nation. We need a critical genealogy of the connection between holistic concepts of culture, language, and nation. See Wolf (1982: 387); and Handler (1987), for some strands implicating anthropology.

6. For archaeological evidence in support of this conclusion, see Rouse (1986).

7. In this connection, I cannot resist mentioning what may be a sign of the changing interpretive times. "Ancient Tribes That Didn't Vanish, They Just Moved" proclaims the headline of a recent article (Barringer, 1990). Archaeologists of the U.S. Southwest believe they have solved a long-standing mystery: What happened to the Anasazi? Cliff dwellers, builders of impressive permanent settlements and road networks, the Anasazi simply "vanished" when at certain moments (1150 A.D. at

Chaco Canyon or 1300 A.D. at Mesa Verde) their sites were abandoned. Given strong evolutionist assumptions about the development of agriculture and cities, the end of these and other developed settlements could be interpreted only as a terminus, a cultural "disappearance" or "death." Thus, no continuous connection could be established between the Anasazi (a kind of catch-all name, actually Navajo in origin, meaning "the old ones") and contemporary cultures with deep historical roots in the region: Hopi, Zuni, Acoma. But in the new interpretive approach, cliff *dwellers* are also cliff *travelers*. "Accumulated evidence" now suggests that the Anasazi moved around in the region, building and leaving settlements of varying complexity right up until European settlers began to invade and contain them in drastic ways. Their recent names are Hopi, Zuni, Acoma. No mysterious absence or death separates the vanished old ones from the current populations, only a complex history of dwelling *and* traveling. Though I am certainly not an expert, I cannot help wondering whether the new conclusion is adequately accounted for by what authorities call an "accumulation of new evidence." Assumptions about spatial continuity and cultural localization are currently being challenged in a wide variety of fields. The global developments reflected in the present chapter certainly have something to do with this general change of perspective.

8. I am grateful to Christina Turner for her very helpful comment. This is its gist, at least as I understood it.

9. The rather limited role that academic anthropology/ethnography has played, so far, in cultural studies (particularly in Britain) is a subject that deserves a discussion of its own. Specific disciplinary and imperial histories would need to be explored. My impression is that current possibilities of interaction are greater in the Americas—although the discipline of cultural studies is still felt as a threat in many anthropology departments, and an (inexpungible?) taint of colonialism makes anthropology untouchable in some progressive and "Third World" milieus.

10. How rare the experience of Alice Fletcher, sent as special government agent in 1889 to survey and allot the lands of the Nez Perce Indians. Fletcher was leader of her expedition, with real power over white men and Indians. Her considerable personal authority was evident in her nickname, "Queen Victoria." For a generous and lucidly ironic account of women on the frontier doing "men's work" in their own way, see the letters by Fletcher's companion E. Jane Gay (1981).

11. Lisa Bloom (1993) has written insightfully on Peary, Henson, Eskimos, and the various efforts by *National Geographic* to retell a deeply contested story of discovery.

12. I am grateful to Paul Gilroy for bringing the work of Rediker and Linebaugh (for example, 1990) to my attention during several very stimulating conversations on commuter trains. For a discussion of *The Black Atlantic,* see Chapter 10.

13. See the recent experiment in ethnographic writing by Karen McCarthy Brown,

Mama Lola: A Vodou Priestess in Brooklyn (discussed in Chapter 3). Also the bifocal study by Grasmuck and Pessar (1991).

3. Spatial Practices

1. For the emergence of this fieldwork norm and its "magic" see the classic account in Stocking (1992, ch. 1). My discussion here is largely limited to Euro-American trends. I join Gupta and Ferguson (1997) in admitting my "sanctioned ignorance" (Spivak, 1988; John, 1989) of many non-Western anthropological contexts and practices. And even within the contested but powerful disciplinary "center," my discussion is primarily focused on North America and, to some extent, England. If the issues raised extend beyond these contexts, they do so with reservations I am not yet able to discuss systematically.

2. Renato Rosaldo, comment at the "Anthropology and 'the Field'" conference, Stanford University, April 18, 1994. The context was a comparison of ethnography by postexotic anthropologists and cultural-studies scholars. What, in the absence of extended co-residence, guarantees interactive "depth"?

3. In his recent survey of emerging "multi-sited ethnography," George Marcus (1995: 100) confronts this question, and argues that such ethnographies are "inevitably the product of knowledge bases of varying intensities and qualities." He adds: "It is perhaps anthropologists' appreciation of the difficulty of doing intensive ethnography at any site and the satisfaction that comes from such work in the past when it is done well that would give them pause when the ethnographer becomes mobile and still claims to have done good fieldwork." Overall, Marcus' important attempt to grasp an emergent phenomenon bypasses the question of *fieldwork*. He simply calls all the new mobile practices *ethnography,* a manifestly interdisciplinary orientation, albeit retaining certain recognizable anthropological features: up-close perspectives, cross-cultural translations, language learning, attention to everyday practices, and the like.

4. Criteria of adequate fieldwork have tended to be enforced through tacit consensus rather than explicit rules. A professional culture recognizes "good" ethnography and ethnographers in ways that can appear obscure, even arbitrary, to an outsider. I am not concerned, however, with distinguishing research of different quality or with showing how specific distinctions function professionally. This would require a history and sociology of the discipline which I am not qualified to supply.

5. A single offering that would attempt to integrate current work in physical anthropology and archaeology is barely conceivable. Most departments sustain separate tracks, with hopes—more or less serious—of cross-fertilization.

6. It is a fraught border that, in the United States at least, is the site of turf wars. On the anthropological side, there has been recurrent grumbling about misuse of the culture concept and superficial ethnography. Moreover, some embattled an-

thropologists have been tempted to dismiss cultural studies as just more trendy "postmodernism." This reflex is currently visible in negative reactions to the new editorial policies of Barbara and Dennis Tedlock at the discipline's flagship journal, *American Anthropologist*. A motion to censure the journal's "postmodern turn" was introduced (and defeated) at the annual meeting of the American Anthropological Association. Expressing a more ambivalent sense of the fraught border, Dale Eickelman (quoted by the *Chronicle of Higher Education*) finds a recent "photo-studded article on the marketing of religious kitsch in Cairo [to be] something 'radically new' for the journal, work that 'recaptures some of the territory appropriated by cultural studies'" (Zalewski, 1995: 16). Handler (1993) gives a judicious account of the cultural-studies border, from the anthropological side.

7. One thinks of the Chicago School. More recently, the work of Becker (e.g., 1986), Van Maanen (1988), Burawoy et al. (1991), and Wellman (1995) explicitly addresses anthropological debates about ethnographic authority. Anthropology has, until relatively recently, been distinguished from sociology by a research *object* (the primitive, the tribal, the rural, the subaltern—especially non-Western and premodern). Michèle Duchet (1984) has traced the emergence of anthropology's special object to eighteenth century anthropology-sociology, which divided up the globe according to a series of familiar dichotomies: with/without history, archaic/modern, literate/nonliterate, distant/nearby. Each opposition has, by now, been empirically blurred, politically challenged, and theoretically deconstructed.

8. My comments here are based on conversations with Susan Harding. Indeed, her hybrid research practice was my starting point for reconsidering the "field" in anthropology. Publications from her work in progress include Harding (1987, 1990, 1993).

9. My late colleague David Schneider never tired of reminding me that fieldwork was not the *sine qua non* of anthropology. His general position, a critique of my work among others, appears in *Schneider on Schneider* (1995, esp. ch. 10), a mordant, hilarious, intemperate book of interviews. Schneider argues that famous anthropologists are distinguished by ideas and theoretical innovations rather than by good fieldwork. Ethnography, as he sees it, is a process of generating reliable facts which tend to confirm preconceived ideas or are irrelevant to the work's final conclusions. Fieldwork is the empirical alibi for a questionable positivism. He dismisses claims that field research involves a distinctive or particularly valuable form of interactive learning. But under pressure from his interlocutor, Richard Handler, Schneider retreats from his more extreme points. For example, he accepts that good ethnography and theory are not strictly separable in the forging of reputations and recognizes that anthropologists do (misguidedly) place a special, defining emphasis on fieldwork. He also concedes that work in the field can produce new ideas and challenge presuppositions. He does not comment, however, on how approved ethnography functions in normative ways within the

discipline. Schneider's characteristically vehement strictures are a corrective to the focus of this chapter. And his final position seems to be that if fieldwork is indeed a distinctive mark of sociocultural anthropology, it should not be fetishized. I agree. I do not agree that anthropology is (or should be) the "study of culture." That, too, is a problematic disciplinary life-raft. I miss David's loyal provocations and certainly do not claim the last word in this argument.

10. Malinowski (1961: 11). Lowie's *History of Ethnological Theory* (1937) begins by sharply distinguishing anthropological ethnography from exoticist, "literary" travel. For a critique of this discursive move, see Pratt (1986).

11. The "Sophisticated Traveler" supplements, which feature travel essays by well-known writers, are—along with the weekly Sunday travel section—major sources of advertisement revenue. An introduction by *Times* editors A. M. Rosenthal and Arthur Gelb to the first of a series of anthologies based on the supplements claims an equivalence between sensitive journalism and literary travel writing (Rosenthal and Gelb, 1984).

12. Many "good" bookstores now consecrate the tourist/traveler distinction by maintaining well-stocked, *separate* sections for guidebooks and travel books.

13. Van Maanen (1988) provides a balanced account of new approaches to ethnographic writing and their consequences for fieldwork—anthropological and sociological. The title of his book, *Tales of the Field,* is indicative of my present theme: travelers, not scientists, tell tales.

14. Marcus (1995: 105–110) replaces the image of ethnographic dwelling with that of "following." Multi-sited ethnography ranges widely, and on routes that often cannot be prefigured.

15. The literature is now very extensive. Golde (1986); Moore (1988); Bell, Caplan, and Karim (1993); and Behar and Gordon (1995) indicate the current range of feminist agendas.

16. An exception is the neglected work of Ruth Landes. Sally Cole's illuminating account (1995), which arrived too late to be fully integrated in this essay, confirms, I think, my general approach. Landes gave sustained attention to "race," resisting its subsumption under "culture." She gave prominence to issues of embodiment and sexuality in a fieldwork which was presented in relational, personal terms. She broke the disciplinary taboo on sexual liaisons in the field. Her work on *candomblé* in Bahia, *The City of Women* (1947), was, according to Cole, dismissed by powerful gatekeepers as a "travelogue" (tainted also by association with the devalued genres of journalism and folklore). The work of another casualty of professionalization, Zora Neale Hurston, was marginalized in similar ways, seen as too subjective, literary, or folkloric. Hurston's reception was (and still is) compounded by essentialist notions of racial identity that have construed her negatively as a limited native ethnographer and positively as a conduit for black cultural authenticity. Such receptions, academic and nonacademic, elide the

different worlds and affiliations of race, gender, and class negotiated by her work in the rural South, during the Harlem Renaissance, and at Columbia University. The Hurston literature and debates are now quite extensive. Hernandez (1995) provides a valuable discussion.

17. Boon (1977) is a prescient historical exploration. Anthropologists are beginning to write self-consciously about/in this borderland (Crick, 1985; Boon, 1992; Dubois, 1995).

18. On Flaubert's sexualized orientalist travels, see Behdad (1994). One might also mention Bali as a site for gay sex tourism before 1940.

19. One of the consequences, perhaps, of this taboo on physical sex has been to restrict discussion of the "erotics" of fieldwork. Newton (1993) provides an antidote.

20. I have been using the term "habitus" in the generally recognized social-scientific sense made familiar by Bourdieu (1977). This notion sees the social inscribed in the body: a repertoire of practices rather than rules, a disposition to play the social game. It makes conceptions of social and cultural structure more processual: embodied and practiced. Unlike Defert's usage, it presupposes modern notions of society and culture. The older sense of "habitus" sees subjectivity as a matter of concrete, meaningful gestures, appearances, physical dispositions, and apparel without reference to these determining structures, which became hegemonic only in the late nineteenth century.

21. The case of Isabel Eberhardt is complicated by the coincidence of gender and cultural cross-dressing. See the acute discussion in Behdad (1994).

22. In her gently reflexive ethnography, *Storytellers, Saints, and Scoundrels* (1989), Kirin Narayan provides a photo of herself in the field. The focus of her research was the apartment of Swamiji, a Guru storyteller in West India, and the photo shows several women seated there, on the floor. None is Narayan, though were she seated among them she would not, with her sari and "Indian" features, be easily distinguished from the other South Asian women. The caption reads: "Listening attentively from the women's side of the room. The bag and camera-cover mark my presence." The accoutrements of her trade occupy the ethnographer's discrete place. Indeed, throughout the book, Narayan's tape recorder is an explicit topic of discussion for Swamiji and his followers.

23. "External" appearances are powerful. Dorrine Kondo (1986: 74), in her important exploration of the processes of dissolution and reconstitution of the self in fieldwork encounters, begins her account with a disturbing glimpse of her own image, reflected in a Tokyo butcher's display case as she shops for her Japanese "family." For an instant she is indistinguishable in every particular—clothes, body, gesture—from a typical young housewife, "a woman walking with a characteristically Japanese bend in the knees and sliding of the feet. Suddenly I clutched the handle

of the stroller to steady myself as a wave of dizziness washed over me . . . Fear that perhaps I would never emerge from this world into which I was immersed inserted itself into my mind and stubbornly refused to leave, until I resolved to move into a new apartment, to distance myself from my Japanese home and my Japanese existence." In the border-crossings of fieldwork, a holistic "experience" is mobilized, and at risk. Kondo argues that this embodied experience needs to be brought into explicit ethnographic representation.

24. On the nonidentical, imbricated relationship of indigenous, diasporic, and postcolonial locations, see Chapter 10.

25. I am, of course, referring to normative patterns and pressures. Much fieldwork has, in fact, been done outside the (metonymic) "village" or "field site." In anthropology, this is permitted, so long as the work is seen to be peripheral to a central site of intensive encounter. In other fieldwork traditions—for example, those of elicitation and transcription in linguistics—hotels and even universities can be primary "field" sites. Such practices have been actively discouraged in anthropology.

26. Thus, many anthropologists were stung—or bemused—by attacks such as Deloria's in *Custer Died for Your Sins* (1969). The predatory visitor he described, little better than a tourist, seemed a caricature. Anthropologists were being hostilely "located," roughly shaken out of a self-confirming persona.

27. Thanks to Teresia Teaiwa. For her own very complex "native" location, see joannemariebarker and Teaiwa (1994).

28. I hold to this even in the face of my colleague Chris Connery's comment on Paul Theroux: "Travel narrows!"

5. Four Northwest Coast Museums

1. The name *Kwakiutl,* familiar in the anthropological literature, is currently disputed as a vague "tribal" catch-all. The phonetically more accurate term *Kwagiulth* (or *Kwagu'l*) properly denotes only one of many village communities among the peoples formerly called Southern Kwakiutl on northern Vancouver Island and the nearby islets and inlets of the mainland. Recently, the U'mista Cultural Society of Alert Bay has proposed the name *Kwakwaka'wakw* ("Those Who Speak Kwak'wala") for the larger group. Current usage is fluid. When I use *Kwagiulth,* it refers loosely to native peoples in the regions of Cape Mudge, Alert Bay, and Fort Rupert. Name changes and specifications are occurring throughout Vancouver Island: Hesquiaht, mentioned several times in this essay, is a band in a "tribe" once called Nootka, then Westcoast, and now Nuu-Cha-Nulth.

2. Two recent books recount aspects of this history in the context of current resurgence: Dara Culhane Speck's historical ethnography set in Alert Bay, *An Error in*

Judgment: The Politics of Medical Care in an Indian/White Community (1987), a remarkable work of engaged analysis; and Celia Haig-Brown, *Resistance and Renewal: Surviving the Indian Residential School* (1988).

3. For a sign of the times, see *Muse* (the journal of the Canadian Museums Association) 6, no. 3 (Fall 1988), issue entitled "Museums and the First Nations." The Lubicon Cree boycott of "The Spirit Sings: Artistic Traditions of Canada's First Peoples," a 1988 exhibition at the Glenbow Museum, Calgary, had just sent ripples through the Canadian museum world. For a report on the situation around Vancouver, see Kimmelman (1989).

4. For a discussion of this complex "world of museums," see Chapter 7.

5. If at times I have stressed the oppositional entanglement of the tribal museums, I do not claim that their *essence* is oppositional. Moreover, I have largely avoided calling them minority institutions, though they share characteristics with other locally or ethnically based cultural centers. Tribal status is fortified by an aboriginal claim that "we were here first," before the existence of any multicultural nation, "mosaic," or "melting pot" to contest or enrich. While living tribal institutions must function within (and against) dominant national orders, they also draw on autonomous sources of tradition, power, and identity. The opposition *majority/tribal* that organizes some of my comparisons cannot be reduced to *majority/minority.* (Particular thanks to Nancy Marie Mitchell, who, with several others, pressed me to clarify these issues.)

6. A contrasting example is the Margaret Mead Hall of Pacific Peoples at the American Museum of Natural History in New York. See Clifford (1988) for a critique. On the display of cultural change in museums, see Chapter 6.

7. The relational approach did not go as far as an installation called "At the Western Door," which was on view at the Rochester (New York) Museum and Science Center in 1991. Here the guiding principle was to focus on cultural exchange between Seneca and European society from contact to the present. At every point both white and Native American histories were on display. I am grateful to Margaret Blackman for a slide presentation on the exhibit.

8. See, for example, Doreen Jensen and Polly Sargent, *Robes of Power: Totem Poles on Cloth* (1986), covering mythology, written and oral history, design, and current production. The catalogue is composed largely of blanket makers' statements and reflects in its ordering the sequence of a potlatch.

9. Michael Ames, director of the UBC Museum of Anthropology, has forthrightly articulated the institution's evolving—sometimes difficult and contradictory—position. He has pressed consistently within the Canadian museum establishment for increased responsiveness to Native American concerns, and has sought to articulate compromises between the traditional role of major museums and the growing politicization of their activities. See Ames (1986) and (1987). Ames has

also defended the curatorial autonomy of museums in the face of strong, interventionist political pressure—as in the controversy over the "Spirit Sings" exhibition. See his intervention in *Muse* 6, no. 3 (1988). A cooperative museology presumes some real sharing of curatorial control, beyond simple consultancies (see Chapter 7). A good example is the large exhibit on the potlatch, "Chiefly Feasts," organized by Aldona Jonaitis for the American Museum of Natural History in 1991, for which Gloria Cranmer Webster curated the modern section.

10. Western appreciation (appropriation) of tribal objects as "fine art" dates most importantly from the modernist primitivism of Picasso and his generation. See Rubin (1984). However controversial this appreciation has been, the institution of tribal "art" is currently an important source of native power—and revenue.

11. On *art* as a translation device, both communicating and hiding meaning, see Clifford (1989).

12. On the Cranmer potlatch, see Daisy (My-yah-nelth) Sewid Smith, *Prosecution or Persecution* (1979); and Douglas Cole, *Captured Heritage* (1985).

13. *Potlatch . . . A Strict Law Bids Us Dance* and *Box of Treasures* are available from the U'mista Cultural Centre, Box 253, Alert Bay, B.C., VON lA0, Canada.

14. As told to Ruth Kirk; see Kirk (1986: 15). For an account of similar encounters with old photos—specifically for the way in which research collections from the Hearst Museum at the University of California at Berkeley have become family history for California Pomo Indians—see Margolin (1989).

15. The museum had already collaborated with the Musqueam to display their (recently revived) weaving. See Johnson and Bernick, *Hands of Our Ancestors* (1986).

16. On the "museum set," see Baxandall (1991). The U'mista Cultural Centre's video on the potlatch collection's return (to Alert Bay only) is titled, after an elder's comment on the museum, *Box of Treasures*. The categories "treasure" and "work of art" overlap but do not coincide. "The Storage Box of Tradition" is Ira Jacknis' title for his doctoral dissertation, subtitled "Museums, Anthropology and Kwakiutl Art, 1881–1981." Jacknis writes in his abstract: "The 'storage box of tradition' is an appropriate and resonant Kwakiutl idiom for a museum. Boxes were central to the Northwest Coast emphasis on ranking and the accumulation of wealth, and they were regarded as receptacles, concretely, for inherited artifacts, and, metaphorically, for the transmission of ancestral privileges. The box idiom was used in potlatch oratory to stress the preservation of customs, Boas employed the phrase in trying to explain his work with George Hunt to the Kwakiutl, and it has also been used by contemporary Kwakiutl to refer to their native cultural center" (1988: 3). Jacknis' important thesis goes into historical depth on many of the issues treated in this essay.

17. See the important study by Bill Holm, *Smoky-top: The Art and Times of Willie Seaweed* (1983).

18. The only other sewing machines I saw on display were in the Royal British Columbia installation, where two antique models turned up in a case illustrating the varieties of wealth typically distributed at potlatches: masks, rattles, coppers, crockery, coffeepots, blankets, and so on. The sewing machines make different statements in the cultural history traced at Victoria and the political and familial genealogy told at Alert Bay.

19. For a sensitive presentation of the (California) Hoopa Tribal Museum and a persuasive argument for both the profound differences and possibilities for cooperation between tribal and majority (university) museums, see Davis (1989).

20. For an account of how Northwest Coast objects in a Western museum setting were translated by native (Tlingit) elders into powerful mythic, historical, and political stories and performances, see Clifford (1989); and Chapter 7, below. The elders' performances as consultants to a reinstallation project called deeply into question the classification of traditional masks, rattles, drums, and so on as "objects" (art or artifact).

21. For example, she helped identify and commission contemporary art for the pioneering show and catalogue produced by the Royal British Columbia Museum (Macnair, Hoover, and Neary, 1984).

22. *U'mista Cultural Centre Newsletter,* Alert Bay, April 1987.

23. See also Assu and Inglis (1989: 104–109), for another account reflecting Cape Mudge's role in the repatriation process. The view from Alert Bay counters that, from the beginning of the repatriation movement, many with legitimate claims on the regalia had wanted the museum in Alert Bay. Moreover, the owners of returned regalia were, predominantly, not members of bands from the Cape Mudge area. Most of those in the area with valid claims on parts of the potlatch collection, such as Chief James Sewid (originally from Village Island, and a relative of Emma Cranmer), had migrated to central Vancouver Island from the Alert Bay region only in recent decades. The argument about locating the museum was complicated by counterclaims concerning ownership, sixty years of intermarriage, and migration toward new centers of tribal and economic power.

24. On the somewhat legendary Kwagiulth penchant for diversity and argument, Susan Reid has written: "Anthropology still has a picture of traditional society as based on common consent. The Durkheimian concept of the mechanical society, in which everything and everyone works together to uphold the status quo, is still with us. It would be truer to say of Kwakiutl society that it was based on common dissent. Every member was carefully trained to be able to decide for himself. He was trained to 'look through' the symbolic structures he had accepted in childhood to their meaning. Seeing that they were not given but man-made he learnt to use them creatively, becoming, in his time, a maker for

others" (Reid, 1981: 250). Thanks to Dara Culhane Speck for pointing out this quotation.

6. Paradise

1. O'Hanlon (1993: 80). All subsequent page references to this catalogue are included in the text. I would like to thank Michael O'Hanlon for discussing the exhibition with me, for generously providing me with documentation, and for correcting my account in important ways. He does not, of course, share all my interpretations.

2. As I write this paragraph, my confidence that I can predict anything about actual responses to the show wavers. I think of a well-educated, museum-loving acquaintance who might very well conclude that the Wahgi were indeed in a fallen state and who would see the gum-wrapper headbands, the cross in the *bolyim* house, and the beer-label shields as signs of a new barbarism composed of the worst of several worlds. I can also imagine a quick take on the show: "Oh, those wild and crazy highlanders!" Extravagant hybrid imagery may provoke quite contradictory reactions.

3. The critical and historical literature on museums and collecting has grown rapidly in the past decade. O'Hanlon cites as representative some of my own work (of which more later) and two important collections: Karp and Lavine (1991); and Karp, Lavine, and Kraemer (1992). I would add to his bibliography several risk-taking experiments by a precursor in reflexive museum work, Susan Vogel, at the Center for African Art in New York (1987a, 1987b, 1988).

4. "O wad some Pow'r the giftie gie us / To see oursels as others see us!" as Robert Burns said. A god-like gift indeed!

5. Michael O'Hanlon, personal communication, May 27, 1994. For a photo of "taboo stones" at the collecting camp, see O'Hanlon (1993: 61).

6. See, among others, Jonaitis (1991: 23, 37) for Native Americans' interest and participation in an exhibition of their traditions by a large, distant metropolitan museum. These issues are developed in Chapter 7.

7. Michael O'Hanlon, personal communication, May 27, 1994.

8. For a portrayal of highland social relations which shows the two ideologies in ambiguous tension, see the film *Joe Leahy's Neighbors* (1988), directed and produced by Robin Anderson and Bob Connolly.

9. Michael O'Hanlon, personal communication, May 27, 1994.

10. The process is, of course, not limited to art and aesthetics. All practices of cross-cultural understanding may be seen in the same historically contingent light. In ethnography, for example, one necessarily begins by establishing domains of equivalence—comparative "topics" such as religion, kinship, gender, modernization, mode of production, and so forth. These undergird comparative under-

standing until their partiality and reductivism are made apparent by criticisms both internal and external to their discursive/institutional regimes. A history of ethnographic understanding—a nonprogressive, nondismissive history—would be a story of serious, failed translations.

11. This is an increasingly common critique of "postcolonial" projections; see, for example, Shohat (1992), as well as Chapter 10, note 25, below. Sangari (1987) was my wake-up call in this regard.

7. Museums as Contact Zones

1. Tedlock (1993: 292), writes about Zuni dialogical storytelling: "The problem of the mythographer [here, the consulting curator] is not merely to present and interpret Zuni myths as if they were objects from a distant place and time and the mythographer were a sort of narrow, one-way conduit, but as events taking place among *contemporaries along a frontier that has a long history of crossings*" (emphasis added). Greg Sarris (1993: 39), relating Tedlock's point to California Indian oral texts, stresses that the presence of the interlocutor positions the storytellers so that the stories are interpreted in a specific relational context.

2. For another encounter of native elders, traditional objects, and curators in a museum storage space, see Jonaitis (1991: 66–69).

3. Elsewhere, following Bakhtin, I have called this structure of spatialized time a "chronotope" (Clifford, 1988: 236), a structure now increasingly questioned by "peripheral" art practices. In penetrating discussions of the work of Chilean artist Eugenio Dittborn, Nelly Richard (1993, 1994) explores the different distances and transits which works of art negotiate on their ways to and through exhibitionary centers, routes that both register and destabilize geopolitical relations of center/periphery. Dittborn marks the trajectories of his works by mailing them in envelopes to distant museums: folds and evidence of prior passages are integral to the works, which are thus clearly passing *through* the museum spaces. Dittborn's art calls attention to nonsynchronous, politicized distances of space and memory (Dittborn, 1993). See also Charlotte Townsend Gault (1995: 92), for a discussion of the ways in which the first exhibition of native artists in the National Gallery of Canada marked a critical distance from the museum and the nation at the very moment of inclusion.

4. Asserting the necessity of this termination in strategic areas such as ownership of land and control of heritage is the aim of contemporary "sovereignty" movements. Complete economic and cultural independence is not a realistic option; what is sought, however, is a power base from which to exert some real control over the ongoing interaction.

5. Fred Meyers (1994), writing about Australian aboriginals in the New York art

scene, argues that new "interculture" is created in performances connected to museum exhibits—performances in which the participants have quite different stakes in the interaction.

6. In a similar vein, Richard Bauman and Patricia Sawin (1991: 312) criticize a tendency to think of participants in folklife festivals as display objects. They portray them "as agents, reflexive, adaptive, and critical, crafting the representations in which they are involved, working to figure out what they should and could be doing within a folklife festival, negotiating their way through structures of power and authority, and offering firm, if usually good-humored, resistance when they feel that their own sense of identity and self-worth is impinged upon by others."

7. Bruce Mannheim (1995), in a complex meditation on Fusco and Gomez-Peña, reminds us of the material reality of kidnapping and forced labor that underlies a long-established response: indigenous accounts of Europeans as body snatchers in Latin America (and Africa).

8. Indeed, the analysis of Western hegemony in the display of "exotics" can itself become totalizing, glossing over important differences. Raymond Corbey's valuable discussion runs this risk when it asserts a strong similarity between colonial exhibits and the 1984 Te Maori exhibit in New York at which Maori were present (Corbey, 1993: 359). The reception by museum visitors of Maori chanting and praying in the museum may, in many (though certainly not all) cases, be continuous with the older tradition. But Maori stakes in the performance, as well as the complex tribal/state/museum politics surrounding the exhibit, reflect important ruptures with the past. Coco Fusco runs the same risk by moving seamlessly from Ishi in the Anthropology Museum to "another, lesser-known example": the Mexicans who were taken prisoner by Anglo-Texan secessionists, caged in public plazas, and left to starve (Fusco, 1995: 41).

9. Pauline Turner-Strong (1992) brings these missing narratives sharply into focus. Although she raises crucial issues, her evidence of Indian experiences in Europe is inevitably fragmentary. Her use of oral tradition, especially the Wampanoag legend of the European intruder as cannibal bird, is tantalizing and important. Better documentation is available for more recent "travelers," though information on their complex points of view remains sketchy. Corbey (1993: 348–352) urges the importance of attending to indigenous experience in European "ethnographic showcases" but is limited to a series of questions. The story told by the Sioux Black Elk of his trip to Europe with Buffalo Bill's Wild West Show is an exception (Black Elk, 1979); see also the diary of an Inuit in Germany (Taylor, 1981). The account by Bradford and Blume (1992) of Ota Benga, a pygmy who was exhibited at the St. Louis World's Fair, contains intriguing, if somewhat speculative, accounts of pygmy senses of violated hospitality and their uses of parody and humor to turn the tables on their audiences.

10. See Chapter 5 for current Kwakiutl (Kwagiulth) uses of Curtis' romanticized images—recycled as family portraiture.

11. Terence Turner (1991) provides an acute analysis of cultural self-representation for outsiders by a tribal people (the Kayapo) in the context of ethnic political mobilization and defense.

12. I have adapted these issues from Michael Ames's account of the dispute (Ames, 1991: 9). In his discussion of "Spirit Sings" and "Into the Heart of Africa," he is concerned with the protests' unfairness to the exhibits, and their potential "chilling effect" on curatorial independence and freedom of expression. Although his focused discussion of the two protests is a defense of curatorial interests, the lessons he draws from the debates and the examples he gives of emerging museum practices seem to argue for a renegotiation of curatorial and community control—a general move toward shared planning, power, and a broader conception of the diverse knowledges represented in museums (13–14). Ames's ambivalence reflects the fine line that reformist museum professionals currently walk, in a period of shrinking resources and growing political pressures from contradictory directions.

13. I mean, of course, something more central than adding a gallery or sponsoring a visiting show—including a Hans Haacke installation or a Fred Wilson intervention.

14. The difference is sensitively evoked by Aldona Jonaitis, who worked with Gloria Cranmer Webster, director of the U'mista Cultural Centre, and other Kwakiutl elders on "Chiefly Feasts: The Enduring Kwakiutl Potlatch" at the American Museum of Natural History (Jonaitis, 1991: 66–69).

15. Intensive discussions of repatriation are ongoing in a wide range of museums and government agencies. For a sense of the issues, see the differing positions of the National Museum of the American Indian (1991) and Sturtevant (1991); also Blundell and Grant (1989).

16. Perhaps—as John Urry (1990: 134) and Chris Healy (1994: 35) suggest—the range of projects now covered by the term "museum" is too large to be coherent. Its translation into so wide a variety of contexts may have blurred its meaning beyond recognition. I think, however, that we can still speak of a "world of museums" (not a global "museum world") united by overlapping resemblances, if not by an identity of structure or function.

17. Previously excluded groups may, of course, make inclusion on the Mall a political goal. But this will be one strategy, linked to others, decentralized or otherwise centered, not inscribed in the imagined space of the inclusive nation-state. In this regard it will be important to follow how the new Museum of the American Indian, located in Washington, D.C., and New York, collaborates with a range of tribal institutions. The general vision I am articulating here echoes the "polycentric multiculturalism" of Shohat and Stam, which they distinguish clearly from liberal pluralism (1994: 46–49).

18. Museums' current commercial competitors and alter egos are theme parks and shopping malls. In an effort to provide safe meeting places and edifying middle-class entertainments, some large urban museums have developed their own shops, upscale cafés, and restaurants. As government and local funding bases shrink, many large museums are becoming more corporate and consumer-defined, following a trajectory similar to that of universities. See Readings (1995) for a trenchant analysis of current institutional trends.

19. The "heritage debates" in Britain are ongoing. Patrick Wright's brilliant *On Living in an Old Country* (1985) was quickly followed by Robert Hewison's *The Heritage Industry* (1987) and by many other critiques of a romanticized national past composed of stately country houses, picturesque landscapes, skilled artisans, and industrious workers. Recently, Raphael Samuel (1994) has launched a counterattack which claims a longer and more democratic history for conservationist projects and accuses the critics of snobbism. His own left populist nostalgia has not gone unremarked. So far, the debate has been intensely focused on Britain. Walsh—though he overgeneralizes the Thatcherite context—has the merit of casting the market in heritage as a global phenomenon. I am struck, however, by the multiple investments in "heritage," as articulated in diverse local/global situations. In the spirit of Featherstone's work, we need to recognize that the heritage debate itself is an element of global culture and should not be too firmly resolved on one "side" or another.

20. A relatively modern native institution that is designed for the display of "culture," and that needs to be treated with the same attention to discrepant functions, contexts, and audiences, is the "pow-wow." Drawing on traditional dance and social forms, allied with twentieth-century pan-Indian movements in the United States and Canada, pow-wows are inventive occasions, popular with tourists and natives alike—often for quite different reasons. Blundell (1989) provides a complex account. See also my musings on the Onga Cultural Centre, Highland New Guinea, in Chapter 6.

10. Diasporas

1. A comparable circuit, joining the Dominican Republic and New York, is treated in depth by Grasmuck and Pessar (1991). See also Brown (1991); Fischer and Abedi (1990); and Marcus and Fischer (1986: 94) for multi-locale ethnographic texts.

2. For example, see Pan (1990); also Chow (1992); Ong (1993); and Li (1993).

3. The distinction between immigrant and diasporic experiences, heightened for definitional clarity in this paragraph, should not be overdrawn. There are diasporic moments in classic assimilationist histories, early and late, as new arrivals

maintain and later generations recover links to a homeland. Diasporic populations regularly "lose" members to the dominant culture.

4. On Jewish anti-Zionism, see, for example, the work of "diaspora nationalist" Simon Dubnow (1931, 1958), whose secular vision of "autonomism" projected a cultural/historical/spiritual "national" identity beyond the territorial/political. In an (un)orthodox vein, Jonathan and Daniel Boyarin argue that a rigorous eschatology of "return" at the end of historical time can produce a radical critique of Zionist literalism (1993).

5. In *The Western Abenakis of Vermont, 1600–1800: War, Migration, and the Survival of an Indian People,* historian Colin Galloway (1990) argues that the survival of the Abenaki as a people was accomplished through "diaspora." The mobile family band, not the settled village, was the basic unit of group life. In response to conquest, many Abenaki bands moved to Canada and to sites all over the northeast United States, while some stuck it out in Vermont. When so many villages disappeared, it *seemed* to outsiders that the group had been fatally decimated. In Galloway's perspective, diasporic communities such as Mashpee—where displaced members of several Cape Cod communities came together—seem less aberrant.

6. Recent interest in the oxymoronic figure of the *traveling native* complicates and historicizes, though it does not eliminate, the tension between tribal and diasporic claims to legitimacy. I am drawing here on the insightful work of Teresia Teaiwa. She evokes a long history of Pacific Islander travels (linked to contemporary practices). This mobility can be traced along ancient routes of exchange, such as "the kula ring which linked the east peninsula of mainland New Guinea with the Trobriand Islands and Louisiade Archipelago; the epic voyages between Hawai'i, Tahiti, and Actearca/New Zealand; the consistent migration and exchange within the Fiji-Tonga-Samoa triangle; and the exchange of navigational knowledge among Carolinian and Mariana Islanders. These, of course, are just a few of the circuits within which Pacific Islanders represented/performed their identities as both dynamic and specific—ways they thought about difference through connection" (Teaiwa, 1993: 12).

7. In the U.S. academy, "minority" discourse has been theorized as a resistance practice (JanMohamed and Lloyd, 1990). It is often institutionalized in programs defined by ethnicity/race. Diasporic transnationalism complicates and sometimes threatens this structure, particularly when "minorities" have defined themselves in ethnically absolutist, or nationalist, ways. In Britain, the tension between minority and diaspora articulations of identity takes place in a different context: "minority discourse" has been largely an official discourse.

8. The distinction between old and new, European and non-European immigrants, while critical, should not be overdrawn. Immigrants from Ireland and from central, southern, and eastern Europe have been racialized. And anti-Semitism

remains an often latent, sometimes explicit force. But generally speaking, European immigrants have, with time, come to participate as ethnic "whites" in multicultural America. The same cannot be said, overall, of populations of color—although region of origin, shade of skin, culture, and class may attenuate racist exclusion.

9. Edward Said has used the term "contrapuntal" to characterize one of the positive aspects of conditions of exile: "Seeing 'the entire world as a foreign land' makes possible originality of vision. Most people are principally aware of one culture, one setting, one home; exiles are aware of at least two, and this plurality of vision gives rise to an awareness of simultaneous dimensions, an awareness that—to borrow a phrase from music—is contrapuntal . . . For an exile, habits of life, expression or activity in the new environment inevitably occur against the memory of these things in another environment. Thus both the new and the old environments are vivid, actual, occurring together contrapuntally" (1984: 171–172; see also 1990: 48–50). These reflections on exile apply to experiences of diaspora, but with the difference that the more individualist, existential focus of the former is tempered by networks of community, collective practices of displaced dwelling, in the latter.

10. In a far-reaching historical critique of Pacific Rim discourse and liberal/neoliberal "free-trade" ideologies, Christopher Connery (1994) identifies a danger of imagining counterhegemonic sites of crossing/cosmopolitanism "within the dominant conceptual category of the Ocean, given that it is Capital's favorite myth-element." He calls for a careful historicizing of oceanic discourses, a concern that applies to Gilroy's projection of a black Atlantic, discussed below.

11. For diverse accounts and critiques of the Los Angeles Festival, see Getty Center (1991), particularly Lisa Lowe's comments on the depoliticizing effects of postmodern pluralism/multiculturalism.

12. Of course, men also select and strategize, within their own constraints and privileges. The difference between gendered diaspora predicaments is critical for an emerging comparative perspective. Ganguly's 1992 study of men's and women's memories in the South Asian U.S. diaspora is exemplary; Bottomley (1992) provides an excellent treatment of gender and class articulation in a study of Greek migration as cultural process.

13. Brah (1993), Mohanty (1987), Hall (1988b, 1990), Mercer (1988, 1990), and Radakrishnan (1991), among others, discuss this diasporic space of cross-cutting determinations.

14. On tensions between Caribbean and African American populations in New York, see Foner (1987). The analysis in Velez (1994) of a story by Puerto Rican writer Ana Lydia Vega, "Encancaranublado" (Vega, 1987), very acutely evokes the national/cultural/racial/linguistic differences separating Caribbean immigrants, as well as their common lumping together by the U.S. racial order. Whether this

latter repositioning will lead to new alliances or conflicts in the diasporic economy of struggle and scarcity is left open.

15. Here a parallel with border cultures could be developed, highlighting the constitutive, repeated violence of the arbitrary line, the policed border—and the desperate/utopic crossings that ensue. This ambivalence recalls Nestor Garcia Canclini's conflicting, simultaneous images of transnational "border" cultures: the "airport" and the "garage sale," one institutional and disciplinary, the other popular and improvised (1992). The garage-sale image is derived from the portrayal of border cultures in Renato Rosaldo's *Culture and Truth* (1989: 44).

16. Bhabha tends to equate "diasporic" and "postcolonial" in his discussion. This raises an interesting question that I cannot develop fully here. To what extent are theorizations of postcoloniality projections of specific diasporas? Ella Shohat (1992) links articulations of hybridity in the name of a "postcolonial" condition to diasporic Third World intellectuals writing primarily in First World centers, and Arif Dirlik (1994) links them, in a functionalist account, with the needs of transnational capitalism. To be sure, South Asian theorists are strikingly prominent, notably in Britain and North America. Postcoloniality is not much heard from elsewhere—for example, in Latin America and Africa, where histories of de-, anti-, and neocolonialism are significantly different. If postcolonial theory is historicized in relation to South Asian diasporas, we might usefully distinguish, following Vijay Mishra (1983, 1994), two kinds: the first diaspora, in the late nineteenth century, involved the movement of indentured laborers to places such as Trinidad, Guyana, Surinam, Fiji, Mauritius, South Africa, and Malaysia; the second consisted of postwar "free" migrations to Britain, the United States, Australia, and Canada. The representative writer of the first would be V. S. Naipaul; that of the second, the moment of "postcolonial" visions, Salman Rushdie. Mishra's ongoing work will help flesh out this historicization in detail. Obviously, the substance of postcolonial theorizing is not entirely reducible to the histories of certain South Asian intellectuals. The key concept of hybridity, for example, rhymes with Latin American theorizations of *mestizaje,* or Caribbean *créolité.* These are not identical concepts, and they emerge from distinct historical situations; but they overlap and together denote a domain of complex cultural formations produced by, and partially subverting, colonial dichotomies and hierarchies.

17. *The Black Atlantic* guards, more explicitly, against the problems Mercer finds in Gilroy's concept of "populist modernism," with its implicit culture- and class-based authenticity test. The book's critical countertradition of modernity spans vernacular, "popular" forms and "high" cultural arguments (explicit and implicit) with Enlightenment philosophy.

18. *The Black Atlantic* is pointedly an intervention in the tradition of African *American* intellectual and cultural history. This tradition has canonically meant African

North-American, including those areas of the Caribbean directly connected with the English-speaking United States. New Latino/Chicano readings of the Americas as complex border zones question overly linear diaspora narratives. See, for example, José David Saldívar's reading of Ntozake Shange in terms of magical realism and *mestizaje* (1991: 87–104).

19. See Clifford (1988: 277–346, "Identity in Mashpee") for a similar attempt to portray an interactive culture/identity as something persistently, but not continuously, there. The differences concerning land, oral tradition, travel, racialization, and identity are of course salient. But the general approach to peoples who have managed to prevail through histories overdetermined by cultural, political, and economic power relations is comparable. See Gilroy (1991, 1992b) for the notion of a *changing same* (derived from Leroi Jones / Amiri Baraka). The phrase does not, I think, quite do justice to the tensions and violent discontinuities that are constitutive of the "tradition" he tracks. His most recent formulations struggle against the grain of various organicisms, while asserting a complexly hybrid *historical* continuity. Gilroy (1992b) is explicitly concerned not to privilege appeals to kinship or "family." Stefan Helmreich (1993) asserts the contrary but does not discuss *The Black Atlantic* or a wide range of Gilroy's recent work. Helmreich's suggestive etymological reading of the bias toward male genealogies built into the concept/metaphor of "diaspora" applies better to those strongly linear, genealogical visions of diaspora which Gilroy questions. Despite its general, but not exclusive, emphasis on men, Gilroy's work is not inherently closed to women's experiences or to complex intersections of gender, race, class, and sexuality. Etymology is not destiny. I fully agree with Helmreich's project of "set[ting] in motion to new meanings the term *diaspora*" (Helmreich, 1993: 248).

20. Gilroy's formulation of the interconnected diversity of historical "black" experiences is not reducible to the image of a tree—root, stem, and branches—proposed by St. Clair Drake (1982: 397). This difference distinguishes his diaspora from the "traditional" or "continental" forms evoked by Drake.

21. See Daniel Boyarin (1993a) for a historical account of the symmetrical discursive construction of "woman" and "Jew" in Pauline Christian universalism.

22. Their recent analysis of circumcision marks its subject matter and perspective explicitly as male (Boyarin and Boyarin, 1995).

23. Another area of specification I am not yet prepared to discuss: diasporic sexualities and/or sexualized diaspora discourses. In Brah's idea of "diasporic space," there is room for developing such analyses. And Mercer's work points the way, along with the productions of the Sankofa Film Collective. In commenting on a draft of this essay, Kathleen Biddick reminded me of Sankofa's *Passion of Remembrance* "and the strange place to which the film returns, with the voices and bodies of the man and woman fractured in interesting ways across it" (personal communication, 1993). Diasporic histories may not be necessary conditions for developing

performative visions of gender, sexuality, race, and ethnicity, but their liminal spaces, displaced encounters, and tactical affiliations provide apt settings for such visions. In this vein, it would be interesting to historicize Audre Lorde's complex articulation of race, gender, and sexuality in *Zami: A New Spelling of My Name* (1982) with attention to New York City neighborhoods as diasporic spaces.

24. *Geniza,* in this context, refers to the "storeroom" of the synagogue at Fustat (Old Cairo), where a rich archive of records—business, personal, and religious in nature—survived from the tenth to the nineteenth century. These documents are the basis for Goitein's extraordinary vision of transregional, interactive Jewish life in the Middle Ages (see Goitein, 1967–1993, vol. 1; also Ghosh, 1992; and Cohen, 1994).

25. In many places, Weinreich anticipates current contact perspectives on colonial and neocolonial border zones, processes of "transculturation" and interactive identity formation. Compare, particularly, Pratt's definition of "contact zone," also derived from ethnolinguistic "contact" or "fusion" languages (1992). See also Dubnow (1931) for a historically grounded Ashkenazi vision of interactive Jewishness that presupposes the permanence of diaspora.

26. In the past few years "postcolonial" and "postcoloniality"—terms that often confuse theoretical approaches and historical moments—have been subjected to searching, often skeptical, symptomatic critiques. See especially During (1987), Appiah (1991), Shohat (1992), Chow (1992), Frankenberg and Mani (1993), Miyoshi (1993), Dirlik (1994), and many of the papers in *Social Text,* 31–32 (1992). I cannot here engage the many unresolved issues raised by these arguments, except to say that I am persuaded by Frankenberg and Mani's insistence on a rigorously conjunctural understanding of different ways to be "postcolonial" (1993). Whatever the fate of this term, the sites of complex historical entanglement and agency it provisionally names should not be reduced to epiphenomena of postmodern fragmentation, neocolonial transnationality, or global capitalism. On the connection of postcoloniality with recent diaspora theories, see Frankenberg and Mani (1993: 302). Also for our current purposes, the three possible temporalities that Chow connects to the prefix *post-* are relevant, particularly the third: (1) "having gone through"; (2) "after"; (3) "a notion of time that is not linear but constant, marked by events that may be technically finished but that can only be fully understood with consideration of the devastation they left behind" (Chow, 1992: 152).

References

Abu-Lughod, Janet. 1989. *Before European Hegemony: The World System,* A.D. *1250–1350.* Oxford: Oxford University Press.

———. 1991. "Going beyond Global Babble." In *Culture, Globalization and the World-System,* ed. Anthony King. Binghamton, N.Y.: Department of Art History, State University of New York. 131–138.

Abu-Lughod, Lila. 1991. "Writing against Culture." In *Recapturing Anthropology: Working in the Present,* ed. Richard Fox. Santa Fe: School of American Research. 137–162.

Agar, Michael. 1985. *Independents Declared: The Dilemma of Independent Trucking.* Washington D.C.: Smithsonian Institute Press.

Akmajian, Adrian, et al. 1993. *Linguistics: An Introduction to Language and Communication.* Cambridge, Mass.: MIT Press.

Alcalay, Ammiel. 1993. *After Jews and Arabs: Remaking Levantine Culture.* Minneapolis: University of Minnesota Press.

Alekseev, A. I. 1987. *The Odyssey of a Russian Scientist: I. G. Voznesenskii in Alaska, California and Siberia.* Kingston, Ontario: Limestone Press.

Alpers, Svetlana. 1991. "The Museum as a Way of Seeing." In *Exhibiting Cultures: The Poetics and Politics of Museum Display,* ed. Ivan Karp and Steven Lavine. Washington, D.C.: Smithsonian Institution Press. 25–32.

Alvarez, Robert. 1994. "*Un Chilero en la Academia:* Sifting, Shifting, and the Recruitment of Minorities in Anthropology." In *Race,* ed. Steven Gregory and Roger Sanjek. New Brunswick, N.J.: Rutgers University Press. 257–269.

———. 1995. "The Mexican-U.S. Border: The Making of an Anthropology of Borderlands." *Annual Review of Anthropology,* 24: 447–470.

Ames, Michael. 1986. *Museums, the Public, and Anthropology: A Study in the Anthropology of Anthropology.* Vancouver: University of British Columbia Press.

———. 1987. "Free Indians from their Ethnological Fate: The Emergence of the Indian Point of View in Exhibitions of Indians." *Muse,* 5 (2): 27–35.

———. 1988. "Boycott the Politics of Suppression." *Muse,* 6 (3): 15–16.

———. 1991. "Biculturalism in Exhibitions." *Museum Anthropology,* 15 (2): 7–15.

Amin, Samir. 1994. *Re-reading the Postwar Period: An Intellectual Itinerary.* New York: Monthly Review Press.

Amselle, Jean-Loup. 1989. *Logiques métisses: Anthropologie de l'identité en Afrique et ailleurs.* Paris: Payot.

Anderson, Robin, and Bob Connolly. 1988. *Joe Leahy's Neighbors.* Santa Monica: Direct Cinema.

Anzaldúa, Gloria. 1987. *Borderlands / La Frontera: The New Mestiza.* San Francisco: Spinsters / Aunt Lute.

Appadurai, Arjun. 1988a. "Putting Hierarchy in Its Place." *Cultural Anthropology,* 3 (1): 36–49.

———. 1988b. "Introduction: Place and Voice in Anthropological Theory." *Cultural Anthropology,* 3 (1): 16–20.

———. 1990. "Disjuncture and Difference in the Global Cultural Economy." *Public Culture,* 2 (2): 1–24.

Appiah, Kwame Anthony. 1991. "Is the Post in Postmodern the Post in Postcolonial?" *Critical Inquiry,* 17 (Winter): 336–357.

Asad, Talal. 1982. "A Comment on the Idea of a Non Western Anthropology." In *Indigenous Anthropology in Non-Western Countries,* ed. Hussein Fahim. Durham: Carolina Academic Press. 284–288.

———. 1986. "The Concept of Cultural Translation in British Social Anthropology." In *Writing Culture: The Poetics and Politics of Ethnography,* ed. James Clifford and George Marcus. Berkeley: University of California Press. 141–164.

Assu, Harry. 1989. *Assu of Cape Mudge: Recollections of a Coastal Indian Chief.* Vancouver: University of British Columbia Press.

Bakhtin, Mikhail. 1937. "Forms of Time and the Chronotope in the Novel." In *The Dialogic Imagination,* ed. Michael Holquist. Austin: University of Texas Press, 1981. 84–258.

Bammer, Angelika, ed. 1992. *The Question of 'Home.'"* (Entire issue.) *New Formations* (17).

Barnaby, Joanne, and Nancy Hall. 1990. "The Dene Cultural Institute." *Muse,* 8 (1): 27–28.

Barringer, F. 1991. "Ancient Tribes That Didn't Vanish, They Just Moved." *New York Times* (October 23): C1, C6.

Barthes, Roland. 1981. *Camera Lucida.* New York: Hill and Wang.

Bauman, Richard, and Patricia Sawin. 1991. "The Politics of Participation in Folklife Festivals." In *Exhibiting Cultures: The Poetics and Politics of Museum Display,* ed. Ivan Karp and Steven Lavine. Washington, D.C.: Smithsonian Institution Press. 288–314.

Bauman, Zygmunt. 1989. *Modernity and the Holocaust.* Ithaca, N.Y.: Cornell University Press.

Baxandall, Michael. 1991. "Exhibiting Intention: Some Preconditions of the Visual Display of Culturally Purposeful Objects." In *Exhibiting Cultures: The Poetics and*

Politics of Museum Display, ed. Ivan Karp and Steven Lavine. Washington, D.C.: Smithsonian Institution Press. 33–41.

Becker, Howard. 1986. *Doing Things Together.* Evanston, Ill.: Northwestern University Press.

Behar, Ruth. 1993. *Translated Woman: Crossing the Border with Esperanza's Story.* Boston: Beacon Press.

———— and Deborah Gordon, eds. 1995. *Women Writing Culture.* Berkeley: University of California Press.

Behdad, Ali. 1994. *Belated Travelers: Orientalism in the Age of Colonial Dissolution.* Durham, N.C.: Duke University Press.

Bell, Diane, Pat Caplan, and Wazir Jahan Karim, eds. 1993. *Gendered Fields: Women, Men and Ethnography.* New York: Routledge.

Benjamin, Walter. 1969. "Theses on the Philosophy of History." In *Illuminations,* ed. Hannah Arendt. New York: Schocken. 253–265.

————. 1985. *The Origin of German Classic Drama.* London: Verso.

Benmayor, Rina. 1991. "Testimony, Action, Research, and Empowerment: Puerto Rican Women and Popular Education." In *Women's Words: The Feminist Practice of Oral History,* ed. Shema Berger Gluck and Daphne Patai. New York: Routledge.

————, Ana Juarbe, Celia Alvarez, and Blanca Vasquez. 1987. *Stories to Live By: Continuity and Change in Three Generations of Puerto Rican Women.* New York: Centro de Estudios Puertoriqueños, Hunter College.

Bennett, Tony. 1988. "Museums and 'the People.'" In *The Museum Time Machine: Putting Cultures on Display,* ed. Robert Lumley. London: Routledge.

Bhabha, Homi K. 1990. "DissemiNation: Time, Narrative, and the Margins of the Modern Nation." In *Nation and Narration,* ed. Homi K. Bhabha. London: Routledge. 291–322.

Black, Lydia. 1977. "Aleuts and Russians." *Arctic Anthropology,* 14 (1): 94–107.

————. 1991. *Glory Remembered: Wooden Headgear of the Alaska Seahunters.* Seattle: University of Washington Press.

Black Elk. 1979. *Black Elk Speaks.* As told through John G. Neihardt. Lincoln: University of Nebraska Press.

Blackstone, Sarah. 1986. *Buckskins, Bullets, and Business: A History of Buffalo Bill's Wild West.* New York: Greenwood Press.

Blake, William. 1971. *The Poems of William Blake.* Harlow, England: Longman.

Blaut, J. M. 1993. *The Colonizer's View of the World: Geographical Diffusionism and Eurocentric History.* New York: Guilford Press.

Bloom, Lisa. 1993. *Gender on Ice: American Ideologies of Polar Explorations.* Minneapolis: University of Minnesota Press.

Blundell, Valda. 1989. "The Tourist and the Native." In *A Different Drummer: Readings in Anthropology with a Canadian Perspective,* ed. Bruce Cox, Jacques Chevalier, and Valda Blundell. Ottawa: Carleton University Anthropology Caucus. 49–58.

———— and Laurence Grant. 1989. "Preserving Our Heritage: Getting beyond Boycotts and Demonstrations." *Inuit Art Quarterly,* Winter: 12–16.

Boon, James. 1977. *The Anthropological Romance of Bali, 1597–1972: Dynamic Perspectives in Marriage and Caste, Politics and Religion.* New York: Cambridge University Press.

————. 1990. *Affinities and Extremes.* Chicago: University of Chicago Press.

————. 1992. "Cosmopolitan Moments: Echoey Confessions of an Ethnographer-Tourist." In *Crossing Cultures: Essays in the Displacement of Western Civilization,* ed. Daniel Segal. Tucson: University of Arizona Press. 226–253.

Bottomley, Gillian. 1992. *From Another Place: Migration and the Politics of Culture.* Cambridge: Cambridge University Press.

Bourdieu, Pierre. 1977. *Outline of a Theory of Practice.* Cambridge: Cambridge University Press.

————. 1984. *Distinction.* London: Routledge.

Bowen, Elenore Smith. 1954. *Return to Laughter.* New York: Harper and Row.

Boyarin, Daniel. 1993a. *Carnal Israel: Reading Sex in Talmudic Culture.* Berkeley: University of California Press.

————. 1993b. "Paul and the Genealogy of Gender." *Representations,* 41 (Winter): 1–33.

Boyarin, Daniel, and Jonathan Boyarin. 1993. "Diaspora: Generational Ground of Jewish Identity." *Critical Inquiry,* 19 (4): 693–725.

Boyarin, Daniel, and Jonathan Boyarin. 1995. "Self-Exposure as Theory: The Double Mark of the Male Jew." In *Rhetorics of Self-Making,* ed. Deborah Battaglia. Berkeley: University of California Press. 16–42.

Boyarin, Jonathan. 1992. *Storm from Paradise: The Politics of Jewish Memory.* Minneapolis: University of Minnesota Press.

Bradford, Phillips Verner, and Harvey Blume. 1992. *Ota Benga: The Pygmy in the Zoo.* New York: St. Martin's Press.

Brah, Avtar. 1992. "Difference, Diversity and Differentiation." In *"Race," Culture and Difference,* ed. James Donald and Ali Rattansi. London: Sage.

————. 1993. "Diasporas and Borders." Unpublished manuscript, University of California, Santa Cruz.

Brecher, Jeremy, John Brown Childs, and Jill Cutler, eds. 1993. *Global Visions: Beyond the New World Order.* Boston: South End Press.

Briggs, Jean. 1970. *Never in Anger.* Cambridge, Mass.: Harvard University Press.

Brody, Hugh. 1982. *Maps and Dreams.* New York: Pantheon.

Brown, Karen McCarthy. 1991. *Mama Lola: A Vodou Priestess in Brooklyn.* Berkeley: University of California Press.

Brown, Norman O. 1991. *Apocalypse and/or Metamorphosis.* Berkeley: University of California Press.

Burawoy, Michael, et al. 1991. *Ethnography Unbound: Power and Resistance in the Modern Metropolis.* Berkeley: University of California Press.

Buzzard, James. 1993. *The Beaten Track: European Tourism, Literature, and the Ways to Culture, 1800–1918.* Oxford: Oxford University Press.

Calderón, Héctor, and José Saldívar, eds. 1991. *Criticism in the Borderlands: Studies in Chicano Literature, Culture, and Ideology.* Durham, N.C.: Duke University Press.

Canadian Museums Association. 1988. *Museums and the First Nations.* (Entire issue.) *Muse,* 6 (3).

———. 1990. *The Nature of Northern Museums.* (Entire issue.) *Muse,* 8 (1).

Canclini, Nestor Garcia. 1990. *Culturas híbridas: Estrategias para entrar y salir de la modernidad.* Mexico City: Editorial Grijalbo.

———. 1992. "Museos, aeropuertos y ventes de garage." Paper read at conference entitled "Borders/Diasporas." Center for Cultural Studies, University of California, Santa Cruz.

Cannizzo, Jeanne. 1989. *Into the Heart of Africa.* Ontario: Royal Ontario Museum.

———. 1991. "Exhibiting Cultures: 'Into the Heart of Africa.'" *Visual Anthropology Review,* 7 (1): 150–160.

Chabram, Angie C. 1990. "Chicana/o Studies as Oppositional Ethnography." *Cultural Studies,* 4 (3): 228–247.

Chakrabarty, Dipesh. 1992. "Postcoloniality and the Artifice of History: Who Speaks for the 'Indian' Pasts?" *Representations,* 37 (1): 1–26.

Chaussonnet, Valérie, ed. 1995. *Crossroads Alaska: Native Culture of Alaska and Siberia.* Washington, D.C.: Arctic Studies Center, Smithsonian Institution.

Chevigny, Hector. 1951. *Lord of Alaska: Baranov and the Russian Adventure.* Portland, Ore.: Binford and Mort.

———. 1965. *Russian America: The Great Alaskan Venture, 1741–1867.* Portland, Ore.: Binford and Mort.

Chow, Rey. 1992. "Between Colonizers: Hong Kong's Postcolonial Self-Writing in the 1900s." *Diaspora,* 2 (2): 151–170.

Clifford, James. 1982. *Person and Myth: Maurice Leenhardt in the Melanesian World.* Berkeley: University of California Press.

———. 1986. "On Ethnographic Allegory." In *Writing Culture: The Poetics and Politics of Ethnography,* ed. James Clifford and George Marcus. Berkeley: University of California Press. 98–121.

———. 1987. "Of Other Peoples: Beyond the 'Salvage' Paradigm." In *Discussions in Contemporary Culture,* ed. Hal Foster. Seattle: Bay Press. 121–130.

———. 1988. *The Predicament of Culture: Twentieth Century Ethnography, Literature, and Art.* Cambridge, Mass.: Harvard University Press.

———. 1989. "Interview with Brian Wallis." *Art in America,* 77 (7): 86–87, 152–153.

———. 1990. "Notes on (Field) Notes." In *Fieldnotes: The Makings of Anthropology,* ed. Roger Sanjek. Ithaca, N.Y.: Cornell University Press. 47–69.

———. 1991. "Four Northwest Coast Museums: Travel Reflections." In *Exhibiting Cultures: The Poetics and Politics of Museum Display,* ed. Ivan Karp and Steven Lavine. Washington, D.C.: Smithsonian Institution Press. 212–234.

———. 1992a. "Traveling Cultures." In *Cultural Studies,* ed. Lawrence Grossberg, Cary Nelson, and Paula Treichler. New York: Routledge. 96–116.

———. 1992b. "Museums in the Borderlands." In *Different Voices: A Social, Cultural and Historical Framework for Change in the American Art Museum,* ed. Marcia Tucker. New York: Association of Art Museum Directors. 117–136.

———. 1995. "Paradise." *Visual Anthropology Review,* 11 (1): 92–117.

——— and George Marcus, eds. 1986. *Writing Culture: The Poetics and Politics of Ethnography.* Berkeley: University of California Press.

Cohen, Mark. 1994. *Under Cross and Crescent: The Jews in the Middle Ages.* Princeton: Princeton University Press.

Cohen, Robin. 1987. *The New Helots: Migrants in the International Division of Labor.* Aldershot, England: Gower.

Cole, Douglas. 1985. *Captured Heritage.* Vancouver: Douglas and McIntyre.

Cole, Sally. 1995. "Ruth Landes and the Early Anthropology of Race and Gender." In *Women Writing Culture,* ed. Ruth Behar and Deborah Gordon. Berkeley: University of California Press. 166–185.

Coles, Robert. 1992. *Anna Freud: The Dream of Psychoanalysis.* Reading, Mass. Addison-Wesley.

Connery, Christopher. 1994. "Pacific Rim Discourse: The U.S. Global Imaginary in the Late Cold War Years." *Boundary 2,* 21 (2): 30–56.

Conrad, Joseph. 1957. *Victory.* Garden City, N.Y.: Doubleday.

Coombes, Annie E. 1988. "Museums and the Formation of National and Cultural Identities." *Oxford Art Journal,* 11 (2): 57–68.

Counter, S. Allen. 1988. "The Henson Family." *National Geographic,* 147 (3): 422–429.

Crapanzano, Vincent. 1977. "The Writing of Ethnography." *Dialectical Anthropology,* 2 (1): 69–73.

Crick, Malcolm. 1985. "Tracing the Anthropological Self: Quizzical Reflections on Field Work, Tourism, and the Ludic." *Social Analysis,* 17 (August): 71–92.

Cronon, William, ed. 1995. *Uncommon Ground: Toward Reinventing Nature.* New York: Norton.

Dalby, Lisa. 1983. *Geisha.* Berkeley: University of California Press.

D'Amico-Samuels, Deborah. 1991. "Undoing Fieldwork: Personal, Political, Theoretical and Methodological Implications." In *Decolonizing Anthropology: Moving Further toward an Anthropology of Liberation.* Washington, D.C.: Association of Black Anthropologists and American Anthropological Association. 68–85.

D'Andrade, Roy. 1995. "Moral Models in Anthropology." *Current Anthropology,* 36 (3): 399–408.

Davies, W. D. 1992. *The Territorial Dimension of Judaism.* Minneapolis: University of Minnesota Press.

Davis, Lee. 1989. "Locating the Live Museum." *News from Native California,* 4 (1): 4–9.

Deacon, Bernard. 1934. *Malekula: A Vanishing People of the New Hebrides.* London: Routledge.

de Certeau, Michel. 1984. *The Practice of Everyday Life*. Berkeley: University of California Press.

Defert, Daniel. 1984. "Un genre ethnographique profane au XVIe siècle: Les livres d'habits (essai d'ethno-iconographie)." In *Histoires de l'Anthropologie (XVIe–XIXe siècles)*, ed. Britta Rupp-Eisenreich. Paris: Klincksieck. 25–42.

Deliss, Clémentine. 1995. "The Visual Programme." In *Africa95: A Season Celebrating the Arts of Africa*. London: Richard House.

Deloria, Vine, Jr. 1969. *Custer Died for Your Sins*. New York: Macmillan.

Demallie, Raymond, ed. 1984. *The Sixth Grandfather: Black Elk's Teachings Given to John G. Neihardt*. Lincoln: University of Nebraska Press.

Dening, Greg. 1980. *Islands and Beaches: Discourse on a Silent Land: Marquesas, 1774–1880*. Honolulu: University Press of Hawaii.

Detremery, C., B. Sanguinetti, and H. Gibbs, eds. 1972. *Travels of Ibn Battouta*, A.D. *1325–1354*. Nendeln, Netherlands: Kraus Reprint.

Dhareshwar, Vivek. 1989a. "Toward a Narrative Epistemology of the Post-Colonial Predicament." *Inscriptions*, 5: 135–157.

———. 1989b. "Self-Fashioning, Colonial Habitus and Double Exclusion: V. S. Naipaul's *The Mimic Men*." *Criticism*, 31 (1): 75–102.

Dirlik, Arif. 1994. "The Postcolonial Aura: Third World Criticism in the Age of Global Capitalism." *Critical Inquiry*, 20 (2): 328–356.

Dittborn, Eugenio. 1993. *Mapa: The Airmail Paintings of Eugenio Dittborn, 1984–1992*. London: Institute of Contemporary Art.

Drake, St. Clair. 1982. "Diaspora Studies and Pan-Africanism." In *Global Dimensions of the African Diaspora*, ed. Joseph E. Harris. Washington, D.C.: Howard University Press. 341–404.

Drummond, Lee. 1981. "The Cultural Continuum: A Theory of Intersystems." *Man*, 15 (2): 352–374.

Dubnow, Simon. 1931. "Diaspora." In *Encyclopedia of the Social Sciences*. New York: Macmillan. 126–130.

———. 1958. *Nationalism and History: Essays in Old and New Judaism*. Philadelphia: Jewish Publication Society of America.

Dubois, Laurent. 1995. "'Man's Darkest Hours': Maleness, Travel, and Anthropology." In *Women Writing Culture*, ed. Ruth Behar and Deborah Gordon. Berkeley: University of California Press. 306–321.

Duchet, Michèle. 1984. *Le partage des savoirs: Discours historique et discours ethnologique*. Paris: La Découverte.

Duncan, Carol. 1991. "Art Museums and the Ritual of Citizenship." In *Exhibiting Cultures: The Poetics and Politics of Museum Display*, ed. Ivan Karp and Steven Lavine. Washington, D.C.: Smithsonian Institution Press. 88–103.

———. 1995. *Civilizing Rituals: Inside Public Art Museums*. London: Routledge.

During, Simon. 1987. "Postmodernism or Post-Colonialism Today." *Textual Practice*, 1 (1): 32–47.

Ebron, Paula. 1994. "Subjects in Difference." Paper read at conference entitled "Anthropology and 'the Field': Boundaries, Areas and Grounds in the Constitution of a Discipline." Stanford University and the University of California at Santa Cruz.

———. 1995. "Subjects in Difference: Where and When We Enter." Unpublished manuscript.

———. Forthcoming. "Traffic in Men." In *Cultural Encounters: Gender at the Intersection of the Local and the Global in Africa,* ed. Maria Grosz-Ngate and Omari Kokoli. London: Routledge.

Edwards, David. 1994. "Afghanistan, Ethnography, and the New World Order." *Cultural Anthropology,* 9 (3): 345–360.

Eickelman, Dale, and James Piscatori, eds. 1990. *Muslim Travelers: Pilgrimage, Migration and the Religious Imagination.* Berkeley: University of California Press.

Enloe, Cynthia. 1990. *Bananas, Beaches, and Bases.* Berkeley: University of California Press.

Evans-Pritchard, Edward. 1940. *The Nuer.* Oxford: Oxford University Press.

Fabian, Johannes. 1983. *Time and the Other.* New York: Columbia University Press.

———. 1986. *Language and Colonial Power.* New York: Cambridge University Press.

Fahim, Husein. 1982. *Indigenous Anthropology in Non-Western Countries.* Durham, N.C.: Carolina Academic Press.

Farris, Glenn. 1988. "A French Visitor's Description of the Fort Ross Rancheria in 1839." *News from Native California,* 2 (3): 22–23.

———. 1989a. "Recognizing Indian Folk History as Real History: A Fort Ross Example." *American Indian Quarterly,* 13 (Fall): 471–480.

———. 1989b. "The Russian Imprint on the Colonization of California." In *Columbian Consequences,* ed. David Hurst Thomas. Washington, D.C.: Smithsonian Institution Press. 481–497.

Fienup-Riordan, Ann. 1990. *Eskimo Essays: Yup'ik Lives and How We See Them.* New Brunswick, N.J.: Rutgers University Press.

Finney, Ben. 1994. *Voyage of Rediscovery: A Cultural Odyssey through Polynesia.* Berkeley: University of California Press.

Fischer, Michael M. J., and Mehdi Abedi. 1990. *Debating Muslims: Cultural Dialogues in Postmodernity and Tradition.* Madison: University of Wisconsin Press.

Fitzhugh, William, and Valérie Chaussonnet, eds. 1994. *Anthropology of the North Pacific Rim.* Washington, D.C.: Smithsonian Institution Press.

Fitzhugh, William, and Aron Crowell, eds. 1988. *Crossroads of Continents: Cultures of Siberia and Alaska.* Washington, D.C.: Smithsonian Institution Press.

Flores, Juan, and George Yudice. 1990. "Living Borders / Buscando America." *Social Text,* 24: 57–84.

Foner, Nancy. 1987. "West Indians in New York City and London: A Comparative Analysis." In *Caribbean Life in New York City: Sociocultural Dimensions,* ed. Constance Sutton and Elsa Chaney. New York: Center for Migration Studies. 117–130.

Foster, George, ed. 1979. *Long-Term Field Research in Social Anthropology.* New York: Academic Press.

Frankenberg, Ruth, and Lata Mani. 1993. "Crosscurrents, Crosstalk: Race, "Postcoloniality," and the Politics of Location." *Cultural Studies,* 7 (2): 292–310.

Freud, Sigmund. 1939. *Moses and Monotheism.* New York: Vintage.

Friedman, Jonathan. 1994. *Cultural Identity and Global Process.* London: Sage.

Gallie, W. B. 1964. *Philosophy and the Historical Understanding.* London: Chatto and Windus.

Galloway, Colin. 1990. *The Western Abenakes of Vermont, 1600–1800: War, Migration, and the Survival of an Indian People.* Norman: University of Oklahoma Press.

Gandoulou, Justin-Daniel. 1984. *Entre Paris et Bacongo.* Paris: Centre Georges Pompidou.

Gangulay, Keya. 1992. "Migrant Identities: Personal Memory and the Construction of Selfhood." *Cultural Studies,* 6 (1): 27–50.

Gardner, Margaret. 1984. *Footprints on Malekula: A Memoir of Bernard Deacon.* Edinburgh: Salamander Press.

Gauguin, Paul. 1957. *Noa Noa.* New York: Noonday.

Gay, E. Jane. 1981. *With the Nez Perce: Alice Fletcher in the Field, 1889–1892.* Lincoln: University of Nebraska Press.

Getty Center. 1991. "New Geographies of Performance: Cultural Representation and Intercultural Exchange on the Edge of the Twenty-first Century: Summary Report." Getty Center for the History of Art and the Humanities, Los Angeles, Calif.

Ghosh, Amitav. 1986. "The Imam and the Indian." *Granta,* 20 (Winter): 135–146.

———. 1989a. *The Shadow Lines.* New York: Viking.

———. 1989b. "The Diaspora in Indian Culture." *Public Culture,* 2 (1): 73–78.

———. 1992. *In an Antique Land.* London: Granta Books.

Gibson, James. 1976. *Imperial Russia in Frontier America: The Changing Geography of Supply for Russian America, 1784–1867.* New York: Oxford University Press.

Gilroy, Paul. 1987. *There Ain't No Black in the Union Jack: The Cultural Politics of Race and Nation.* London: Hutchinson.

———. 1991. "Sounds Authentic: Black, Music Ethnicity, and the Challenge of the Changing Same." *Black Music Research Journal,* 2 (2): 111–136.

———. 1992a. "Cultural Studies and Ethnic Absolutism." In *Cultural Studies,* ed. Lawrence Grossberg, Cary Nelson, and Paula Treichler. New York: Routledge. 187–199.

———. 1992b. "It's a Family Affair." In *Black Popular Culture: A Project by Michele Wallace,* ed. Gina Dent. Seattle: Bay Press. 303–316.

———. 1993a. *The Black Atlantic: Double Consciousness and Modernity.* Cambridge, Mass.: Harvard University Press.

———. 1993b. *Small Acts: Thoughts on the Politics of Black Cultures.* London: Serpent's Tail.

Glissant, Edouard. 1981. *Le discours antillais.* Paris: Seuil.

Goitein, Solomon Dob Fritz. 1967–1993. *A Mediterranean Society: The Jewish Communities of the Arab World as Portrayed in the Documents of the Cairo Geniza.* 6 vols. Berkeley: University of California Press.

Golde, Peggy, ed. 1986. *Women in the Field: Anthropological Experiences.* Second edition, expanded and updated. Berkeley: University of California Press.

González, Alicia, and Edith Tonelli. 1992. "*Compañeros* and Partners: The CARA Project." In *Museums and Communities: The Politics of Public Culture,* ed. Ivan Karp, Christine Mullen Kraemer, and Steven Lavine. Washington, D.C.: Smithsonian Institution Press. 262–284.

Gordon, Deborah. 1993. "Worlds of Consequences: Feminist Ethnography as Social Action." *Critique of Anthropology,* 13 (4): 429–443.

Gordon, Richard. 1994. "Internationalization, Multinationalization, Globalization: Contradictory World Economies and New Spatial Divisions of Labor." Working Paper 94-10, Center for the Study of Global Transformations, University of California, Santa Cruz.

Grasmuck, Sherri, and Patricia R. Pessar. 1991. *Between Two Islands: Dominican International Migration.* Berkeley: University of California Press.

Grewal, Shabnam, ed. 1988. *Charting the Journey: Writings by Black and Third World Women.* London: Sheba Feminist.

Gupta, Akhil. 1992. "The Song of the Nonaligned World: Transnational Identities and the Reinscription of Space in Late Capitalism." *Cultural Anthropology,* 9 (1): 63–79.

——— and James Ferguson. 1997. "Discipline and Practice: 'The Field' as Site, Method, and Location in Anthropology." In *Anthropological Locations: Boundaries and Grounds of a Field Science,* ed. Akhil Gupta and James Ferguson. Berkeley: University of California Press.

Gupta, Rahila. 1988. "Women and Communalism, a Tentative Inquiry." In *Charting the Journey: Writings by Black and Third World Women,* ed. Shabnam Grewal. London: Sheba Feminist. 23–29.

Haig-Brown, Celia. 1988. *Resistance and Renewal: Surviving the Indian Residential School.* Vancouver: Tillacum Library.

Hall, Stuart. 1986a. "Gramsci's Relevance for the Study of Race and Race and Ethnicity." *Journal of Communication Inquiry,* 10 (2): 5–27.

———. 1986b. "On Postmodernism and Articulation: An Interview with Stuart Hall." *Journal of Communication Inquiry,* 10 (2): 45–60.

———. 1988a. *The Hard Road to Renewal: Thatcherism and the Crisis of the Left.* London: Verso.

———. 1988b. "New Ethnicities." In *Black Film, British Cinema,* ed. Kobena Mercer. London: Institute of Contemporary Arts. 27–30.

———1990. "Cultural Identity and Diaspora." In *Identity: Community, Culture, Difference,* ed. Jonathan Rutherford. London: Lawrence and Wishart. 222–237.

———. 1991. "The Local and the Global: Globalization and Ethnicity." In *Culture, Globalization and the World-System,* ed. Anthony King. Binghamton: Department of Art and Art History, State University of New York. 19–40.

Handler, Richard. 1985. "On Dialogue and Destructive Analysis: Problems in Narrating Nationalism and Ethnicity." *Journal of Anthropological Research,* 41 (2): 171–182.

———. 1985. "On Having a Culture: Nationalism and the Preservation of Quebec's *Patrimoine.*" *History of Anthropology,* 3: 192–217.

———. 1987. *Nationalism and the Politics of Culture in Quebec.* Madison: University of Wisconsin Press.

———. 1993a. "An Anthropological Definition of the Museum and Its Purpose." *Museum Anthropology,* 17 (1): 33–36.

———. 1993b. "Anthropology Is Dead! Long Live Anthropology!" *American Anthropologist,* 95 (4): 991–999.

Hannerz, Ulf. 1991. "Scenarios for Peripheral Cultures." In *Culture, Globalization and the World-System,* ed. Anthony King. Binghamton: Department of Art History, State University of New York. 107–128.

———. 1992. *Cultural Complexity: Studies in the Social Organization of Meaning.* New York: Columbia University Press.

Haraway, Donna. 1988. "Situated Knowledges: The Science Question in Feminism and the Privilege of Partial Perspective." *Feminist Studies,* 14: 575–599.

———. 1989. *Primate Visions: Gender, Race, and Nature in the World of Modern Science.* New York: Routledge.

———. 1992. "The Promises of Monsters: A Regenerative Politics for Inappropriate/d Others." In *Cultural Studies,* ed. Lawrence Grossberg, Cary Nelson, and Paula Treichler. New York: Routledge. 295–337.

Harding, Susan. 1987. "Convicted by the Holy Spirit: The Rhetoric of Fundamental Baptist Conversion." *American Ethnologist,* 14 (1): 167–181.

———. 1990. "If I Should Die Before I Wake: Jerry Falwell's Pro-Life Gospel." In *Uncertain Terms: Renegotiating Gender in American Culture,* ed. Faye Ginsburg and Anna Tsing. Boston: Beacon Press. 76–97.

———. 1993. "Born-Again Telescandals." In *Culture, Power, History,* ed. Nicholas Dirks, Geoffrey Eley, and Sherry Ortner. Princeton: Princeton University Press. 539–556.

———. 1994. "Further Reflections." *Cultural Anthropology,* 9 (3): 276–278.

Harris, Neil. 1990. *Cultural Excursions: Marketing Appetites and Cultural Tastes in Modern America.* Chicago: University of Chicago Press.

Harrison, Faye. 1991. "Anthropology as an Agent of Transformation: Introductory Comments and Queries." In *Decolonizing Anthropology: Moving Further toward an*

Anthropology for Liberation. Washington, D.C.: Association of Black Anthropologists and American Anthropological Association. 1–14.

Harvey, David. 1989. *The Condition of Postmodernity: An Inquiry into the Origins of Cultural Change.* Oxford: Blackwell.

Hau'ofa, Epeli. 1982. "Anthropology at Home: A South Pacific Islands Experience." In *Indigenous Anthropology in Non-Western Countries,* ed. Hussein Fahim. Durham, N.C.: Carolina Academic Press. 213–222.

———, Vijay Naidu, and Eric Waddell, eds. 1993. *A New Oceania: Rediscovering Our Sea of Islands.* Suva, Fiji: School of Social and Economic Development, University of the South Pacific.

Healy, Chris. 1994. "Histories and Collecting: Museums, Objects and Memories." In *Memory and History in Twentieth-Century Australia,* ed. Kate Darian-Smith and Paula Hamilton. Melbourne: Oxford University Press. 33–54.

Helmreich, Stefan. 1993. "Kinship, Nation, and Paul Gilroy's Concept of Diaspora." *Diaspora,* 2 (2): 243–249.

Helms, Mary. 1988. *Ulysses' Sail: An Ethnographic Odyssey of Power, Knowledge, and Geographical Distance.* Princeton: Princeton University Press.

Hernandez, Graciela. 1995. "Multiple Subjectivities and Strategic Positionality: Zora Neale Hurston's Experimental Ethnographies." In *Women Writing Culture,* ed. Ruth Behar and Deborah Gordon. Berkeley: University of California Press. 148–165.

Hicks, Emily. 1991. *Border Writing: The Multidimensional Text.* Minneapolis: University of Minnesota Press.

Hill, Tom, and Trudy Nicks, eds. 1994. "Turning the Page: Forging New Partnerships between Museums and First Peoples." Report of the Task Force on Museums and First Peoples. Ottawa: Assembly of First Nations and Canadian Museums Association.

Hiller, Susan. 1995. *After the Freud Museum.* London: Bookworks.

———. Forthcoming. *Thinking about Arts.*

Hodgson, Marshall. 1993. *Rethinking World History.* Cambridge: Cambridge University Press.

Holm, Bill. 1983. *Smoky-Top: The Art and Times of Willie Seaweed.* Seattle: University of Washington Press.

——— and George Irving Quimby. 1980. *Edward S. Curtis in the Land of the War Canoes: A Pioneer Cinematographer in the Pacific Northwest.* Seattle: University of Washington Press.

hooks, bell. 1989. "Critical Interrogation: Talking Race, Resisting Racism." *Inscriptions,* 2: 159–164.

———. 1990. *Yearning: Race, Gender, and Cultural Politics.* Boston: South End Press.

Horne, Donald. 1984. *The Great Museum: The Re-presentation of History.* London: Pluto Press.

Houlihan, Patrick. 1991. "The Poetic Image and Native American Art." In *Exhibiting*

Cultures: The Poetics and Politics of Museum Display, ed. Ivan Karp and Steven Lavine. Washington, D.C.: Smithsonian Institution Press. 205–211.

Hulme, Peter. 1986. *Colonial Encounters: Europe and the Native Caribbean, 1492–1797.* London: Methuen.

Hutcheon, Linda. 1994. "The Post Always Rings Twice: The Postmodern and the Postcolonial." *Textual Practice* 8 (2): 205–238.

Irving, Sue, and Lynette Harper. 1988. "Not Another Fur Trade Exhibit? An Inside Look at *Trapline Lifeline.*" *Muse,* 6 (3): 38–40.

Istomin, Alexei. 1992. *The Indians at the Fort Ross Settlement: According to the Censuses by Kuskov, 1820–1821.* Fort Ross, Calif.: Fort Ross Interpretive Association.

Ivy, Marilyn. 1995. *Discourses of the Vanishing: Modernity, Phantasm, Japan.* Chicago: University of Chicago Press.

Iyer, Pico. 1988. *Video Night in Kathmandu, and Other Reports from the Not-So-Far East.* New York: Vintage.

Jacknis, Ira. 1988. "Museums, Anthropology and Kwakiutl Art: 1881–1981." Diss., University of Chicago.

James, C. L. R. 1984. *Beyond a Boundary.* New York: Pantheon.

Jameson, Fredric. 1984. "Postmodernism, or the Cultural Logic of Late Capitalism." *New Left Review,* 146: 53–92.

JanMohamed, Abdu, and David Lloyd, eds. 1990. *The Nature and Context of Minority Discourse.* New York: Oxford University Press.

Jensen, Doreen, and Polly Sargent. 1986. *Robes of Power: Totem Poles on Cloth.* Vancouver: University of British Columbia Press.

joannemariebarker, and Teresia Teaiwa. 1994. "Native Information." *Inscriptions,* 7: 16–41.

John, Mary E. 1996. *Discrepant Dislocations: Feminism, Theory, and Postcolonial Histories.* Berkeley: University of California Press.

———. 1989. "Postcolonial Feminists in the Western Intellectual Field: Anthropologists and Native Informants." In *Traveling Theorists, Traveling Theories: Inscriptions 5,* ed. James Clifford and Vivek Dhareshwar. Santa Cruz: Center for Cultural Studies, University of California at Santa Cruz. 49–74.

Johnson, Elizabeth Lominska, and Kathryn Bernick. 1986. *Hands of Our Ancestor.* Vancouver: University of British Columbia Museum of Anthropology.

Jonaitis, Aldona. 1991. "Chiefly Feasts: The Creation of an Exhibition." In *Chiefly Feasts: The Enduring Kwakiutl Potlatch,* ed. Aldona Jonaitis. Seattle: University of Washington Press. 21–69.

Jones, Ernest. 1953–1957. *The Life and Work of Sigmund Freud.* 3 vols. New York: Basic Books.

Jordan, June. 1985. "Report from the Bahamas." In *On Call: Political Essays.* Boston: South End Press. 39–49.

Kalifornsky, Peter. 1991. "A Dena'ina Legacy: K'tl'egh'i Sukdu." *The Collected Writings of Peter Kalifornsky.* Ed. James Kari and Alan Boraas. Fairbanks: Alaska Native Language Center, University of Alaska.

Kaplan, Caren. 1986. "The Poetics of Displacement in Alicia Dujoune Ortiz's *Buenos Aires.*" *Discourse,* 8: 84–100.

———. 1994. "The Politics of Location as Transnational Feminist Practice." In *Scattered Hegemonies: Postmodernity and Transnational Feminist Practices,* ed. Inderpal Grewal and Caren Kaplan. Minneapolis: University of Minnesota Press. 137–151.

———. 1996. *Questions of Travel: Postmodern Discourses of Displacement.* Durham, N.C.: Duke University Press.

Kari, James. 1983. "Kalifornsky: The Californian from Cook Inlet." *Alaska in Perspective,* 5 (1): 1–11.

Karp, Ivan, and Steven Lavine, eds. 1991. *Exhibiting Cultures: The Poetics and Politics of Museum Display.* Washington, D.C.: Smithsonian Institution Press.

Karp, Ivan, Steven Lavine, and Christine Mullen Kraemer, eds. 1992. *Museums and Communities: The Politics of Public Culture.* Washington, D.C.: Smithsonian Institution Press.

Kearney, Michael. 1995. "The Local and the Global: The Anthropology of Globalization and Transnationalism." *Annual Review of Anthropology,* 24: 547–565.

Khlebnikov, K. T. 1990. *The Khlebnikov Archive: Unpublished Journal (1800–1837) and Travel Notes (1820, 1822, and 1824).* Fairbanks: University of Alaska Press.

Kimmelman, Michael. 1989. "Erasing the Line between Art and Artifact." *New York Times* (May 1): B1.

Kincaid, Jamaica. 1988. *A Small Place.* New York: Farrar, Straus, Giroux.

Kingston, Maxine Hong. 1976. *The Woman Warrior: Memoirs of a Girlhood among Ghosts.* New York: Knopf.

Kirk, Ruth. 1986. *Tradition and Change on the Northwest Coast.* Seattle: University of Washington Press.

Koh, Barbara. 1994. "In the Magic Grove." *San Jose Mercury News* (September 16): 1B–2B.

Komes Peres, Maruch, and Diana Rus. 1991. *Ta Jlok'ta Chobtik Ta K'u'il (Récit d'une tisserande de Chamula).* San Cristóbal de las Casas, Mexico: INAREMAC.

Kondo, Dorinne. 1986. "Dissolution and Reconstitution of Self: Implications for Anthropological Epistemology." *Cultural Anthropology,* 1 (1): 74–88.

———. 1990. *Crafting Selves: Power, Gender and Discourses of Identity in a Japanese Workplace.* Chicago: University of Chicago Press.

Krauss, Michael. 1994. "Crossroads? A Twentieth-Century History of Contacts across the Bering Strait." In *Anthropology of the North Pacific Rim,* ed. William Fitzhugh and Valérie Chaussonnet. Washington, D.C.: Smithsonian Institution Press, 365–379.

Kuhn, Thomas. 1970. *The Structure of Scientific Revolutions.* Enlarged, second ed. Chicago: University of Chicago Press.

Kuklick, Henrika. 1997. "After Ishmael: The Fieldwork Tradition and Its Future." In

Anthropological Locations: Boundaries and Grounds of a Field Science, ed. Akhil Gupta and James Ferguson. Berkeley: University of California Press.

Kurin, Richard. 1991. "Cultural Conservation through Representation: Festival of India Folklife Exhibitions at the Smithsonian Institution." In *Exhibiting Culture: The Poetics and Politics of Museum Display,* ed. Ivan Karp and Steven Lavine. Washington, D.C.: Smithsonian Institution Press. 315–343.

Landes, Ruth. 1947. *The City of Women.* New York: Macmillan.

Lave, Jean, Paul Duguid, Nadine Fernandez, and Eric Axel. 1992. "Coming of Age in Birmingham." *Annual Review of Anthropology,* 21: 257–282.

Lavie, Smadar. 1990. *The Poetics of Military Occupation: Mzeina Allegories of Bedouin Identity under Israeli and Egyptian Rule.* Berkeley: University of California Press.

———. 1992. "Blow-Ups in the Borderlands: Third World Israeli Authors' Gropings for Home." *New Formations,* 18: 84–106.

Leenhardt, Maurice. 1947. *Do kamo: La personne et le mythe dans le monde mélanésien.* Paris: Gallimard.

Leiris, Michel. 1934. *L'Afrique fantôme.* Paris: Gallimard.

Levine, Lawrence. 1988. *Highbrow/Lowbrow: The Emergence of Cultural Hierarchy in America.* Cambridge, Mass.: Harvard University Press.

Lévi-Strauss, Claude. 1977. *Tristes Tropiques.* New York: Washington Square Press. Orig. pub. 1955.

———. 1985. *The View from Afar.* New York: Basic Books.

Lewin, Ellen. 1995. "Writing Lesbian Ethnography." In *Women Writing Culture,* ed. Ruth Behar and Deborah Gordon. Berkeley: University of California Press. 322–325.

Li, Xiaoping. 1993. "New Chinese Art in Exile." *Border/Lines,* 29–30: 40–44.

Lightfoot, Kent, Thomas Wake, and Ann Schiff. 1991. *The Archaeology and Ethnohistory of Fort Ross, California.* Vol. 1: *Contributions of the University of California Archaeological Research Facility, No. 49.* Berkeley: Archaeological Research Facility, University of California at Berkeley.

Limón, José. 1994. *Dancing with the Devil: Society and Cultural Poetics in Mexican-American South Texas.* Madison: University of Wisconsin Press.

Linebaugh, Peter, and Marcus Rediker. 1990. "The Many-Headed Hydra: Sailors, Slaves, and the Atlantic Working Class in the Eighteenth Century." *Journal of Historical Sociology,* 3 (3): 225–252.

Lorde, Audre. 1982. *Zami: A New Spelling of My Name.* Trumansburg, N.Y.: Crossing Press.

Lowie, Robert. 1937. *The History of Ethnological Theory.*

Lutkehaus, Nancy. 1995. "Margaret Mead and the 'Rustling-of-the-Wind-in-the-Palm-Trees School' of Ethnographic Writing." In *Women Writing Culture,* ed. Ruth Behar and Deborah Gordon. Berkeley: University of California Press. 186–206.

Lyman, Christopher. 1982. *The Vanishing Race and Other Illusions: Photographs of Indians by Edward Curtis.* New York: Pantheon.

MacCannell, Dean. 1976. *The Tourist: A New Theory of the Leisure Class.* New York: Schocken.

Mackey, Eva. 1995. "Postmodernism and Cultural Politics in a Multicultural Nation: Contests over Truth in the *Into the Heart of Africa* Controversy." *Public Culture* 7 (2): 403–432.

Macnair, Peter, Alan Hoover, and Kevin Neary. 1984. *The Legacy.* Vancouver: Douglas and McIntyre.

Malinowski, Bronislaw. 1922. *Argonauts of the Western Pacific.* New York: Dutton.

———. 1935. *Coral Gardens and Their Magic.* Bloomington: University of Indiana Press.

———. 1976. *A Diary in the Strict Sense of the Term.* New York: Harcourt, Brace and World.

Mannheim, Bruce. 1995. "On the Margins of 'The Couple in the Cage.'" *Visual Anthropology Review,* 11 (1): 121–127.

Marcus, George. 1995. "Ethnography in/of the World System: The Emergence of Multi-Sited Ethnography." *Annual Review of Anthropology,* 24: 95–117.

——— and Michael M. J. Fischer. 1986. *Anthropology as Cultural Critique: An Experimental Moment in the Human Sciences.* Chicago: University of Chicago Press.

Margolin, Malcolm. 1989. "California Indian Library Collections." *News of Native California,* 3 (3): 7–8.

Marshall, Paule. 1981. *Brown Girl, Brownstones.* New York: Feminist Press.

Martinez, Antoinette. 1995. "Excavation of a Kashaya Pomo Village Site in Northern California." *Berkeley Archaeology,* 3 (1): 1, 11.

Matthaeli, Julie, and Teresa Amott. 1990. "Race, Gender, Work: The History of Asian and Asian American Women." *Race and Class,* 31 (3): 61–80.

McDougall, Walter. 1993. *Let the Sea Make a Noise: Four Hundred Years of Cataclysm, Conquest, War and Folly in the North Pacific.* New York: Basic Books.

McEvilley, Thomas. 1993. *Fusion: West African Artists at the Venice Biennale.* New York: Museum for African Art.

McLendon, Sally, and Robert Oswalt. 1978. "Pomo: Introduction." In *Handbook of North American Indians: California,* ed. Robert Heizer. Washington, D.C.: Smithsonian Institution Press. 274–288.

McLuhan, T. C. 1975. *Edward C. Curtis: The Shadow Catcher.* Phoenix, Ariz.: Mystic Fire Video.

Menocal, Maria Rosa. 1987. *The Arab Role in Medieval Literary History.* Philadelphia: University of Pennsylvania Press.

Mercer, Kobena. 1988. "Diaspora Culture and the Dialogic Imagination." In *Blackframes: Celebration of Black Cinema,* ed. Mbye Cham and Claire Andrade-Watkins. Cambridge, Mass.: MIT Press. 50–61.

———. 1990. "Black Art and the Burden of Representation." *Third Text,* 10 (Spring): 61–78.

Meyers, Fred. 1994. "Culture-Making: Performing Aboriginally at the Asia Society Gallery." *American Ethnologist,* 21: 679–699.

Middleton, Dorothy. 1982. *Victorian Lady Travellers.* Chicago: Academy.

Miller, Daniel. 1987. *Material Culture and Mass Consumption.* Oxford: Blackwell.

———. 1994. *Modernity—An Ethnographic Approach: Dualism and Mass Consumption in Trinidad.* Oxford: Berg.

———. 1995. "Consumption and Commodities." *Annual Review of Anthropology,* 24: 141–161.

Mills, Sara. 1990. "Discourses of Difference." *Cultural Studies,* 4 (2): 128–140.

———. 1991. *Discourses of Difference: An Analysis of Women's Travel Writing and Colonialism.* London: Routledge.

Mishra, Vijay. 1983. "The Girmit Ideology Reconsidered." In *Language and Literature,* ed. Satendra Nandan. Suva, Fiji: University of the South Pacific.

———. 1994. "Theorizing the Literature of the Indian Diaspora: The Familiar Temporariness (V. S. Naipaul)." Paper read at the Center for Cultural Studies, University of California, Santa Cruz.

Mitter, Swasti. 1986. *Common Fate, Common Bond: Women in the Global Economy.* London: Pluto.

Miyoshi, Masao. 1993. "A Borderless World? From Colonialism to Transnationalism and the Decline of the Nation-State." *Critical Inquiry,* 19 (Summer): 726–751.

Mohanty, Chandra. 1987. "Feminist Encounters: Locating the Politics of Experience." *Copyright,* 1 (Fall): 30–44.

Moore, Henrietta. 1988. *Feminism and Anthropology.* Minneapolis: University of Minneapolis Press.

Morris, Meaghan. 1988. "At Henry Parkes Motel." *Cultural Studies,* 2 (1): 1–47.

Mudimbe, V. Y. 1988. *The Invention of Africa: Gnosis, Philosophy and the Order of Knowledge.* Bloomington: University of Indiana Press.

Nader, Laura. 1972. "Up the Anthropologist: Perspectives Gained from Studying Up." In *Reinventing Anthropology,* ed. Dell Hymes. New York: Pantheon. 284–311.

Naficy, Hamid. 1991. "Exile Discourse and Televisual Fetishization." *Quarterly Review of Film and Video,* 13 (1–3): 85–116.

Naipaul, V. S. 1976. *The Mimic Men.* Harmondsworth: Penguin.

Narayan, Kirin. 1989. *Storytellers, Saints and Scoundrels: Folk Narrative in Hindu Religious Teaching.* Philadelphia: University of Pennsylvania Press.

———. 1993. "How Native Is a Native Anthropologist?" *American Anthropologist,* 95: 19–34.

National Museum of the American Indian. 1991. "National Museum of the American Indian Policy Statement on Native American Human Remains and Cultural Materials." *Museum Anthropology,* 15 (2): 25–28.

Needham, Rodney. 1975. "Polythetic Classification." *Man,* 10: 349–369.

Newton, Esther. 1993a. *Cherry Grove, Fire Island: Sixty Years in America's First Gay and Lesbian Town.* Boston: Beacon Press.

————. 1993b. "My Best Informant's Dress." *Cultural Anthropology,* 8 (1): 3–23.

O'Hanlon, Michael. 1989. *Reading the Skin: Adornment, Display and Society among the Wahgi.* London: British Museum Publications.

————. 1993. *Paradise: Portraying the New Guinea Highlands.* London: British Museum.

Omi, Michael, and Howard Winant. 1986. *Racial Formation in the United States from the 1960s to the 1980s.* New York: Routledge.

Ong, Aihwa. 1993. "On the Edge of Empires: Flexible Citizenship among Chinese in Diaspora." *Positions,* 1 (3): 745–778.

————. 1995. "Women out of China: Traveling Tales and Traveling Theories in Postcolonial Feminism." In *Women Writing Culture,* ed. Ruth Behar and Deborah Gordon. Berkeley: University of California Press. 350–372.

Oswalt, Robert. 1964. *Kashaya Texts.* University of California Publications in Linguistics, vol. 36. Berkeley: University of California Press.

————. 1988. "History through the Words Brought to California by the Fort Ross Colony." *News from Native California,* 2 (3): 20–22.

Ottenberg, Simon. 1991. "Into the Heart of Africa," *African Arts* 24 (3): 79–82.

Pan, Lynn. 1990. *Sons of the Yellow Emperor: A History of the Chinese Diaspora.* Boston: Little, Brown.

Patterson, Orlando. 1987. "The Emerging West Atlantic System: Migration, Culture, and Underdevelopment in the United States and the Circum-Caribbean Region." In *Population in an Interacting World,* ed. W. Alonso. Cambridge, Mass.: Harvard University Press. 227–260.

Philip, Marlene Nourbese. 1992. *Frontiers: Essays and Writings on Racism and Culture.* Stratford, Ontario: Mercury Press.

————. 1993. "Black Jewish Relations." *Border/Lines,* 29–30: 64–69.

Porter, Dennis. 1991. *Haunted Journeys: Desire and Transgression in European Travel Writing.* Princeton: Princeton University Press.

Potts, Lydia. 1990. *The World Labour Market: A History of Migration.* London: Zed Books.

Pratt, Mary Louise. 1986. "Fieldwork in Common Places." In *Writing Culture: The Poetics and Politics of Ethnography,* ed. James Clifford and George Marcus. Berkeley: University of California Press. 27–50.

————. 1992. *Imperial Eyes: Travel Writing and Transculturation.* London: Routledge.

Pullar, Gordon, and Richard Knecht. 1995. "Alutiq." In *Crossroads Alaska: Native Cultures of Alaska and Siberia,* ed. Valérie Chaussonnet. Washington, D.C.: Smithsonian Institution, Arctic Studies Center. 14–15.

Rabinow, Paul. 1977. *Reflections on Fieldwork in Morocco.* Berkeley: University of California Press.

Radakrishnan, R. 1991. "Ethnicity in an Age of Diaspora." *Transition,* 54: 104–115.

Raine, Kathleen. 1970. *William Blake.* London: Thames and Hudson.

Readings, Bill. 1995. "The University without Culture?" *New Literary History* 26: 465–492.

Reagon, Bernice Johnson. 1983. "Coalition Politics: Turning the Century." In *Home Girls: A Black Feminist Anthology*, ed. Barbara Smith. New York: Kitchen Table, Women of Color Press. 356–368.

Rediker, Marcus. 1987. *Between the Devil and the Deep Blue Sea: Merchant Seamen, Pirates, and the Anglo-American Maritime World, 1700–1750*. Cambridge: Cambridge University Press.

Reid, Susan. 1981. "Four Kwakiutl Themes on Isolation." In *The World Is as Sharp as a Knife: An Anthology in Honor of Wilson Duff*, ed. Donald N. Abbot. Victoria: British Columbia Provincial Museum.

Rich, Adrienne. 1986. "Notes toward a Politics of Location." In *Blood, Bread and Poetry: Selected Prose, 1979–1985*. New York: Norton. 210–231.

Richard, Nelly. 1993. "Nosotros / The Others." In *Mapa: The Airmail Paintings of Eugenio Dittborn, 1984–1992*, ed. Eugenio Dittborn. London: Institute of Contemporary Arts. 47–65.

———. 1994. "La problematica de la distancia en el contexto de lo translocal." Paper read at conference entitled "Sinais de Turbulencia." Encuentro da Rede Interamerica de Estudor Culturais, Rio de Janeiro.

Riding, Alan. 1995. "African Creativity on Europe's Stage." *New York Times* (October 4): B1, B4.

Rivière, Georges-Henri. 1985. "The Ecomuseum: An Evolutive Definition." *Museum* 148: 182–183.

Rosaldo, Renato. 1980. *Ilongot Headhunting, 1883–1974: A Study in Society and History*. Stanford: Stanford University Press.

———. 1989. *Culture and Truth: The Remaking of Social Analysis*. Boston: Beacon Press.

Rosenthal, A. M., and Arthur Gelb. 1984. "Introduction." In *The Sophisticated Traveler: Beloved Cities—Europe*, ed. A. M. Rosenthal and Arthur Gelb. New York: Penguin.

Ross, Andrew. 1992. "New Age Technoculture." In *Cultural Studies*, ed. Lawrence Grossberg, Cary Nelson, and Paula Treichler. New York: Routledge.

Rouse, Irving. 1986. *Migrations in Prehistory*. New Haven: Yale University Press.

Rouse, Roger. 1991. "Mexican Migration and the Social Space of Postmodernism." *Diaspora*, 1 (1): 8–23.

Rubin, William, ed. 1984. *"Primitivism" in Twentieth-Century Art: Affinity of the Tribal and the Modern*. 2 vols. New York: Museum of Modern Art.

Ruffins, Fath Davis. 1992. "Mythos, Memory, and History: African American Preservation Efforts, 1820–1990." In *Exhibiting Cultures: The Poetics and Politics of Museum Display*. Ed. Ivan Karp and Steven Lavine. Washington, D.C.: Smithsonian Institution Press. 506–611.

Rus, Diana. 1990. "La crisis economica y la mujer indigena: El caso de Chamula, Chiapas." In *Documento INAREMAC 038-VIII-90*. San Cristóbal de las Casas, Mexico: INAREMAC.

Rushdie, Salman. 1989. *The Satanic Verses.* New York: Viking.

Russell, Mary. 1986. *The Blessings of a Good Thick Skirt.* London: Collins.

Safran, William. 1991. "Diasporas in Modern Societies: Myths of Homeland and Return." *Diaspora,* 1 (1): 83–99.

Sahlins, Marshall. 1988. "Cosmologies of Capitalism: The Trans-Pacific Sector of the World-System." *Proceedings of the British Academy,* 74: 1–51.

Said, Edward. 1978. *Orientalism.* New York: Pantheon.

———. 1984. "Reflections of Exile." *Granta,* 13: 159–172.

———. 1990. "Third World Intellectuals and Metropolitan Culture." *Raritan,* 9 (3): 27–50.

Saldívar, José David. 1991. *The Dialectics of Our America: Genealogy, Cultural Critique, and Literary History.* Durham, N.C.: Duke University Press.

Samuel, Raphael. 1994. *Theatres of Memory.* Vol. 1: *Past and Present in Contemporary Culture.* London: Verso.

Sanchez, Luis Rafael. 1984. "The Airbus." *Village Voice,* 39–43.

Sangari, Kum Kum. 1987. "The Politics of the Possible." *Cultural Critique,* 7: 157–186.

Sarris, Greg. 1993. *Keeping Slugwoman Alive: A Holistic Approach to Native American Texts.* Berkeley: University of California Press.

Sassen-Koob, Saskia. 1982. "Recomposition and Peripheralization at the Core." *Contemporary Marxism,* 5: 88–100.

Schepper-Hughes, Nancy. 1995. "The Primacy of the Ethical: Propositions for a Militant Anthropology." *Current Anthropology,* 36 (3): 409–420.

Schildkraut, Enid. 1991. "Ambiguous Messages and Ironic Twists: *Into the Heart of Africa* and *The Other Museum.*" *Museum Anthropology,* 15 (2): 16–23.

———. 1996. "Kingdom of Gold: Ghana Recycles Its Heritage." *Natural History* (February): 36–47.

Schiller, Nina Glick, Linda Basch, and Cristina Blanc-Szanton, eds. 1992. *Towards a Transnational Perspective on Migration: Race, Class, Ethnicity, and Nationalism Reconsidered.* New York: New York Academy of Sciences.

Schneider, Peter. 1983. *The Wall Jumper.* New York: Random House.

Scott, David. 1989. "Locating the Anthropological Subject: Postcolonial Anthropologists in Other Places." *Inscriptions,* 5: 75–85.

Shaw, Rosalind, and Charles Stewart. 1994. "Introduction: Problematizing Syncretism." In *Syncretism/Anti-syncretism: The Politics of Religious Synthesis,* ed. Charles Stewart and Rosalind Shaw. London: Routledge. 1–26.

Shohat, Ella. 1988. "Sephardim in Israel: Zionism from the Standpoint of Its Jewish Victims." *Social Text,* 19 (20): 3–45.

———. 1989. *Israeli Cinema: East/West and the Politics of Representation.* Austin: University of Texas Press.

———. 1992. "Notes on the Post-Colonial." *Social Text,* 41–42: 99–113.

——— and Robert Stam. 1994. *Unthinking Eurocentrism: Multiculturalism and the Media.* London: Routledge.

Shyllon, Folarin. 1982. "Blacks in Britain: A Historical and Analytical Overview." In *Global Dimensions of the African Diaspora,* ed. Joseph E. Harris. Washington, D.C.: Howard University Press.

Smith, Daisy (My-yah-nelth) Sewid. 1979. *Prosecution or Persecution.* Cape Mudge, British Columbia: Nuyumbalees Society.

Speck, Dara Culhane. 1987. *An Error in Judgment: The Politics of Medical Care in an Indian/White Community.* Vancouver: Talonbooks.

Spivak, Gayatri Chakravorty. 1988. "Can the Subaltern Speak?" In *Marxism and the Interpretation of Culture,* ed. Lawrence Grossberg and Cary Nelson. Urbana: University of Illinois Press. 271–313.

———. 1989. "Who Claims Alterity?" In *Remaking History,* ed. Barbara Kruger and Phil Mariani. Seattle: Bay Press. 269–292.

Stainbrook, Lynda S. 1979. *Fort Ross Orchards: Historical Survey, Present Conditions and Restoration Recommendations.* Sacramento: California Department of Parks and Recreation.

Standing Bear, Luther. 1928. *My People the Sioux.* Lincoln: University of Nebraska Press.

Starr, Frederick, ed. 1987. *Russia's American Colony.* Durham, N.C.: Duke University Press.

Stellar, Georg Wilhelm. 1988. *Journal of a Voyage with Bering, 1741–1742.* Ed. O. W. Frost. Stanford: Stanford University Press.

Stevens, John L. 1969. *Incidents of Travel in Central America, Chiapas and Yucatan.* Vol. 1. New York: Dover.

Stewart, Charles, and Rosalind Shaw. 1994. *Syncretism/Anti-syncretism: The Politics of Religious Synthesis.* London: Routledge.

Stewart, Kathleen. 1988. "Nostalgia: A Polemic." *Cultural Anthropology,* 3 (3): 227–241.

———. 1996. *A Space on the Side of the Road: Cultural Poetics in an "Other" America.* Princeton: Princeton University Press.

Stocking, George. 1992. "Philanthropoids and Vanishing Cultures: Rockefeller Funding and the End of the Museum Era in Anglo-American Anthropology." In Stocking, *The Ethnographer's Magic and Other Essays in the History of Anthropology.* Madison: University of Wisconsin Press. 178–211.

Sturtevant, William. 1991. "New National Museum of the American Indian Collections Policy Statement: A Critical Analysis." *Museum Anthropology,* 15 (2): 29–30.

Sutton, Constance, and Elsa Chaney, eds. 1987. *Caribbean Life in New York City: Sociocultural Dimensions.* New York: Center for Migration Studies.

Taussig, Michael. 1980. *The Devil and Commodity Fetishism in South America.* Chapel Hill, N.C.: University of North Carolina Press.

———. 1987. *Shamanism, Colonialism, and the Wild Man: A Study in Terror and Healing.* Chicago: University of Chicago Press.

Taylor, J. Garth. 1981. "An Eskimo Abroad, 1880: His Diary and Death." *Canadian Geographic,* October–November: 38–43.

Teaiwa, Teresia. 1993. "Between Traveler and Native: The Traveling Native as Performative/Informative Figure." Unpublished paper. University of California, Santa Cruz.

Tedlock, Dennis. 1983. *The Spoken Word and the Work of Interpretation.* Philadelphia: University of Pennsylvania Press.

Thomas, Nicholas. 1991. *Entangled Objects: Exchange, Material Culture and Colonialism in the Pacific.* Cambridge, Mass.: Harvard University Press.

Tikhmenev, P. A. 1978. *A History of the Russian-American Company.* Ed. Richard Price. Seattle: University of Washington Press.

Tölölian, Khachig. 1991. "The Nation State and Its Others: In Lieu of a Preface." *Diaspora,* 1 (1): 3–7.

Townsend-Gault, Charlotte. 1995. "Translation or Perversion? Showing First Nations Art in Canada." *Cultural Studies,* 9 (1): 91–105.

Tsing, Anna. 1993. *In the Realm of the Diamond Queen: Marginality in an Out-of-the-Way Place.* Princeton: Princeton University Press.

———. 1994. "Discussant's Comments." Paper read at conference entitled "Anthropology and 'the Field,'" Stanford University.

Turner, Terence. 1991. "Representing, Resisting, Rethinking: Historical Transformations of Kayapo Culture and Anthropological Consciousness." *History of Anthropology,* 7: 285–313.

Turner-Strong, Pauline. 1992. "Captivity in White and Red: Convergent Practice and Colonial Representation on the British-Amerindian Frontier." In *Crossing Cultures: Essays in the Displacement of Western Civilization,* ed. Daniel Segal. Tucson: University of Arizona Press. .

Urbain, Jean-Didier. 1991. *L'idiot du voyage: Histoires de touristes.* Paris: Plon.

Urry, John. 1990. *The Tourist Gaze: Leisure and Travel in Contemporary Societies.* London: Sage.

Van Maanen, John. 1988. *Tales of the Field: On Writing Ethnography.* Chicago: University of Chicago Press.

Vega, Ana Lydia. 1987. "Encancaranublado." In *Encancaranublado y otros cuentos de naufragio.* Rio Piedras, Puerto Rico: Editorial Antillana. 73–79.

Velez, Diana L. 1994. "We Are (Not) in This Together: The Caribbean Imaginary in 'Encancaranublado' by Ana Lydia Vega." *Callaloo,* 826–833.

Visweswaran, Kamela. 1994. *Fictions of Feminist Ethnography.* Minneapolis: University of Minnesota Press.

Vogel, Susan. 1987a. *Perspectives: Angles on African Art.* New York: Center for African Art and Harry F. Abrams.

———. 1987b. *Art/Artifact.* New York: Center for African Art and Prestel Verlag.

———. 1988. *The Art of Collecting African Art.* New York: Center for African Art.

Waldron, Arthur. 1990. *The Great Wall of China*. Cambridge: Cambridge University Press.

Wallis, Brian. 1989. "The Global Issue: A Symposium." *Art in America,* 77 (7): 86–87, 152–153.

Walsh, Kevin. 1992. *The Representation of the Past: Museums and Heritage in the Post-Modern World*. London: Routledge.

Webster, Gloria Cranmer. 1988. "The 'R' Word." *Muse,* 6 (3): 43–46.

Weinreich, Max. 1967. "The Reality of Jewishness versus the Ghetto Myth: The Sociolinguistic Roots of Yiddish." In *To Honor Roman Jakobson*. The Hague: Mouton.

Wellman, David. 1995. *The Union Makes Us Strong: Radical Unionism on the San Francisco Waterfront*. Cambridge: Cambridge University Press.

West, Cornel. 1993. *Race Matters*. Boston: Beacon Press.

Weston, Kath. 1997. "The Virtual Anthropologist." In *Anthropological Locations: Boundaries and Grounds of a Field Science,* ed. Akhil Gupta and James Ferguson. Berkeley: University of California Press.

White, Hayden. 1987. *The Content of the Form: Narrative Discourse and Historical Representation*. Baltimore: Johns Hopkins University Press.

Williams, Raymond. 1966. *Culture and Society, 1780–1950*. New York: Harper and Row.

Willis, Paul. 1977. *Learning to Labour: How Working Class Kids Get Working Class Jobs*. Farnborough, England: Saxon House.

Winichakul, Thongchai. 1994. *Siam Mapped: A History of the Geo-Body of a Nation*. Honolulu: University of Hawai'i Press.

Wolf, Eric. 1964. *Anthropology*. New York: Norton.

———. 1982. *Europe and the People without History*. Berkeley: University of California Press.

Wolff, Janet. 1993. "On the Road Again: Metaphors of Travel in Cultural Criticism." *Cultural Studies,* 7 (2): 224–239.

Wright, Patrick. 1985. *On Living in an Old Country: The National Past in Contemporary Britain*. London: Verso.

Ybarra-Frausto, Tomas. 1992. "The Chicano Movement / The Movement of Chicano Art." In *Exhibiting Cultures: The Poetics and Politics of Museum Display,* ed. Ivan Karp and Steven Lavine. Washington, D.C.: Smithsonian Institution Press. 128–149.

Zalewski, Daniel. 1995. "Can This Journal Be Saved?" *Lingua Franca,* 5 (5): 15–16.

Sources

Previously published chapters of this book are reprinted unchanged or with minor revisions.

Chapter 1: *Cultural Studies,* ed. Lawrence Grossberg, Cary Nelson, and Paula Treichler. New York: Routledge, 1992. Reprinted by permission of the publisher.

Chapter 2: *Times Literary Supplement,* November 16, 1984. Reprinted by permission.

Chapter 3: *Anthropology and "the Field": Boundaries, Areas, and Grounds in the Constitution of a Discipline,* ed. Akhil Gupta and James Ferguson. Berkeley: University of California Press, 1997. Reprinted by permission of the publisher.

Chapter 4: *Sulfur,* 32 (1993): 64–72.

Chapter 5: *Exhibiting Cultures: The Poetics and Politics of Museum Display,* ed. Ivan Karp and Steven D. Lavine. Washington D.C.: Smithsonian Institution Press, 1991. Reprinted by permission of the publisher.

Chapter 6: *Visual Anthropology Review,* 11, no. 1 (1995): 92–117. Reprinted by permission of the American Anthropological Association.

Chapter 7: Published for the first time in this volume.

Chapter 8: *Museum Anthropology,* 17, no. 3 (1993): 58–66. Reprinted by permission of the American Anthropological Association.

Chapter 9: *Displacements: Cultural Identities in Question,* ed. Angelika Bammer. Bloomington: Indiana University Press, 1994. Reprinted by permission of the publisher.

Chapter 10: *Cultural Anthropology,* 9, no. 3 (1994): 302–338. Reprinted by permission of the American Anthropological Association.

Chapter 11: *Sulfur,* 37 (1995): 32–52.

Chapter 12: Published for the first time in this volume.

Acknowledgments

Writing these essays, I have been helped by many friends and colleagues, in agreement and disagreement.

My early thinking on travel received special stimulus from the work of four people: Daniel Defert, Mary Louise Pratt, Lee Drummond, and Caren Kaplan. I'm grateful, also, to participants in the Fall 1990 Luce Faculty Seminar at Yale University, where I was able to develop preliminary ideas in an atmosphere of friendly rigor. I will always associate that productive atmosphere with my host at the Whitney Humanities Center, Peter Brooks.

Chapter 3 received useful critical readings from James Ferguson, Akhil Gupta, Susan Harding, Michelle Kisliuk, Ann Kingsolver, William Ladusaw, and David Schneider.

For help with Chapter 5, I am grateful to Michael Ames, Ira Jacknis, Aldona Jonaitis, Nancy Marie Mitchell, Dan Monroe, Dara Culhane Speck, and Gloria Cranmer Webster.

Michael O'Hanlon was a generous interlocutor on Chapter 6, which also profited from readings by Daniel Miller, Rosalind Shaw, and Charles Stewart.

Different parts of Chapter 7 were stimulated by exchanges with Chris Healy, Jim Mason, Johanna Mizgala, Dan Monroe, Ruth Phillips, Chris Pinney, Mary Louise Pratt, Nelly Richard, Renato Rosaldo, and Enid Schildkraut.

Chapter 10 was conceived in the context of a reading group on diasporas at the Center for Cultural Studies, University of California, Santa Cruz. My thanks to its participants: Gordon Bigelow, Susan Harding, Galen Joseph, Katie Stewart, Anna Tsing, and especially Avtar Brah. I also received useful critical readings from Kathleen Biddick, Jonathan Boyarin,

Iain Chambers, Paul Gilroy, Barbara Kirshenblatt-Gimblett, Vijay Mishra, and David Schneider.

Susan Hiller and Jane Rollo (of *Bookworks,* London) graciously provided materials for Chapter 11.

All those who helped with the research for Chapter 12 are acknowledged in its appendix. Important readings of an earlier draft were provided by Norman O. Brown, Chris Connery, Donna Haraway, Chris Healy, and Hayden White.

Over the years I have benefited from my association with *Sulfur: A Literary Bi-Annual of the Whole Art.* My thanks to its editor, Clayton Eshleman, for welcoming my experiments (some of which appear in this volume), and to Eliot Weinberger for his encouragement.

Lindsay Waters of Harvard University Press has provided steady support and good advice. Maria Ascher offered many useful editorial suggestions.

The production of the book manuscript was much advanced by my research assistant Anniken Hoyer-Nielsen and by Cheryl Van De Veer of the Word Processing Center at the University of California, Santa Cruz.

During the time these essays were produced, I served as director of a research organization, the Santa Cruz Center for Cultural Studies, and became a father. These two absorbing occupations kept me agreeably diverted, and they account, I'm sure, for something of the book's paratactic style. Thanks to all the visitors, staff, and participants at the Center for their many stimulating interventions. Thanks to Ben for the same, and to Judith Aissen for steadfast love and honest readings.

Index